Gender and Law in the Japanese Imperium

Gender and Law in the Japanese Imperium

EDITED BY
Susan L. Burns
AND
Barbara J. Brooks

University of Hawai'i Press
Honolulu

Printed in the United States of America

19 18 17 16 15 14 6 5 4 3 2 1

Library of Congress Cataloging-in-Publication Data

Gender and law in the Japanese imperium / edited by Susan L. Burns and Barbara J. Brooks.
pages cm
Most of the papers in this volume are from a conference held in May 2006 at the University of Chicago.
Includes bibliographical references and index.
ISBN 978-0-8248-3715-0 (cloth : alk. paper)
1. Women's rights—Japan—Case studies—Congresses. 2. Domestic relations—Japan—Case studies—Congresses. 3. Prostitution—Law and legislation—Japan—Case studies—Congresses. 4. Sex and law—Japan—Case studies—Congresses. 5. Women—Legal status, laws, etc.—Japan—Case studies—Congresses. I. Burns, Susan L., [date] editor of compilation. II. Brooks, Barbara J., 1953–2013, editor of compilation.
HQ1236.5.J3G46 2014
305.420952—dc23
2013029036

University of Hawai‘i Press books are printed on acid-free paper and meet the guidelines for permanence and durability of the Council on Library Resources.

Designed by Josie Herr

Printed by Sheridan Books, Inc.

Contents

Part III Colonial Law and the Problem of the Family

Acknowledgments

This volume is the result of a collaborative effort that involved not only the authors whose work is included here but also many others who as readers and interlocutors pushed us to sharpen our analysis, widen our perspective, and polish our prose. While many of us were not trained as legal historians, our work on gender, social, political, and intellectual history compelled us to take up the problem of law. In 2006, the Japan Committee of the University of Chicago sponsored a conference that brought many of us together for the first time. We gratefully acknowledge the contributions of all those who participated in this initial event. Although the papers presented by David Ambaras, Marnie Anderson, Loren Edelson, Suzanne O'Brien, Holly Sanders, and Leila Wice are not a part of this volume, we benefited greatly from their involvement in the workshop. Chen Chao-ju, Daniel Botsman, and Matsutani Motokazu were unable to attend the conference but graciously contributed their papers for discussion. We also wish to James Ketelaar, Norma Field, Katsuhiko Endo, and Tomomi Yamaguchi, who chaired the panels and offered invaluable questions, comments, and suggestions. Mamiko Suzuki, Tanya Maus, Patti Kameya, and Fei-hsien Wang, graduate students at the time of the conference, not only helped with its organization but were also thoughtful and critical participants. The path toward publication was a long one, and we gratefully acknowledge the patience and goodwill of our contributors, including Darryl Flaherty, who joined us several years after our initial gathering. We are grateful to Patricia Crosby of the University of Hawai'i Press for her support of the project and to the anonymous readers of the Press whose advice prompted us to rethink and rewrite. We also thank Grey Osterud, who carefully edited three of the essays, and Wendy Bolton, our copy editor. The Japan Committee of the University of Chicago provided a subvention to support publication.

Sadly, Barbara Brooks died after a long and courageous battle with cancer just as this volume was going into production. Her passionate engagement with her work and her devotion to her family were an inspiration to all who knew her. The essay in this volume is a testament to her groundbreaking research on issues of gender in the Japanese empire. This book is dedicated to her daughter, Isadora Brooks Jaffee, and my own, Hannah Burns Tomio. When we began this project, they were girls; now they are young women, poised to enter a world where, we hope, law will be used to further the goal of gender equality.

Note on East Asian Names and Terms

Throughout this volume, names are written following the East Asian practice of listing the family name followed by the given name, except when the original publication adopted the Western practice. Chinese names and terms are romanized in pinyin except in the case of individuals who published under or are otherwise well known by names romanized differently. Taiwanese terms are romanized following the Taiwanese Romanization System. In the case of historical sources, we have followed the romanization used by the original author. For Japanese publications, the place of publication is omitted for Tokyo-based publishers.

Introduction

Susan L. Burns

Beginning in the nineteenth century, law as practice, discourse, and ideology became a powerful means of reordering gender relations in modern nation-states and their colonies around the world. In France, the Civil Code of 1804 and the Napoleonic Code of 1810 ended a remarkable period of legal experimentation in gender equality that followed the revolution. As modern patriarchy was instantiated in law, there were new restrictions on access to birth control and increased penalties for abortion, while men who declined to marry their pregnant sexual partners or abandoned their families faced criminal prosecution.[1] In the United States, even in the absence of a national code, lawmakers at the level of individual states began to formulate new legal policies that, taken together, redefined gender roles within and outside the family. Marriage, which Republican discourse had regarded as an issue of private consent, became a public matter as states defined standards for marriage. Race, health, and intelligence were addressed by state statutes that sought to define "fitness" for marriage. If marriage became more difficult, so too did divorce, as states began to require legal evidence of "wrongdoing" in order to grant divorce.[2] In Great Britain, too, new laws were enacted that sought to regulate gender relations. While women gained the right to initiate divorce and to retain custody of their children, acting upon these new statutes was difficult, since the concept of economic support lagged far behind.[3] Beyond the family, new laws that aimed to regulate prostitution threatened to turn an occasional occupation into a stigmatizing label.[4]

These metropolitan developments were deeply implicated in the formation of the new colonial order of the nineteenth century. In European colonies in Asia and Africa, the "intimate" relations of colonizer and colonized became an important site where ideas about race, class, gender, and sexuality were articulated and contested. As works by Anne Laura Stoler and Durba Ghosh have demonstrated, the existence of mixed-race children in particular challenged the colonial relations of power that relied upon the visible "difference" of colonizer and colonized.[5] At the same time, however, the nineteenth century conjugal ideal of female domesticity within monogamous marriage that was instantiated in metropolitan systems of family law made it possible for some colonized women to begin to challenge indigenous forms of patriarchy. The diffusion of conjugal modernity did not, however, go uncontested as colonial authorities, nationalists, and traditional sources of authority all struggled to regulate marriage, families, and sexuality to their own advantage.[6]

This volume aims to put the situation in Japan and its colonies in dialogue with these global developments and with the scholarship that examines it. Through a series of case studies that engage with issues of reproductive and human rights, sexuality, cultural notions of femininity and masculinity, gendered agency, and the family, the contributors explore the impact of civil, administrative, and criminal laws upon the lives of both Japanese citizens and Japan's colonial subjects. We argue for the importance of law and legal discourse: in Japan, as elsewhere in the modern world, it was a fundamental means of creating and regulating gendered subjects and social norms about sexuality and the family. In focusing on the Japanese "imperium," our aim is to suggest the interconnectedness of the processes of legal reform in Japan proper and its colonies. Not only did metropolitan and colonial law unfold more or less synchronically, in both cases jurists and officials pursued multiple and conflicting goals. The problem of "custom," for example, was an issue for Japanese jurists who sought to define new statutes for Japan by referencing European codes, but it was equally an issue in the colonial context as the "customary practices" of the native Taiwanese or Koreans were evaluated in reference to the new Japanese civil procedures that were themselves the product of a comparative process. At the same time, we also argue that the relationship between the emergent Japanese legal system and European and American legal regimes cannot be understood simply in terms of "reception" and "adaptation." Instead, Japanese officials, jurists, legal scholars, politicians, and activists were part of a transnational flow of ideas about gender, the family, criminality, social order, and the role of law.

It is undeniable, however, that this transnational flow was always marked by the imperial relations of power that shaped relations between the West and Japan from the 1850s through the Occupation period. Legal reform began in the aftermath of the political revolution of 1868 that overthrew the Tokugawa shogunate. It was a pressing concern for the new government not only because of the need to restore social order, but also because the creation of a new judicial system was seen as necessary for the project of nation building and for renegotiating the unequal treaties of the 1850s. The latter, by granting extraterritoriality to the citizens of Western nation-states, authorized the creation of a system of consular courts that were a tangible symbol of Japan's compromised sovereignty. However, Western governments refused to consider the renegotiation of the treaties, arguing that Japanese law was not in accord with principles of the "civilized" practices of modern nations. Legal reform thus always had ideological significance: it was used to signify Japan's progress toward modernity.

Initially, the government simply issued edicts (*fukoku* and *futatsu*) to carry out fundamental reforms. The establishment of the household registration system, the abolition of the early modern status system, and the banning of a host of quotidienne practices newly viewed as "backward," from mixed bathing and cross-dressing to the wearing of swords and the selling of amulets and charms, were addressed in this way. While the establishment of national codes was the goal, the process of legal reform proved challenging as individuals and groups within and outside of government debated the aims and expected outcomes of various legal frameworks.[7] The result was that the creation of a modern legal system unfolded in a distinctly nonlinear manner. Between 1868 and 1908, four separate criminal codes were enacted, and even after the 1908 code went into effect, major reforms continued. Most notably, between 1928 and 1943, Japan experimented with jury trials in criminal cases.

The establishment of civil law was equally tumultuous. In 1890, the first civil code was finally promulgated, but it met with so much resistance from legal scholars and others who criticized its "slavish" reliance on the French civil code that the government was forced to withdraw it before it went into effect. The family law provisions were targeted for particular criticism: conservative critics argued that the civil code threatened to "destroy" traditional values such as loyalty and filial piety that supported both the family and the so-called "family-state."[8] It was not until eight years later that a substantially revised code finally went into effect in 1898. As Ueno Chizuko has argued, although the provisions in the 1898 code bolstering patriarchal authority were celebrated as "traditional," in fact they represented the formation of a modern system of patriarchy that departed significantly from long-established practices. The new civil code rendered women legal minors even after marriage, with the result that they lost the right to manage property, to initiate divorce, and to retain custody of their children.[9]

The fluidity of the codes and statutes notwithstanding, a working legal system of regional and appellate courts with the High Court of Review (Daishin'in) in Tokyo as its pinnacle was in place by 1873 and functioned without interruption from that point forward. These early courts were not merely an empty display of state authority but quickly became an important element of civic life. In 1875 and 1876, for example, regional courts heard more than 300,000 civil cases, and more than 100,000 cases on average were adjudicated each year until the end of the Meiji period. Beginning in the late 1910s, the number of cases rose again to well over 200,000 per year, before dropping dramatically in the 1930s.[10] While more work needs to be done to understand the reasons behind such dramatic shifts in popular recourse to the courts, the numbers alone reveal that the new courts were an important site where Japanese citizens engaged directly with representatives of the modern state—its prosecutors and judges.

The project of legal reform in the metropole had implications as well for Japan's expanding empire. In both Taiwan, colonized in 1895, and Korea, colonized in 1910, colonial officials, legal scholars, and jurists debated whether the civil and criminal codes of Japan proper could be transferred intact to the colonies. At stake in the debate were the incompatible ideological requirements to distinguish "enlightened" Japanese colonialism from "oppressive" European colonialism while maintaining the claim of Japanese modernity in relation to less "civilized" Taiwanese and Koreans. As this suggests, the Japanese formulation of colonial law, no less than metropolitan law, was ordered by the discourse on civilization that privileged European political and social forms. The result was the establishment of a hybrid legal system in the Japanese colonies. Departing from the British and French policy of setting up separate courts for colonial subjects under the control of colonized elites, there was only one system of courts in the Japanese colonies. They were staffed by Japanese judges who adjudicated cases involving both Japanese and non-Japanese.[11] At the same time, it was eventually concluded that laws had to be tailored to the specific social and cultural requirements of the colonized peoples. Under this policy, although the premise was that the Japanese criminal codes should be enforced in the colonies, the governor-generals of Japan and Korea were given the right to suspend those laws they regarded as inapplicable to colonial subjects and enact ordinances (*seirei*) specifically for the colonies under their control.[12]

In regard to civil law, until 1923, judgments were to be based upon custom, and even after the Japanese civil code was extended to the colonies following more than a decade of debate, matters of family law were excluded: marriage, divorce, succession, and inheritance were to continue to follow the customary practices of the Taiwanese and Koreans. However, as Marie Seong-hak Kim has argued in several articles, and Chen Chao-ju's contribution to this volume demonstrates, "custom was less a sociological than a judicial artifact."[13] Not only did colonial officials conduct ethnological research that sought to create a stable body of knowledge about "Korean" or "Taiwanese" customs that ignored their real diversity, Japanese judges were ultimately given authority to make judgments based upon "custom." The codification of custom in the colonies replicated a similar procedure used in Japan itself: in the 1870s in preparation for the drafting of the civil code, the Ministry of Justice had undertaken a similar research project within Japan, calling upon local officials to compile information about practices regarding marriage, divorce, and child custody.[14]

In the aftermath of Japan's defeat in 1945, the occupation era ushered in another period of intense legal reform. Largely a product of American authorship, the postwar Japanese constitution of 1947 gave women the right to vote for the first time, and the U.S.-endorsed vision of gender equality led to changes in both the civil and criminal codes. Although the bulk of the prewar civil code was unchanged, the fifth and sixth sections that dealt with family law and inheritance were extensively revised based upon the new principle, articulated in article 1b, that "this code shall be interpreted on the basis of the dignity of the individual and the fundamental equality between the sexes."[15] Yet, these ideals notwithstanding, key elements of prewar family law were retained.[16] The survival of the household registration system meant that women, in most cases, continue to be required to abandon their surnames and adopt those of their husbands. And while the revised code allows men to remarry immediately after divorce, women are required to wait six months and any child born within three hundred days of the divorce is considered to be a product of the former marriage, provisions that aimed to guarantee paternal rights to any children conceived during the marriage. Moreover, while inheritance laws no longer privileged sons over daughters, children born within marriage continued to be privileged over their "illegitimate" siblings, until a 1995 court decision struck down this provision of the postwar civil code.

The situation with criminal law was also complicated. While much of the 1907 code was initially retained, key policies were targeted for revision. The criminalization of adultery (the topic of Harald Fuess' chapter) was abandoned, and although the crime of abortion statute remained on the books, the 1948 Eugenics Protection Law provided for the de facto legalization of abortion. Yet, the criminal code continued to be marked by gender asymmetry. The provisions regarding sexual violence are a case in point: the statutes on rape were written in such a way as to exclude the possibility of a male victim and to disallow the possibility of rape within marriage.[17]

As this outline history suggests, the relationship between gender and law is both complex and profound, but perhaps because of the powerful postwar myth of Japanese nonlitigiousness, the field of legal history has been largely moribund until quite recently. In Japan, legal historians have focused almost exclusively on struggles among officials, jurists, and academics, and on the legal debates that accompanied the framing of the civil and criminal statutes and institutional reforms. The cultural and social history of law has been almost ignored, a situation that partially explains the paucity of historical work on gender and law. Only in the late 1990s did that situation begin to change as a new generation of historians, many of them feminist in their orientation, published groundbreaking work. An important milestone was Fujime Yuki's *Sei no rekishigaku: Kōshō seido dataizai taisei kara baishun bōshihō yūsei hogohō e* (The History of Sex: From the System of Legal Prostitution and Criminalized Abortion to the System of the Prevention of Prostitution Law and the Eugenics Protection Law).[18] In her comprehensive study of the regulation of sexuality in Japan from the nineteenth century to the postwar period, Fujime focuses on the powerful role of the state, arguing that by policing abortion and prostitution, it sought to control the reproductive lives of poor women. Fujime's work sparked much new interest in law in relation to issues of reproduction, prostitution, labor, and marriage.[19] Recently, a number of important works on gender and law have appeared in English, including Harald Fuess' work on divorce,

Tiana Norgren's study of postwar legislation on abortion and contraception, Marnie Anderson's work on women's political rights in the Meiji period, and Mark D. West's multiple works on law and everyday life in contemporary Japan.[20]

Taking inspiration from this new literature, the contributors to this volume adopt an explicitly revisionist perspective that aims to push both legal history and gender history in new directions. While the standard textbooks of modern Japanese history now incorporate issues of gender, they typically make mention of "milestone" laws such as the 1882 criminalization of abortion, the 1890 ban on female participation in political activities, the 1892 educational ordinance that created a separate female track, and the patriarchal provisions of the 1898 civil code and place these developments in a narrative of teleological design that is ordered by increasing state oppression and heroic efforts at resistance.[21] In contrast, rather than regarding law as only a technology of state control, we see it as fluid and relational, subject to negotiation, interpretation, and contestation at every level of its formulation and deployment, and productive of new gendered subjectivities. To explore law as a contested set of discourses and practices, the chapters here utilize new kinds of sources, including court records, legal handbooks, and popular reportage, to greater contextualize law in cultural, political, and social terms. The result is a new, more complicated chronology that foregrounds the agency of the various actors who shaped the legal process, from judges who interpreted the statutes in flexible ways, to the ordinary people who as defendants and plaintiffs deployed laws and the legal process to their advantage, to the journalists who through their reporting shaped the public understanding of modern legal culture. While discourse analysis is a fundamental methodological tool employed by all the authors in this volume, an emphasis on agency and practice defines many of these essays. We are interested in the material realm of social life that was shaped by institutions, policies, and individuals, as well as by discourse and regimes of representation.

The organization of the volume is thematic and, within this framework, chronological. The three themes addressed are: (1) prostitution, law, and human rights; (2) gender and criminality; and (3) colonial law and the family. But across these thematic frames, the essays explore other key issues, including the interplay between law as an international and national phenomenon, the tension between law as an ideological construct and law as practice, and the social, economic, and political imperatives that shaped legal efforts to regulate gender, sexuality, and the family.

Part I brings together two works that address the beginning and the end of Japan's modern system of legalized prostitution. Douglas Howland's chapter, "The *Maria Luz* Incident: Personal Rights and International Justice for Chinese Coolies and Japanese Prostitutes," explores a seminal moment in the history of modern prostitution. The *Maria Luz* was a Peruvian cargo ship that was transporting Chinese coolies to Peru when it put into Yokohama in 1871. When one of the Chinese ran away to seek asylum, his plight became an international incident. Japanese officials subsequently freed the coolies on board the *Maria Luz* on the basis of the illegality of their contracts, but Peru's legal representative quickly sued. He argued that indentured prostitution in Japan was a practice equivalent to the coolie "trade," so there was no legal basis for Japanese actions. Ōe Taku (1847–1921), the judge who presided over the *Maria Luz* case, agreed that the two practices were similar violations of individual rights and that both represented a subversion of the justice demanded by international norms. In the wake of his decision in the *Maria Luz* case, Ōe issued the first Meiji era ruling intended to improve the condition of prostitutes in Japan. Howland argues that while the resulting changes may seem superficial, the modern prostitution system must be understood in the context of Japan's positions on labor contracts in the age of indentured labor and on its desire to participate in international law. Conceptually, if not in practice, female prostitutes, no less than male coolies, were endowed with the right to control their own labor by entering into contracts, now subject to legal oversight by the modern state.

In "Disputing Rights: The Debate over Anti-Prostitution Legislation in 1950s Japan," Sally Hastings also takes up prostitution as an issue of human rights and international law but in a different historical moment, the 1950s. In February 1946, in response to an American occupation order, the Japanese government abolished the laws that had supported the system of licensed prostitution since the late nineteenth century. This did not bring an end to prostitution; rather, what was termed "voluntary" prostitution flourished in both the former brothel districts and in new ones that sprang up to serve the hundreds of thousands of U.S. soldiers and civilian officials then in Japan. With the end of the Occupation era in 1952, prostitution became a pressing social and political issue as advocates for criminalization vied with those who called for a return to the prewar system. Hastings focuses on the role of the first generation of female Diet members who advocated for the criminalization of prostitution, which they characterized as a violation of women's human rights even as they called for penalties for those who engaged in it, female prostitutes as well as their male clients. Coalitions of brothel owners, a prostitute's union, and conservative politicians, however, also adopted the rhetoric of "rights," championing the right of women as free agents to choose their own form of employment, while also positioning regulated prostitution as a social necessity that satisfied male sexual needs, controlled the spread of venereal disease, and offered protection to women. Hastings concludes that the 1956 law, which criminalized solicitation, procurement, and contracts for prostitution but not the act itself, was a "limited symbolic victory" that made it possible for the trade in sex to continue while depriving it of the state support that had allowed prostitution to be conceptualized as a legitimate form of female labor since the time of Ōe's landmark decision.

The essays in Part II all address the issue of gender in relation to criminal and penal law. As recent work by scholars such as Christine Marran and William Johnston has illuminated, fascination and fear of female criminality was a cultural phenomenon throughout the prewar period, as stories of "poison women" became front-page news and trial transcripts became best-sellers.[22] The essays in this section seek to push the study of gender and criminality in new directions by looking beyond literary sources and sensational cases to explore how cultural conceptions of femininity and masculinity shaped the formulation and applications of laws and the processes of adjudication and punishment.

In "Gender in the Arena of the Courts: The Prosecution of Abortion and Infanticide in Early Meiji Japan," Susan L. Burns traces the history of abortion law from the early modern period and analyzes trial records of abortion and infanticide cases from the 1870s and '80s in order to intervene in the debate over the motives and the impact of the criminalization of abortion and infanticide in the modern period. Burns argues that the new laws and the social arena of the courts compelled a rethinking of individual agency in relation to reproductive choices as defendants were required to articulate who had acted and why. In responding to these statements, judges were remarkably flexible in their judgments, with women receiving widely varying sentences for the same act. Generally, young women who acted outside of patriarchal authority (young working women who were sexually active) were treated harshly for ending a pregnancy but so too were their male sexual partners. In contrast, wives and daughters who represented themselves as deferring to husbands and fathers were treated more generously, but this could result in punishment for the men who were implicated. Burns suggests that while the statutes defined stiff penalties for reproductive crimes, the adjudication of cases suggests that judges were less concerned with promoting pronatalism than with regulating sexuality, morality, and patterns of familial authority.

Like Burns, Harald Fuess too argues that the ideological value of the statutes offers only a partial picture of how law functioned to regulate gender roles. In his essay, "Adultery and Gender Equality in Modern Japan, 1868–1948," Fuess explores the legal status of adultery in the modern period. From 1868 until 1948, adultery was a criminal offense—but only in the case of a married woman who engaged in extramarital sexual relations. Adultery by a married man was not criminalized, even when the man maintained a concubine or fathered children outside of marriage. Similarly, within the civil code, adultery by a wife was grounds for a divorce, while that of a husband was not. Fuess explores the discussions and debates that surrounded this legal sexual double standard in light of European practice and the early modern Japanese legal tradition and notes that both provided justification for the gender inequality embodied in the adultery laws. By tracing these debates as well as the case law, Fuess argues that in practice jurists sought to mitigate the asymmetry of divorce laws by interpreting adultery by husbands as "grave cruelty," thus allowing women, under the terms of the civil code, to divorce their adulterous husbands. Moreover, he notes that in discussion of the criminal provisions, the key concern of the courts changed over time, from regulating the sexuality of wives to concern about containing male sexuality and enforcing monogamy. As a result, while the adultery law in the criminal code went unrevised, the number of prosecutions and convictions declined dramatically after 1912. Fuess argues then that the postwar abolition of adultery penalties should be viewed less as an imposition by Occupation reformers and more as the expected outcome of the prewar legal process.

Like Burns and Fuess, Daniel Botsman too contextualizes modern laws in relation to both pre-Meiji practices and developments in Europe. In "Of Pity and Poison: Imprisoning Women in Modern Japan," he traces the forms of punishment to which women were subjected in the period from the mid-eighteenth century to the 1930s. Botsman argues that while penal methods were transformed during this period, they were always gendered. In the early modern period, while men were beaten or banished, female criminals were often punished by confinement, either in jailhouses or in the brothel district of Yoshiwara, where they were forced to work as prostitutes. In the 1870s, as modern prisons were constructed, special facilities for women were established, and after 1900 a gender-specific discourse on female prisoners took form, reflecting a new concern for rehabilitation. Influenced by eugenics and class-based notions of femininity, prison officials debated how best to reform female prisoners so that they could become "future mothers of our country." Then, in the 1920s and '30s, the number of female prisoners began to decline dramatically, a development Botsman concludes may have been related to the medicalization of female criminality.

The discourses on femininity and female criminality are also at the heart of Darryl Flaherty's essay. In "Burning Down the House: Gender and Jury in a Tokyo Courtroom, 1928," Flaherty explores the trial of Yamafuji Kanko, a wife, mother, and small-business owner who was charged with arson. He argues that while Yamafuji's crime was commonplace, her trial attracted the attention of the public, legal officials, intellectuals, and politicians, as well as the press, because Yamafuji was the first defendant to be judged by a jury during Japan's brief experiment with jury trials between 1928 and 1943. Because women were excluded from jury service and male jurors were subject to age, tax, and residency restrictions, her case was adjudicated by twelve men who were representatives of Tokyo's old and new middle classes. Flaherty argues that these jurors came to stand in for the (male) public, with the result that ideas about women, their place in society, and their potential for criminality came into play in Yamafuji's trial. The prosecution called for jurors to ignore Yamafuji's gender, even as it cast her as a bad mother and unchaste wife. In contrast, the defense made Yamafuji's gender the focus of their case, portraying her as a loving mother, loyal wife, and filial daughter. Flaherty suggests that while casting Yamafuji as the victim ultimately may have aided in her acquittal, it also served to affirm theories of female weakness that allowed the patriarchal state to deny women political rights

As the essays by Burns, Fuess, Botsman, and Flaherty suggest, even beyond the realm of family law, conceptions of gender roles within the family and concerns about familial authority came into play in Japan's new courts and prisons. The works by Chen, Brooks, and Matsutani focus explicitly on issues of the family while shifting our attention to the Japanese colonies of Korea and Taiwan. In the last decade and half, studies of colonial law have become a vibrant new field of interest among scholars of empire and colonialism.[23] The essays in this volume put the Japanese case in dialogue with this literature and contribute to a new cross-cultural exploration of colonial governance, gender, and modernity. Like scholars working on other colonial sites, their work takes up the tensions that emerged as new legal definitions of modern familial relations clashed with "tradition" and "custom" and as the boundary between colonizer and colonized was challenged by sexual, conjugal, and parental relationships.

In her essay, "*Sim-pua* under the Colonial Gaze: Gender, 'Old Customs,' and the Law in Taiwan under Japanese Imperialism," Chen Chao-ju examines tensions in Japanese colonial legal policy toward the widespread Taiwanese custom of *sim-pua* marriage, whereby a girl was adopted at a very young age and raised in the family of her intended husband and then married in her teens to that adoptive brother. Chen's paper contextualizes colonial policy toward this practice within the debate on whether the Japanese civil code should be extended to Taiwan. She notes that in the aftermath of the 1923 decision to continue to use customary law to rule on family matters, courts struggled to reconcile the "civilizing mission" that authorized Japanese colonial rule with the requirement to respect custom. However, while colonial courts tended to position themselves as liberators of victimized colonial women, they would not have been able to "rescue" the victims of custom without their action. Through the careful reading of cases, Chen explores how *sim-pua,* their natal families, and adoptive brothers/would-be husbands used the colonial courts to assert their agency.

Building upon Ann Stoler's discussion of the tensions that emerged in relation to race and sexual intimacy in colonial societies, Barbara Brooks takes up the issues of mixed marriages and "hybrid" children through the examination of legal handbooks that were published in prewar Japan and Korea to guide public officials through the complications of the household registration system. The *koseki,* or household registration system, was divided into metropolitan (*naichi*) and colonial (*gaichi*) registers, and throughout the colonial period policing the divide between these two systems was a challenge for officials. The essay further explores why Japanese women so often appear to be at the sexual divide between colonizer and colonized, in contrast to the dynamics elucidated in European scholarship on gender and colonial culture. Marginal Japanese women flowed into Korea and northeast China to take up menial work, often in the sex trade. Rules regarding intermarriage between colonial and metropolitan subjects changed with time, but the trend was to deny metropolitan status to Japanese women who married colonial men. Over the course of the colonial period, not only most offspring of hybrid unions, but their mothers as well, could find themselves consigned to colonial status in the *gaichi* registers.

Matsutani Motokazu's groundbreaking work takes up one of the most reviled of Japanese colonial policies. This, the so-called name-changing policy, has been widely seen as aimed at forcing Korean families to give up their native Korean-language surnames in favor of entirely Japanese surnames in a harsh culmination of decades of assimilationist policies that included the Japanese-language education of Korean children and compulsory Korean worship at Shinto shrines. However, Matsutani carefully reviews the ordinances, their actual effects, and a new body of revisionist scholarship and argues that the policy actually aimed to unify Korean nuclear families, especially through the elevation and better integration of the wife/mother in family units. By undermining the patriarchal clan structure in Korea, the colonial state hoped to mobilize Korean families as socials units, and Korean women within those units, to fulfill wartime exigencies. Matsutani points out that, postcolonial nationalist accounts notwithstanding, some Korean women and men praised the ordinances because they viewed these laws as liberating them from the oppressive patriarchal clans.

As these summaries suggest, these nine essays taken together contribute to the recent revitalization of interest in law as an object of research by alerting readers to new sources, new problems, and new methodologies. Japan's courts continue to be a powerful social site where men and women not only embrace the potential of law to protect and define rights but also to contest the restrictions that laws have imposed. In 1992, for example, in what is known as the "Fukuoka Case," a female employee won a groundbreaking judgment against a male colleague for sexual harassment in the workplace. This case and those that followed it eventually prompted the amendment of the Equal Employment Opportunity Act to specifically address instances of sexual harassment.[24] However, legal challenges to the gender asymmetry created by law continue. Early in 2011, five Japanese citizens filed suit to change the legal requirement that couples share a surname, a law established well over a century ago.[25] Notably, both these cases point to the ongoing interaction between international norms and national laws that the authors in this volume address. Japan's sexual harassment law was modeled on those of the United States and Western Europe, and in 2009, the UN Convention on the Elimination of All Forms of Discrimination against Women urged the Japanese government to amend the code and drop the one-surname requirement as discriminatory.[26] With developments such as these in mind, we look forward to further work, by historians, political scientists, sociologists, and others, that will elucidate the complicated and continuing role of law in mediating the relationship between states, individuals, ideologies, and everyday life.

Notes

1. On law, the family, and gender in France, see Jacques Donzelot, *The Policing of Families* (Baltimore: Johns Hopkins University Press, 1997); Suzanne Desan, *The Family on Trial in Revolutionary France* (Berkeley: University of California Press, 2004); and Kristen Childers, *Fathers, Families, and the State in France, 1914–1945* (Ithaca, NY: Cornell University Press, 2003).

2. On the U.S. case, see Michael Grossberg, *Governing the Hearth: Law and the Family in Nineteenth-Century America* (Chapel Hill: University of North Carolina Press, 1985); Hendrik Hartog, *Man and Wife in America: A History* (Cambridge, MA: Harvard University Press, 2000); and Nancy Cott, *Public Vows: A History of Marriage and the Nation* (Cambridge, MA: Harvard University Press, 2002). For an insightful study of the history of miscegenation laws in the United States, see Peggy Pascoe, *What Comes Naturally: Miscegenation Law and the Making of Race in America* (New York: Oxford University Press, 2010).

3. For an interesting analysis of marriage and divorce laws that puts legal and literary discourse in dialogue, see Kelly Hager, *Dickens and the Rise of Divorce* (Burlington, VT: Ashgate, 2010).

4. Judith Walkowitz, *Prostitution and Victorian Society: Women, Class, and the State* (Cambridge: Cambridge University Press, 1982).

5. Ann Laura Stoler, *Carnal Knowledge and Imperial Power: Race and the Intimate in Colonial Rule* (Berkeley: University of California Press, 2002); Durba Ghosh, *Sex and the Family in Colonial India: The Making of Empire* (Cambridge: Cambridge University Press, 2008).

6. See Rochona Majumdar, *Marriage and Modernity: Family Values in Colonial Bengal* (Durham, NC: Duke University Press, 2009); and Mytheli Sreeni-

vas, *Wives, Widows, and Concubines: The Conjugal Family Ideal in Colonial India* (Bloomington: Indiana University Press, 2008).

7. For an overview of the reforms of the late nineteenth century, see Ryōsuke Ishii, *Japanese Legislation in the Meiji Era,* translated and adapted by William J. Chambliss (Tokyo: Pan-Pacific Press, 1958); and Wilhelm Röhl, ed., *History of Law in Japan since 1868* (Leiden: Brill, 2005).

8. For a collection of sources on the debates surrounding the 1890 code, see Hoshino Tōru, ed., *Minpōten ronsō shi* (Nihon Hyōronsha, 1944).

9. Ueno Chizuko, "Modern Patriarchy and the Formation of the Japanese Nation State," in *Multicultural Japan: Paleolithic to Postmodern,* ed. Donald Denoon et al. (Cambridge: Cambridge University Press, 2001), 213–233.

10. Hayashiya Reiji, "Meiji Shonen no minji soshō shin jukensū no kōsatsu," in *Meiji zenki no hō to saiban,* ed. Hayashiya, Ishii Shirō, and Aoyama Yoshimitsu (Shinsensha, 2002), 93.

11. On colonial law in Korea, see Marie Seong-hak Kim, "Customary Law and Colonial Jurisprudence in Korea," *American Journal of Comparative Law* 57, no. 1 (2009): 213–247; and Marie Seong-hak Kim, "Law and Custom under the Choson Dynasty and Colonial Korea," *Journal of Asian Studies* 66, no. 4 (November 2007): 1067–1097. On colonial law in Taiwan, see Taysheng Wang, *Legal Reform in Taiwan under Japanese Colonial Rule (1895–1945): The Reception of Western Law* (Seattle: University of Washington Press, 2000).

12. Wang, *Legal Reform in Taiwan under Japanese Colonial Rule,* 47.

13. Kim, "Law and Custom under the Choson Dynasty and Colonial Korea," 1070.

14. On the problem of custom and early Meiji statutes on the family, see Susan L. Burns, "Local Courts, National Laws, and the Problem of Patriarchy in Meiji Japan: Reading 'Record of Civil Rulings' from the Perspective of Gender History," in *Interdisciplinary Studies in the Taiwan Colonial Court Archive,* ed. Wang Tay-Sheng (Taipei: Angle Publishing, 2009), 285–309.

15. Quoted in Ronald Frank, "The Civil Code," in *History of Law in Japan,* 204.

16. On the postwar reform of family law, see Nishimura Nobuo, *Sengo Nihon no kazokuhō no minshūka,* 2 vols. (Kyoto: Hōritsu Bunkasha, 1978–1991).

17. Rape was defined narrowly as forcible intercourse involving a vagina and a penis, a definition that excluded many acts of sexual violence including anal and oral intercourse. The result was that instances of male-male sexual violence were not deemed rape. Forcible anal and oral intercourse involving a woman were also excluded. These kinds of crime were treated

under the obscenity statutes, which carried far lighter punishments. For a discussion of problems in Japan's rape laws and international criticism, see Morikawa Yasutaka, "Kakuron: Gōkanzai no mondaiten," *Hōgaku seminā* 43, no. 10 (October 1998): 29–32.

18. Fujime Yuki, *Sei no rekishigaku: Koshō seido, dataizai taisei kara baishun boshihō, yusei hogohō taisei e* (Fuji Shuppan, 1997).

19. See, for example, the works by Kanazu Hidemi and Ishikawa Shōko on the criminalization of abortion cited by Burns in Chapter 3, as well as Mitsunari Miho, *Jendā no hikakuhō shigaku: Kindaihō chitsujo no saikentō* (Suita: Osaka Daigaku Shuppankai, 2006); and Murakami Kazuhiro, *Nihon kindai kekkonhō shiron* (Kyoto: Hōritsu Bunkasha, 2003).

20. Harald Fuess, *Divorce in Japan: Family, Gender, and the State* (Stanford, CA: Stanford University Press, 2004); Tiana Norgren, *Abortion before Birth Control: The Politics of Reproduction in Postwar Japan* (Princeton, NJ: Princeton University Press, 2001); Marnie S. Anderson, *A Place in Public: Women's Rights in Meiji Japan* (Cambridge, MA: Harvard University Asia Center, 2010); and Mark D. West, *Law in Everyday Japan: Sex, Sumo, Suicide, and Statutes* (Chicago: University of Chicago Press, 2005) and *Lovesick Japan: Sex/Marriage/Romance/Law* (Ithaca, NY: Cornell University Press, 2011). An important work on gender and law that predates the post-2000 "boom" is J. Mark Ramseyer, "Indentured Prostitution in Imperial Japan: Credible Commitment in the Commercial Sex Industry," *Journal of Law, Economics, and Organization* 17, no. 1 (Spring 1991): 89–116.

21. See, for example, James L. McClain, *Japan: A Modern History* (New York: W. W. Norton and Company, 2002), 256–259; and Andrew Gordon, *A History of Modern Japan: From Tokugawa Times to the Present,* 2nd ed. (New York: Oxford University Press, 2003), 87–89.

22. William Johnston, *Geisha, Harlot, Stranger, Star: A Woman, Sex, and Morality in Modern Japan* (New York: Columbia University Press, 2004); Christine L. Marran, *Poison Woman: Figures of Female Transgression in Modern Japanese Culture* (Minneapolis: University of Minnesota Press, 2007).

23. In addition to the works cited in notes 7 and 8, see Richard L. Roberts, *Litigants and Households: African Disputes and Colonial Courts in the French Soudan, 1858–1912* (Portsmouth, NH: Heinemann Educational Books, 2005); Elsbeth Locher-Scholten, *Women and the Colonial State: Essays on Gender and Modernity in the Netherland Indies, 1900–1942* (Amsterdam: Amsterdam University Press, 2000); and Sally Engle, *Colonizing Hawai'i: The Cultural Power of Law* (Princeton, NJ: Princeton University Press, 2000).

24. There is an extensive literature on the Fukuoka case and its after-

math. Huen's overview article is useful: see Yuki P. Huen, "Workplace Sexual Harassment in Japan: A Review of Combating Measures Taken," *Asian Survey* 47, no. 5 (September/October 2007): 811–827.

25. The surname suit was filed in January 2011. Information on the case is available on the website maintained by a group called the Association to Support the Separate Surname Suit (*Bessei soshō o sasaeru kai*) available at http://www.asahi-net.or.jp/~dv3m-ymsk/index.html (accessed on July 9, 2012).

26. Chika Shinohara and Christopher Uggen, "Sexual Harassment: The Emergence of Legal Consciousness in Japan and the U.S.," *Sociological Quarterly* 50, no. 2 (2009): 201–234.

PART I

Prostitution, Law, and Human Rights

CHAPTER 1

The *Maria Luz* Incident

Personal Rights and International Justice for Chinese Coolies and Japanese Prostitutes

Douglas Howland

For its handling of the *Maria Luz* incident in 1872, Japan received international acclaim as a humanitarian supporter of international law. The case concerned the Peruvian transport of Chinese coolies on the *Maria Luz* into the Japanese port of Yokohama, and invited the participation of Japan in international efforts to suppress the coolie trade. Japan freed the coolies on board the *Maria Luz,* but in their defense of Peru's practice of shipping Chinese coolies, Peru's legal representatives pointed out that indentured prostitution in Japan was an equivalent practice. Since Japan allowed domestic indentured prostitution, how could it disallow Chinese coolie bondage in Peru? In the wake of his ruling in the *Maria Luz* case, Kanagawa assistant governor Ōe Taku (1847–1921) agreed that the two practices were similar violations of personal rights and represented a common subversion of the justice anticipated by the international civilization to which the new Japan aspired. Ōe subsequently promoted the first of Meiji laws intended to rectify the conditions of prostitutes in Japan.

Accordingly, the *Maria Luz* incident has been routinely presented as a beginning for the reform of prostitution in modern Japan.[1] This essay downplays such a reading of the prostitution reform laws of 1872, which invariably criticizes the laws as insufficient. Instead, this essay returns attention to the parallel drawn between coolies and prostitutes in order to stress the point of justice that prompted Ōe to instigate a reform of prostitute contracts. In that context, the conclusions drawn by the three most prominent readings of the *Maria Luz* incident seem to miss the point of international justice. First, the work of anti-prostitution reformers in the 1880s and '90s, many of whom joined the movement out of Christian goodwill, argued that the law had simply not done enough to eradicate a social evil subversive of public morality.[2] A second interpretation, which starts with the assumption that prostitution is a natural and lasting element of human society, seems to apologize for prostitution in that it argues that laws like those of 1872 could have little effect on what was so profound a social custom; such scholars believed that change could arise not by means of laws decreed from on high but only through popular reform of Japanese customs.[3] And a third interpretation is the more recent one offered by scholars of Japanese women and prostitution, who criticize the 1872 laws as simply inadequate and see a cynical government doing as little as possible to change the situation.[4] My own position is closest to this third perspective—as I will argue, the 1872 laws offer evidence of a paternalistic state safeguarding the institution of prostitution.

The peculiar similarity between the male Chinese coolie and the female Japanese prostitute was the fact that, in the context of nineteenth-century capitalist development, both were an intermediate category of labor. Neither was free or enslaved; rather, each was a captive group placed in a specific site of productivity.[5] Both the plantation, where the coolie was usually bonded, and the brothel, where the prostitute was bonded, were sites outside of the patriarchal (and increasingly nuclear) family structure strongly encouraged by national government sanctions. While this was true of many categories of labor at the time—sailors, miners, and certain factory employees—the coolie was marked racially, for Chinese coolies as a group differed from the rest of the population of their tropical host country.[6] Likewise, prostitutes were a marked population located in brothel districts segregated to some degree from so-called respectable Japanese society.

Feminist scholars have pointed out that the colonial state and its legal regimes in the nineteenth century ensconced paternal authority at the head of the state, which attempted to reproduce itself within the family by sponsoring a legal form of the patriarchal family. In the same way that the patriarch protected his wife and offspring by managing their persons and property, as well as their labor contribution to the well-being of the family, the state too guaranteed the profitability of entrepreneurs in plantations and brothels with its structure of laws. For both Chinese coolie and Japanese prostitute, the legal regime of property relations dominated their labor, and the two fundamental principles of this labor and legal regime were servitude according to contract and the repayment of debts.[7] In the end, the 1872 order to liberate prostitutes was an unsuccessful experiment: the business losses sustained by freeing prostitutes from their debts raised more concern than the conditions of the women themselves, and the law was reversed in 1875.

This essay argues that rather than place the 1872 laws at the start of a movement to reform prostitution in Japan, we should see these laws as an effort to reform labor contracts in the larger international context informed by notions of personal rights, justice and equity, and the expansion of enlightened civilization. We look first at the *Maria Luz* incident and then examine the coolie trade in the third quarter of the nineteenth century and the corresponding practice of bonded prostitution in early Meiji Japan. Finally, we turn to the consequences of Ōe Taku's legal judgments against bonded labor.

The *Maria Luz* Incident

On July 9, 1872, the *Maria Luz,* a Peruvian ship carrying 230 bonded Chinese laborers from Macao, docked unexpectedly in the Japanese port of Yokohama; the ship urgently needed to repair a foremast—damaged in a typhoon—before proceeding to its destination in Peru.[8] Within a few days of the ship's arrival, one of the Chinese passengers jumped overboard and sought refuge on a British naval ship in the harbor, the *Iron Duke.* The Chinese man, Mok-hing, reported that he and his fellow passengers were being seriously mistreated on the *Maria Luz,* but after a consultation between the captain of the *Iron Duke* and the British chargé d'affaires, Robert G. Watson, the man was transferred to Japanese authorities, who subsequently returned him to his ship. Both Watson and the chargé d'affaires for the United States, Charles O. Shepard, believed that the *Maria Luz* was involved in the coolie trade, and on August 3, following a few more such incidents, they urged Japanese foreign minister Soejima Taneomi to investigate the ship, first, because of the barbarity of the coolie trade, which Britain, France, and the United States had been attempting to eliminate, and, second, because this was perhaps an opportunity for Japan to bolster good relations with China.[9]

Japanese leaders were initially reluctant to interfere with Peru, a foreign power with whom Japan had no treaty. On the one hand, Soejima argued that the ship was in Japanese territorial waters and Japan had jurisdiction; on the other hand, Etō Shinpei, minister of justice, felt that the *Maria Luz* was a foreign ship and not subject to Japanese jurisdiction. But Soejima was supported by Prime Minister Sanjō Sanetomi, and so, at Soejima's request, officials G. W. Hill and Hayashi Dōsaburō (Gontenji) of the Kanagawa prefectural government conducted an investigation on board the *Maria Luz* on August 7, which so raised the suspicions of Japanese investigators that they removed the Chinese passengers from the ship for further questioning.

A special inquiry was conducted August 17–24 under the authority of the Kanagawa government. Governor Mutsu Munemitsu had resigned rather than intervene in Peruvian affairs, so the proceeding was put in the hands of Ōe Taku, an assistant governor. Several of the Chinese coolies testified against Captain Ricardo Herrera: that he had subjected his passengers to cruel treatment, including beatings and the cutting of their queues; that there had been insufficient food and space on the ship; and that several of their group had been kidnapped and forced to sign their contracts after the ship had left Macao. In his defense, Herrera and his English lawyer, Frederick V. Dickins, argued that: (1) Japan had no jurisdiction in Macao or China, or on the high seas regarding the *Maria Luz* or Captain Herrera. (2) None of Herrera's actions constituted piracy according to the law of nations. (Piracy was the charge laid against transporters of slaves.) (3) Neither slavery nor the coolie trade was prohibited by the law of nations or by Japan, and contracts such as those between the Chinese and Peruvians were common in all countries. Moreover, Japanese law allowed the analogous practice of indentured prostitution. (4) Herrera refused to recognize what he claimed were the irregular proceedings of the Kanagawa court. And (5) the *Maria Luz* should be allowed to depart and an indemnity paid to Herrera for his additional expenses that had accrued from his delay in Japan and the loss of his passengers.[10]

Ōe pronounced his "finding and recommendation" on August 26. He upheld against Captain Herrera the charges of cruel treatment, which he insisted had occurred in Japanese waters and within the jurisdiction of Kanagawa prefecture. But he pardoned the Captain from any further punishment and allowed him to go his way.

Meanwhile, a group of foreign consuls protested against the Kanagawa court procedure. Led by Eduard Zappe, acting consul general for the German Federation, and including the representatives of Denmark, Poland, and Italy, they claimed that Japan was not competent to punish offenses committed on the high seas by Peru, nor was Japan competent to decide on the validity of a contract made between foreigners in places outside of Japan. Moreover, they asserted the right, by virtue of their countries' respective treaty provisions for extraterritorial privileges, to assist the court since the case concerned a foreign power in Japan. According to a memorandum regarding the Yokohama foreign settlement signed in October 1867, the Kanagawa government was to prosecute the criminal offenses of resident Chinese and non–treaty power foreigners (such as Peru) in consultation with a committee of foreign consuls. Zappe and his fellows were concerned that Ōe's actions could constitute a precedent that might later challenge the principle of extraterritoriality. The British consul, however, did not support the move, nor did the representatives of the United States and Holland. As Ōe and the Japanese government successfully argued, because they were not residents neither Captain Herrera nor the Chinese passengers of the *Maria Luz* fell under the rules of the 1867 memorandum. Moreover, the memorandum did not restrict Japan's independence in such criminal matters.[11]

Consequently, a second, civil lawsuit took place from September 18 to 27, with Herrera as plaintiff and the Kanagawa prefectural government as defendant. Ōe Taku again presided. Herrera offered a more meticulous articulation of the validity of the labor contracts for his Chinese coolies, asserting that they were valid under the law of nations and Chinese law, and enforceable according to Japanese custom—in the same manner as prostitution contracts. But the judgment handed down in favor of the Kanagawa government on September 27 reconfirmed the earlier judgment against Herrera. Ōe found that the contracts took Chinese persons out of their native jurisdiction against their consent, and thus the contracts were not duly executed and thus not valid nor enforceable. (I return to this point in the discussion of prostitution in Japan below.) Ōe also found that the contracts were *contra bonos mores* and thus Japan was not obliged to enforce them, and that the contracts were rendered void by Herrera's substandard treatment of his passengers.[12] In the wake of this decision, Herrera deserted his ship, and eventually the *Maria Luz* was sold at auction and the proceeds were forwarded to the ship's owner in Peru.[13] The Chinese coolies were returned to China, and, as British diplomats had hoped, the Chinese government expressed its gratitude for Japan's kindness toward China's unfortunate subjects.[14]

Peru's continuing dissatisfaction over the outcome of the trial prompted the Peruvian government to send a mission to Japan, led by Aurelio García y García, whose purpose was both to resolve the *Maria Luz* incident and to negotiate a treaty of friendship and trade between Peru and Japan.[15] Because that set of negotiations became deadlocked over the *Maria Luz* dispute, the two governments agreed to seek international arbitration of their differences, which were taken up by Czar Alexander II of Russia. In March 1875, Peruvian and Japanese legal advisors presented their cases to the czar: Peru insisted upon the legality of both coolie contracts and the shipping of coolies through Japanese waters, as well as Japan's want of jurisdiction and the illegal constitution of the Kanagawa prefectural court. In its defense, Japan asserted its jurisdiction over the *Maria Luz,* particularly in the interests of the well-being of both its port of Yokohama and the Chinese passengers on the ship, and argued that Captain Herrera's demand that Japan return the Chinese passengers to the ship was a legal matter of extradition. In the absence of an extradition treaty, Japan was not obliged to do so. In June 1875, Alexander II pronounced his judgment in favor of Japan. With Japan vindicated, the case was ostensibly closed.[16]

The Chinese Coolie Trade

The traffic in Chinese coolies began in the second quarter of the nineteenth century, sponsored primarily by British shippers interested in cheap labor for the sugar plantations in British Guiana.[17] As much scholarship has pointed out, the coolie trade was created to replace the African slave trade, outlawed in the British Empire through a series of prohibitions during the first half of the nineteenth century: from the slave trade (1807) to slavery (1833), to ultimately all exportation of slaves (1841).[18] Insofar as the coolie trade developed simultaneously with these efforts to curtail the slave trade, it was always a source of national moral contradiction, for it was judged comparable to, if not worse than, African slavery—particularly the voyage from China to the Americas and the conditions of coolie labor in the Americas. And although British prohibitions began to curtail the slave trade, slavery nonetheless remained legal in several countries to which Chinese coolies were transported; slavery was not abolished in Peru until 1854, in Cuba until 1883, and in Brazil until 1888. Although slavery was eventually abolished, the conditions of capitalism that had encouraged slavery persisted well beyond the nineteenth century. Large numbers of inexpensive laborers were needed in the sugar plantations of Cuba and Brazil, and in the cotton plantations and guano beds of Peru. As African slaves became less available, they were replaced by Chinese coolies.[19]

Three conditions encouraged the expansion of the coolie trade in the 1840s. In the first place, both Peru and Spain revised their immigration laws so as to permit the inflow of laborers from China. Spain was particularly motivated on behalf of its colonies such as Cuba.[20] Second, Chinese officials continued to turn a blind eye to emigration: as Hosea Morse put it, emigration was "unregulated because illegal, and unrestricted because unregulated."[21] Although emigration remained technically illegal until 1860, the reciprocity implicit in China's treaties with the Western powers after 1842 acknowledged the rights of person and property for overseas Chinese, certainly those of merchants and "free" laborers. Most free laborers emigrated to the United States or Australia.[22] And third, the conditions of extraterritoriality established in the wake of the first Opium War between China and Great Britain created those independent zones of contact that facilitated and encouraged the coolie trade—the treaty ports on China's southern coast. Indeed, extraterritoriality both facilitated the rise of the coolie trade and also served to restrain it, a point to which I will return. But even after the formal cessation of coolie labor shipments in 1875, coolies continued to be shipped illegally from Chinese ports southward to plantations in the Dutch East Indies, the Straights Settlements, and the Malay States.[23]

The coolie trade was intimately linked, in its most unregulated and abusive phase, to the shipments to Peru and Cuba largely during the third quarter of the nineteenth century. From 1847 to 1875, between 250,000 and 500,000 Chinese laborers were shipped from southern ports, primarily Macao after 1855, bound mainly for Peru and Cuba (as well as Brazil, Chile, Hawai'i, and several Caribbean and Central American ports).[24] These estimates vary widely, in part because of deliberately muddled ship records, and in part because of the mortality rates in transit. And in fact, it was the terrible mortality on some voyages that brought the coolie trade to the attention of British officials in Hong Kong.[25] Watt Stewart, who completed the most extensive analysis of the case of Peru, estimated that between 80,000 and 100,000 Chinese coolies reached Peru between 1849 and 1875. The average mortality on the voyages between 1860 and 1863 was 30.44 percent, and that between 1870 and 1874, 6.5 percent. Stewart's average mortality for the decade from 1860 to 1870 was 10.74 percent.[26] By comparison, Hosea Morse noted a range of mortality rates for particular voyages from 14 percent to 45 percent; his average for the nearly 24,000 Chinese shipped from Hong Kong to Cuba between 1847 and 1857 was a mortality of 14 percent, or 3,342 persons.[27] Working from records in Cuba, Duvon Corbitt observed a similarly wide range of mortality rates among specific voyages, but overall estimated a mortality rate of 15.2 percent for 50,123 coolies shipped between 1847 and 1859: reportedly 42,501 arrived in Cuba and 7,722 died en route.[28] Merely on its passage from Macao to Yokohama, the *Maria Luz* lost at least 6 coolies to yellow fever.[29]

In the typical process, collecting agents (or "crimps") brought laborers to the coolie depots (or "barracoons") where the coolies signed contracts that bound them to eight years of labor service. As nearly all coolie laborers were illiterate, their signatures were more often than not an "X"—if formal, written contracts were used at all. According to Nicholas Hannen, a British judge in the Kanagawa consular court, illiteracy was further complicated by the linguistic challenges facing exporters of coolies—in addition to working between Spanish and Portuguese, interpreters also had to deal with the three different Chinese languages used among the coolie population: Hakka, Fujianese, and Cantonese. It was difficult to say if any coolie understood what he was signing. The investigation in the *Maria Luz* case, for example, found that the contracts in the possession of the coolies on board ship had not been signed and hence were not valid contracts, that many of the coolies were minors whose guardians had allegedly signed on their behalf, and that the contracts could be assigned to anyone at any future date. Ōe concluded that the contracts created a relationship of personal servitude, which, except for the eight-year time limit, encouraged a labor system quite similar to slavery. Moreover, there was no oversight as to the legality of coolie contracts. The coolie in Cuba may have had a right to appeal to Spanish courts for enforcement of his rights in case of maltreatment, but critics noted that there was no instance on record of such a proceeding. In Peru as well, justice was not forthcoming. The coolies on the *Maria Luz* were utterly unaware of whatever Portuguese or Peruvian law might have given them redress, and Ōe was dismayed when neither Captain Herrera nor his legal counsel could produce a copy of the law in court. Simply put, the shipping agents in charge of the barracoons paid the crimps a fee for each man brought in and advanced an initial payment to each coolie, a payment that began a series of expenses defrayed on the coolie's behalf and repayment of which routinely extended his years of service beyond the contracted eight. Upon entering the barracoon, in other words, the coolie was no longer a free contractor.[30]

But many men had not arrived freely at the outset. Reports on coolie supply indicate that the three major sources included, first, men taken prisoner in clan fights in Guangdong province and sold to Chinese or Portuguese crimps, and, second, villagers or fishermen seized by kidnappers along the southern coast. The third source were those unfortunates who, having lost at gambling, paid their debts with their persons by contracting with the crimps.[31] Again, reports vary widely. Samuel Wells Williams, who examined the record of coolie labor in Cuba, claimed that of the more than 142,000 coolies who landed in Havana during the quarter century in question, roughly two-thirds went abroad willingly, if ignorantly. But the Cuba Commission, sent by the Chinese government to investigate conditions in Cuba in 1874, reported that four-fifths of the coolies interviewed declared that they had been kidnapped or decoyed against their wills.[32] Many of the coolies aboard the *Maria Luz* complained that they had been kidnapped, and even if not all of them had been interviewed, the fact that their contracts were not in order invited Ōe's suspicion that they were not willing emigrants. In the subsequent preparations for arbitration before Czar Alexander II, the Japanese government took the position that the coolies had been kidnapped, and from the point of view of British common law, Captain Herrera's abusive treatment of his passengers constituted "continuous trespass" within the jurisdiction of Japan and was deserving of punitive action.[33]

At the barracoon, the shipping agent then contracted with ship captains to transport the coolies to the Americas. Sailing conditions were reportedly substandard, if not miserable: the first few years of coolie shipments gained such notoriety that the ships were described commonly as "floating hells."[34] The *Maria Luz* was typical in that regard. Ship captains such as Herrera represented labor brokers in Peru or Cuba, to whom the coolies were transferred upon arrival at a Peruvian port such as Callao. There the coolies were auctioned, in the same manner as African slaves had once been auctioned, their contracts transferred to their new owners, and their persons distributed to their new work sites. In Peru, many coolies were sent to work in the guano beds, even though many contracts had stipulated that they would not be working there. Labor conditions resembled those of slaves, for the coolies were confined to dormitories, their movements restricted, and their behavior disciplined with harsh punishment. One Peruvian writer maintained that although Peru's Civil Code specifically granted a number of rights to former Negro slaves—including recompense for work performed, food, protection, medical assistance in case of illness, and many others—the Chinese coolie had no such rights under Peruvian law.[35] Suicide and rebellion were the primary alternatives to work, the latter such a problem in 1870 in Peru that local critics argued that the coolie trade had become a source of national disgrace.[36]

Internationally, officials in the British and U.S. diplomatic service took the lead in attacking the coolie trade and working for its suppression.[37] Once the wretched conditions of transport operations became widely known, the first focus of legislation was to attempt to restrict transport. The British Passenger Acts of 1852 and 1855 included provisions for the security of ship passengers regarding their contracts, and this effectively closed Hong Kong to the coolie trade. Consequently, Macao under Portuguese control became the primary port of departure. In 1862, the United States prohibited the transport of coolies in U.S. vessels.[38] Since these prohibitions did little to curtail the coolie trade, Britain attempted to use the most-favored-nation clause of the treaty system with China. The Coolie Convention of 1866, signed by China, Great Britain, and France, mandated standards for each step of the coolie trade—recruitment, retention in depot, transport, conditions of work and payment, and repatriation of contract immigrants—and the signees expected that all other nations joined in treaties with China were bound to respect the Convention. The United States and Russia publicly agreed to do so, but Spain, Portugal, and Peru passively resisted, even though the official policy of the Chinese government, articulated by Prince Gong of the Zongli yamen (Foreign Office), was that coolie labor could only be contracted according to the Convention of 1866.[39]

Accordingly, the years from 1866 to 1872 were a period of heightened tension surrounding the coolie trade. Two infamous incidents immediately preceding the case of the *Maria Luz* incited international outrage. One scandal that rocked Peru in 1868 was the incident of the "branded 48": forty-eight Chinese coolies had been branded by their Peruvian master in order to identify them if they ran away. The incident drew such condemnation from Britain that the governor of Macao was induced to suspend the emigration of Chinese from Macao in November 1868. But six months later, the transports had resumed.[40] The second scandal was the case of the *Nouvelle Penelope,* a French-registered ship transporting coolies from Macao in September 1870. Shortly after departure, the coolies took control of the ship, killed the captain and eight members of the crew, and sailed back to China. Most of the coolies escaped, but sixteen were executed at the request of the French consul in Canton, and that action prompted one of the escapees, Kwok-a-sing, to seek a trial in his own defense. His English attorney and the governor of Hong Kong conducted a thorough investigation of the incident, which revealed the wretched conditions on the ship and the maltreatment of the Chinese on the part of the captain and crew. Kwok was released and the court magistrate judged, first, that the commerce in coolies was a slave trade—were the captain still alive he should be punished for piracy—and, second, that being forced to emigrate against one's will permitted one to exercise one's right to use violence for the sake of self-preservation. This judgment prompted, on the one hand, the U.S. Minister to China, Frederick Low, to suggest that self-preservation under international law be used against the governments of Portugal and Macao to end the coolie trade, and, on the other hand, a consular convention on the part of Peru and Portugal in February 1872 in order to confirm each other's rights in maritime transports.[41]

Thus the *Maria Luz* incident offered a key opportunity in the efforts of Britain and the United States to suppress the coolie trade. The Japanese judgment against Peru, which was undertaken with the sanction of Britain and contrary to the usual British commitment to extraterritoriality—and which was subsequently upheld in international arbitration—signaled the end of the coolie trade. Ships transporting coolies to the Americas were no longer safe from interference. In 1873, the Spanish minister to China abruptly resigned when the Chinese government refused to allow any coolies to emigrate to Cuba; Spain's request would be considered only if Spain heeded the 1866 Convention and improved conditions for Chinese laborers in Cuba. Worse for Spain, China insisted on sending a commission to Cuba to investigate labor conditions there, and the report submitted by Chen Lanbin in 1874 condemned Spanish and Cuban officials and their policies regarding Chinese laborers.[42] At the same time, as a direct consequence of the *Maria Luz* incident, Peru negotiated a treaty of friendship and trade with China that agreed to Chinese demands regarding the emigration of laborers to Peru and their working conditions there; this was followed by a mission of investigation that similarly reported back to China on the outrageous treatment of Chinese laborers in Peru. Macao decreed an end to the coolie trade in March 1874, and thereafter only free laborers emigrated to Peru, Cuba, and other ports in the Americas.[43] The coolie trade became illegal in the eyes of the law of nations and, accordingly, became a furtive practice.

Prostitution in Early Meiji Japan

Bonded prostitution in 1870s Japan bears a number of striking similarities to the coolie trade, from procurement and the legal niceties of a labor contract to conditions surrounding labor and the rather ineffectual legal attempts to end the practice.[44] In 1868, the new and westernizing Meiji state inherited a widespread practice of licensed prostitution from the preceding Tokugawa shogunate; if anything, the economic changes directed by the Meiji state encouraged the growth of prostitution well into the twentieth century. Available numbers do not go as far back as the 1870s, but it is clear that the number of licensed prostitutes in Tokyo's Yoshiwara district more than doubled between 1883 and 1906, from reportedly 3,156 to 6,834 women; nationally the number of prostitutes increased from 27,559 in 1887 to 52,410 in 1899.[45] Indeed, the *Maria Luz* incident prompted the first official attempt to moderate the growth of prostitution in Japan. Frederick Dickins' affront to the Kanagawa court in his defense of Captain Herrera—when he pointed out the hypocrisy of Japan in allowing bonded prostitution—persuaded Ōe Taku and then Etō Shinpei, minister of justice, to take action on behalf of young Japanese women. The result was a pair of regulations in late 1872: the "Order to Liberate Prostitutes" and the "Regulations Concerning Brothels and Prostitutes."

Employment as a prostitute in Japan during the late 1800s was associated with a number of occupations available for young women at the time, especially those of domestic servant and machine operator in a silk or cotton-spinning factory. Young women were brought into each of these trades in much the same manner: impoverished rural families, many of whom became poor tenant farmers as a result of the economic reconstruction of the 1880s, hired out, sold, or mortgaged their daughters to a factory or brothel for a number of years, in exchange for a cash advance on the daughter's wages. The family arranged the hiring out; the father as head of household signed a contract committing his daughter to, typically, from three to seven years of labor; and the young woman's father, as guarantor, was liable for a penalty if she should run away or otherwise fail to fulfill the terms of the contract. Apart from this usual contractual arrangement, women were also transferred, sold, tricked, or kidnapped into work as prostitutes; this was especially true of women in domestic service. By the 1920s, a significant number of Japanese prostitutes claimed to have "graduated" from work in cotton mills to work as prostitutes; one researcher estimates that between 11 and 30 percent of prostitutes had originally left home to work in silk or cotton mills.[46]

A number of points are salient here. As Ōe discovered with many of the coolies on board the *Maria Luz,* a young woman was sent into prostitution under the authority of her family guardian; this typically male head of household was confirmed in the sobriety of his decision by the officially patriarchal form of the family. In that regard, the Meiji state sanctioned prostitution as labor insofar as it confirmed the patriarchal order of the Japanese family. At the same time, much like the Chinese coolie, poor tenant farmers and their daughters tended to be illiterate, so that the labor contracts that legalized the commitment were easily fraudulent; some young women who learned the content of their contracts subsequently protested their servitude. Moreover, like the Chinese coolie, women worked as prostitutes under conditions that were often miserable, marked by poor food, an absence of health care (mitigated only minimally by the spread of contagious diseases regulations in the late 1870s), confinement to the brothel, and an incremental growth of expenses defrayed by the brothel owner, repayment of which necessitated the extension of a prostitute's length of service. The alternatives were few; absconding was difficult and suicide grim.[47]

It is worth noting that scholars of Chinese prostitution have argued that the shipment of Chinese women overseas for prostitution was early on coordinated with the coolie trade. Women were shipped to California and Southeast Asia to service coolies indentured to plantations there.[48] Similarly, as Japanese companies invested in China and Southeast Asia, Japanese women too were shipped to Shanghai, Hong Kong, Singapore, Batavia, Manila, Saigon, and elsewhere. Although the peak of traffic in these Japanese women, known as the *karayuki-san,* occurred between 1890 and 1935, J. F. Warren, who has completed the most extensive study of prostitution in Singapore, noted that fourteen Japanese prostitutes were registered in Singapore already by 1877. And a significant population of 276 Japanese women was present in Siberia in 1884. In other words, overseas traffic began well before officials in Japan became aware of the trend.[49]

In any case, the benefits of these employment arrangements were praised throughout the Meiji period. To work as a prostitute was a fate more dire than factory employment for young women from poor families, but all recognized that the wages advanced for such young women were significantly higher than those for textile factory recruits. Otherwise unemployed young women had a means to contribute to the improvement of their impoverished households, and a family's increased prosperity in the absence of a daughter absolved the stigma attached to the reason for that daughter's absence. The statesman Itō Hirobumi declared in 1896 that licensed prostitution was "a splendid arrangement" insofar as it allowed filial daughters to assist their parents.[50]

Itō's comment underscores the great ambivalence among Meiji leaders regarding prostitution. As I have already noted, a number of scholars charge the Meiji state with complicity in the maintenance of prostitution. The state sanctioned patriarchal authority within the family, the state's land tax policy ruined vast numbers of peasants, and the state was either unable or unwilling to introduce economic measures that might have ameliorated the plight of Japan's poorest peasants. Japan's efforts to industrialize in the 1870s depended on the creation of a proletariat culled from the countryside, and the young women who went into factories and brothels represented a deliberate and significant effect of those government policies. The demands of a national economy, in other words, supported the traffic in young women.

At the same time, public opinion on the matter of prostitution was quite divided in the 1870s. For example, the scholars, educators, and government officials associated with the Meiji Six Society, a debating society that set itself the goal of enlightening Japanese society, broached the issue of prostitution in two general contexts. First of these was the nature of marriage in a civilized society. Ideally, Japanese in an enlightened age should be developing toward monogamy in marriage, which meant the elimination of the traditional practice of concubinage. A man should have only one wife, and the practice of maintaining a concubine should no longer be acceptable. Mori Arinori, Tsuda Mamichi, and Sakatani Shiroshi advocated the elimination of concubines as a way to strengthen the nuclear family. Without the interference of concubines, a man's primary wife and his legally recognized children with her could be secure in their patrimony; in addition, her love and position as wife and mother would be secure. Mori, Tsuda, and Sakatani recommended that Japan recognize the equal rights of husbands and wives, as a means to strengthen monogamy in marriage. However, given the perennial problem of male lust and the fact that a poor laborer in Japan was unable to support a wife and family, prostitution offered an outlet for men.[51] The educator Fukuzawa Yukichi, for example, praised prostitution for its salutary effect in maintaining safety and order in civilized society—even though, he added, it is shameful and hateful work and should be secluded from society. Both Fukuzawa and Sakatani imagined that morality would grow with enlightenment, so that monogamy would eventually become the norm.[52]

But a second context for public opinion was Japan's national reputation. Tsuda castigated prostitution as a national disgrace, reporting in late 1875 that he was shocked to discover on a summer trip to the central mountains northwest of Tokyo that, contrary to what one might expect, the spread of enlightenment in Japan was accompanied by a vast increase in the number of prostitutes along the main thoroughfares to and from the capital. Prostitution, he charged, was a sign of the people's ignorance, demoralization, and disease; it weakens their physical strength and exhausts their wealth, it reflects the poverty and weakness of the nation and its army, and it portends national humiliation among the civilized nations of the earth. He urgently recommended that it be abolished. In response, some of his colleagues soberly reminded him that the civilized nations of Europe, too, supported systems of licensed prostitution.[53]

Clearly, Japanese leadership was divided over prostitution and its meaning for the nation. On the one hand, it was a positive effect of national economic policy; on the other, it was a detrimental mark on Japan's international standing. In both cases, prostitution was a matter of national concern for Japan's development as a civilizing nation. Before turning to the legal effects on prostitution that arose from the *Maria Luz* incident, I would point out the surprising absence of descriptions of prostitution in 1870s Japan, in contrast to the thorough and contemporaneous investigations of coolie labor. Why were there no examinations of prostitution? Apart from the fact that coolie traffic was better documented because it was an international trade, it is clear that the Japanese state had not yet engaged issues that had prompted more detailed studies of prostitution in other places. Two conditions at least can be noted. One is concern over syphilis—the contagious diseases acts in Britain and British colonies produced public records of prostitution. J. F. Warren was able to identify fourteen Japanese prostitutes in Singapore by 1877 because of the imposition of a contagious diseases act there in 1870; records had been thereafter maintained. In Japan, such acts were not in place in major cities until the late 1870s, so that records of prostitutes are not available until the 1880s. A second factor that spurred inquiries into the practice was parliamentary debate over the age of consent; determining the age at which men could have sexual access to women frequently served as a national means to monitor information on prostitutes.[54] This was not forthcoming during the early Meiji period.

The Pursuit of Personal Rights, Justice, and Civilization

When, in the course of the civil trial over the *Maria Luz* incident, lawyer Frederick Dickins urged Ōe Taku to see that Japan "free its slaves," it is clear that Ōe took that advice to heart.[55] Ōe dismissed the analogy as inapplicable: prostitution contracts concern the commitment of laborers within Japan and are thus a purely domestic matter, while the coolie contracts concern the transport of laborers to alien territory, where they cannot have recourse to their own authorities. Coolie contracts are thus under the jurisdiction of international law, which was at issue in the *Maria Luz* case. Nonetheless, Ōe conceded,

> A peculiar domestic institution may exist in a state, and to an extent receive its countenance without any intention of encouraging its establishment abroad or forcing it upon the attention of the world. . . . The contracts referred to by the counsel are a peculiar feature of a strictly domestic institution, and it is not supposed that, even were it possible they could in any manner come before a foreign tribunal, that they would be regarded as having any force.[56]

Accordingly, five days after his judgment in the *Maria Luz* case, on October 2, 1872, Ōe issued a prohibition on human trafficking and bonded prostitution for Kanagawa prefecture; a week later, on October 9, this was sanctioned and expanded by the Ministry of Justice as a national "Order to Liberate Prostitutes." Collectively these orders did the following: (1) They prohibited the buying and selling of persons, and warned that moneys paid to purchase women for work as prostitutes, geisha, or servants could be confiscated. (2) They condemned the prostitutes' and geishas' loss of rights, and decreed that moneys paid for their purchase or upkeep may not be called by creditors. (3) They condemned the sale of children as an especially severe matter that would meet with dire penalty. And (4) they allowed for the continuance of contracted labor, provided that such contracts were properly written and limited to no more than seven years, and decreed that all contracts made prior to the Order were in effect void, so that prostitutes were free to leave their brothels. The Tokyo municipal government issued a similar order on October 4.[57]

As several scholars of the history of both women and prostitution in Japan have noted, these laws did not do much of significance to eliminate prostitution in Japan. They were a failed experiment, particularly as the Japanese state reaffirmed in 1875 the validity of debts owed to procurers and brothel owners. At best, the 1872 laws made it illegal to buy and sell human beings, and they eliminated the father or other familial guarantor from the demands of creditors. Women were henceforth independent contractors for their own labor, and presumably could have recourse to Japanese courts if their employers failed to observe the terms of their contracts.[58] In fact, the subsequent "Regulations Concerning Brothels and Prostitutes" (October 1872) made a point of the legality of women entering into such contracts by their own free will. Such language seemingly anticipated a protest aimed against restrictions on prostitution in 1877, in which supporters of prostitution argued that in a civilized society, people have freedom of occupation (announced in the Meiji "Charter Oath" of 1868), and thus the choice of prostitution should be considered a legitimate exercise of that freedom.[59] Not until 1902 did Japan's Supreme Court recognize a prostitute's right to leave a brothel.[60]

But as Fujime Yuki and others have argued, the pretext that prostitution was based on freely entering into contractual labor simply underscores the state's continued complicity with the system of legalized prostitution. The "Regulations Concerning Brothels and Prostitutes" established the systematic issuing of licenses and fixed monthly licensing fees at five yen per month for brothels and two yen a month for prostitutes. From 1876, each prefectural police department was given the authority to regulate prostitution in its respective area, and the income from licensing fees quietly encouraged the growth of licensed prostitution. According to U. G. Murphy, who attempted to bring prostitute cases before Japanese courts at the turn of the century in Nagoya, the police were outright indifferent or complicit with brothels. The main effect of the 1872 laws, in other words, was to eliminate the family from a woman's labor contract and to begin the process of restricting unlicensed prostitution, making prostitution a legally contractual form of labor maintained with state approval and the threat of sanctions. The paternal impulse overseeing prostitution shifted from the family to the state.[61]

Thus my purpose in this essay is not to lament that the legal conjuncture of Chinese coolie and Japanese prostitute contracts before the Kanagawa court failed to eliminate prostitution in Japan. Instead, I am interested in what Ōe Taku did accomplish, particularly since his biographers describe him as a "humanitarian" sincerely committed to the marginalized members of Japanese society in the 1870s—prostitutes, declassed samurai, and burakumin—and, in fact, he served a prison sentence for his support of the samurai rebels in the Satsuma Rebellion.[62] But rather than understand Ōe's judgments during and after the *Maria Luz* case as solely a pair of humanitarian gestures on behalf of coolies and prostitutes, it is appropriate to locate his judgments in their original context of international law. Ōe's decision against Captain Herrera was a mark of Japan's membership in the civilized family of nations, an important and strategic mark of alliance with Britain and the United States, the two countries most influential in international affairs and most likely to assist Japan in undoing the unequal treaties that had invited the insult and interference of Zappe and the other consuls on the grounds of extraterritorial privileges. Likewise, the 1872 laws on prostitution that Ōe had instigated were responding quite carefully and directly to the objections raised by Dickins in the *Maria Luz* case. As with the coolie trade, traffic in women and children for purposes of prostitution, insofar as it resembled slavery, was henceforth abolished, and Japan's treatment of women moved closer to what was expected of civilized nations. Like coolies, Japanese women could no longer be duped into becoming responsible for a contract they did not comprehend. Legally, a measure of personal right and justice had been attained—even though it proved temporary. As Ōe asserted in a reminiscence of 1911, it was a moral victory for Japan.[63]

The common thread here is Japan's eagerness to attain an international standard of civilization, for that was the measure by which the unequal treaties had been imposed in the 1850s and by which those treaties would be revised. Justice for coolies and prostitutes was secondary to the overall national goal of international parity. Japan's commitment to international law was informed by the same impulse as Japan's commitment to a national industrial policy: the desire for national autonomy. In a world order marked by imperialism and growing colonial conflict, international law and national economic policy joined to free bonded laborers from fraudulent contracts. Ōe's humanitarian efforts thus raised Japan's status in the eyes of the leaders of the civilized world.

Notes

Author's note: I thank Luise White, Holly Sanders, Barbara Brooks, and Marnie Anderson for comments on an earlier draft of this essay; I remain grateful to the University of Chicago Center for East Asian Studies for support of the research informing this work.

1. An exception is Oikata Sumio's argument that, in light of Justice Minister Etō Shinpei's prior plans to reform prostitution in Japan, the *Maria Luz* incident was not that relevant: "Nihon kindai kokka no seiritsu to baishō mondai," in *Nihon joseishi ronshū,* ed. Sōgō joseishi kenkyūkai, vol. 9, *Sei to karada* (Yoshikawa Kōbunkan, 1998), 75–109. Morita Tomoko has responded that, in spite of Etō's plans, Japanese officials were influenced by the input of British lawyers during the *Maria Luz* case and the newspapers certainly publicized the connection; see "Maria Rusu gō jiken to geishōgi kaihō rei," in *Onna to shakai shi,* ed. Ōguchi Yujirō (Yamakawa Shuppansha, 2001), 245–264.

2. See, for example, Itō Hidekichi, *Nihon haishō undōshi* (Fuji Shuppan, 1931), 23–27; and John R. Black, *Young Japan: Yokohama and Yedo,* vol. 2 (London: Trubner & Co.; Yokohama: Kelly & Co., 1880–1881), 377–378.

3. See J. E. De Becker, *The Nightless City, or the History of the Yoshiwara Yūkwaku,* 5th ed., revised [1905] (Rutland, VT: Tuttle, 1971), 300–301. A variant of this argument was that the laws would help to "civilize" Japan; see Morita, "Maria Rusu gō jiken to geishōgi kaihō rei," 257–258.

4. Fujime Yuki, "The Licensed Prostitution System and the Prostitution Abolition Movement in Modern Japan," *positions: east asia cultures critique* 5, no. 1 (Spring 1997): 135–170; Karen Colligan-Taylor, "Translator's Intro-

duction," in Yamazaki Tomoko, *Sandakan Brothel No. 8,* trans. Karen Colligan–Taylor (Armonk, NY: M. E. Sharpe, 1999), xvii–xx.

5. See the insightful analysis of labor and the "slave contract" in Carole Pateman, *The Sexual Contract* (Stanford, CA: Stanford University Press, 1988), 62–76, 142–153.

6. See Evelyn Hu–DeHart, "Chinese Coolie Labour in Cuba in the Nineteenth Century: Free Labour or Neo-slavery?," *Slavery and Abolition* 14, no. 1 (April 1993): 67–83; and Moon-Ho Jung, *Coolies and Cane: Race, Labor and Sugar in the Age of Emancipation* (Baltimore: Johns Hopkins University Press, 2006), 6–8, 19, 218, 222–225.

7. M. Jacqui Alexander, "Erotic Autonomy as a Politics of Decolonization," in *Feminist Genealogies, Colonial Legacies, Democratic Futures,* ed. M. Jacqui Alexander and Chandra Mohanty (New York: Routledge, 1997), 63–100 (esp. pp. 63–78); Kathleen Canning, *Gender History in Practice* (Baltimore: Johns Hopkins University Press, 2006), 5–6, 36–38; Chandra Mohanty, "Introduction: Cartographies of Struggle," in *Third World Women and the Politics of Feminism,* ed. Chandra Mohanty, Ann Russo, and Lourdes Torres (Bloomington: Indiana University Press, 1991), 1–47 (esp. pp. 15–28); Carole Pateman, both *The Sexual Contract,* 10–14, 116–142 passim, and (with Charles Mills) *Contract and Domination* (Cambridge: Polity, 2007), 222–227.

8. An official Japanese account of the incident was written by an assistant to the Kanagawa government, George Wallace Hill, although he is not credited as author: *The Peruvian Barque "Maria Luz": A Short Account of the Cases Tried in the Kanagawa Kencho . . .* (Kanagawa kenchō, 1874); this was translated by Japanese officials as *Peirokoku Maria Roshi sen saiban ryakki* (Kanagawa Kenchō, 1874), repr. *Meiji bunka zenshū,* vol. 11, *Gaikō hen,* ed. Meiji Bunka Kenkyūkai (Nihon Hyōronsha, 1968), 29–60. Official documents are gathered in *Nihon gaikō monjo,* ed. Gaimushō (Gaimushō, 1955), vol. 8 [1872], 412–540, vol. 9 [1873], 479–553, vol. 10 [1874], 494–537, and vol. 11 [1875], 374–481; and Republica del Peru, *Colección de los tratados, convenciones capitulaciones, armisticios, y otros actos diplomáticos y políticos celebrados desde la independencia hasta el día, precedida de una introducción que comprende la época colonial,* ed. Ricardo Aranda (Lima: Imprenta del estado, 1890–1911), vol. 10. See also Great Britain, Foreign Office Archives, F.O. 84/1442 ("Slave Trade—Fugitive Slave Commission. No. 29. Escape of Coolie Emigrants from the Peruvian Ship 'Maria Luz' on Board Her Majesty's Ship 'Iron Duke' in Japan in 1872"); and *Foreign Relations of the United States,* 1873, vol. 1 (Washington, DC: Government Printing Office, 1874), 524–630.

9. The most exacting discussions of the *Maria Luz* incident are Morita Tomoko, *Kaikoku to chigai hōken* (Yoshikawa Kōbunkan, 2005), 140–198; Tabohashi Kiyoshi, "Meiji gonen no 'Maria Rusu' jiken," *Shigaku zasshi* (1929): 40, no. 1: 98–114, 40, no. 3: 102–113, 40, no. 4: 87–112; and Takeda Yasumi, *Maria Rusu jiken: Ōe Taku to dorei kaihō* (Yokohama: Yurindō, 1981). See also Suzanne Crawford, "The *Maria Luz* Affair," *Historian* 46, no. 4 (1984): 583–596; C. Harvey Gardiner, *The Japanese and Peru, 1873–1973* (Albuquerque: University of New Mexico Press, 1975), 7–17; Hiroshi Mitani, *Maria Luz Affair and Public Opinion in the World* (Nagoya: Nanzan University, Centro de Estudios de America Latina, 1985); Robert L. Irick, *Ch'ing Policy toward the Coolie Trade, 1847–1878* (Taipei: Chinese Materials Center, 1982), 221–231; Wayne C. McWilliams, "Soejima Taneomi: Statesman of Early Meiji Japan, 1868–1874" (PhD diss., University of Kansas, 1973), 166–185; Ōyama Azusa, "Maria Rūsu gō jiken to saiban tetsuzuki," in his *Nihon gaikōshi kenkyū* (Ryōsho Fukyūkai, 1980), 55–79; Shimomura Fujio, *Meiji ishin no gaikō* (Ōyasu Shuppan, 1948), 163–172; Tanaka Tokihiko, "Maria Ruzu gō jiken," in *Nihon seiji saiban shiroku*, vol. 1, *Meiji zen*, ed. Wagatsuma Sakae (Daiichi Hōki Shuppan, 1968), 273–298; and Payson Treat, *Diplomatic Relations between the United States and Japan, 1853–1895* (Stanford, CA: Stanford University Press, 1932), vol. 1, 455–463.

10. On F. V. Dickins, see Peter F. Kornicki, "Frederick Victor Dickins (1838–1915)," in *Britain and Japan: Biographical Portraits*, vol. 3, ed. J. E. Hoare (Richmond, Surrey: Japan Library, 1999), 66–77; and idem, "Introduction," to Frederick Victor Dickins, *Collected Works of Frederick Victor Dickins* (Bristol: Ganesha, 1999), vol. 1, ix–xxxi.

11. *Foreign Relations of the United States*, 1873, vol. 1, 599–600; *Nihon gaikō monjo*, 8: 462–467; Shimomura, *Meiji ishin no gaikō*, 166–168; Tabohashi, "Meiji gonen no 'Maria Rusu' jiken," [part 2], 102–103, 106; Takeda, *Maria Rusu jiken*, 75–76, 134–136. In fact, British authorities insisted from the beginning that Japan had jurisdiction over the ship; see Robertson to Watson, 17 July 1872, in F.O. 84/1442: [4–6].

12. An English transcript of both trials was published "by the authority of the Foreign Department, Tokio, Japan" as *Case of the Peruvian Barque Maria Luz; with Appendix* (Yokohama, 1872); a copy is included in F.O. 84/1442: [220–226]. Takeda asserts that this pamphlet was printed for the Iwakura Mission to circulate in Europe; see *Maria Rusu jiken*, 183. Matsumura Masayoshi reprints the pamphlet and develops its purpose as "public diplomacy" in "Maria Rusu gō jiken no kōhō gaikō teki seikaku," *Teikyō kokusai bunka*, no. 9 (1996): 1–52.

13. *Foreign Relations of the United States*, 1873, vol. 1, 548–552; *Nihon gaikō monjo*, 8: 502–510.

14. See Wen Qing, comp., *Chouban yiwu shimo: Tongzhi chao* (Peiping: Palace Museum, 1929–1930), *juan* 88: 49a–51b; Wade to Granville, 17 November 1872, enclosing a memo from the Zongli Yamen, in F.O 84/1442: [259–264]; and Wayne C. McWilliams, "East Meets West: The Soejima Mission to China, 1873," *Monumenta Nipponica* 30, no. 3 (1975): 237–275.

15. On the García y García mission to Japan and China, see Morita, *Kaikoku to chigai hōken*, 227–245; Watt Stewart, *Chinese Bondage in Peru: A History of the Chinese Coolie in Peru, 1849–1874* (Durham, NC: Duke University Press, 1951), 160–205; and Treat, *Diplomatic Relations between the United States and Japan*, vol. 1, 487–493.

16. See Tabohashi, "Meiji gonen no 'Maria Rusu' jiken," [part 3], 93–105; *Foreign Relations of the United States*, 1873, vol. 1, 586–594, 609–616; *Nihon gaikō monjo*, 11: 395–437; Republica del Peru, *Colección de los tratados*, 152–177; Yasuo Ishimoto, "International Arbitration in the Meiji Era," *Japan Annual of International Law* 7 (1963): 30–37; and Ishimoto Yasuo, "Meijiki ni okeru chūsai saiban no senrei (1)," *Ōsaka shiritsu daigaku hōgaku zasshi* 7, no. 4 (1961): 50–78. For an analysis of the administrative decisions leading to the arbitration process and its relation to the subsequent Russo-Japanese Treaty resolving territorial differences, see Kasahara Hidehiko, "Maria Rusu gō jiken no saikentō: Gaimushō 'inen' to chūsai saiban," *Hōgaku kenkyū* 69, no. 12 (1996): 117–138. For the official English translation of the czar's judgment, see John Bassett Moore, *History and Digest of the International Arbitrations to which the United States has been a Party* (Washington, DC: Government Printing Office, 1898), vol. 5, 5034–5036.

17. Edward Jenkins, *The Coolie, His Rights and Wrongs* (London: Strahan & Co., 1871), 1–54, 162–200; Jung, *Coolies and Cane*, 5–6, 11–19; Arnold J. Meagher, *The Coolie Trade: The Traffic in Chinese Laborers to Latin America, 1847–1874* (N.p.: Xlibris, 2008), 27–48.

18. See Chaim D. Kaufmann and Robert A. Pape, "Explaining Costly International Moral Action: Britain's Sixty-Year Campaign against the Atlantic Slave Trade," *International Organization* 53, no. 4 (1999): 631–668.

19. On the coolie trade, see Chen Zexian, "Shijiu shiji shengxing de qiyue huagong shi," *Lishi yanjiu*, no. 1 (1963): 161–179; Duvon Clough Corbitt, *A Study of the Chinese in Cuba, 1847–1947* (Wilmore, KY: Asbury College, 1971); Cuba Commission, *Chinese Emigration: Report of the Commission Sent by China to Ascertain the Condition of Chinese Coolies in Cuba* (Shanghai: Imperial Maritime Customs Press, 1876), 6–34; M. Foster Farley, "The Chinese

Coolie Trade, 1845–1875," *Journal of Asian and African Studies* 3, nos. 3–4 (July and October 1968): 257–270; Hu-DeHart, "Chinese Coolie Labour"; Irick, *Ch'ing Policy*, 8, 201–212; Meagher, *The Coolie Trade*; Hosea Ballou Morse, *The International Relations of the Chinese Empire* (New York: Longmans, Green, & Co., 1910–1918), vol. 2, 166–181; Stewart, *Chinese Bondage in Peru*, 25–54; Mauro García Triana and Pedro Eng Herrera, *The Chinese in Cuba, 1847–Now*, ed. and trans. Gregor Benton (Lanham, MD: Rowman & Littlefield, 2009), 141–184; Wu Jianxiong, *Haiwai yimin yu Huaren shehui* (Taibei: Yunchen wenwhua shiye youxian gongsi, 1993), 17–42; and Yen Ching-hwang, *Coolies and Mandarins: China's Protection of Overseas Chinese during the Late Ch'ing Period (1851–1911)* (Singapore: Singapore University Press, 1985), 36–71.

20. Corbitt, *A Study of the Chinese in Cuba*, 1–17; Stewart, *Chinese Bondage in Peru*, 8. On Chinese emigration to Cuba generally, see Wu Jianxiong, *Haiwai yimin yu Huaren shehui*, 49–107.

21. Morse, *The International Relations*, vol. 2, 164.

22. Irick, *Ch'ing Policy*, 11–15, 148–150, 389–414; Harley Farnsworth MacNair, *The Chinese Abroad: Their Position and Protection, A Study in International Law and Relations* (Shanghai: Commercial Press, 1933), 2, 211 (see also pp. 1–27, 104–150); Yen, *Coolies and Mandarins*, 19–31.

23. Meagher, *The Coolie Trade*, 92–128, 245–273.

24. MacNair, *The Chinese Abroad*, 210; Tabohashi, "Meiji gonen no 'Maria Rusu' jiken," [part 3], 106–108; Samuel Wells Williams, *Chinese Immigration: A Paper Read before the Social Science Association of Saratoga, September 10, 1879* (New York: Scribner's Sons, 1879), 9. Chen Zexian gives a figure of 1,280,000 for the total number of Chinese persons leaving China between 1851 and 1875: "Shijiu shiji shengxing de qiyue huagong shi," 177.

25. See Great Britain, House of Commons, *Hong Kong: Copies or extracts of correspondence between the Colonial Department and the governor of Hong Kong . . . on the subject of emigration from Hong Kong and from the Chinese Empire to the British West Indies . . . since the 1st day of January 1853. Part I* (London: n.p., 1858).

26. Stewart, *Chinese Bondage in Peru*, 62–75.

27. Morse, *The International Relations*, vol. 2, 171.

28. Corbitt, *A Study of the Chinese in Cuba*, 51–59; see chart on p. 52 and note that Corbitt's totals err by one hundred. Specific details of ships to Cuba are presented in Wu Jianxiong, *Haiwai yimin yu Huaren shehui*, 69–84, and Meagher, *The Coolie Trade*, 168–173, 371–405.

29. See excerpt from the *Japan Mail* of July 13, 1872, included in F.O.

84/1442: [9]. Others reported that 8 of 238 coolies died en route to Yokohama, two possibly from suicide.

30. Corbitt, *A Study of the Chinese in Cuba*, 21–46, 63–86; Cuba Commission, *Chinese Emigration*, 22–25; Richard Henry Dana Jr., *To Cuba and Back* [1859], in *Two Years before the Mast and Other Voyages* (New York: Library of America, 2005), 429, 447, 500–502, 522–523; Hannen to Watson, 9 September 1872, in F.O. 84/1442: [85–90]; Edmund Hornby, "Memorandum," in F.O. 84/1442: [69–79]; Hornby to Watson, 22 September 1872, in F.O. 84/1442: [180–184]; Hu-DeHart, "Chinese Coolie Labour in Cuba," 76; MacNair, *The Chinese Abroad*, 211; Meagher, *Coolie Trade*, 71–81; *The Peruvian Barque "Maria Luz": A Short Account*, 45–48, 55–56; Stewart, *Chinese Bondage in Peru*, 108–110.

31. Cuba Commission, *Chinese Emigration*, 6–11; Hornby, "Memorandum," F.O. 84/1442: [70]; MacNair, *The Chinese Abroad*, 210–211; Morse, *The International Relations*, vol. 2, 178.

32. Cuba Commission, *Chinese Emigration*, 8; Morse, *The International Relations*, vol. 2, 179; Williams, *Chinese Immigration*, 9.

33. *Nihon gaikō monjo*, 11: 404–407; Tabohashi, "Meiji gonen no 'Maria Rusu' jiken," [part 3], 100–101.

34. Stewart, *Chinese Bondage in Peru*, 18; Meagher, *The Coolie Trade*, 153–168.

35. Stewart, *Chinese Bondage in Peru*, 118–119; see also MacNair, *The Chinese Abroad*, 214, 221; Morse, *The International Relations*, vol. 2, 176; and *American Diplomatic and Public Papers: The United States and China*, Ser. II, *The United States, China, and Imperial Rivalries, 1861–1893*, vol. 12, *The Coolie Trade and Outrages against the Chinese*, ed. Jules Davids (Wilmington, DE: Scholarly Resources, 1979), 92–93.

36. See Stewart, *Chinese Bondage in Peru*, 104–105, 120–124.

37. On British and U.S. policy, see Eldon Griffin, *Clippers and Consuls: American Consular and Commercial Relations with Eastern Asia, 1845–1860* (Ann Arbor, MI: Edwards Bros., 1938), 98–100, 194–199; Irick, *Ch'ing Policy*, 15–20, 47–57, 60–68, 81–101; and Alexander Michie, *The Englishman in China* (Edinburgh: Blackwood & Sons, 1900), vol. 2, 168–174.

38. Stewart, *Chinese Bondage in Peru*, 19; *American Diplomatic and Public Papers*, Ser. II, vol. 12, 92; Great Britain, House of Commons, *Hong Kong: Copies or extracts of correspondence between the Colonial Department and the governor of Hong Kong . . .* (1858), 24–30.

39. *American Diplomatic and Public Papers*, Ser. II, vol. 12, 124; Great Britain, House of Commons, *Coolie Emigration* (London: n.p., 1868), 5; Irick,

Ch'ing Policy, 137–140, 151–181 (esp. pp. 167–171); MacNair, *The Chinese Abroad*, 213–214; Morse, *The International Relations*, vol. 2, 177; Tabohashi, "Meiji gonen no 'Maria Rusu' jiken," [part 2], 100, and [part 3], 106–107.

40. Irick, *Ch'ing Policy*, 213–214; Stewart, *Chinese Bondage in Peru*, 148–150.

41. Irick, *Ch'ing Policy*, 214–218; Stewart, *Chinese Bondage in Peru*, 48–52; Meagher, *The Coolie Trade*, 174–192; Morse, *The International Relations*, vol. 2, 179–180; *American Diplomatic and Public Papers*, Ser. II, vol. 12, 132–138; Great Britain, House of Commons, *Hong Kong Coolie Trade* (London: Wm. Clowes & Sons, 1873), 22–23, 27.

42. See *Foreign Relations of the United States*, 1874 (Washington: Government Printing Office, 1875), 203–208; Irick, *Ch'ing Policy*, 291–317; Morse, *The International Relations*, vol. 2, 179–180; Stewart, *Chinese Bondage in Peru*, 36–37; Triana and Herrera, *The Chinese in Cuba*, 142–144; Yen, *Coolies and Mandarins*, 122–128; and the Cuba Commission, *Chinese Emigration*.

43. See Great Britain, House of Commons, *China, no. 3 (1875). Correspondence Respecting the Macao Coolie Trade: 1874–1875* (London: Harrison and Sons, 1875); Irick, *Ch'ing Policy*, 233–238, 257–272, 317–367 passim; Mitani, *Maria Luz Affair*, 10–13; Morse, *The International Relations*, vol. 2, 180–181; Stewart, *Chinese Bondage in Peru*, 160–205; and Yen, *Coolies and Mandarins*, 129–134.

44. On prostitution in the Meiji period, see De Becker, *The Nightless City*; Mikiso Hane, *Peasants, Rebels, and Outcastes: The Underside of Modern Japan* (New York: Pantheon, 1982), 207–225; Fujime, "The Licensed Prostitution System"; Itō Hidekichi, *Nihon haishō undōshi*; U. G. Murphy, *The Social Evil in Japan*, 4th ed., revised (Tokyo: Methodist House, 1908), 1–38; Sotozaki Mitsuhiro, *Nihon fujinron shi* (Domesu Shuppan, 1986); and Yamamoto Shun'ichi, *Nihon kōshō shi* (Chūō Hōki Shuppan, 1983).

45. Hane, *Peasants, Rebels, and Outcastes*, 208; Murphy, *The Social Evil in Japan*, 35; see also Fujime Yuki, *Sei no rekishigaku: Koshō seido, dataizai taisei kara baishun boshihō, yusei hogohō taisei e* (Fuji Shuppan, 1997), 96.

46. Hane, *Peasants, Rebels, and Outcastes*, 174–193; E. Patricia Tsurumi, *Factory Girls: Women in the Thread Mills of Meiji Japan* (Princeton, NJ: Princeton University Press, 1990), 62–67, 125–128, 181–189; De Becker, *The Nightless City*, 84–94, 305–311, 380–386; James Francis Warren, *Ah Ku and Karayuki-san: Prostitution in Singapore, 1870–1940* (New York: Oxford University Press, 1993), 184–190; Yamazaki, *Sandakan Brothel No. 8*, 181–194. See also Sharon L. Sievers, *Flowers in Salt: The Beginnings of Feminist Consciousness in Modern Japan* (Stanford, CA: Stanford University Press, 1983), 62–79; and

Barbara Molony, "Activism among Women in the Taishō Cotton Textile Industry," in *Recreating Japanese Women, 1600–1945*, ed. Gail Lee Bernstein (Berkeley: University of California Press, 1991), 216–238. The 1920s statistic is cited in Tsurumi, 145n73.

47. J. Mark Ramseyer has disputed this interpretation of prostitution in nineteenth-century Japan: "Indentured Prostitution in Imperial Japan: Credible Commitments in the Commercial Sex Industry," *Journal of Law, Economics, and Organization* 7, no. 1 (1991): 87–116. But his data are confined to the 1920s and '30s and do not warrant comment on the Meiji period.

48. Sue Gronewald, *Beautiful Merchandise: Prostitution in China, 1860–1936*, published as *Women and History*, no. 1 (1982); Lucie Cheng Hirata, "Free, Indentured, Enslaved: Chinese Prostitutes in Nineteenth-Century America," *Signs: Journal of Women in Culture and Society* 5, no. 1 (1979): 3–29; and Warren, *Ah Ku and Karayuki-san*, 35.

49. Warren, *Ah Ku and Karayuki-san*, 85; Kanō Mikiyo, "Manshū to onnatachi," in *Iwanami kōza: Kindai Nihon to shokuminchi*, vol. 5, *Bōchōsuru teikoku no jinryū* (Iwanami Shoten, 1993), 203. See also Fujime, *Sei no rekishigaku*, 56–60; Takeda, *Maria Rusu jiken*, 172; Yamazaki, *Sandakan Brothel No. 8*, passim; and League of Nations, *Commission of Enquiry into Traffic in Women and Children in the East: Report to the Council* (Geneva: League of Nations, 1933), 67–79.

50. Itō Hirobumi, quoted in Tsurumi, *Factory Girls*, 182.

51. *Meiroku Zasshi: Journal of the Japanese Enlightenment*, trans. William Reynolds Braisted (Cambridge, MA: Harvard University Press, 1976), 104–105, 143–144, 252–253, 278, 393–397.

52. Fukuzawa Yukichi, "On Morality," in *Fukuzawa Yukichi on Japanese Women: Selected Works*, trans. Eiichi Kiyooka (Tokyo: University of Tokyo Press, 1988), 87–101; *Meiroku Zasshi*, 397. See also Fujime, *Sei no rekishigaku*, 24–28; and Sievers, *Flowers in Salt*, 10–25.

53. *Meiroku Zasshi*, 393, 517–518.

54. The best general discussions of social and legal issues surrounding prostitution are Mark Thomas Connelly, *The Response to Prostitution in the Progressive Era* (Chapel Hill: University of North Carolina Press, 1980); and Luise White, *The Comforts of Home: Prostitution in Colonial Nairobi* (Chicago: University of Chicago Press, 1990). See also Pateman, *The Sexual Contract*, 189–218.

55. Osatake Takeki, "*Peirokoku Maria Roshi sen saiban ryakki* kaidan," in *Meiji bunka zenshū*, vol. 11, *Gaikō hen*, ed. Meiji bunka kenkyūkai (Nihon

Hyōronsha, 1968), 6–10; Morita, *Kaikoku to chigai hōken,* 253–257; Itō Hidekichi, *Nihon haishō undōshi,* 81.

56. *Foreign Relations of the United States,* 1873, vol. 1, 549. Ōe's interpretation of the coolie and prostitute contracts was informed by Nicholas Hannen, British judge at the Kanagawa consular court; see his account of the *Maria Luz* hearings, as an attachment to Hannen to Watson, 9 September 1872, in F.O. 84/1442: [112–113]; and Morita, "Maria Rusu gō jiken to geishōgi kaihō rei," 249–250. See also Morita's evaluation of Hornby's input in *Kaikoku to chigai hōken,* 199–226.

57. De Becker, *The Nightless City,* 91–93; Itō Hidekichi, *Nihon haishō undōshi,* 82–83; Maki Hidemasa, *Jinshin baibai* (Iwanami Shoten, 1971), 194–197; Ōe Taku, "Baido no heifū sainen semugosuru o fusegubeshi," *Kakusei / The Purity* 1, no. 4 (October 1911): 18–25; Sotozaki, *Nihon fujinron shi,* 43–44; Yamamoto, *Nihon kōshō shi,* 88–106; Yoshimi Kaneko, *Baishō no shakaishi,* rev. ed. (Yūzankaku, 1992), 18–20.

58. De Becker, *The Nightless City,* 300–301; Fujime, "The Licensed Prostitution System," 140–141; Fujime, *Sei no rekishigaku,* 90–92; Sotozaki, *Nihon fujinron shi,* 40–42.

59. Sotozaki, *Nihon fujinron shi,* 48.

60. Fujime, "The Licensed Prostitution System," 140; Murphy, *The Social Evil in Japan,* 115–119; Ramseyer, "Indentured Prostitution in Imperial Japan," 98–100.

61. Fujime, "The Licensed Prostitution System," 141–142; Fujime, *Sei no rekishigaku,* 92–93; Maki, *Jinshin baibai,* 198–200; Murphy, *The Social Evil in Japan,* 63–82, 82–101 passim; Sotozaki, *Nihon fujinron shi,* 41–42; Yamamoto, *Nihon kōshō shi,* 121–156; Yoshimi, *Baishō no shakaishi,* 23–27.

62. See Takeda, *Maria Rusu jiken,* 30–32, 70–72, 97; David L. Howell, *Geographies of Identity in Nineteenth-Century Japan* (Berkeley: University of California Press, 2005), 84, 217n13; and Daniel Botsman, "Freedom without Slavery? 'Coolies,' Prostitutes, and Outcastes in Meiji Japan's 'Emancipation Moment,'" *American Historical Review* 116, no. 5 (2011): 1323–1347.

63. Ōe, "Baido no heifū sainen semugosuru o fusegubeshi," 18–20.

CHAPTER 2

Disputing Rights

The Debate over Anti-Prostitution Legislation in 1950s Japan

Sally A. Hastings

When the Prostitution Prevention Law was enacted on May 21, 1956, the press hailed the legislation as a triumph for the cause of human rights in Japan. The *Asahi* celebrated Japan's entry into the company of progressive nations, in which "prostitution should vanish just as slavery did."[1] The *Nippon Times* described the passage of the bill in the upper chamber as "a momentous day in the history of Japan," an event that removed the stigma of association with legal prostitution.[2] An editorial in the same paper proclaimed, "A new sense of moral conscience has been born in Japan," bestowing credit for the passage of the bill on "newly enfranchised women." The writer traced the origins of the bill, which had finally passed after many failed attempts, to the efforts of women legislators in 1947.[3]

In reality, the 1956 Prostitution Prevention Law was a compromise measure that glossed over the many types of rights that were contested. Reformers for whom prostitution was an issue parallel to slavery wanted to guarantee to women the right to be free from sale as property. For feminist activists among the reformers, the passage of an anti-prostitution law represented a significant exercise of the political rights for which women had fought for decades. The brothel owners parried arguments about women's right to equality with arguments based on the right to livelihood, also guaranteed in the 1947 Constitution. Also at stake in the debate over prostitution was the freedom of men to engage in commercial sex with impunity. This freedom, which was never explicitly demanded in terms of rights, was preserved in the negotiation over punishments. The anti-prostitution activists demanded punishments for those who engaged in the act of prostitution, including male customers. The bill that the Liberal Democratic Party sponsored in 1956 did not make the act of prostitution illegal and thus did not impose punishment on either party to a commercial sexual transaction.

This examination of the anti-prostitution debate begins in 1953, when women in the Diet consciously allied across party lines to secure anti-prostitution legislation, and continues the story to 1956, when the Diet unanimously passed a government-sponsored anti-prostitution bill. The emphasis of this essay is on the concern of women legislators for human rights. As elected representatives, they were exercising political rights that women had not possessed a decade earlier. In the legislature, women politicians were subject to the disparaging remarks of male colleagues who questioned their legitimacy. Although the discourse on anti-prostitution legislation was not entirely free of judgmental moral rhetoric that sparked class resentments, the debate centered primarily on rights that were assumed to be universal. Changing Japanese law to protect those rights was a matter of national pride.

The Setting

The debate over prostitution was structured by Japan's experience of defeat and occupation. In response to an American Occupation order on January 21, 1946, to end licensed prostitution, the Japanese government abolished all laws regulating prostitution on February 2, 1946. Prostitution itself, however, was not criminalized and "voluntary" prostitution flourished in designated restaurants and bars, the red light districts. Geisha houses became known as blue districts, while streetwalkers plied their trade in areas called white light zones.[4] The red, white, and blue theme was appropriate, since American soldiers were among the chief customers for the industry.

Anti-prostitution legislation emerged as a pressing issue when the American Occupation came to an end in April 1952. Women leaders feared that with the restoration of national autonomy and the end of the political purges some of the legal reforms of the Occupation era, for instance, Japan's renunciation of war, would be overturned if conservatives achieved the two-thirds majority of the Diet necessary for constitutional revision.[5] They worried that conservative forces might rescind the reforms that made women equal to men before the law and that freed the younger generation from the authority of the household. They were apprehensive that the Women's and Minors' Bureau might be eliminated or reduced in status. They also viewed with dismay the possible reinstitution of licensed prostitution in Japan. The issue of prostitution was particularly pressing because of the lively sex trade that flourished without benefit of a licensing system, fueled by the continued American military presence in Japan.

The Japanese women reformers of the 1950s were, of course, successors to an abolition movement that dated back to the nineteenth century. Asai Saku, president of the Woman's Christian Temperance Union (WCTU), presented a petition for the abolition of licensed prostitution to the first session of the Japanese Diet in 1890.[6] Her arguments that licensed prostitution failed to control venereal disease, violated human rights, and endangered youth were echoed repeatedly by the postwar reformers. There were strong linkages between women's demand for political rights and their fight to abolish prostitution. The WCTU supported women's political rights as a means to reforming society. In the 1920s and 1930s, non-Christian women's groups formed to demand women's rights also called for the abolition of prostitution and the regulation of cafes and dance halls.[7]

The issues that a broad range of reformers wanted to address through anti-prostitution bills were laid out in a report that the Women's and Minors' Bureau published in December 1952, the product of an investigative commission on prostitution chaired by Kamichika Ichiko.[8] The report invoked the rhetoric of democracy to declare the flourishing state of prostitution in Japan an obstacle to the emancipation of women, the protection of women's human rights, and the improvement of women's status. The commission recommended passage of an anti-prostitution law, protection and rehabilitation for prostitutes, measures to prevent ordinary women from falling into prostitution, and cooperation between the United States and Japan regarding military bases.

Underlying the report was the assumption that, despite the official abolition of licensed prostitution, the postwar "red-line zones" in fact functioned in exactly the same manner as the old licensed quarters.[9] The report denounced the idea that officially supervised prostitution isolates vice and protects ordinary women. Private prostitution had spread outward from the special zones, proving that such zones do not halt the spread of venereal disease. On the contrary, special zones promoted prostitution by numbing the moral outrage usually associated with the practice. Rejecting the notion that the women in the red-line zones were independent workers engaging in a series of economic transactions with customers, the report regarded the women as minor employees in the profitable brothel industry, which appropriated a high percentage of the women's income.[10]

The report recommended a national law banning prostitution. All participants in the prostitution industry—the prostitutes, their customers, and the brothel owners—would be subject to penalties such as fines and imprisonment, with the heaviest penalties reserved for those who profited from the prostitution of others. Recognizing that women became prostitutes for economic and other reasons, the members of the commission asked for support for rehabilitation facilities and for educational programs that would stress the right of every human being to be free from prostitution and would promote good male–female relationships conducive to stable homes.[11]

Citing a 1949 public opinion poll that showed that 70 percent of the Japanese polled said that prostitution was necessary, the report called for a new conceptualization of the institution of prostitution. First, the report rejected the claim that prostitution is necessary to satisfy male sexual desire, arguing that such desire was not inherent but rather the product of poor male–female relations and the artificial stimulation of the red-light districts. Second, the authors reiterated their stance that the concept that the flesh of some women provides a barrier that protects the majority of women was a violation of human rights. They argued, on the contrary, that the legal operation of red-light districts actually created the danger that ordinary women might stray into prostitution or even be taken by force. Third, they noted, licensed prostitution does not inhibit the spread of venereal disease; overconfidence in the efficacy of the weekly medical examinations administered in the licensed quarter merely created a false sense of immunity.[12]

The presence of American military bases in Japan was unquestionably a factor in the urgent call for a law against prostitution. In 1952, it was clear that the restoration of national sovereignty had not freed the country from foreign troops and that foreign military bases would be part of Japanese society for the foreseeable future. The reformers hoped that the American authorities would forbid soldiers to consort with prostitutes, but they also wanted the Japanese government itself to deal firmly with the problem. The concerns that the Japanese reformers expressed about the negative effects of military bases on the youth of the surrounding areas resonate with the findings of Cynthia Enloe,

Katherine Moon, and others on the social problems around military bases in Asia, where large numbers of young men with money to spend make prostitution a lucrative job in a poor economy.[13] The question of national pride also loomed large in the movement to abolish prostitution. The reformers suggested that without an anti-prostitution law, Japan could not take its place in the ranks of civilized nations.[14]

The fact that prostitution around military bases was the primary zone in which Americans intersected with Japanese society created anxieties about Japan's international standing. The report reminded the officials of the Labor Ministry that "Throughout the world all civilized countries have anti-prostitution laws."[15] Testimony in the U.S. Senate that described Japan as a country with a tradition of prostitution was another indication that Japan's international reputation was at stake.[16] Moreover, the reformers used knowledge of international conditions to refute the argument that the prostitution of a few women protects the virtue of the rest. They pointed out that "There is no example among foreign countries of the abolition of public prostitution increasing the number of rapes." They further argued that in the world at large anti-prostitution laws have resulted in better conditions for women: "It is generally thought that trivializing women's bodies is immoral and rape is a serious crime."[17]

The government-commissioned report did not prompt a government-sponsored anti-prostitution bill; rather, women Diet members were instrumental in converting the recommendations of the report into legislative bills. On March 3, 1953, Miyagi Tamayo and four other members of the upper house presented a bill to penalize prostitution to the fifteenth Diet.[18] The bill itself stated that the purpose of the penalties was to prevent disruptions in social morality, to protect the human rights of women, and to maintain social order. Thus, both in spirit and in language, it drew on the 1952 report of the investigative commission of the Women's and Minors' Bureau. When the Diet dissolved on March 14, the bill had not yet been debated. During the national election campaign that followed the dissolution, a women's group called the Committee to Promote the Enactment of a Prostitution Penalty Law (CPEPPL, Baishun Kinshi Seitei Sokushin Iinkai) worked to build legislative support for a prostitution penalty law. Members of the organization distributed questionnaires to the fifteen hundred candidates and garnered expressions of support from a hundred and fifty.[19]

Women Legislators Take the Initiative

The possibility that women legislators could get anti-prostitution legislation to the floor of the Diet increased in the fall of 1953 when women in both houses of the Diet formed nonpartisan groups to support issues important to women. The elections held for both houses of the Diet in April 1953 brought new women leaders to the legislature, among them Ichikawa Fusae, the prominent leader of the prewar suffrage movement, to the upper house and Kamichika Ichiko, the chair of the investigative commission on prostitution, to the lower house. Ichikawa had always advocated that women should join forces across the political spectrum, and she was instrumental in the formation of this new alliance of women Diet members in November 1953. The women resolved to oppose the abolition or reduction of the Women's and Minors' Bureau and to work for a law that would wipe out prostitution.

Through cooperative efforts across party lines, an anti-prostitution bill was introduced to the lower house of the nineteenth Diet on May 10, 1954. The twelve sponsors of the bill were eight of the nine women members of the lower house (the exception was Nakayama Masa) and four men: Ii Seiichi and Inomata Kōzō, both socialist lawyers; Yamamoto Katsuichi, a socialist faculty member; and Takahashi Teiichi, a conservative lawyer.[20] The stated aims of the bill were exactly the same as in the bill submitted to the fifteenth Diet, including protection of the fundamental human rights of women. When the Diet session came to an end on June 2, it was decided to carry the bill over into the next session for further examination.

At the end of the tumultuous twentieth Diet, a special session, on December 9, 1954, the bill expired. On December 14, the bill was introduced into the twenty-first Diet. The Diet dissolved on January 24, 1955, before the bill could be considered.[21] Although the bill never came up for a vote in the Diet, it did provoke opposition. The euphemistically named National Association for the Prevention of Venereal Disease (Zenkoku Seibyō Yobō Jijikai), an organization founded by the brothel owners, issued a statement on June 25, 1954, expressing its firm opposition to the bill on the grounds that it was an inappropriate approach to the problem of public morality.[22] The legislation would punish women who were simply the victims of economic distress, argued brothel owners and conservative pundits. This eloquent defense of economically disadvantaged women masked the fact that the real objection of conservative men was the imposition of penalties upon customers. Instead of rallying support to the standard of the male right to commercial sex, the conservatives recast the debate in terms of the gallant defense of impoverished women under attack from unrealistic, moralistic, female reformers.

An article that Kamichika Ichiko, one of the sponsors of the 1954 bill, wrote for a legal journal in the summer of 1954 shows what the sponsors of the bill were trying to accomplish and the type of opposition they faced.[23] Kamichika approved the basic aims of the law: maintaining social order, preventing disruption of public morality, and defending the fundamental human rights of women. She recognized as threats to the social order the health problems of citizens weakened by venereal disease, the inducements to crime, the disruption of education, and the undermining of the work ethic. The provisions of the law were intended to reform the lives of the prostitutes and to punish two categories of individuals: the men who were their customers and the entrepreneurs who exploited them. Such punishments would make brothels unprofitable and thus unlikely to stay in business. Kamichika conceded that the 1954 law was not precisely what the commission she headed had recommended, but she believed it was essential to support the law nevertheless.[24]

Kamichika addressed one major criticism of the 1954 bill, the absence of any provision for the protection or rehabilitation of prostitutes. The commission on which Kamichika had served had, of course, recommended such measures. The reason the 1954 bill did not include relief measures was that the government would not appropriate funds for rehabilitation facilities. Kamichika argued that since one might have to wait as long as a century for the government to come up with the funds, supporters of the bill should move ahead without the rehabilitation facilities. Once prostitution was illegal, some means would be found to fund the rehabilitative facilities. She cited the U.S. May Act as a precedent for such a course. Named for its sponsor, Andrew J. May, the congressman from Kentucky who sponsored the legislation, the May Act of 1938 (renewed 1941) made prostitution near military installations a federal offense.[25]

Kamichika argued that criminalizing prostitution would be one step toward reform. She cited the expert opinion of Segawa Yasō, the Salvation Army officer who headed the National League of Women's Shelters, that efforts to reform women had been hampered in Japan by the legality of prostitution.[26] Invoking her long-held concern for the dignity of labor, Kamichika argued that to protect individuals who had lost their work ethic was to impose pressure on the lives of those who labored. Kamichika was arguing, of course, from a defensive position. She in fact favored such facilities; her commission had recommended them. She would not allow, however, government budget priorities to undermine the fundamental importance of human rights.

In her published articles in support of the 1955 anti-prostitution bill, Kamichika did not blame the women working as prostitutes for the institution of prostitution. She distinguished clearly between the entrepreneurs of the prostitution industry and the prostitutes, whom she regarded as victims of Japan's disordered postwar economy. She hoped that they could be rescued and reformed. She supported, of course, the penalties for those who engaged in prostitution, both the prostitute and her customer, that were included in the bills submitted to the fifteenth, nineteenth, and twenty-second Diets. As noted above, the intention was to punish the entrepreneurs and the customers and to rehabilitate the women. She made crystal clear that the object of the punishment was the customer and that even without provisions for rehabilitation in the anti-prostitution law, under the revised penal code the female prostitutes should be sentenced to rehabilitation. The penalties for habitual offenders would be applied only to women who spread venereal diseases, committed additional crimes, or in other ways constituted poor candidates for reform.[27]

Kamichika and her allies were attempting nothing less than the reconstruction of Japanese ideas about prostitution. One important tenet in their assault on the existing mode of thought was that they, the anti-prostitution forces, spoke for all women. Two rhetorical strategies that they used to establish their majority position were the invocation of the voices of ordinary women and the deployment of statistics. Kamichika described how women from all parts of the country—Fukushima in the northeast, Niigata and Toyama on the Japan Sea, and Nagano in central Japan—expressed their concerns to her about the prostitution problem and asked what could be done. She gave a particularly vivid account of how young elementary school teachers from Iwakuni near Hiroshima struck up a conversation with her on a train. They complained to her about the social disorder that resulted from the presence of an American military base in their area. The teachers, who had investigated some of the local prostitutes, assured Kamichika that the women did not want to work in prostitution but were forced into it by the need to support themselves. Kamichika responded that she thought that prostitution was a disease ravaging Japan, but she did not know how to change the law.[28]

One of the statistics that Kamichika brandished in her advocacy of an anti-prostitution bill was the number of women in Japan working as prostitutes, but this figure was a contested one. A white paper issued by the Labor Ministry in July 1955 gave the figure of half a million prostitutes working in Japan.[29] Kamichika Ichiko was already using the rhetoric of half a million in 1954, and the figure appears repeatedly in her writing.[30] The Democratic Party used that figure to defend its opposition to the 1955 anti-prostitution bill.[31] When the government sponsored its own anti-prostitution bill in 1956, various government sources put the figure considerably lower. In 1956, the Labor Ministry said that 140,000 women in Japan relied on prostitution to earn a living.[32] On the eve of the enactment of the anti-prostitution bill in May 1956, the press estimated that 200,000 women would be thrown out of jobs.[33]

In their appeal to the general public to identify with the anti-prostitution cause, Kamichika and her allies presented the prostitution industry as a danger to young women, the daughters of the nation. In 1952, the Women's and Minors' Bureau reported that the number of incidents of child selling were increasing and that 93.3 percent of the children sold were girls.[34] Precisely because prostitution was profitable, brokers lured young girls into their service and provided a market for parents who wanted to raise cash by selling their daughters. Such parents were among the targets of the anti-prostitution bill.[35] Kamichika's appeal, then, was not simply to parents but to all citizens, to defend the rights of the young.

The Concerted Effort of 1955

The sessions of the Diet in which the anti-prostitution bill languished were the same ones in which Hatoyama Ichirō was fighting to oust Yoshida Shigeru from his long tenure in the position of prime minister. Hatoyama had promised the socialists as a condition for their support in his struggle against Yoshida that he would hold new elections when he took office. Only after those elections had taken place on February 27, 1955, were women legislators able to renew their efforts to secure passage of an anti-prostitution law.

Dramatic events helped the women Diet members keep the issue of anti-prostitution in the public eye. The "Matsumoto Incident" referred to events in Kagoshima in August 1954. Matsumoto Michio, the head of a construction company whose wife ran an inn known as the Matsumoto-ya, received many lucrative contracts from the prefecture. It was discovered that his favored status derived from his having supplied officials with young women, some of them high school students dressed in their school uniforms. Telling their parents that they were staying with a friend, the girls used their income to pay for movies, cosmetics, and eating out. The second incident occurred in Ōta Ward in Tokyo in April 1955 when the owner of a geisha house was found to be using a seventeen-year-old girl as a prostitute; the owner was charged with violations of the child protection law.[36] These incidents illustrated the contention of Kamichika and other women reformers that prostitution was a danger to the daughters of Japan.

The Matsumoto Incident, in which young women entering prostitution for reasons other than desperate economic need, undermined the conservative argument that prostitution was simply a product of Japan's status as a poor country. In an article for a woman's magazine, Kamichika stressed that the Matsumoto Incident showed that young girls could become entangled in prostitution, simply drawn in by their curiosity or vanity. There was no question, she argued, that the young girls in this incident were objects of the men's desire, nothing but meanly exploited tools. Nevertheless, the brothel owners, the perpetrators of this inhuman treatment, were given very light sentences. Kamichika asserted that the sentences reflected the attitude in Japan that pimping was perfectly legal. She ended the article with a resounding declaration that the Matsumoto Incident was her motivation to enact, with the support of all Japanese women, an anti-prostitution bill. The bill would be one weapon to protect women's rights and overthrow the old system that had treated women as nothing.[37]

On June 10, 1955, Kamichika Ichiko and eighteen others introduced to the twenty-second Diet a bill to penalize prostitution. Although this bill did not win passage, its popularity set the stage for the government-sponsored bill that passed without opposition in 1956. The 1955 debates, then, offer the best opportunity to examine the discourses about legal rights. On the same day, the Women's and Minors' Bureau launched a nationwide movement to stamp out prostitution and released figures that showed half a million prostitutes in Japan.[38]

The early press reaction to the bill was less than enthusiastic. Arguing that prostitution is the product of poverty and ignorance, the editors of the conservative *Yomiuri* newspaper questioned the value of the law. With their declaration that "in order to root out the practice of prostitution, it will be vital to wipe out poverty and ignorance," they branded the bill unrealistic. They also suggested that the proposed law would be ineffective: "Mere punishments as contemplated in the bill in question will be far from wiping out prostitution."[39]

The two conservative parties, however, raised hopes that the bill might pass. On June 15, both the Democratic and the Liberal parties gave their members freedom to vote on this bill in accordance with their individual views. By Kamichika's count, if proponents of the bill could secure thirty-three more votes than they already anticipated, they could assure its passage.[40] The bill was sent to the Judicial Affairs Committee of the lower house on June 15. As the brothel owners, pursuing their economic interests, lined up opposition to the bill, they inadvertently stirred up public controversy. Sekō Kōichi, chair of the Judicial Affairs Committee, suggested that the committee needed to take into account the "right to live" of the brothel owners. The editors of the *Mainichi* newspaper declared that it was absurd to recognize the right to engage in white slavery. They urged the members of the Diet to take a more positive view of the legislation and to enact it as soon as possible.[41] According to a survey conducted in Tokyo and published on July 7, 62.7 percent of those polled favored the anti-prostitution bill. Of those, 70.4 percent were women. Only 15.8 percent of the sample opposed the bill. Those who favored licensed prostitution were mainly laborers and industrial workers.[42]

On July 6, members of the Judicial Affairs Committee who opposed the law had an opportunity to question the sponsors of the bill. Shiina Takashi of the Democratic Party asked whether mistresses or "onlies" (prostitutes who were faithful to a particular American serviceman) would be included in the definition of prostitution. Inomata Kōzō responded that they would not. Shiina then suggested that omitting any punishment for mistresses was inconsistent with the claims of the women Diet members that they wished to rid Japan of prostitution in order to establish proper relationships between men and women. Kamichika acknowledged the inconsistency but suggested that the problem of mistresses should be handled by slight revisions in the civil code regarding bigamy rather than by stipulations in the anti-prostitution law.[43]

Shiina then suggested that anti-prostitution laws, applicable to half a million human beings, were unenforceable; passing one would extinguish respect for the law among the general population and thus inflict injury on eighty-five million people (the entire population of Japan). He noted that efforts to abolish prostitution in Japan dated from the Tokugawa era, but the Tokugawa reformers, the Salvation Army, and the Purity Society (Kakuseikai) had all failed. Moreover, in countries such as France, England, and the United States where the practice had long been illegal, prostitution still survived.[44]

In her reply, Kamichika raised the issue of Japan's international standing. She assured Shiina that she was well aware of the failures of the anti-prostitution movement in Japan. Quite apart from the six hundred thousand women concerned (she thus raised her usual figure for the number of prostitutes by a hundred thousand), Japan's prostitution problem was an embarrassing matter internationally. At a time when only countries such as Turkey and Costa Rica still had licensed prostitution, Japan had a semi-official system. Former Justice Minister Inukai Ken had already indicated that prostitution was one of the domestic issues that would have to be settled before Japan could join the United Nations. Wherever a legal bridgehead existed, Kamichika said, she and her allies would promote laws related to human rights.[45]

Furuya Sadao, another sponsor of the bill, supplemented Kamichika's reply; he emphasized the low consciousness in Japan that there was anything wrong with prostitution, a phenomenon he attributed to influences from Japan's feudal era. He said that the traditional Japanese attitude, that it was perfectly appropriate for families to sell daughters into prostitution as a sacrifice on behalf of the household, was a serious error from the point of view of fundamental human rights. The most important aim of the bill was to develop a consciousness in the general population that prostitution was wrong. He rejected Shiina's argument that passing the bill would extinguish respect for the law. Furuya's mention of sexual morality prompted Shiina to argue again that, if morality was the issue, then mistresses should be included in the scope of the law.[46]

After an exchange between Shiina and Inomata on the close relationship between poverty and prostitution, Shiina returned to the imperfections of the bill under consideration, saying that there were many matters that required further investigation. Narrating the history of prostitution and its opponents, mentioning emperors Nintoku, Shōmu, and Shirakawa, he concluded that nowhere, either in the East or in the West, had prostitution ever been extinguished. If the law were implemented three months after it passed, what would the brothel owners do? Inomata had expressed concern about how the prostitutes would eat. Were not men and brothel owners also human beings? In defiance of Kamichika's suggestion that Japan's semi-official system of prostitution was an international disgrace, Shiina argued that foreigners liked Japanese women. The members of the British Far Eastern Squadron had in the nineteenth century and the American soldiers did now. The families of prostitutes depended upon their earnings; were they not entitled to a guarantee of livelihood? No law would be able to contain the *panpan,* the streetwalkers.[47]

Kamichika responded somewhat sarcastically that she was surprised that Shiina had become such a scholar. She thought, however, that the system of prostitution in the day of Nintoku, long before the establishment of a free society in Japan, was irrelevant. What concerned her was Japan's reputation. At a recent Asian Conference in India, members of the upper house carried a message to the women of Asia. Japanese women's groups reported that thanks to Japan's becoming a democratic country, they were beginning to take action on issues such as an anti-prostitution law. The women at the conference expressed great surprise that a progressive country such as Japan, one they wanted to emulate, had not yet solved the problem of prostitution.[48]

The next day, July 7, the members of the Judicial Affairs Committee listened to the testimony of nine outside authorities, five of them participants in the prostitution industry. The first to testify was Mogi Shōsaku, a member of the National Federation of Restauranteurs' Associations, who opposed the bill. Speaking for the owners and employees of the blue zones, Mogi said that passage of the law would destroy their livelihoods, businesses they had founded in the terrible poverty right after the war. Echoing Kamichika's rhetoric from the day before, he described the bill as a bridgehead for a cultural revolution, and he complained that he and his fellow workers were being sacrificed for this cause. He lamented the absence of any provision of work for women who would lose their jobs if prostitution were abolished, but he made no mention of punishment for customers. The women, he predicted, would turn to private prostitution and streetwalking. As a result, venereal disease would spread into the general population. Mogi urged the politicians in judging the bill to "consider the consequences without simply taking into account the abstract question of morality."[49] Mogi's arguments recapitulated, of course, the traditional view that prostitution protected respectable women from sexual advances and the entire population from venereal disease.

Suzuki Akira, chairman of the board of directors of the Yoshiwara Café Association and a representative of the National Association for the Prevention of Venereal Disease, opposed the bill in the name of the new democratic order. Speaking for sixteen thousand owners and the sixty-some thousand women they employed, he positioned himself as a tax-paying citizen who had engaged in democratic self-government right after the war when licensed prostitution was abolished. At the behest of various officials, he had organized the industry so as to minimize problems such as venereal disease and illegal restraint. Suzuki opposed the bill because, he said, it did not take into account the point of view of the women. Because of the abolition of licensed prostitution by the American Occupation, prostitutes were autonomous employees who worked of their own free will. The sponsors of the bill, who blamed only the brothel owners for prostitution, ignored the fact that postwar prostitution was different from that in the prewar period. He opposed legislation that interfered with the right of the women to work. "They have no other way to live," he said.[50] Togano Satoko, a socialist woman, obviously skeptical of his claims, questioned Suzuki at length about the age of his employees, the circumstances of their employment, and the percentage of their wages that he appropriated.[51]

The remainder of the witnesses supported the bill. The two prostitutes from the Yoshiwara said they had fled from work that allowed them no freedom of movement and in which their earnings never were adequate to pay off their debt. The chair of the Nagasaki Federation of Entertainment Rooms Employees Association also favored the bill, although she asked that there be provision for the women who would be thrown out of work by the legislation. Other expert witnesses who supported the bill were Yamataka Shigeri, a member of the Committee to Promote the Enactment of a Prostitution Penalty Law; Itō Hidekichi, a social worker; Ichikawa Tokuji, a physician and professor at Tokyo University; and Kanzaki Kiyoshi, a well-known social critic.[52]

Two decisions reached on July 14 affected the fate of the bill. First, the Judicial Affairs Committee decided to put the bill to a vote at its executive meeting schedule for July 19. Second, the Policy Board of the ruling Democratic Party decided that it would cut off discussion on the current bill by submitting to the committee a resolution that the government would present an anti-prostitution bill to the next session of the Diet.[53] On Saturday, July 16, in a step clearly intended to discourage passage of the bill, Welfare Minister Kawasaki Hideji informed the members of the Judicial Affairs Committee that he had no financial resources to look after the women who would be unemployed if the anti-prostitution bill were to pass immediately.[54]

The deliberations of the Judicial Affairs Committee on July 19 were lengthy and debilitating. The committee began its work at 10:27 in the morning. Before the evening was over, one member of the audience, Fujiwara Michiko of the upper house, had fainted in exhaustion.[55] The room was packed with several hundred women and brothel owners who had come to hear the proceedings. The size of the crowd reflected an escalation in partisan interest in the bill. Ichikawa Fusae noted that when the brothel owners began showing up in higher numbers, women increased their participants to match. Kamichika records that by mid-morning on July 19 there were forty owners lined up outside the inappropriately small room scheduled for the day. The owners somehow had visitor's passes that should not have been distributed until early afternoon. Arrangements were made for a larger room and observers from both sides were seated, but the day began in an intense atmosphere of rivalry.[56]

The first speech of the day was in opposition to the bill. Shiina Takashi of the Democratic Party acknowledged that prostitution was a significant social problem, but he raised several objections to this particular bill. First, there was no money in the budget for the expenses the bill would entail. "Even if this law is born," he said, "it will not live to grow up." "If the law were passed but not implemented," he said, "that would undermine the confidence of the citizens in any laws." Moreover, the law would victimize millions of citizens—the half million prostitutes and those dependent upon them. Shiina criticized the failure of the law to criminalize women who were partners of American military personnel.[57]

In her testimony before the committee, Kamichika observed that the position of the conservative parties was to allow prostitution to continue under its current conditions. Freely admitting that the current bill had flaws, she asked why, if the conservative parties had objections, did they not propose compromises? Instead, they dismissed as utopian talk the efforts of practical political participants who wanted to move forward step by step. She pointed out that except in a communist paradise, passing a perfect bill would be impossible. She urged compromise rather than political party intrigue and she called for cooperation among various ministries in order to deal with half a million violations of human rights. The reality was that in the red-line and blue-line districts, the human rights of half a million women were being trampled. The women had no freedom of action and they were cruelly exploited. She cited a study of the Women and Minors' Bureau that reported that 90 percent of the women working in prostitution hoped to be rehabilitated as soon as possible.[58] The violation of these women's rights was an immediate problem and should be dealt with now. To the claim of her opponents, that other countries had no anti-prostitution laws, Kamichika replied that Japan needed such a law precisely because it was a country in which leading politicians referred to the system of licensed prostitution as a "beautiful national custom" and a "pillar of the country." In Christian countries, where religion taught that prostitution was a sin, there was no need for the same kind of law.[59]

In her allotted time before the committee, Togano Satoko emphasized the broad public support for this bill, especially among women and young people and deplored the fact that some Diet members opposed the bill. What, she asked, was the reasoning of those who opposed the bill? Their first objection was the absence of rehabilitative facilities, a concern she shared. She argued, however, that in politics one must move forward one step at a time. Once prostitution was illegal, it would be easier to get funding for rehabilitation. If opponents of the bill really supported its aims, they should suggest specific revisions that would make the bill acceptable. Togano's critique of the conservative politicians was particularly apt, coming as it did right after a speech by Fukui Shōta, who endorsed the aims of the bill but argued against it on rather vague grounds that there was still preparation to be done.[60]

Togano then more explicitly attacked the Democratic and Liberal parties. Although members of the two major parties privately expressed support for this popular bill on an important social problem that affected Japan's standing in the international community, they nevertheless spoke against it in the committee. Togano said that she had heard rumors that some members of the conservative parties had pledged support for both sides, and she wondered whether perhaps the rumors were true. Another rumor was that because the bill was so popular, some members did not want to speak against it. Instead, they planned to let the bill fail in committee and then blame the committee. If members of the committee were supporting the brothel owners, Togano argued, they should just say so; to do anything else was to disparage the Diet system of committees. Such behavior was particularly regrettable when Japan was handicapped in its efforts to establish a place for itself in international society by its infamy as a country of prostitution. She finished by saying that if the bill did not pass, the indignation of the bill's supporters would increase and they would pledge themselves to fight to the end to achieve their goal.[61]

When Togano finished speaking, the chair of the committee called for the vote. As the newspapers had forecast, when the bill failed to win approval, Yamamoto Kumekichi of the ruling party made a motion to pass a resolution that the government should establish a council to look into the prostitution problem and, if a bill should be found necessary, to present one to the next session of the Diet. Furuya Sadao raised the question of how the motion for a government bill rather than amendment of the proposed legislation related to the right of Diet members to initiate legislation. He also questioned postponing the bill yet again, arguing that the members' bill had failed not because research was lacking but because there was a fundamental disagreement as to whether or not prostitution was wrong.[62]

When the question period ended, Fukuda Masako summed up for the Japan Socialist Party (JSP) the arguments against the Democratic Party resolution. The ruling party, she said, submitted this strange resolution when the committee had not thoroughly discussed the members' bill and was still debating it. One could take this as proof of the government's lack of respect for the right of Diet members to propose and to debate legislation. Fukuda pointed out that the bill that the Judicial Affairs Committee had just failed to approve was the fifth anti-prostitution bill to be introduced in the postwar era and that it was now the eighth year since the first bill was introduced in 1948. In Japan, the number of prostitutes was increasing and the brothel owners were flourishing. From the point of view of other countries, she said, these figures seemed to indicate that Japan wanted the infamy of being the land of prostitution. Thus it was exceedingly regrettable that when Japan urgently needed some kind of policy to control prostitution, the ruling party cut off debate on the Prostitution Penalty Bill and submitted this resolution. Although the number of poor households was on the increase, the amount of money budgeted for poor relief had decreased. In the recent budget, the government reduced the amount of money for rehabilitation, funds that would prevent young women from falling into prostitution. It was clear that the Hatoyama Cabinet did not have a burning interest in prostitution policy. These figures also demonstrated the unparalleled cold-heartedness of the cabinet's rehabilitation policy for prostitutes.[63]

Asserting that all virtuous women in Japan had been hoping for passage of the Prostitution Penalty Law, Fukuda emphasized the unity of Japanese women on this issue. Tens of millions of women would be disappointed and pessimistic when they learned that the Diet had failed to pass the anti-prostitution bill and that the government had submitted this resolution in its place. She ended her oration by reminding her listeners that under the new constitution men and women had equal rights. The debate on this bill, however, created the impression that some of the male members of the Diet were maintaining into the present the attitude of despotic male dominance that prevailed for many centuries. She invited the male members of the chamber to cast aside their male privilege and stand in the position of a prostitute for even one day.[64]

When the testimony before the committee ended and debate began at 10:30 p.m., Shiina Takashi reiterated the same themes he had set in the morning. He was scathing in his denunciation of the bill that was doomed to die young. "It violates the law-abiding spirit, and even as human rights, it is not interesting." In a common tactic of the conservatives, he suggested, in defiance of polls showing that women supported the bill, that the women legislators were out of touch with ordinary women. "Women come to my office, perhaps from your districts, to ask that the actions of the women's groups who have gone too far be undone." Kamichika replied, "We are not talking about some distant utopia; what shall we do about the fact that women's rights are being trampled now? Even if this bill is defeated, we will submit it as many times as we need to until it passes."[65] When the vote was taken in the Judicial Affairs Committee of the lower house late on the evening of July 19, the committee voted 18 to 11 against it. The bill failed in the full house on July 21, 142 in favor and 191 against.

As soon as the bill failed in committee, the JSP issued a statement, blaming the Democratic and Liberal parties for allying with the brothel owners.[66] The press was equally indignant that the anti-prostitution bill had failed. The *Nippon Times* accused the conservative parties of voting "to prolong Japan's shame" and "in favor of organized crime." The

Nippon Times and the *Tokyo Shinbun* concurred in their judgment that the excuses the conservative parties had offered for voting against the bill—that the bill would be ineffective and that it lacked rehabilitation for prostitutes—were illogical and inadequate. "If we follow this reasoning," the editors of the *Nippon Times* wrote, "crime should not be eradicated because many criminals and policemen would have to find other means of livelihood." The *Mainichi* accused the conservative parties of indifference to human rights.[67] The *Jiji* regretted that the bill had fallen victim to party politics.[68]

The Democratic Party had not, of course, taken a stance in absolute opposition to an anti-prostitution bill. The substitute resolution that so infuriated the supporters of the 1954 bill called for the establishment of a deliberative council to study the prostitution issue and, if the council found an anti-prostitution law to be necessary, the introduction of such a bill to the next Diet.[69] On Monday, July 25, Katō Shizue had the opportunity to direct questions to members of the government in the upper house. In the face of widespread criticism of its role in defeating the anti-prostitution bill, the Democratic Party used these queries as an opportunity to affirm its commitment to future legislation. Prime Minister Hatoyama conceded, in response to a question asked by Katō, that it would be a disgrace to retain a system of prostitution that "violates the dignity of women." Justice Minister Hanamura Shirō reiterated the promise of the government to act on the recommendation of the proposed deliberative council, and Finance Minister Ichimata Hisato promised funds to improve the social welfare systems so as to eradicate prostitution.[70]

On August 15, Hatoyama's Democratic Party issued a statement explaining why it had opposed the anti-prostitution law.[71] The party argued that precisely because there were so many women working as prostitutes—half a million, most of them from economic necessity—it would be wrong to pass a law that punished prostitution. Seventy percent of the prostitutes worked to support themselves, their children, their parents, or their siblings. Fewer than 10 percent had entered the profession out of curiosity or vanity. Most were simply victims of war, repatriation, flood, or famine. Thus, the party argued, prostitution was a problem that arose from Japan's status as a poor country and the national failure to provide protection and relief for the victims of poverty. Prostitutes were women who had made the ultimate sacrifice for their children or family.

The party statement concluded by spelling out the points on which the party disagreed with the bill that Kamichika Ichiko and others had sponsored. Although the leaders of the ruling party acknowledged that prostitution was a moral and social evil, they simply did not believe that prostitution should be a crime punishable by law, parallel to fraud or larceny. Rejecting the reformers' sense of urgency, they insisted that existing laws already addressed various aspects of the problem of prostitution. The statement ended with a reiteration of the promise that the ruling party would submit an anti-prostitution bill of its own to the Diet.

The showdown between the conservative and the progressive parties ended, then, with both sides committed to the passage of an anti-prostitution bill. The women legislators and the women's groups had failed to sustain cooperation across party lines, but in the process of getting the bill to the Diet floor, they had stirred up public opinion to the point where the conservative parties had to take a stand on the issue. The voices of the prostitutes were not absent from the arguments of the reformers. Two former workers testified in the public hearings before the lower house Judicial Affairs Committee. Kamichika provided sympathetic evidence of their point of view from her discussions with the schoolteachers in Iwakuni. She also cited survey data on the views of the prostitutes, usually emphasizing their economic problems and their desire for dignified labor. In the summer of 1955, however, the conservative parties succeeded in representing themselves as the protectors of the prostitutes.

The Prostitutes' Union

In the next stage of the debate, a prostitutes' union took shape that claimed to represent the voices of the prostitutes themselves. The union that Shiga-Fujime has described so well was founded in September 1955, shortly after the member-sponsored anti-prostitution bill failed in July. Just as the passage of a government-sponsored prostitution bill seemed likely in the near future, two members of the JSP, Iwauchi Zensaku and Takahara Asaichi, called together prostitutes, brothel owners, and labor leaders. Their purpose was to organize a union to defend the right to earn a living through prostitution. Their logic was that "it has become a world where one must resort to prostitution in order to survive."[72]

The logic and vocabulary that Takahara and Iwauchi used resonated with those of the brothel owners. The newly formed Alliance of Tokyo

Women Employees' Unions (Tōkyō-to Joshi Jūgyōin Kumia Rengōkai) used the same word for employee (*jūgyōin*) that Suzuki Akira had in his testimony before the Judicial Affairs Committee to refer to the women working in the establishments of the red-light districts. The proclamation presented at a preparatory meeting on December 19, 1955, defined the aims of the alliance in terms of the constitutional guarantees of fundamental human rights and a civilized life (*bunka seikatsu*). Echoing the claims of Suzuki Akira and others in the Diet, the members of the alliance asserted that they were law-abiding, healthy (free from venereal disease), tax-paying citizens. Wishing to transcend feudal social rights, the members emphasized the greater importance of the right to live. Pledging cooperation between employers and union members, they planned attacks on middlemen they characterized as evil and called for the government to provide adequate social security.[73] The formal inauguration of the organization was a meeting attended by fifteen hundred women at the Asakusa Assembly Hall on January 21, 1956. The JSP sent observers, Kamichika Ichiko among them, to the meeting.[74]

Iwauchi, Takahara, and the Alliance of Tokyo Women Employees' Unions launched a national organization on March 26, 1956, by summoning women employed in red-light districts anywhere in Japan to a meeting at the Ryōgoku Memorial Hall in Tokyo. The representatives from nearly two hundred districts formed the National Service Employees Union Alliance (Zenkoku Sekkyaku Joshi Jūgyōin Renmei). Perhaps by coincidence, the national alliance took shape two days after the JSP submitted an anti-prostitution bill to the Diet.[75]

The formation of the prostitutes' union draws attention, of course, to the fact that the prostitutes did not identify with the leadership of the women elected to national office. An oft-quoted remark of Kamichika's in defense of the reformist position must be set in the context of the contentious debate over rights. Kamichika wrote, "We must punish the estimated five hundred thousand prostitutes to protect the lifestyle of forty million housewives."[76] The word that has been translated "lifestyle" here is *seikatsu,* or "livelihood." In this sentence, Kamichika was reasserting the importance of rights in response to critics such as Iwauchi and Takahara, who argued that the reformers overemphasized rights and thus neglected livelihood (*seikatsu*). Kamichika used specific numbers, not to assert the dominance of one class over another, but rather to emphasize the importance of rights to all women. Eighty million was the rhetorical shorthand for the entire population of Japan, of which presumably forty million were women. The application of legal penalties for certain acts was, Kamichika said, a small price to pay to guarantee the human rights of all women.

To be sure, prostitutes took offense at some of Kamichika's rhetoric. Parrying the arguments of brothel owners positioned as defenders of poverty-stricken women, Kamichika argued for better welfare provisions. Focusing on young girls tempted into prostitution in the 1950s, Kamichika mentioned vanity and curiosity as motives, infuriating women who hated the implication that they enjoyed the distasteful work they had taken on to support their families.[77] Moreover, there were genuine class resentments. The prostitute Masuda Sayo asked rhetorically, "Among those making the laws, were there any women like us, who couldn't have survived if they hadn't prostituted themselves?" When she watched a newsreel, Masuda was put off by the women legislators, "all done up in their finery, mincing about so proudly on their tour of the red-light district."[78] The tours women Diet members took of the Yoshiwara seem to have provoked particular resentment. Gaye Rowley has translated a poem in which one of the prostitutes expresses her resentment of the "lady bigwigs wearing chrysanthemum badges" who made speeches to the assembled women about soiled hearts and politics.[79] An articulate leader of the prostitutes expressed irritation at the probing questions and the condescending attitude of a delegation from the upper house. She complained that she was treated as if she were a first grader.[80] Despite such resentments against the abolitionists, most prostitutes wished to quit as soon as possible.[81]

Iwauchi and Takahara were undoubtedly sincere in their desire to help the prostitutes articulate their needs to the government. As Shiga-Fujime points out, both men had long years of experience in organizing working women in mines and in textile factories.[82] Their conviction that access to income was more important than abstract rights was consonant with dialectical materialism. The two were ideologically committed to labor unions as a means of securing better working conditions. There is no question, of course, as to why the owners would agree to join the alliance. With the commitment of the two conservative parties to the passage of anti-prostitution law, they had lost their best allies in their struggle to preserve brothels as legitimate businesses. The importance of the prostitutes' union should not be exaggerated. The efforts of Iwauchi and Takahara took place within a very limited period of time and had little effect on the passage of anti-prostitution legislation. The arguments by which they supported the prostitutes had already been advanced by the owners with the help of the two conservative parties. Their union did not exert significant influence on the fate of the anti-prostitution legislation, nor was it a long-lasting organization. The last public act of the National Service Employees Union Alliance was in 1957.[83]

The 1956 Prostitution Prevention Law

On March 7, 1956, the Hatoyama Cabinet, in fulfillment of its promise to sponsor an anti-prostitution bill, established a Council on Prostitution Policy (Baishun Taisaku Shingikai). The twenty-five members of the council overlapped only slightly with the sponsors of the earlier anti-prostitution bills. There were only seven women on the council, but four of them (Kamichika Ichiko, Fujiwara Michiko, Nakayama Masa, and Miyagi Tamayo) were among the ten council members from the Diet. The three women newly appointed to the council were Tanabe Shigeko (1903–1986), a law professor at Tokyo University; Ōhama Hideko, a family court mediator; and Mimaki Akiko, vice president of the Housewives' League. On March 14 the council, chaired by Sugawara Tsusai, with Tanabe Shigeko as vice-chair, held its first meeting to discuss the merits of a draft prepared by members of the bureaucracy.[84] Kamichika Ichiko protested vehemently that this bill differed in significant ways from the ones she had sponsored earlier. The proposed law made no provision to punish either women who engaged in acts of prostitution or their customers.[85]

The report that the Council on Prostitution Policy submitted on April 9 provided the basis for the bill that the recently formed Liberal Democratic Party (LDP) submitted to the twenty-fourth Diet on May 2. The bill differed from the earlier proposals in two important respects. First, although the new law called for penalties for procurers and brothel owners, it did not criminalize the act of prostitution itself. Second, the bill provided that the law would not take effect until April 1, 1957. The penalties stipulated by the law would not be imposed until April 1, 1958, thus giving the owners and their employees two years to find alternate employment.[86]

Given the likelihood that a government-sponsored bill would pass, the hearings on the bill were much more perfunctory in 1956 than in 1955. When the chair of the upper house Judicial Affairs Committee reported to the plenary session of the chamber on the provisions of the bill, the only questions came from the women members. Yokoyama Fuku, a member of the ruling party, asked about the absence of penalties for acts of prostitution and the two-year delay in implementation. Justice Minister Matsubara's reply revealed a major shift in the conceptualization of the anti-prostitution measures. He said that out of respect for women's rights the bill would protect rather than punish. In this simple exchange, we see that punishments for the male customers have simply vanished from the discourse. His answer obscures, of course, the fact that the earlier bills were equally committed to rehabilitation. The punishments had been directed at the male customers of the prostitutes. A reporter for the *Asahi* noted that most of the male members did not even bother to listen to the proceedings; the total attendance in the house dropped to under forty.[87]

Passage of the bill was virtually assured when the Judicial Affairs Committee of the lower house approved the bill unanimously on May 12. The JSP immediately made clear that its cooperation was less than enthusiastic. The party issued a statement that it "approved the unsatisfactory Government-sponsored bill only because opponents spearheaded by brothel keepers had threatened to influence the Liberal-Democratic legislators into shelving the bill."[88] The critic Tanaka Sumiko opined that the bill had been eviscerated, but she still supported its passage. With the reluctant socialist votes, a plenary session of the lower house gave its unanimous approval on May 15. To be sure, as Ichikawa Fusae pointed out in an editorial piece in the *Asahi,* this unanimity was achieved by the failure of the chair to recognize any dissenting votes.[89] The upper house provided its unanimous approval on May 21, again with only perfunctory discussion.

Although the 1956 bill passed without opposition, supporters of every stripe harbored reservations about its provisions. Sugawara Tsusai, chair of the Council on Prostitution Policy, admitted that the law was full of loopholes but declared it better than nothing. At the same time, he left the door open for the restoration of licensed prostitution when he said, "If [the law] is found to be completely unworkable, then all we have to do is scrap it. People might even think then that licensed prostitution is the only answer."[90] Ichikawa Fusae conceded in her newsletter to her supporters that the bill was flawed. She expressed regret that the law failed to punish the act of prostitution and that enforcement of the new legislation would be postponed for two years.[91] The socialist and independent women who had worked together to secure an anti-prostitution bill continued to support the anti-prostitution legislation even when under government sponsorship the bill became much weaker that they desired. Their support, however, was not the crucial factor in the passage of the bill. Their bloc of votes, insufficient to pass a bill in 1955, was not strong enough to block a bill in 1956.

The crucial factor in the passage of the 1956 bill was, of course, the sponsorship of the LDP. A number of observers, among them Tanaka Sumiko and Kamichika Ichiko, suggested that the LDP about-face was related to concerns about women's votes in the upcoming upper house elections.[92] An editorial in the *Nippon Times* maintained that if no election had been scheduled, the anti-prostitution bill would have died yet again. The editors hypothesized that the party leaders thought that women's votes would outweigh the electoral support the party stood to lose from the brothel owners and their employees.[93]

Conclusion

The 1956 Prostitution Prevention Law was a limited symbolic victory for those who argued that women should be free from the indignity of being treated as property that can be bought and sold. Although acts of prostitution were never declared illegal, the government did not lend to them the legitimacy of formal regulation. Selling a daughter was no longer legal.

The reformers' hope that they could transform societal attitudes toward prostitution was not achieved. The law criminalized solicitation, procurement, and contracts for prostitution but not the act of prostitution itself. This omission placed male customers beyond the reach of the law and made enforcement difficult. The demand for sexual services in Japan has remained high, and the supply has not lagged far behind. The law did nothing to diminish the collusion between proprietor and police that was vividly described in Diet debate.[94] In search of pleasures no longer legally available in Japan, Japanese men embarked on sex tours to Korea and Southeast Asia.

Certainly the rights of the owners to earn a living were not impaired. The immediate solution to the claims of the brothel owners and the prostitutes to the right to a livelihood was postponement of the imposition of penalties for two years. In the long run, the proprietors evaded a law that prohibited male–female sexual intercourse by selling other sexual services instead in enterprises categorized as adult entertainment businesses.[95] Given the ongoing high demand for their services, female sex workers could exercise their right to earn a living, but their working conditions were not necessarily better. The reformers did not get the level of rehabilitation funding that they desired. The absence of contracts made the position of sex workers yet more vulnerable.

In the 1950s discourse on prostitution, the fundamental question was whether prostitution should be legal. Each side presented arguments about how its position would promote the welfare of the workers and reduce the spread of venereal disease, but the law was not a coherent program for solving either problem. The fight against exploitation and sexually transmitted diseases is unending. After 1956, however, Japan was no longer a land of prostitution, a place where the sale of male–female intercourse was legal.

Notes

1. As quoted in the *Nippon Times,* May 23, 1956.
2. *Nippon Times,* May 22, 1956.
3. Ibid., May 20, 1956.
4. Yuki Tanaka, *Japan's Comfort Women: Sexual Slavery and Prostitution during World War II and the US Occupation* (London: Routledge, 2002), 161; Shiga-Fujime Yuki, "The Prostitutes' Union and the Impact of the 1956 Anti-Prostitution Law in Japan," *U.S.-Japan Women's Journal, English Supplement,* no. 5 (1993): 8–9.
5. For treatment of this problem as a women's issue, see Kamichika Ichiko, "Fujin wa heiwa e no suishinryoku de aru," *Shakai kyōiku* 8, no. 3 (March 1953): 8–11. Kamichika explicitly voiced her concern about the return to politics of those who had been purged.
6. Elizabeth Dorn Lublin, *Reforming Japan: The Woman's Christian Temperance Union in the Meiji Period* (Vancouver: University of British Columbia Press, 2010), 107.
7. Sheldon Garon, *Molding Japanese Minds: The State in Everyday Life* (Princeton, NJ: Princeton University Press, 1997), 196–197.
8. The report appears in Ichikawa Fusae, ed., *Nihon fujin mondai shiryō shūsei* (Domesu Shuppan, 1976–1980), 1:577–582. Hereafter cited as NFMSS.
9. For a scholarly description of the relationship of the old system to the new, see Garon, *Molding Japanese Minds,* 198.

10. NFMSS 1:578.

11. Ibid., 1:578–579.

12. Ibid., 1:579–580.

13. See, for instance, Cynthia Enloe, *The Morning After: Sexual Politics at the End of the Cold War* (Berkeley: University of California Press, 1993); and Katharine H. S. Moon, *Sex among Allies: Military Prostitution in U.S.-Korea Relations* (New York: Columbia University Press, 1997).

14. Survey data indicated that national pride was far more important as a motive for opposition to American bases than was concern about "harm to public morals." Douglas H. Mendel Jr., "Japanese Attitudes toward American Military Bases," *Far Eastern Survey* 28, no. 9 (September 1959): 132–133.

15. NFMSS 1:578.

16. Ibid., 1:580. The specific date provided for the testimony was July 23, 1952.

17. NFMSS 1:580.

18. For the text of the bill, see NFMSS 1:582–584. One of the other sponsors of the bill was the socialist writer Kaneko Yōbun.

19. Kamichika Ichiko, *Sayonara ningen baibai* (Gendaisha, 1956), 240.

20. NFMSS 1:593.

21. Kamichika, *Sayonara ningen baibai,* 244–245.

22. For the text, see NFMSS 1:595. For the connection of the brothel owners to the organization opposing the bill, see Kanzaki Kiyoshi, *Baishun Ketteiban Kanzaki repōto* (Gendaishi Shuppankai, 1974), 391.

23. Kamichika Ichiko, "Shin no tsukareru sōron: Baishun shobatsu hōan no teiansha to shite," *Toki no hōrei,* no. 138 (July 3, 1954): 20–23.

24. Kamichika, "Shin no tsukareru sōron," 22–23.

25. Kamichika, who referred to the law as if it were named for the fifth month, clearly did not know about its sponsor. She may have overestimated its use. The first instance in which federal officials invoked the law was in Nashville, Tennessee in May 1942. Robert G. Spinney, "Municipal Government in Nashville, Tennessee, 1938–1951: World War II and the Growth of the Public Sector," *Journal of Southern History* 61, no. 1 (February 1995): 85.

26. A native of Kanazawa, Segawa Yasō (1890–1977) was especially active in his late years on behalf of the women of Okinawa. *Kirisutokyō jinmei jiten* (Nihon Kirisutokyōdan Shuppankyoku, 1986), 807.

27. Kamichika Ichiko, "Baishun nado shobatsu hōan wa naze fuketsu sareta," *Fujin kōron* 40, no. 9 (September 1955): 66–68. Another assertion that women engaged in prostitution for economic reasons appears in Kami-

chika Ichiko, "'Matsumoto jiken' to chihō seiji no fuhai," *Fujin kōron* 40, no. 7 (July 1955): 201.

28. Kamichika Ichiko, *Waga seishun no kokuhaku* (Mainichi Shinbun, 1957), 69–72.

29. *Nippon Times,* June 11, 1955.

30. See for instance Kamichika, "Shin no tsukareru sōron," 23; and Kamichika, "Baishun nado shobatsu hōan wa naze fuketsu sareta," 68.

31. NFMSS 1:661.

32. *Nippon Times,* May 1, 1956.

33. Ibid., May 22, 1956.

34. Kanzaki, *Baishun,* 225–226.

35. Kamichika, "Baishun nado shobatsu hōan wa naze fuketsu sareta," 67–68.

36. These incidents are mentioned in Kamichika, *Sayonara ningen baibai,* 249, and *Fujin taimuzu,* May 14, 1955. On the Matsumoto Incident, see also Kamichika, "Matsumoto jiken," 198–201.

37. Kamichika, "Matsumoto jiken," 201.

38. Kamichika, *Sayonara ningen baibai,* 246–247; *Nippon Times,* June 11, 1955.

39. As summarized in *Nippon Times,* June 13, 1955.

40. Kamichika, *Waga seishun no kokuhaku,* 76–77.

41. As summarized in *Nippon Times,* July 5, 1955.

42. *Nippon Times,* July 8, 1955. The results of the poll first appeared in *Tokyo shinbun.*

43. Shiina Takashi, *Dai nijūni tokubetsu kokkai baishun mondai* (Yōyōsha, 1955), 131–133.

44. Shiina, *Dai nijūni tokubetsu kokkai baishun mondai,* 135–136. On the Kakuseikai, see Garon, *Molding Japanese Minds,* 98–99. The exchange about "onlies" was reported in *Nippon Times,* July 8, 1955.

45. Shiina, *Dai nijūni tokubetsu kokkai baishun mondai,* 136–137.

46. Ibid., 138–140.

47. Ibid., 141–145.

48. Ibid., 145–146.

49. *Nippon Times,* July 8, 1955; NFMSS 1:609–610.

50. NFMSS 1:614–615.

51. Ibid., 1:633–635.

52. *Nippon Times,* July 8, 1955.

53. Ibid., July 15, 1955.

54. Ibid., July 17, 1955.

55. NFMSS 1:639; *Nippon Times,* July 20, 1955.

56. Kamichika, *Waga seishun no kokuhaku,* 83–84; NFMSS 1:664; *Nippon Times,* July 20, 1955.

57. NFMSS 1:639–640.

58. Ibid., 1:640–642.

59. Ibid., 1:642–643.

60. Ibid., 1:646. Fukui's testimony appears on pages 644–646.

61. Ibid., 1:647–648.

62. Ibid., 1:648–650.

63. Ibid., 1:652–653.

64. Ibid., 1:654–655.

65. Ibid., 1:660.

66. NFMSS 1:656–657.

67. *Nippon Times,* July 21, 1955.

68. Ibid., July 25, 1955.

69. Ibid., July 20, 1955.

70. Ibid., July 26, 1955.

71. NFMSS 1:661–663.

72. Shiga-Fujime, "Prostitutes' Union," 11.

73. NFMSS 1:677.

74. Shiga-Fujime, "Prostitutes' Union," 19; Kamichika, *Sayonara ningen baibai,* 99.

75. Shiga-Fujime, "Prostitutes' Union," 21.

76. Ibid., 10.

77. For the anger of prostitutes at Kamichika, see Holly Vincele Sanders, "Prostitution in Postwar Japan: Debt and Labor" (PhD diss., Princeton University, 2005), 181–182.

78. Masada Sayo, *Autobiography of a Geisha,* trans. G. G. Rowley (New York: Columbia University Press, 2003), 158.

79. G. G. Rowley, "Prostitutes against the Prostitution Prevention Act of 1956," *U.S.-Japan Women's Journal, English Supplement,* no. 23 (2002): 49.

80. Kanzaki, *Baishun,* 109–110. The prostitute singled out Fukagawa Tamae for particular criticism.

81. Sanders, "Prostitution in Postwar Japan," 184.

82. Shiga-Fujime, "Prostitutes' Union," 14–17.

83. Ibid., 24.

84. The order establishing the council and the list of its members is given in NFMSS 1:682–683. On Tanabe, see Haga Noboru, *Nihon josei jinmei jiten* (Nihon Toshō Sentaa, 1993), 680.

85. Kamichika, *Sayonara ningen baibai,* 105–106.

86. *Asahi shinbun,* May 1, 1956.

87. Ibid., May 10, 1956.

88. *Nippon Times,* May 13, 1956.

89. *Asahi shinbun,* May 18, 1956.

90. Quoted in Kiyoaki Murata, "Outlawing of Prostitution: Newly Passed Law Will Only Drive Prostitutes Underground," *Nippon Times,* May 28, 1956.

91. *Watakushi no kokkai hōkoku,* no. 4 (December 1956), 6.

92. On Tanaka Sumiko's opinion, see *Asahi shinbun,* May 13, 1956. Kamichika describes the view that the major parties had passed the 1956 bill to buy off women's anger because of the failure of the 1955 bill in Kamichika, *Sayonara ningen baibai,* 98.

93. *Nippon Times,* May 27, 1956.

94. Sarah C. Kovner, "Prostitution in Postwar Japan: Sex Workers, Servicemen, and Social Activists, 1945–1956" (PhD diss., Columbia University, 2004), 164–165, 173.

95. For a description of Turkish baths, soaplands, and sex tourism, see Sanders, "Prostitution in Postwar Japan," 215–217.

PART II

Crime, Punishment, and Gender

CHAPTER 3

Gender in the Arena of the Courts

The Prosecution of Abortion and Infanticide in Early Meiji Japan

Susan L. Burns

IN 1949 JAPAN became the first country in the world to legalize abortion based upon socioeconomic grounds, a legislative innovation that Tiana Norgren has described as "a marked departure from international norms."[1] But the legalization of abortion was also a remarkable departure from almost eight decades of Japanese criminal law. The first modern law on abortion went into effect in 1873 when the law code known as the Amended Criminal Regulations (*Kaitei ritsurei*) was promulgated. Article 114 of this code made it a crime both to procure an abortion for oneself and to encourage or aid another person in procuring one and provided for a maximum sentence of one hundred days of penal servitude for a conviction of either crime.[2] In 1882, when a new criminal code (now known as *kyukeihō*) went into effect, abortion was again defined as a crime, and the maximum prison sentence was extended to six months.[3] Then, in 1908, when the criminal code was revised again, the sentence for obtaining an abortion was extended to as long as one year.[4] Abortion was only one subject of a network of laws promulgated in this period that intervened in the reproductive lives of Japanese women. Infanticide too was deemed a crime in the Amended Criminal Regulations and, as in the case of abortion, with subsequent legal reform came increasingly severe penalties.[5]

In her influential book *Sei no rekishigaku: Kōshō seido dataizai taisei kara baishun bōshihō yūsei hogohō e* (The History of Sexuality: From the System of Legal Prostitution and Criminalized Abortion to the System of the Prevention of Prostitution Law and the Eugenics Protection Law), Fujime Yuki has characterized what she termed the "licensed prostitution–criminalized abortion system" as fundamental to the formation of the modern Japanese state.[6] According to Fujime, motivated by the desire to forge a "rich nation, strong army," as a popular slogan put it, beginning in the late nineteenth century the Japanese government deployed a new bio-politics that promoted female fertility by criminalizing abortion and controlling access to contraception, while affirming male sexuality through the establishment of a system of licensed prostitution. However, writing in Fujime's wake, other scholars have challenged her conclusions. Most notably, in a series of articles Ishizaki Shōko has argued that Fujime's emphasis on the continuity of state reproductive policy from the late nineteenth century through the 1930s obscures important changes in both policy and ideology. She suggests that it was not until the 1930s, as the pace of Japanese expansionism quickened, that pro-natalism reflected concern for population growth as a source of national strength.[7] In the late nineteenth century, in contrast, the regulation of reproduction through law was prompted by concerns about social disorder and the decline in popular morals that arose in the wake of the Meiji Restoration.

This chapter seeks to contribute to the debate over the intent and impact of the criminalization of abortion and infanticide by shifting the focus from the requirements of the statutes and the intent of those who formulated them to an examination of how they were actually deployed within the new social space of the modern courts. While the statutes, of course, had a symbolic value that cannot be dismissed, their ideological significance has to be evaluated in light of the social reality of their use in practice. To explore the relationship between the statutes and their application, this essay takes up an important but relatively unexamined moment in Japan's legal history, that is, the decade before the criminal code of 1882 took effect.[8] While the 1882 and 1908 codes were at the center of Fujime's work, the prosecution of abortion and infanticide had begun in the 1870s. By 1875 a functioning legal system of regional and appellate courts with the Daishin-in or High Court of Review as its pinnacle was in place. The case records of criminal convictions of abortion and infanticide preserved by the high court offer a glimpse into the struggles that accompanied attempts to adjudicate the newly defined reproductive crimes.[9]

I begin by examining how abortion and infanticide were dealt with in the Tokugawa period as a necessary first step to understanding the unprecedented nature of the Amended Criminal Regulations. I next turn to review the code itself and the new legal regime that first defined reproductive crimes. This forms the basis for an analysis of the adjudication of specific cases both at the local level and by the high court in Tokyo. I argue that ideas about sexuality, gendered social roles, and authority within families and between sexual partners came into play in determining culpability and punishment, compelling a new concern for individual agency in relation to reproductive decision making. In contrast to Fujime's work, which portrayed the prewar judicial system as little more than a technology of social control that consistently oppressed women, I conclude that the pattern of judgments suggest an evolving juridical stance toward reproductive crimes that had consequences for both men and women.

Reproductive Crimes and the Tokugawa-Meiji Divide

Even before the promulgation of the early Meiji codes, both abortion and infanticide were already problematic acts, commonplace to be sure and yet subject to frequent denunciation from Confucian moralists and others and repeated bans by the bakufu and some domains. In the city of Edo, the earliest town edict (*machibure*) on abortion dates from the 1640s. It simply stated, "techniques for aborting a child are forbidden." An edict issued twenty years later offered a more elaborate denunciation. It described "women doctors" (*onna isha*) who performed abortions as "immoral in the extreme" and states that both these practitioners and their clients should be punished. There is, however, little evidence of overt efforts to police these practices until the late eighteenth century. The official record of crimes and punishments (*Onshioki saikyochō*) compiled in the early eighteenth century makes mention of abortion in only three cases. Each involved the death of a woman and the "provider" was charged not for the abortion itself but for involvement in the woman's death.[10] No mention of either abortion or infanticide appears in the 1742 Rules for Determining Criminal Matters (*Kujikata osadamegaki*), the bakufu's attempt to systematize the punishment of criminal offenses, although by this time doctors who specialized in inducing abortion, many associated with the medical "school" known as Chūjōryū, were practicing openly in Edo and other cities, sometimes advertising their services by posting notices in public toilets.[11] In 1842, the town magistrate of Edo, apparently concerned about the visibility of this trade, submitted an inquiry to his superiors asking whether it should be allowed to continue, although he noted that abortion providers offered legitimate midwifery services as well. In response the bakufu issued a new ban and for the first time delineated specific punishments: in the case of an abortion both the man and woman involved in the pregnancy should be expelled from the city proper while the doctor who aided them was subject to the harsher punishment of banishment.[12]

By the time this edict was announced in Edo, some domains had been attempting to prevent or alternatively to discover and punish acts of abortion and infanticide for several decades. In the 1780s, a devastating famine caused a dramatic loss of population in northern Honshu as tens of thousands starved and others fled. In the aftermath, domainal governments in the hardest hit areas concluded that abortion and infanticide were responsible for the failure of population to rebound. They developed policies that aimed to insure that pregnancies resulted in live births. In Sendai, for example, village officials were required to compile records of pregnancies within the village and to investigate cases of miscarriage and stillbirth. However, one of the most stringent systems of pregnancy surveillance was deployed in Tsuyama domain in western Japan, an area not directly affected by the famine. Proclaiming the need to improve the morals of the populace, the domainal government ordered village and town officials to compile monthly reports on the pregnant women within their jurisdiction. If a suspicious miscarriage or stillbirth occurred, not only the pregnant woman but also her family, her neighbors, and the heads of the "five man group" to which her household belonged were all subject to punishment. Initially, this took the form of fines and confinement, but after 1834, the domain resorted to harsher measures. The man and woman held responsible for an act of infanticide were to be reduced to outcaste (*hinin*) status.[13] These new efforts to police abortion and infanticide were accompanied by the rise of a moral discourse critical of these practices. Confucianists, Buddhist priests, and local officials published and circulated broadsheets, pamphlets, and votive tablets that denounced abortion and infanticide as evil and inhumane acts committed by depraved women who valued ease and comfort over their children.[14]

The overthrow of the Tokugawa shogunate in 1868 was followed by a new wave of restrictions on abortion, infanticide, and child abandonment at the level of the newly created prefectures. In 1869 the new governor of Kōchi announced that abortion and infanticide were prohibited, and soon after the prefectural governments of Iwate, Hita (later part of Oita Prefecture), Kisarazu (later part of Chiba Prefecture), Kagoshima, Wakamatsu, and Aomori followed with similar proclamations of their own.[15] Ishizaki Shōko has looked closely at two of these sites, Hita and Kisarazu, and argues that in both governors appointed by the new government issued restrictions on these practices as part of a larger campaign to "reform custom" and "control behavior" after the breakdown of social order during the turbulent 1860s, an era marked by widespread unrest in the form of cultivator rebellions and so-called "world renewal" uprisings.[16] Oriented by the Confucian conception of the family as a crucial building block of an orderly society, samurai officials at the prefectural level sought to use reproductive policies to encourage those in their jurisdiction to concentrate on diligent and productive labor, the raising of children, and the prosperity of their families.

In contrast to Fujime's emphasis on the powerful role of the Meiji state in policing reproduction, Ishizaki's research suggests that the abortion and infanticide restrictions of the early Meiji codes reflected a different process, one in which officials in Tokyo looked to local initiatives as they forged new national policies. But while this may be the case for specific statutes, there is no denying that legal reform was fundamentally a "top-down" process that was driven by national concerns—the desire to create a central administration that would instantiate the ideology of imperial rule and the need to counter Western criticism of Japan's "backward" penal practices. In 1871, as a provisional solution to the need to create a new national legal system, the government promulgated the Outline of the New Criminal Code (*Shinritsu koryō,* hereafter referred to as the "Outline"), a set of legal guidelines compiled by Mizumoto Narumi, Tsuruta Akira, and Murata Tamotsu, scholars trained in Confucian thought who drew upon the statutes of the Chinese codes of the Ming and Qing periods. However, criticism of the "Outline" soon followed as local officials found its general principles offered little guidance for dealing with actual cases and foreign observers criticized its reliance on corporal punishments. As a result, Etō Shinpei, who became Minister of Justice in 1872, was charged with the revision of the "Outline." The result was the Amended Criminal Regulations of 1873, which supplemented the earlier code by offering a more concise definition of crimes and their punishments and replaced floggings and banishment with prison terms and fines.[17]

In the "Outline" abortion was not identified as a crime, although a common if unintended consequence of the act was that the section on homicide specified punishment for the male partner of an "unchaste woman" (*kanpu*) who died as the result of an abortion. The Amended Criminal Regulations contained the same provision: according to Article 198 of the statutes on homicide, if a woman pregnant as a result of an "illicit" sexual relationship died because of an abortion, her sexual partner was to be sentenced to penal servitude for three years.[18] But the revised code also specifically designated abortion itself as a crime. Article 114 came in the section on household statutes that addressed crimes against children: Article 113 addressed child abandonment by parents, while Article 115 criminalized the practice of fostering children, presumably for a fee, and then abandoning them. The Amended Criminal Regulations also specifically addressed infanticide (*eijisatsu*) but directed that it be treated in light of the general statutes on homicide. According to Article 164: "as for the person who kills an infant, he or should be punished according to the specific degree of kinship and based upon the provisions for premeditated murder (*bōsatsu*) and manslaughter (*kosatsu*). If a midwife kills an infant based upon the request of another person, she is guilty of the same crime as the one who made the request."[19]

The distinction between premeditated murder and manslaughter thus became essential to the adjudication of infanticide cases. The former was defined an act of homicide in which the participant had prepared for the act in advance and acted with deliberation, while the latter was carried out in a state of emotion in which the intent to kill was conceived at the time of the act and there was no preparation or planning.[20]

The code also distinguished between varying degrees of culpability when multiple people were involved in a criminal act. The term "accomplice" (*jūhan*) was used to describe someone who assisted in carrying out a homicide but at the instigation of some other person, labeled the "principal offender" (*shuhan*). The principal offender with whom the intent to commit the crime had originated was to be punished more harshly than an accomplice, even if he or she was not directly involved in committing the act itself.[21] As we shall see, this distinction was to become a central issue in the infanticide cases heard by the courts, as judges and prosecutors no less than defendants struggled to make sense of the often murky issue of who had acted, who had not, and why.

A third factor involved in the prosecution of infanticide cases was the familial relationship of those involved. Like the Chinese codes it was based upon, the Amended Criminal Regulations reflected Confucian principles of social hierarchy by defining different degrees of punishment based upon the relationship of the perpetrator to his or her victim when acts of violence occurred between family members. Commenting on the Chinese codes' exhaustive delineation of penalties according to who did what to whom, one scholar has declared that within premodern Chinese law acts of homicide had nothing in common but a dead body.[22] While the general principle was that "juniors" who committed acts of violence against "seniors" were treated more harshly than in the reverse case, the degree of kinship complicated this general principle.[23] In cases in which a "junior" injured or killed a "senior" kinsmen, the closer the familial relationship, the harsher the punishment. In contrast, if a "senior" injured or killed a "junior," the closer the relationship, the less severe the punishment.[24] Needless to say, it was this second principle that came into play in cases of infanticide.

A final feature of the code that had significance for the adjudication of both abortion and infanticide was the concept of mitigation. While the Amended Criminal Regulations defined specific punishments for specific crimes, it also gave judges great latitude to determine punishments based upon the circumstances of the crime in question. Punishment could be reduced by one to five degrees based upon a variety of factors such as the offender's age, gender, health, and status as a male heir or an only child.[25] However, some statutes specified that one or more factors could not be considered in determining mitigation. Article 114 stated that, "Even in the case of a woman, it is not allowed to commute the punishment."[26]

That Fujime and others have overlooked the codes of the 1870s is not surprising: they were in effect for only a decade, and from their inception they were criticized by some government officials and members of the new civil elite who were already advocating the emulation of more "civilized" Western-style laws. Although this seems to be a transitory and discontinuous moment in Japanese legal history, the new national laws supplanted the patchwork of local attempts at regulating reproduction with clearly defined criminal acts and specific punishments, and the prosecutions that occurred under them marked the beginning of the state's involvement in policing the reproductive lives of its citizens. The aggressiveness of these efforts is remarkable. As Table 1 reveals, after 1876, the first year for which there are records, hundreds of men and women were prosecuted each year under the abortion statutes of the Amended Criminal Regulations.[27]

In fact, the still nascent state of the Japanese legal system notwithstanding, the number of abortion prosecutions under the Amended Criminal Regulations was among the highest in the modern period. As Graph 1 suggests, prosecutions rose sharply after the passage of each major revision of the criminal code, probably because increased policing followed legal reform.[28]

The period of 1878–1881 was the first of these sharp peaks, another occurred in 1883–1884, and then a third in the early 1910s. It was not until the 1920s that the number of prosecutions began a sharp and steady decline. Whether the rates for infanticide were similar is difficult to discern since such cases were treated as homicides and no specific statistics were compiled.[29] Also difficult to quantify is the cultural impact of this first wave of prosecutions. As early as 1875, Japan's new newspaper began to frequently report on convictions for reproductive crimes, often in terms that mocked and shamed those involved.[30] The implication of the new legal process for popular perceptions of abortion and infanticide needs further study, but the intense reportage in this period suggests that what were once private and commonplace acts were rendered public and problematic through the mediation of the new courts.

While the late 1870s thus clearly marked the first moment when the fledgling Japanese state began to intervene in a sustained way in the reproductive lives of its citizens, the nature and impact of this interven-

Table 1 Abortion-Related Crimes under Article 114 of the Amended Criminal Regulations

Year	Total number of people charged	Women for aborting	Men as *jūhan*	Women as *jūhan*	Male "providers"	Female "providers"
1876	394					
1877	297					
1878	718/618	262	173	60	60	63
1879	597/540	347	72	20	43	58
1880	551/621	306	108	56	72	79
1881	536/437	165	107	61	48	56

tion has yet to be fully explored. To consider this issue, I have analyzed the records of the Daishin'in. Between 1877 and 1882, the five or more judges of this final court of appeal reviewed sixteen cases of reproductive crimes involving twenty-two defendants: eleven abortion cases, four infanticide cases, and one case involving both abortion and infanticide. In only one of the abortion case was the woman who ended her pregnancy the defendant; the others involved either "providers" (who had performed the procedure or supplied abortifacients or instruction) or the male sexual partners of the women who had undergone an abortion. In the four infanticide cases, two involved multiple female defendants (in both cases, the grandmother and great-grandmother of the infant), while two involved fathers charged with killing their children. To be sure, the cases that came before the high court represent only a tiny fraction of the prosecutions that occurred at the local level. For example, in 1878, a year in which at least 628 people were charged with crimes related to acts of abortion, only one case involving abortion was reviewed by the high court. However, while the number of appealed cases was small, the very fact that they came before the high court sug-

Graph 1 Rates of Prosecution and Conviction for Abortion-related crimes, 1876–1924

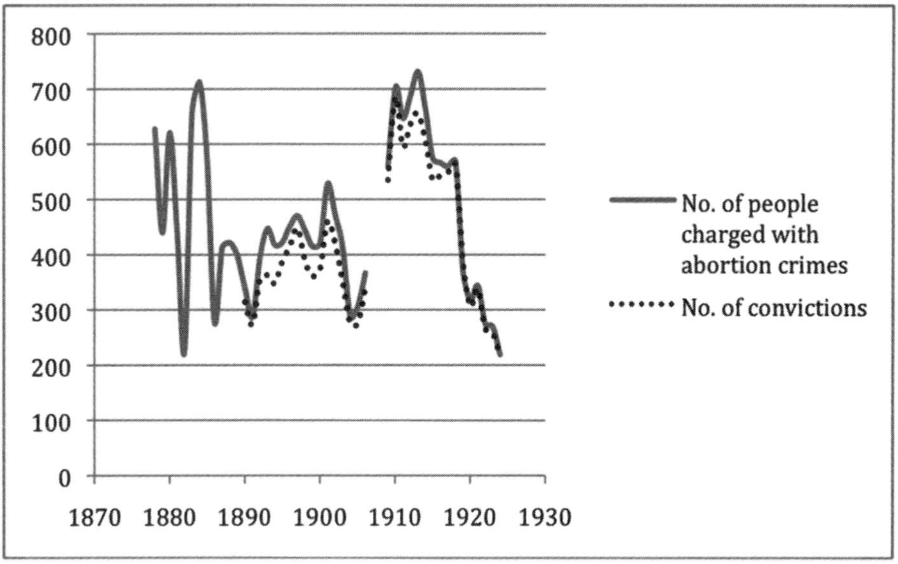

gests that some issue of legal significance or some dispute over the nature of the justice rendered was involved.

In analyzing these cases, my aim is neither to attempt to determine what "really" happened nor to comment on the quality of the justice rendered by the Meiji courts. Rather, taking a hint from the work of Natalie Zemon Davis, I want to read the records as a set of conflicting stories told about an act of abortion or infanticide.[31] The Daishin'in records are not verbatim transcripts of the proceedings; they are summaries that were compiled by officials of the court. However, they incorporated lengthy summaries of the testimony offered in the original court by the accused, sometimes including direct quotations in colloquial language. The defendant's testimony was followed by the judgment of the lower court and its sentence. Attached to this record was a statement detailing the basis of the appeal: here another story is told as either the defendant or the prosecutor (both could initiate an appeal) explained how the original judgment conflicted with the statutes or with the evidence. The record concluded with the response of the high court to this statement and its decision to either uphold or revise the judgment of the local court. Read as a set of competing narratives, the case records offer a glimpse into the struggles that accompanied attempts to explain and evaluate these intimate and no doubt desperate acts in light of new and unfamiliar legal norms.

Telling Tales in the Courtroom

Of the twenty-two cases reviewed by the Daishin'in, perhaps the most complicated—and compelling—was that involving Kikuchi Ryūhei's family of Iwai-gun in Iwate. The dossier on the Kikuchi case is one of the lengthiest in the records of the high court, stretching over eleven pages in the modern print edition. Ryūhei himself; his wife, Kotono; his mother, Kan, and his son, Sōjirō, as well as a local doctor, Katsuta Gen'ei, were all charged in the death of an infant born to Ryūhei's unmarried daughter, Etsu, in 1877.[32] As Kotono related the story of this family crisis in her testimony, sometime in August 1877, she became suspicious that Etsu was pregnant: the girl was not eating as usual and seemed bothered by stomach problems. Then one day, she saw Etsu binding her stomach with a long cloth known as *hara-obi,* an act typically performed by women in their fifth month of pregnancy. She questioned Shio, the wife of Sōjirō, who related that Etsu had been intimate with a young man—this in spite of the fact that her family had recently entered into marriage negotiations with another family.

All but certain that Etsu was indeed pregnant, Kotono stated that she then conferred with her husband. They agreed that the pregnancy would not only bring an end to this marriage proposal but also ruin Etsu's chances for a good marriage in the future and damage the reputation of the family as a whole. It was decided that Etsu would be taken to a local physician, Katsuta Gen'ei, and if she was indeed pregnant, an abortion would be performed. When Katsuta confirmed Etsu's pregnancy, Kotono told him of the family's concerns and asked him to help abort the fetus. He advised her that an abortion would be difficult since Etsu was already at least five months pregnant but agreed to provide an herbal compound that would induce a miscarriage. After returning home, Kotono informed Ryūhei of what had transpired, and—according to her account—he continued to insist that an abortion was the only solution. Etsu then took the three packets of medicine Katsuta had provided but to no effect. Several days later Katsuta was consulted again, and he responded by providing another oral abortifacient, and when this too failed he turned to another common method of inducing an abortion, the insertion of a foreign object into the uterus. When this final effort was ineffective, Katsuta advised Kotono that an abortion was not possible and suggested that she raise Etsu's child as her own. In her statement, Kotono related that she again conveyed the doctor's opinion to her husband and the rest of the family but that Ryūhei in particular continued to voice concern for the disrepute this birth would bring to the family.

On December 31, Etsu's labor began, and Katsuta was called to attend to her. When it became apparent that Etsu was having difficulty delivering the child, Katsuta asked that another doctor be summoned to assist him, but the family refused. Finally, the next morning, Etsu's baby was born. Kotono stated that the infant did not cry and moved its arms and legs weakly. Believing that it would not survive in any case, she asked Kan, her mother-in-law, to kill it, whereupon Kan smothered the infant with some old rags. After the departure of Katsuta, Kotono told Ryūhei and the other members of the family that the infant had died as the result of its difficult birth. A relieved Ryūhei then told Sōjirō to bury the infant in the family garden. Kotono concluded her statement with the declaration that, with the exception of Katsuta and Kan, no one else had any knowledge of how the infant died.

Katsuta Gen'ei denied involvement in the infant's death. According to his testimony, from the first he was convinced that an abortion was impossible because of the advanced state of Etsu's pregnancy, and thus he had advised Kotono early on to resign herself to raising the infant. In fact, Katsuta claimed that none of the herbal medicines he had supplied presented any danger to Etsu or her fetus—an assertion that was confirmed by another physician who offered testimony. Katsuta stated that he had provided harmless drugs in order to placate the family until they accepted the inevitability of the birth. As for the death of the infant, Katsuta cast further blame on the family: although Etsu's life was in danger, they refused to call in another doctor to aid him in the hope of keeping the birth a secret, and he became aware of Kan and Kotono discussing the need to dispose of the infant even as Etsu labored. Shortly after he had finished attending to Etsu, he realized that they had in fact smothered the newborn. Katsuta acknowledged that he should have reported this to the authorities at once. He had not, because "in any case it would not have revived the child."

The record does not reveal how the judges of the Morioka Court came to their decision, but the sentences they issued were far lighter than the statutory requirements. Kotono was determined to be the principal offender and sentenced to three years, the term specified by the homicide regulations for parents and grandparents who kill their child or grandchild, but this was then reduced to a mere one hundred days, in recognition of what was vaguely described as "the circumstances" (*jōjō*) of her act.[33] Kan was treated as a midwife and received the same reduced sentence as her daughter-in-law. Ryūhei also benefited from the court's largess: while it recognized that he had "incited" the initial efforts to abort, he was sentenced to only thirty days because in the end the attempts at abortion had failed. Moreover, even this sentence was reduced to a fine of two yen and twenty-five sen. Ryūhei was not found guilty of any involvement in the infant's death but was fined one additional yen for his role in its unlawful burial. Sōjirō too was found guilty of aiding in the burial, but his fine was the paltry sum of five sen. In contrast, the doctor, Katsuta, was treated with relative harshness. While the court accepted his argument that his drugs had had no ill effect, it held him responsible for not attempting to prevent Kan's act, citing the statute that made it a crime to fail to intervene to prevent an act of violence. He was sentenced to ninety days, but this was reduced to forty days based upon mitigation, and this sentence was then commuted to a fine of three yen.

The case did not end, however, with these rather lenient sentences. The prosecutor of the Morioka Court, Takeuchi Naoyoshi, disagreed with what he characterized as their undue lightness and appealed the lower court's rulings. In his lengthy statement to the high court, Takeuchi spoke contemptuously of the Morioka judges' affirmation of the Kikuchi family's concern for reputation and argued that none of those involved should have been granted a reduction of the statutory sentences. In regard to Kotono, Takeuchi argued that she had decided to kill her grandchild merely in order to conceal her daughter's misconduct, behavior for which she, as Etsu's mother, was ultimately responsible. He contrasted Kotono's lack of concern for the life of the infant, with the motivation of impoverished parents who, in a misguided attempt to provide for their child, abandon it at the gate of a wealthy household. Noting that acts of child abandonment were punished by one hundred days of penal servitude, Takeuchi asked, can the act of Kotono be weighed the same? As for Kan, Takeuchi argued that she could not be treated as a mere midwife: she was the great-grandmother of the dead infant and should be treated accordingly. He dealt harshly with Ryūhei as well, pointing out that whatever the outcome, his intention had been that Etsu end her pregnancy. Ryūhei's failure to report the birth and death of the child as required by the household registration system and his involvement in its illegal burial were clear evidence of his complicity. Given this, there was no basis for reducing his sentence to a fine. As for Katsuta, Takeuchi argued that not only had he failed to intervene to stop the murder of infant, he had also failed to report it. There was no basis for reducing his sentence to a mere fine.

In the end, however, the high court confirmed the right of the lower court judges to determine degrees of mitigation. It made no response to the outraged prosecutor's charge, but its verdicts fell far short of the stiff punishments he had requested, suggesting that the judges in Tokyo, like those in Morioka, had some sympathy for the family. It confirmed the sentences of the lower court in relation to Kotono and Katsuta. In regard to Ryūhei, the court apparently dismissed the charge under the abortion statute, presumably because no abortion had in fact occurred. Instead it found him guilty, as Takeuchi requested, of violating the household registry laws that required the registration of births and deaths. However, the fine it imposed was the same as that in the original judgment. In the end, it was sixty-two-year-old Kan who was made to bear the greatest responsibility for the death of Etsu's child.

The judges of the high court agreed with Takeuchi that she could not be treated as a midwife under the provisions of Article 164. The correct statute was Article 225, which addressed injury or murder of junior family members by their senior relatives of the third degree or beyond and stipulated a sentence of death by strangulation or a life sentence.[34] The court convicted Kan under this statute but reduced her sentence to a term of two a half years of penal servitude, again on the basis of "circumstances."

Absent from the case record is any testimony attributed to Etsu herself. We never learn what she thought of her family's increasingly frantic efforts to end her pregnancy or of their involvement in the death of her child. The silence of Etsu within the court records is not unusual. In fact, the records of other cases suggest that when abortion and infanticide took place within the context of a family, responsibility for this decision was assumed to rest with someone other than the young pregnant woman herself. Older relatives, including both parents and grandparents in the multigenerational households of the time, were deeply involved in reproductive decision making, a pattern that posed difficulty for judges attempting to implement the new statutory guidelines.

This is evident from another case that also originated in Iwate, which involved the death of a female infant born to Terakura Banzō and his wife, Tatsu.[35] Charged with the death were Terakura Tami, the mother of Banzō; Terakura Fuyo, his maternal grandmother; and Furutachi Tsuru, the mother of Tatsu. According to the statement offered by Tami to the Morioka Court, all three women were present when Tatsu gave birth to her second child, a girl. After conferring with Fuyo and Tsuru—but not with Tatsu, who is described as "tired from the birth and unaware"—she smothered the infant. Her justification, echoed by her co-defendants in their own testimony, was that the baby girl was born before her sickly older brother was weaned, and she believed that Tatsu would be unable to successfully nurse both children. The lower court convicted all three women of manslaughter, but their sentences differed: Tami was identified as the principal offender and sentenced to three years of penal servitude, Fuyo and Tsuru to life sentences that were reduced in both cases to two and a half years. As in the case of Kikuchi Kan, the harsh sentences of Tsuru and Fuyo reflect the principle that distant relatives should be punished more harshly than close ones for acts of violence against their junior relations.

In this case too the appeal was brought by the prosecutor, who argued that the sentences were too lenient. He stated that Tami should have been found guilty of intentional murder, that there was no basis for reducing Fuyo's sentence, and that Tsuru's sentence should only have been reduced to three years. But again the high court disagreed. It confirmed the legality of the lower court's decision in relation to Tami and Fuyo—but ordered a further reduction of Tsuru's sentence to only one year. In her statement to the high court, Tsuru asserted that when the issue of the infant's fate came up soon after her own daughter had given birth, she in fact was opposed to smothering it because she had few grandchildren and wanted another, but since her daughter had married into this family she felt she could not strongly protest and that ultimately the decision was Tami and Fuyo's to make. It seems that this argument proved convincing: the judgment of the court was that Tsuru's passive stance was understandable, if still criminal, and thus reduced her sentence.

As these two cases reveal, the statutes notwithstanding, there was no easy consensus even among judges and prosecutors—the representatives of the new state's legal regime—on how to adjudicate cases of infanticide. The moral outrage voiced by the prosecutor, Takeuchi, stands in sharp contrast to the judges' willingness to acknowledge "circumstances." Not only were judges at every level lenient in sentencing, they were also quite flexible in their interpretation of the statutes when a defendant successfully appealed to a seemingly shared cultural norm. Thus, Tsuru's evocation of her "outsider" status within the household of her daughter's husband seems to have resonated with judges of the Daishin'in, with the result that she fared far better than Kan, whose defense was that she had acted at the direction of her daughter-in-law.

These two cases, and in particular the treatment of Kikuchi Ryūhei, who paid a fine while his wife and mother went to prison, might seem to suggest that women were held responsible for reproductive decision making. But in fact, men involved in acts of infanticide and abortion tended to be treated quite harshly by the courts. The case of Iwase Shigehachi, a resident of Chiba, is instructive. When Shigehachi and his wife divorced in 1875, she was pregnant, but an agreement was reached that Shigehachi would raise the child after its birth, an arrangement common in some regions that was affirmed by the regulations for child custody issued in the early 1870s.[36] Two days after its birth in April 1876 the infant was brought to Shigehachi, who resided with his parents and siblings. In his initial confession, later to be recanted, Shigehachi stated that, fearing the child would be a burden to his parents and an obstacle to his own remarriage, he smothered it during the first night it was in his care and announced to his startled parents the next morning that the child had sickened and died. Although the family quickly buried the infant, its death caught the attention of the village authorities, who then contacted the police. Initially suspicion fell on Shigehachi's mother, who was taken into custody for questioning and soon admitted her guilt. At that point, Shigehachi came forward and confessed that he was responsible. Based on this confession, the Chiba Court convicted him of manslaughter and sentenced him to three years. Shigehachi's appeal rested on the grounds that his confession had been a fiction, concocted to protect his mother. He denied any role in the infant's demise, arguing that as far as he knew the death resulted from natural causes. Statements from both his parents, however, called this claim into question. Both stated that Shigehachi had admitted to smothering the child, and his mother explained her admission of guilt as a desperate attempt to shield her son. In the end, the high court accepted this version of events and confirmed the decision of the lower court. Significantly, in this case there was no mention of extenuating circumstances: Shigehachi was ordered to serve his full term.

Even men whose involvement in a reproductive crime was seemingly tenuous could be judged culpable apparently based upon the principle of male authority within the family. Nakajima Matabei was tried and convicted in the Himeji court for participating in the murder of an infant born to Nishigaki Maki, his wife's niece.[37] Sentenced to three years of penal servitude, Nakajima appealed his case to the Daishin'in. According to the case record, Maki had lived with Matabei and his wife, Rie, for several years before her marriage in 1879. However, the marriage soon failed, and when Maki returned to the Nakajima home early in 1880, she was pregnant. When the child was born three months later, Rie smothered the infant, an act that resulted in her conviction for manslaughter. Matabei was convicted of failing to intervene to stop this crime and was sentenced to ten years (the lengthy sentence reflects the distance of the kinship relation), which was then reduced to three years. In his appeal, Matabei argued that although he was present in the home at the time of the birth, he was drunk and knew nothing of what went on, that his wife told him the child was stillborn, and so he had buried it. He insisted that his wife had implicated him to lighten her own sentence. To this, the prosecutor countered by citing the story Matabei himself had told upon his arrest: when Rie had questioned him about what to do with Maki's infant, he had replied, "do what you want" (*katte ni shiro*). In the end, the Daishin'in apparently concluded that, drunk or not, Matabei bore responsibility for the crime, given that his wife had consulted him. His original sentence was confirmed.

Matabei's charge that his wife implicated him merely to lessen her own culpability was not without some foundation. In fact, the high court did show leniency to a married woman who argued that she had deferred to her husband in the decision to end a pregnancy. This was the argument that won Takenaka Shika, a thirty-seven-year-old woman who resided in Osaka prefecture, a reduced sentence.[38] Shika had been convicted of procuring an abortion and sentenced to one hundred days by the Osaka Court, but this decision was appealed by none other than the prosecutor himself, who asserted that the sentence was overly harsh in that Shika, a married woman, had sought out an abortion at the insistence of her husband, Shōgorō, who felt the family's poverty made it impossible to support the child. The prosecutor argued that the lower court had failed to consider the involvement of her husband, arguing that this was not her crime alone, but "a crime of family complicity" (*ikka kyōhan*). The response by the Daishin'in was to point out that Article 114 of the Amended Criminal Regulations specifically held that women were to be held accountable for this crime, and that, while the court could distinguish between principal offender and accomplice, there was no foundation upon which to assert "family complicity." That being said, the high court judges, while affirming Shika's conviction, reduced her sentence to only sixty days.

The new legal system thus situated reproductive crimes within a new regime of justice: one in which legal principles concerning intention and motive were brought to bear on the complex inner workings of the family. In conceptualizing the difference between early modern and modern policies toward reproductive crimes, Sakurai Yuki has argued that in the Tokugawa era abortion and infanticide were treated as "crimes of the family" (*kazoku no tsumi*), while in the Meiji period they began to be viewed as "crimes of individuals" (*kojin no tsumi*).[39] Sakurai is correct in her recognition that the new legal system of the 1870s required a new and unfamiliar consideration of individual agency. But the transition she identified was not an easy one, and even those responsible for regulating reproduction found themselves at times unwilling to embrace the concept of individual culpability as the Himeji prosecutor's evocation of "family complicity" reveals.

Those charged with meting out justice clearly struggled to balance the intricacies of family life with the abstract requirements of the codes. In rendering their judgments, the courts had to address the complicated relations of power within the family, evaluating the authority and autonomy of husbands and wives, children and parents, women and their mothers-in-law in relation to one another. The result was not a simple and straightforward pattern of the oppression of women and the validation of male authority but rather a series of often opaque judgments that reflect not only the requirements of the statutes and the facts of each case but also contesting assumptions about how families actually "worked" and about the ethicality of their actions.

Illicit Sex and the Morality of Motives

If acts of abortion and infanticide that occurred within families resulted in a pattern of flexible judgments and reduced sentences, those that occurred as a result of what were termed "illicit" sexual relationships (*mittsū, kantsū,* and *shitsū*) were treated both more uniformly and more severely. As the Osaka prosecutor's sympathy for the impoverished Shika and the Muraoka prosecutor's scathing dismissal of Kikuchi Kotono's concern for reputation suggest, the motives that prompted an act of abortion or infanticide factored significantly into how a case was adjudicated. While prosecutors and judges showed leniency toward obedient wives and timid grandmothers, they regarded much more harshly men and women who sought abortions in order to conceal sexual relationships outside of marriage. This was not necessarily a "traditional" stance. Sawayama Mikako has suggested that in early modern Tsuyama, married couples were punished more severely than unmarried couples for abortion and infanticide, because officials thought it "natural" that people should be ashamed of and seek to hide the consequences of an illicit relationship. A married couple, on the other hand, had no such excuse, since the principal purpose of marriage was to produce descendents.[40] Of the eleven cases involving abortion heard by the high court, five involved men found guilty of "instigating" an abortion in such circumstances. As Table 1 reveals, these men were not isolated cases: in 1878, for example, 173 men were found guilty of either encouraging an abortion or participating in its planning. Presumably most of these men were the sexual partners of the women who had procured the abortion. The appeals of the five men rested upon the assertion that the decision to abort had in fact been made by the pregnant women themselves and that they were uninvolved.

The appeal of Takagi Hisakichi revolved around this claim.[41] Takagi, a twenty-one-year-old man who resided in a village in Osaka Prefecture, was convicted in the Sakai Branch of the Osaka District Court in 1881. According to the original charge, Takagi and a young woman named Machitani Masu had conspired together to procure an abortion for Machitani when she became pregnant as a result of their sexual relationship. In appealing his one-hundred-day sentence, the maximum allowed under Article 114, Takagi stated that the decision to abort had been entirely Machitani's and that he himself knew well that "human life was not something to be killed." Without his knowledge or consent, she had secretly sought out an abortion. In its decision, the Daishin'in simply rejected Takagi's appeal without comment and confirmed the original sentence.

The high court was equally unresponsive to the suits of the other men. In each case, the male defendant was subject to the maximum sentence with no provisions for mitigation due to extenuating circumstances, the rule rather than the exception in cases in which multiple family members were involved in a reproductive crime. Evidence that ordinary citizens recognized that an illicit sexual relationship was a legal liability comes from the case of Ishioka Komekichi, who was charged under Article 198, which held an "unchaste man" responsible when his sexual partner died after an abortion.[42] Ishioka was sentenced to the required three-year term of penal servitude after the death of Natsumi Shina. In his appeal, Ishioka raised several objections, including the characterization of his relation with Shina as "illicit." He argued that Shina was in fact his wife, that while the marriage had not been registered, their relatives and neighbors acknowledged them as husband and wife. He also denied that he had been a party to the decision to procure an abortion after Shina became pregnant. According to Ishioka, he had urged Shina to carry on with the pregnancy, because of the ill effects that abortions were known to have. Finally, he suggested that the abortion may not even have been the cause of Shina's death. In the aftermath of the abortion, he claimed, she had recovered completely, even performing household chores and farm work without difficulty.

In response to Ishioka's claim that he and Shina were married, both the Kyoto Court and the Dai'shinin noted that there was clear evidence that Ishioka had fraudulently attempted to register the marriage after Shina's death, by conspiring with a local physician to alter the date of her death certificate so that it would appear that the two had legalized their relationship by filing the marriage registration days before her death. Ishioka, in fact, admitted the forgery in his appeal but insisted that he had done this only because he feared their relationship would be misinterpreted. In his statement to the high court, Ishioka stressed the anxiety and intimidation that he, "a cowardly farmer," felt when questioned by the police. It was fear that led him to lie, not guilt. In the end, the high court accepted Ishioka's representation of his relationship with Shina but not his denial that he was involved in the decision to end her pregnancy. As in the case of Takenaka Shika, the high court affirmed the culpability of husbands in reproductive decision making. Although the original three-year sentence was rejected, like Takagi, Ishioka too was sentenced to one hundred days for his involvement in the abortion.

Thus, these cases suggest that concern for regulating sexuality was one of the imperatives underlying the prosecution of reproductive crimes. Unlike Etsu and Tatsu, the young women involved in these "illicit" relationships appear to have been in service (*hōkōnin*): that is, they were employed as household servants or as workers in family enterprises and thus no longer living within their natal households, where presumably their parents exercised some degree of control. It is unclear whether the judges in fact believed that young women were unlikely to have acted on their own to end their pregnancies, as the male defendants claimed, or were simply unwilling to have the men who figured in these relationships walk away unpunished. Certainly, little sign of sympathy for the women involved appears in the legal records of these cases. In court documents, prosecutors, judges, and their former lovers as well routinely refer to the woman in question not by name, but by the disparaging term "unchaste woman" (*kanpu*).

Reproductive Crimes and the Japan "Case"

The view that sexual partners, married or not, shared responsibility for reproductive decision making had implications not only for judgments in particular cases but also for the still evolving legal issue of how to adjudicate acts of infanticide and abortion. The Daishin'in case records were published at regular intervals and distributed to the lower courts in order to guide the decisions of judges.[43] Thus, they represented an unfolding body of legal opinion about reproductive and other crimes, how and why they were committed and how culpability should be assessed for purposes of punishment. This body of information came into play as the Japanese government initiated the process of legal reform that culminated in the 1882 criminal code. The central figure in this process was a French legal scholar, Gustave Boissonade de Fontarabie, one of several Europeans hired by the Japanese government to aid Ministry of Justice officials in producing modern criminal and civil codes. In 1872 Tsuruta Akira, one of the scholars involved in drafting the Amended Criminal Regulations, was sent to Europe to do research on European legal systems. In France, he met Boissonade, whose hiring he recommended to the Meiji government. Boissonade arrived in Japan in 1873, and by 1876 he had produced a first draft of a new criminal code. However, the process of its revision, which involved lengthy consultation with Japanese officials within the Ministry of Justice, required almost another five years.

Complicating this process was the position taken by Tsuruta and other Ministry of Justice officials that European laws could not be simply translated and transplanted to Japan but had to be modified and adapted in light of Japanese customs and social norms, a position maintained two decades later when Japan turned to developing colonial laws for Taiwan and then Korea, as the essays by Chen and Matsutani in this volume reveal.

Boissonade disagreed, arguing that French law was expressive of the civilized and universal norms of the advanced West. The abortion statute was one of the issues of contention.[44] The "crime of abortion" law drafted by Boissonade reflected the harsh provisions of Article 317 of the French Criminal Code, which stipulated that a woman who procured an abortion or attempted to perform one on herself was subject to a prison term of six months to two years and a fine of 360 to 20,000 francs. Boissonade made the penalties even stiffer in his initial version of the article on abortion in the Japanese draft code. It stated, "the pregnant woman who uses some food or drink or some other method to have an abortion should be sentenced to confinement for between two and five years and to a fine of fifty to five hundred yen."[45] Boissonade's interlocutor in relation to this draft statute was none other than Tsuruta

Akira, who strenuously objected to the proposed penalties. In a note to Boissonade, Tsuruta defended the terms of Article 114, noting that "in our current code, the crime of abortion carries a sentence of one hundred days" and argued that the stiff fines were inappropriate because "in Japan, it is only poor people and those who have engaged in illicit sex who have abortions. If they are sentenced to this kind of heavy fine, then they will never be able to pay it."[46]

In response, Boissonade argued that abortion was rightfully considered homicide, which at the time carried a sentence of three years when carried out by a parent against his child. Nonetheless, in his next draft, the punishment was reduced with the prison sentence newly defined as six months to two years and the fine set at five to fifty yen. However, Tsuruta objected that this proposed sentence was still too harsh and again he referenced the particularities of the Japanese "case" to explain his stance:

> In Japan, there are poor people in distant mountainous areas who rely upon abortion as a custom. They do not know that it is a serious crime. Since there is no one who has an abortion with this kind of understanding [of its serious nature], it must be punished a bit more lightly than under the French criminal code. . . . In the mountainous areas, when poor people have several children and it is difficult for them to raise them, then . . . husbands and wives will discuss it together and decide to abort the fetus.[47]

Tsuruta's view—that in Japan abortion occurred as a result of poverty or shame, that men and women were jointly involved in the decision, and that it was a crime that required some leniency—was one shared by his fellow jurists, as we have learned from the case records of the Daishin'in. Similarly, Tsuruta's assertion that motive mattered was reflected in the pattern of judgments in the courts. In evaluating the criminality of an act of abortion or infanticide, the judges viewed some motives as more valid than others: poverty was a mitigating factor, a desire to conceal illicit sexual activity was not. In the end, Boissonade and Tsuruta agreed that the punishment for abortion should be reduced to a prison sentence of one to six months with no fine, establishing a minimum sentence that was significantly less than the one hundred days imposed by Article 114.

Conclusion

The records of the Daishin'in offer a new perspective on the goals, impact, and trajectory of the criminalization of abortion and infanticide in the Meiji period. What Fujime characterized as a state-sponsored "system" that with increasing severity sought to control women's sexual and reproductive behavior now appears to have been a fragmented, tentative, and even divisive process that had consequences for both men and women who found themselves subject to a new and unfamiliar regulatory regime. While the courts were implicated in the formation of a new social and sexual order, their rulings did not simply seek to impose Confucian gender norms on an unruly populace, as Ishizaki has implied. Instead, the patterns of judgments suggest that judges attempted to balance the requirements of the statutes with their own assumptions about how and why reproductive crimes occurred and relied upon the principle of mitigation to soften potentially harsh punishments. There is evidence that the tendency toward lenient sentencing for women so prevalent in the 1870 rulings would continue to be the norm throughout the prewar period, the revisions of 1882 and 1908 notwithstanding. In the 1920s, Okamoto Harimatsu, a professor of forensic medicine at Kyoto University, analyzed the outcome of 310 abortion cases prosecuted between 1899 and 1917, before and after the 1908 revision of the criminal code that raised the maximum prison sentence for abortion to one year. According to Okamoto's analysis, most female defendants convicted after 1908 in fact received a sentence of only one month, and in the overwhelming number of cases, even that was suspended.[48] In practice, then, sentences for abortion became lighter, rather than harsher, over time.

Yet if the early courts attempted to balance responsibility for reproductive crimes between family members and sexual partners, the new legal system simultaneously required that the "crimes" of abortion and infanticide be viewed as acts committed by individuals—a position most explicitly demonstrated in the explicit rejection of the concept of "family complicity" by the high court. As the stories told to the Daishin'in reveal, the new arena of the law pitted family members against one another, requiring them to rethink, to articulate, and to identify in a public forum who had made the decision about whether a pregnancy was to continue or not, whether an infant was to live or die. The result of the early codes was to set in motion the reconceptualization of abortion and infanticide into acts of "choice" on the part of newly self-conscious subjects. Historians of abortion and infanticide in Europe and North America have most often explored the prosecution of reproductive "crimes" as an issue of female bodily self-determination, arguing that from the nineteenth century onward women's natural desire to control their own fertility for financial, health, or other reasons came into conflict with state and civic forms of authority, among them religious institutions acting upon changing definitions of fetal life and medical professionals attempting to establish their control over reproductive strategies.[49] But the case of Japan forces us to recognize that the concept of "choice" too clearly "has a history"—it took form as new conceptions of gendered social subjects were being produced and enacted. It remains to be studied how Japanese women, newly endowed with legal responsibility for their sexual and reproductive choices, navigated the modern reproductive culture that emerged at the intersection of state policy and ideology, the emergent capitalist economy, medicine, and the mass media.

Notes

1. Tiana Norgren, *Abortion before Birth Control: The Politics of Reproduction in Postwar Japan* (Princeton, NJ: Princeton University Press, 2001), 3.

2. Ishii Shirō and Mizubayashi Takeshi, eds., "Shinritsu kōryō Kaitei ritsurei," in *Nihon kindai shisō taikei,* vol. 7, *Hō to chitsujo* (Iwanami Shoten, 1992), 211–212.

3. Ōta Tenrei, *Datai kinshi to yūsei hogohō* (Ningen Kagakusha, 1976), 26–30.

4. Ibid., 32–33.

5. For an overview of the laws regarding infanticide as well an a discussion of sentencing, see Uematsu Tadashi, "Eijisatsu ni kansuru hanzaigakutekina kenkyū," in *Keijihō no riron to genri: Ono Hakushi kanreki kinen,* vol. 2, ed. Uematsu Tadashi and Ono Seiichirō (Yuhikaku, 1951), 183–231.

6. Fujime Yuki, *Sei no rekishigaku: Koshō seido, dataizai taisei kara baishun boshihō, yusei hogohō taisei e* (Fuji Shuppan, 1997), chap. 3.

7. Ishizaki Shōko, "Nihon dataizai no seiritsu," *Reikishi hyōron* 571 (1997): 53–70; "Kindai Nihon no sanji chōsetsu to kokkai seisaku," *Sōgo joseishi kenkyū* 15 (1998): 15–32; "Meiji Ishin to seishoku rinri," in *Esunishiti, jenda kara miru Nihon no rekishi* (Yoshikawa Kōbunkan, 2002), 313–337. Following Ishizaki, Iwata Shigenori also criticizes Fujime in his work

"Inochi" wo meguru kindaishi: Datai kara jinkō ninshin chūzetsu e (Yoshikawa Kōbunkan, 2009).

8. For example, neither Norgren nor Fujime makes any mention of the 1873 statutes or the prosecutions that occurred under them in their work.

9. I became aware of the Daishin'in case records through my reading of Tama Yasuko, "Datai to satsujin no aida: senzen ni okeru datai eijisatsu no hanketsu kara," in *Kindai Nihon no bunkaron,* vol. 6, *Hanzai to fūzoku,* ed. Aoki Tamotsu et al. (Iwanami Shoten, 2000), 179–209.

10. Cited in Koizumi Eiichi, *Dataizai kenkyū* (Ganshōdō Shoten, 1934), 49.

11. On the Chūjōryū, see Hayashi Yōko, "Chūjōryū," *Joseishi kenkyū* 20 (1985): 27–31.

12. Sakurai Yuki, "Mabiki to datai," in *Nihon no kinsei,* vol. 15, *Josei no kinsei,* ed. Hayashi Reiko (Chūō Kōronsha, 1993), 120–122.

13. See Sakurai above, 104–119, and Sawayama Mikako, *Shussan to shintai no kinsei* (Keisō Shobō, 1998), chaps. 3–5.

14. On the anti-infanticide discourse, see Susan L. Burns, "The Body as Text: Confucianism, Reproduction, and Gender in Early Modern Japan," in *Rethinking Confucianism: Past and Present in China, Japan, Korea and Vietnam,* ed. Benjamin Elman, Herman Ooms, and John Duncan (Los Angeles: UCLA Asia Pacific Monograph Series, 2002), 178–219; and Fabian Drixler, Infanticide and Fertility in Eastern Japan: Discourse and Demography, 1660–1880 (PhD diss., Harvard University, 2008). A variety of anti-infanticide tracts are collected in Takahashi Bonsen, *Datai mabiki no kenkyū* (Daiichi Shobō, 1981); and Ōta Motoko, *Mabiki kankō shiryō shūsei* (Tōsui Shobō, 1997).

15. Morinaga Eisaburō, "Dataizai shikō, ge," *Nihon hanzai gakkai zasshi* 2, no. 2 (1936): 52–62.

16. Ishizaki, "Meiji Ishin to seishoku rinri," 328.

17. On the formulation of the two early Meiji codes, see Mizubayashi Takeshi, "Shinritsu kōryō to Kaitei ritsurei no seikai," in *Nihon kindai shisō taikei,* vol. 7, *Hō to chitsujo* (Iwanami Shoten, 1992), 454–551; and Tezuka Yutaka, *Meiji shoki keihō shi no kenkyū* (Keiō Gijuku Daigaku Hōseigaku Kenkyūkai, 1956). In English, see Paul Heng-chao Ch'en, *The Formation of the Early Meiji Legal Order: The Japanese Code of 1871 and its Chinese Foundation* (Oxford: Oxford University Press, 1981), 3–30. Many of the statutes are available in English translation in Joseph H. Longford, "A Summary of the Japanese Penal Codes," *Transactions of the Asiatic Society of Japan* 5, part 2 (1877): 1–114.

18. Ishii and Mizubayashi, ed., *Hō to chitsujo,* 262–263.

19. Ibid., 244.

20. Ibid., 494–500.

21. Ibid., 501–507.

22. M. J. Meijer, *Murder and Adultery in Late Imperial China: A Study of Law and Morality* (Leiden: Brill, 1991), 24.

23. Ishii and Mizubayashi, ed., *Hō to chitsujo,* 140–141. The codes delineated multiple degrees of kinship: an individual's first-degree relatives were parents and adoptive parents, the husband (in the case of a woman), children and adopted children; second-degree relatives included grandparents, grandchildren, siblings, wives and concubines, and paternal uncles and aunts; while great-grandparents, cousins, and illegitimate children were classified as third-degree relations.

24. For useful charts illustrating the relationship between degrees of kinship and the increase or reduction in penalties, see Ishii and Mizubayashi, ed., *Hō to chitsujo,* 276, 531, 532.

25. Ibid., 530–537.

26. Ibid., 212.

27. This table draws on statistical data provided by two sources: Hōmushō Chōsa Tōkeika, ed., *Kensatsu tōkei 100-nen* (Hōmusho, 1976), 3; Naimushō, ed., *Naimushō nenpō hōkokusho,* bekkan 1 (San'ichi Shobō, 1982), 82. *Kensatsu tōkei 100-nen* provides the total number of those charged for all abortion crimes for the period 1876–1881, while the *Naimusho nenpao hōkokusho* (reprints of the Meiji era Home Ministry reports) provides that number for the period from 1878–1881. These numbers do not agree, however, and so I have indicated both in the chart. The first number is from the *Kensatsu tōkei 100-nen;* the second, from *Naimushō nenpō hōkokusho.* The additional information on the nature of the crime and gender of the accused is from the latter source.

28. This graph was constructed using numbers drawn from several sources. For the periods 1876–1881 and 1931–1944 I have relied upon *Kensatsu tōkei 100-nen,* 3 and 49; for the period 1882–1888, I used the statistical information in Morinaga, 61; information on the period 1890–1924 comes from Mogi Yōichi, "Kindai Mie-ken iki in okeru datai torishimari no suii nit suite," *Chiken nenpō* 13 (2007): 2. No records are available for 1907–1908. As indicated in note 27, the statistical data varies somewhat from source to source, although usually by less than 10 percent.

29. The only data I have found on rates of prosecution for infanticide comes from Uematsu Tadashi who provides a chart detailing the number

of convictions per year for the period 1918–1943 in "Eijisatsu ni kansuru hanzaigakutekina kenkyū," 191. Uematsu does not cite the source of this information, but if his numbers are correct, far fewer people were convicted for infanticide than for abortion. These are numbers for the period addressed by Graph 1: 1918: 181; 1919: 158; 1920: 137; 1921: 176; 1922: 129; 1923: 151; 1924: no information.

30. For example, between 1875 and 1880, the *Yomiuri Shinbun* reported on more than forty convictions for abortion-related crimes. As examples of this kind of reportage, see *Yomiuri shinbun,* April 14, 1875, 1; August 23, 1875, 1; October 30, 1875, 1; March 27, 1876, 2; May 3, 1876, 1; November 28, 1876, 3. Many of the articles took up cases involving couples involved in "illicit" relationships that were transgressive in nature (i.e., a priest and a parishioner, a widow and her son-in-law, and the like).

31. Natalie Zemon Davis, *Fiction in the Archives: Pardon Tales and Their Tellers in Sixteenth Century France* (Stanford: Stanford University Press, 1987).

32. Daishin'in, ed., *Meiji zenki Daishin'in keiji hanketsu roku,* vol. 6 (Shihōsho, 1875–1887; repr., Bunsei Shoin, 1987), 23–34.

33. Ishii and Mizubayashi, ed., *Hō to chitsujo,* 277–278.

34. Ibid., 275–276.

35. *Meiji zenki Daishin'in keiji hanketsu roku,* vol. 11, 363–368.

36. On the problem of child custody in the Meiji period, see Susan L. Burns, "Local Courts, National Laws, and the Problem of Patriarchy in Meiji Japan: Reading 'Records of Civil Rulings' from the Perspective of Gender History," in *Interdisciplinary Studies on the Taiwan Colonial Court Records Archive,* ed. Wang Tay-sheng (Taipei: Angle Publishing, 2009), 285–309.

37. *Meiji zenki Daishin'in keiji hanketsu roku,* vol. 15, 294–295.

38. Ibid., vol. 18, 24–25.

39. Sakurai, "Mabiki to datai," 126.

40. Sawayama Mikako, "Umukoto/umanaikoto: Datai mabiki wo meguru kenryoku," in *Ningen keisei no zentai shi: Hikaku hattatsu shakaishi e no michi,* ed. Nakauchi Toshio et al. (Ōtsuka Shoten, 1998), 170–171.

41. *Meiji zenki Daishin'in keiji hanketsu roku,* vol. 19, 222–223.

42. Ibid., vol. 16, 32–33.

43. Compilations of cases were published once in 1875–1877, twice in 1878, four times in 1879, eight times in 1880, and monthly until 1884.

44. For an in-depth analysis of the process of drafting the abortion statute, see Kanazu Hidemi, "Kindai Nihon ni okeru 'datai no tsumi' no seiritsu," *Josei shigaku* 16 (1996): 26–43.

45. Waseda Daigaku Tsuruta Bunsho Kenkyūkai, ed., *Nihon keihō sōan kaigi hikki,* vol. 3 (Waseda Daigaku Shuppanbu, 1997), 1908.

46. Ibid.

47. Ibid., 1903.

48. Okamoto Harimatsu, "Honkoku ni okeru datai ni kansuru tōkei-teki chōsa no ippan," *Kyōto igakkai zasshi* 26, no. 8 (1929): 551–581; no. 9 (1929): 778–794; no. 10 (1929): 861–878.

49. This is the dominant narrative in the histories of abortion in the United States. See, for example, James C. Mohr, *Abortion in America* (New York: Oxford University Press, 1978), and Janet Farrell Brodie, *Contraception and Abortion in Nineteenth-Century America* (Ithaca, NY: Cornell University Press, 1994).

CHAPTER 4

Adultery and Gender Equality in Modern Japan, 1868–1948

Harald Fuess

THIS CHAPTER EXAMINES how Japanese developed, applied, and contested adultery laws in the period between 1868 and 1948. Perhaps more than any other legislation, laws on adultery were explicitly phrased in gendered terms that clearly differentiated the actions of a husband from those of a wife. This sort of distinction was not unique to Japan, but Japanese adultery laws were created, maintained, and justified at the same time that similar regulations were being criticized and abolished in Western Europe, so these laws offer a particularly useful way to explore how and to what degree the formation of the Japanese legal framework was influenced by foreign models and interacted with local perceptions and social practices. In Japan, as elsewhere, adultery laws often served as an expression of ideal behavior and embodied social values that the state was willing to endorse or enforce. Critics and supporters frequently debated adultery laws as if they were not only visible symbols of the double standard regarding men's and women's sexual and social behavior but also a sign of a society's progress and civilization.

The definition of adultery seems self-evident, but given the variety of terms Japanese used to name this act, a short overview is in order. Today in Japan when a married person engages in sexual intercourse with a person of the opposite sex the act is generally considered adultery and described as an "illicit relationship" (*furin*). Before 1948, however, Japanese laws treated only the sexual relationship of a married woman with another man as adultery. During the Meiji period this act was usually referred to as "illicit sex" (*kantsū*) in legal texts or "illicit sex by a married woman" (*yūfukan*) in Supreme Court verdicts. According to court cases and social customs, under certain circumstances the behavior of a husband could also be treated as a form of adultery, but public and legal opinions were divided on this issue. The most common circumstances under which a husband would be considered as committing *kantsū* were when he took a secondary wife, fathered children with another woman, or squandered family resources by visiting prostitutes. The Chinese character *kan* in *kantsū* was also included in the word to describe illicit consensual relationships (*wakan*) between a man and a woman that were considered socially problematic because they transgressed community norms, which included premarital sexual activities and unions formed without parental approval, as well as customary marriages not registered with offices of the Meiji government. The compound that stood for nonconsensual sexual intercourse involving force—that is, rape—was *gōkan*.

As adultery provisions in criminal and civil legislation evolved in Meiji Japan, the crucial relationship in question was that of a wife and her extramarital lover. In criminal law the key variation was the extent to which the government prosecuted adultery and what kind of punishment it deserved, whereas in civil law the important issues were how adultery influenced the terms of divorce. A sexual double standard existed in both processes: the transgressions of a married woman were subject to scrutiny, while a married man became subject to chastisement only when he had sexual relations with the wife of another man. Although the same basic distinction existed in both types of law, definitions of mitigating circumstances varied, as did the laws' implementation. As regulations evolved at different times and were drafted by different groups, the gender ideology at work was not always consistent. But by the turn of the twentieth century lawmakers and lawyers agreed that adultery of the wife was a legal problem only if the husband made it one. To do so, however, was his patriarchal privilege.

Despite various attempts at revision and reinterpretations to mitigate the gender gap, this basic legal consensus remained in place until the postwar legal reforms. As adultery laws evolved, change did not proceed exclusively in a linear fashion as a story of women's liberation, nor did all the Western models that were evoked support notions of gender equality. European legal traditions concerning adultery varied from the more unequal Roman law to the more equal canonical law.[1] Adultery in modern Japan has received only cursory attention; legal scholars and historians have for the most part neglected the topic of law and gender, and the few studies in Japanese describe the law's development rather than interpreting the historical and comparative social significance of adultery regulations.[2] One of the few American historians to even mention the issue contextualizes the existence of the double sexual standard in late Meiji laws in terms of the modern state's policies to control potentially subversive female sexuality and to confine married women to the home.[3] This view is plausible considering that the official slogan of "good wife, wise mother" (*ryōsai kenbo*), proclaimed in 1899 as a guideline for female higher education, emphasized women's contribution to state and society mainly through their domestic roles and the fact that the government, in the best known example of discrimination in the prewar era, denied them suffrage until 1946. The exclusive access of husbands to the bodies of their wives and the unilateral female duty of chastity may be interpreted as a necessary condition for the stability of the modern patriarchal family and the maintenance of the authoritarian state. After all, the Meiji civil code reinforced the notion that men were the official heads of the household, and Japanese ideologues often linked "natural" domestic roles in the family with the distribution of political power.

Gender relations in society have often been conceived and construed as a reflection of the structure of public power. In her classic essay on gender as a useful category of historical analysis, Joan Wallach Scott explains: "Gender has been employed literally and analogically in political theory to justify and criticize . . . the relationship between ruler and ruled."[4] The drawback of interpreting late Meiji adultery laws only in this way, however, is an exaggerated emphasis on the symbolic values and politico-ideological reading of specific codes without scrutinizing the laws' implementation and social consequences. Moreover, when stressing the "modern" and "Japanese" dimensions of these kinds of gendered laws of adultery, we tend to lose sight both of their premodern roots and their international context.

While a sexual double standard existed in both criminal and civil codes, this chapter focuses primarily on adultery in criminal legislation, legal debate, and jurisdiction. Compared to contemporary European countries, adultery was a less prominent problem in Japanese civil law because of its different approach to divorce. In Japan, establishing the "fact" of a spouse's adultery was unnecessary to dissolve a marriage because a court judgment based on fault grounds was not a precondition for divorce. Even after the creation of Japan's first civil code in 1898, more than 99 percent of divorces were by simple registration. Among those who terminated their marriages with the help of a court between 1900 and 1940, only 641 invoked an adultery clause.[5] By contrast, Japanese criminal legislation contained effective penalties for adulterers until the early postwar years.

This study of the legal framework of adultery, understood as extramarital sexual relationships of husbands and wives, is divided into two broadly chronological parts. First, it analyzes the influences of early modern Japanese, Chinese, and especially European legal and social thought during the forty years it took to create the last Meiji penal code in 1908. Second, it looks at the subsequent forty years until the legal reforms enacted under the American Occupation, when legal changes no longer took place through the amendments to the codes but through their critique and reinterpretation and through new modes of application.

Codifying the Sexual Double Standard

The period from 1868 until the codification of criminal law in 1882 was marked by legal transition and experimentation, as Japanese regulations from the Tokugawa period were mixed with ancient and contemporary Chinese moral models as well as some elements of Western legal philosophy. Among these three streams of thought, which all contained elements of a sexual double standard, Japanese indigenous ideas of adultery prosecution were by far the strictest. The 1742 Rules for Determining Criminal Matters (*Kujikata osadamegaki*), also known as the Hundred Articles or *Hyakkajō,* mandated the death penalty for adulterers. Capital punishment was not one of several possible alternatives but the only sentence available to the magistrates. Article 48 stated unequivocally, "If a married woman commits adultery, she should be put to death," and "If a man commits adultery with a married woman, he should be put to death."[6] As with many of the strict rules during the Tokugawa period, the state's bite was less painful than its bark since magistrates usually encouraged the parties to settle issues privately, although there are examples in fact and fiction of the bakufu executing adulterous wives, even against the will of the wronged husband. Officials treated adultery as a crime against the social and political order, not just as a private issue to be resolved by the spouses, their families, and the local community.[7] Besides criminalizing adultery and threatening adulterers with capital punishment, the Rules for Determining Criminal Matters also took a lenient attitude toward a husband's killing his adulterous wife and her lover. Article 3 specified that a husband "should receive no penalty" if he slaughtered them; indeed, it was not merely the husband's prerogative but actually his duty to execute adulterers wherever and whenever he caught them. Permitting the husband to engage in what might be categorized as revenge killing put adultery in the same category as the other crime for which a legal vendetta was permissible in the Tokugawa world, namely murder.[8] Specific to the Tokugawa period was a differentiation in the severity of the official punishment, even in the forms of the death penalty, in terms of the degree to which one had violated status boundaries. In practice, most adultery squabbles seem to have been resolved in the community through letters of apology and compensation payments.[9]

During its initial years, the Meiji government used the Rules for Determining Criminal Matters as a source of reference, since the first set of criminal regulations, the Preliminary Criminal Code (*Kari Keiritsu*) of 1868, was rudimentary in form. In December 1868, the government encouraged all domains and prefectures to follow the regulations of the Rules for Determining Criminal Matters, which had previously only guided the administration under direct control of the bakufu. Moreover, an 1869 report by the Justice Ministry confirmed that the decapitation of an adulterous wife and her lover was the appropriate sentence for adultery.[10] This harsh penalty applied to both parties. Initially, the revolutionary samurai who were consolidating their power over the country did not redefine the official policy toward adultery, most likely because the new political and social order they were envisioning did not involve a reconsideration of the gender hierarchy.

The Outline of the New Criminal Code (*Shinritsu kōryō*) of 1871, a more deliberate and detailed piece of legislation with 192 articles, departed from several legal traditions of the Tokugawa period. It was the first penal code in Japan that was officially made public, breaking with the Tokugawa policy of officially keeping legal precedents and regulations secret, even while their contents often became widely known in practice.[11] Adultery was addressed in the section regulating sexual offenses, such as rape and consensual sex between unmarried persons. The new penal code abolished the death penalty for adultery but retained the Confucian notion that the heinousness of a crime depended on the relative social status of the perpetrator to his victim. A wife now received three years of penal servitude for extramarital sex.

A servant who had consensual sexual intercourse with his master's wife was punished by "third-degree exile." When the same deed was committed with the master's daughter, with no reference to her marital status, the sentence was only "first-degree exile." Exile, then considered a more severe sentence than prison, was abolished a year later.[12] What is noteworthy is that the penalties varied only for the man involved, while the married woman received the same "ordinary punishment," presumably because he was regarded as the instigator of the sexual relationship and therefore the legally more responsible person.[13] Like the Rules for Determining Criminal Matters, the 1871 Criminal Code declared a husband who killed his adulterous wife and her lover to be innocent. However, unlike the Tokugawa regulations it superseded, a new proviso stipulated that the killing must be in response to the husband discovering them in the "act of adultery," with the result that the deed no longer served as a blanket excuse for the murder of a wife or her alleged lover. If the husband only killed one of the parties, the other was still to receive his or her usual punishments, which were more severe for the man than the woman. Moreover, the penal code decreed that for all types of crimes, under certain circumstances a female offender could avoid implementation of the punishment, a provision that offered convicted wives the opportunity to have their sentences reduced.[14]

While the 1871 Criminal Code broke with some important Japanese legal traditions, it closely followed Chinese laws on illicit sexual relations both in the sequence of its articles and in the wording of particular offenses. The Chinese criminal codes of the Ming (1368–1644) and Qing (1644–1911) dynasties, which had also been a source for policies during the Tokugawa period, were less brutal in their suppression of female sexuality than the Rules for Determining Criminal Matters. For example, the Chinese codes mandated one year of penal servitude or seventy to eighty blows with a bamboo stick for adultery and allowed for leniency toward a husband who killed his wife and her lover only when he reacted in anger upon discovering them engaged in a sexual act.[15]

Unlike these older Chinese models or Japanese traditions, early Meiji penal codes limited what European visitors were quick to criticize as "barbaric" corporal punishments. In the Amended Criminal Regulations (*Kaitei ritsurei*) of 1873 corporal punishments such as beating with a bamboo stick were banned, and legislators shortened the period of penal servitude for both adulterers from three years to one, a reduction also in line with Chinese codes.[16] Another European-influenced innovation, or clarification, in the early Meiji legal order of adultery was a May 1874 notification by the Justice Ministry that the prosecution of adultery required a complaint by the injured husband and should not proceed based upon a third-party report. An eminent Japanese legal historian explains this measure as intended to avert "the host of evils caused by the many unwarranted accusations of adultery involving married women."[17] From this point, it became the exclusive right of the husband to sue his wife for adultery.[18] Thus, while in the early Meiji years, as in the Tokugawa period, adultery was considered a public crime worthy of state prosecution, in contrast to earlier times only the wronged husband retained the privilege to file a suit. Laws became more explicitly centered on the maintenance of patriarchal authority in the family, and the role of the community or the state in regulating marital sexuality was weakened.

The second wave of Meiji criminal codification was shaped more visibly by European influence as the Japanese government became increasingly aware of the importance of bringing its codes into greater conformity with those of European nations in order to achieve its overarching domestic and foreign policy goal of the revision of unequal treaties, which failed in 1887 because of foreign skepticism toward Japanese criminal law.[19] The French Napoleonic Code became a model for the Criminal Code of 1882, and German legal thought was an inspiration for the revised Criminal Code of 1908. As a result, both the 1882 and 1908 codes incorporated the new principle of fundamental equality before the law, in contrast to the previous concern for basing penalties on status. The well-known exceptions to this principle were the clause of lèse-majesté that derived from the French code and the Confucian-influenced notion that patricide was a particularly heinous crime requiring harsher punishment than other forms of murder. In addition, Western conceptions of familial relationships were incorporated into both the criminal and civil codes. The 1882 Criminal Code no longer recognized a concubine as a legally defined conjugal partner, with the result that men were no longer able to punish their secondary wives for infidelity, and in 1898 the civil code explicitly outlawed bigamy by both men and women.

One of the legacies of the 1870s for both the 1882 and 1908 Criminal Codes was that imprisonment became the central "means of correction" for adultery, a policy that was explicitly justified as the common European practice.[20] Contrary to the popular expectation that Western influence made penalties more humane, the 1882 Code increased the maximum sentence for adultery to two years from the mandatory sentence of one year established in 1873. At the same time, Article 353 of the 1882 Code introduced a minimum sentence of more than six months, enabling courts to vary their verdicts depending on circumstances.[21] The minimum penalty disappeared completely in 1908, so courts no longer had to send convicted adulterers to jail. In 1905 a penal reform introduced a new probation system of suspending sentences of one year or less, which further decreased the legal requirement for imprisonment and facilitated the practical decriminalization of adultery.[22]

This series of reforms culminated in the Criminal Code of 1908. It embodied the late Meiji political, legal, and social consensus on adultery in Article 183, which remained on the books until 1947: "When a married woman commits adultery, she should be sentenced to penal servitude (*chōeki*) of up to two years. The same applies to the other adulterous party. These offenses are only prosecuted on demand of the husband, but if the husband has condoned the act of adultery (*kantsū o shōyō*) his suit will not be accepted."[23] This regulation supported the husband's privilege to sue in accord with earlier legislation, with the new restriction that he could not make an accusation if he had previously permitted or encouraged the affair, a rule also found in French law. Although Article 183 derived from established legal concepts in Japan and in fact newly constrained the rights of the patriarch, some scholars have interpreted it as reflective of the new gender ideology formulated after the 1890s as a part of the government's emphasis on wives' duty and prerogative to manage their households and children. In fact, it was by no means an innovative policy created from scratch, but it did reaffirm the sexual double standard and provided it with renewed legitimacy by referencing Western modernity.

The main difference between the treatment of adultery in the 1882 and 1908 codes was the elimination of the leniency clause for a husband who executed his adulterous wife and her partner. Article 311 of the 1882 Code stated that a husband's killing of his wife or her lover would be excused "if done spontaneously at the location where he discovers the adulterous act" and if he had no previous knowledge of the affair. Japanese legal experts justified this particular privilege with reference to "the grave insult to the husband's right and honor," but as early as 1884 some worried that granting the husband who killed his wife immunity amounted to granting him the right to adjudicate.[24] Objections to the husband's power also came from traditional Confucian corners. Murata Tamotsu asked in a Senate meeting in 1880 why children who avenged their parents received the death sentence, but not a man who killed his wife's lover.[25] The 1908 Criminal Code no longer contained an explicit provision for a husband's killing his adulterous wife, but during deliberations committee members questioned whether the general clause on extenuating circumstances (Art. 36) might be stretched to include the old privilege. State officials subsequently denied this interpretation, but legal experts continued to be divided on this issue.[26] The state's restriction of the husband's prerogative enhanced the status of women, but this outcome may not have been the main motivating factor for reform. A more plausible explanation is that the husband's right to kill his adulterous wife, which from the Tokugawa period onward appeared to be an extension of state power, now conflicted with the modern state's insistence on maintaining a monopoly over violence.

While there was a Japanese precedent for Article 311, we cannot overlook the fact that the influential French jurist Gustave Boissonade de Fontarabie, who arrived in Japan in November 1873 to act as a legal advisor to the government and is often credited with convincing the Meiji state to abolish judicial torture, was one of its main supporters. In an 1886 treatise he defended the possibility of leniency against murderous husbands acting in "insurmountable anger" against the wife who had "cheated his confidence, hurt his affection and insulted his dignity" as a provision found in "all foreign legislation." To be sure, he emphasized that husbands should not have blanket rights to kill their wives and that it was necessary to ascertain that they had indeed acted in rage. Nevertheless, Boissonade argued vehemently against a similar leniency for the enraged wife who reacted with violence toward her adulterous husband. According to Boissonade, there was an "enormous difference" in the "social damage" of male adultery, because there was no possibility of introducing illegitimate children into the family. It was this danger that explained greater male anger; "without injustice" the murder by the husband can be excused but not that by the wife.[27] Although Boissonade's published opinions do not prove that he was responsible for the inclusion of this discriminatory provision, his sweeping yet incorrect claim that such regulations existing everywhere in the Western world was certainly used to justify them. A detailed study of the process of drafting the 1882 Penal Code by a Japanese scholar has concluded that Boissonade himself inserted Article 311, which he modeled after French law, into the Japanese code.[28]

The sexual double standard in adultery law provoked little debate in late nineteenth-century Japan among foreign or Japanese lawyers. Boissonade led the way in justifying Article 311:

> One should not be surprised considering that morality for a long time authorized the husband to look for opportunities to increase his chances of having male descendants, even outside of marriage. Without a doubt this tolerance does not have the same explanatory value when the husband had already fathered numerous male children from his legitimate wife; but one should not expect a rigorous logic in matters of morality and custom, especially regarding such a subject.[29]

In addition to stressing the "real danger" of female adultery—the possibility that unrelated offspring would enter the family—he also stressed that straying wives undermined the "dignity" of the husband and patriarch. Therefore, he argued, female adultery deserved punishment even if the wife was sterile, was beyond childbearing age, or failed to conceive after committing adultery.

Boissonade's concern for the maintenance of patriarchal authority in the home led him to characterize female adultery as a "private crime" against the rights of the husband and the interests of the family rather than a crime against "society or the public order." From this perspective, he supported the husband's ability to withdraw his suit against his wife and argued that the public prosecutor should be prohibited from pursuing adultery charges except when demanded by the husband. The law should respect the husband's interest in avoiding scandal and dishonor. Boissonade wanted to treat adultery merely as a misdemeanor in Japan as in France, since to him it was not a major social problem.[30]

Other foreign legal experts also defended the sexual double standard in Japanese law. Writing twenty years after Boissonade, the Englishman Joseph Ernest De Becker emphasized that true gender equality could only be assured by legally distinguishing between husbands and wives in order to recognize the different consequences of their adultery:

> The law insists upon the wife fulfilling towards her husband her marital promise of fidelity, but, for physical and social consider-

> ations, allows the husband greater freedom of action. Whether this is sound legislation or otherwise is, of course, a question worthy of grave consideration, in as much as the opposing arguments advanced are numerous and weighty, but without wishing to dogmatize, it would seem that consequences of a man breaking his marriage vows are far less harmful and far-reaching. The husband is not the child-bearer, and his lapse from virtue does not so seriously affect the status of the home, while the wife's sin actually destroys it; and it cannot be denied that as the physical conditions are so different, equity demands a differential treatment of each sex.[31]

While De Becker also endorsed patriarchal authority, he was less concerned with male pride and privilege than with the new ideals of social equity and biological differences. De Becker's views may reflect discursive shifts in emphasis, but his discussion suggests that foreign commentators on Japanese law for the most part accepted the sexual double standard as reasonable and just.[32]

Contesting Gender Inequality

Few Japanese criticized the laws for their gender inequality during the late nineteenth century. Even around the turn of the century, the majority interpreted the changes in the legal status of women as a sign of Japan's progress toward civilization. Tokyo Imperial University professor Hozumi Nobushige, an eminent legal scholar, praised the Meiji Civil Code on which he had worked. In a lecture to a foreign audience, Hozumi spoke of a "great advance" and even a "revolution" in the legal position of women. He stressed that either spouse was free to demand divorce according to specified grounds, "so that husband and wife are now placed on an equal footing." He simply ignored the differential treatment of adultery.[33] His view of recent legislation as liberating for women was probably shared by most of his contemporaries. Few Japanese legal commentators questioned the sweeping view that gender equality had been fully realized. In his lengthy commentary of 1898, Okamura Tsukasa, law professor at Kyōto Imperial University, criticized differential adultery clauses in the civil code as unjust (*fusei*) and unfair (*fukōhei*) and proof of Japan's extremely low morals. Recognizing that older French laws accepted a man's adultery as a legal reason for divorce only when a husband introduced a concubine into the family home, Okamura pointed out that in recent years the laws in France, Germany, and England were revised to enable either spouse to sue for divorce on the grounds of adultery. In Japan, he emphasized, the husband had sexual relations with other women, typically prostitutes or widows, Despite legal monogamy, the husband could engage in the "evil" of maintaining a public concubine without legal sanction. His wife was unable to divorce him even if he had a relationship with another married woman, unless her husband was sued and convicted for this deed.[34] Other male legal experts urged similar revisions of the criminal code to improve morality and to enhance the position of women in marriage. Nishimura Kannosuke and Iwano Shinpei argued that if the crime of adultery destroyed a marriage based on "the virtuous ideal of monogamy," a husband's adultery should also be treated as a crime, as it was already in the penal law of the Austro-Hungarian Empire, though not in Germany, Russia, or Sweden. They saw the "evil custom" of "honoring men and despising women" manifest in the keeping of concubines as proof that Meiji Japan still retained legacies of a feudal society.[35]

Organized women, who were a novel political force prior to the turn of the twentieth century, argued publicly for sexual and gender equality. From the margins of the state, without the right to attend political meetings until 1922, women's groups had to find male allies in the parties and the bureaucracy.[36] Legal experts repeatedly referred to the lobbying activities of the Japan branch of the Women's Christian Temperance Union, which was rooted ideologically in American Protestantism. Surprisingly, they often professed sympathy for these women's reform agenda and criticized Diet members who called them "stupid" for wanting men not to engage in extramarital relations.[37] Nevertheless, lawyers also distanced themselves from female activists by describing them as Japanese women with Western hairstyles (*sokuhatsu fujin*) advocating feminism (*fueminizumu*).[38] By the 1930s, some began to express self-consciousness about their gender as male experts and admitted that they did not want women to complain that "law is made by men."[39] Postwar legal authors praised the prewar women's movement as pioneers of spousal equality (*fūfu byōdō*).[40]

The Women's Christian Temperance Union (WCTU) began its political lobbying even before the civil and criminal codes had been finalized. A petition to the Diet on November 30, 1891, signed by 700 people urged the revision of these legal drafts. Over the years the submission of such proposals as well as their official rejection became a matter of routine. By 1929, the WCTU had written 47 petitions "to reform the difference in the level of virtue between men and women."[41] The 1899 version advocated a criminal code punishing both husband and wife and their respective lovers with severe imprisonment. It defined adultery in a gender-blind way as a sexual act of a husband or wife with a married or unmarried person and explicitly included the husband's maintaining a concubine. It also advocated for either husband or wife to be able to sue for divorce. But one of the proposed consequences of adultery was an unusually stiff fine of "half the assets." The group's vision of gender equality was closely connected with improving men's morals, which must have alienated many of those in power. Invoking the trope of progress, one petition claimed that current laws ignored women's human rights and that marriage should be based on the notion of an independent man and an independent woman joined together through love based on the principles of (a presumably Christian) heaven.[42] The WCTU failed to achieve adultery law reform in the prewar period, probably because it connected demands for spousal sexual equality in the family with more threatening and far-reaching goals of moral reform of society and marriage. Nevertheless, its repeated efforts and demands influenced popular debates, court decisions, legislative actions, and legal opinions.[43]

While the laws remained constant after 1908, judges responded to demands for change and in the long term mitigated the gender gap. Initially the courts showed conservative caution. On October 1, 1903, the Daishin'in or High Court of Review affirmed that the husband should expect chastity from his wife and that infringement constituted a violation of his rights.[44] In 1909 a court for the first time declared adultery to be a form of grave cruelty and thereby a ground for divorcing a husband under the civil code.[45] Later several other courts began to construct a concept that might be called "aggravated adultery" based on the civil code's grave cruelty clause (Art. 813.5), creating an avenue for wives to divorce unfaithful husbands. Aggravated adultery usually meant abandoning the wife, fathering children with other women, or bringing secondary wives into the home.[46] Courts also started awarding wives tort damages if husbands had relationships with other women while abandoning wife and children.[47] Judges often disregarded cases when men committed "simple adultery." By contrast, wives were punished on the evidence of having gone on a trip to a hot spring resort with a manservant or staying overnight at an inn with another man.[48] But the most significant shift in the legal philosophy of courts toward gender equality took place in the late 1920s when the Daishin'in affirmed that "husbands also have the duty of chastity."[49]

The state instituted several committees to review criminal and civil law, partly as a reactionary effort to strengthen the legal institution of the patriarchal family. However, contrary to government intentions, legal experts with more liberal persuasions sometimes won over their committees. A criminal code review committee that began in 1913 submitted a contested proposal to eliminate the sexual double standard in the penal law by making both husband and wife punishable for adultery, just as the WCTU had proposed. Several successive civil code review committees (1919–1927, 1929, and 1943) recommended a change in the grounds for divorce. A legal scholar characterized the overall approach of the majority on a 1919 committee as wishing to "break down" the family system by making "radical changes" in the law. But the Diet never passed any of these proposals, which continued to be drafted into the early 1940s.[50]

Early twentieth-century legal debates on adultery tended to center around the problem of male sexuality instead of the more traditional focus on controlling married women. Criminal lawyer and prison reformer Ogawa Shigejirō (1863–1924) published the first article on adultery reform to which later legal experts, who were also mostly members of the elite trained at Tokyo Imperial University, frequently referred. Since his piece has been lost, his views are only known through the words of his critics and commentators. Others cited his arguments for the creation of consistency in criminal and civil codes verbatim. Criticizing the fact that Japanese law only punished women for the crime of adultery, he argued for an amendment of "this irrational law" so that either a husband should also be punished for adultery or this act should be decriminalized for both spouses. Adultery, he said, should also become a reason for divorce for both men and women.[51]

Katō Hiroyuki (1836–1916), then retired from the presidency of Tokyo Imperial University, rebuked Ogawa's suggestions and took a more pragmatic approach in an article published ten months ahead of the implementation of the new criminal code on October 1, 1908. He attributed the fact that "since old times" the mere adultery of the wife had been punished to the "selfishness of men," and one-sided punishment remained a "serious inequality" in "today's civilized world" where adultery was an exceedingly grave deed because it was a crime against the "family" (*katei*), which he called "the basis of society." Without a law there was no protection against adultery. But Japanese customs did not yet treat male and female adultery in the same way because of the difference of power between the sexes. Despite his egalitarian insights, he concluded that change was still "too early," since it was impossible "to reform male customs." Moreover, the "natural results" were different, as a wife's adultery could lead to a soiling of the lineage. Nevertheless, Katō felt that a change in the penal code so a husband would be jailed for adultery—which he specified as relations with a concubine, secondary wife, or prostitute—was too "abrupt." Therefore he argued against an amendment of the criminal law. In contrast, he supported a change in divorce laws, a reform he thought would be widely approved by the public, especially by wives. Admitting that some legal "discrimination" would remain, he recommended his proposal as reasonable and convenient.[52]

Within a month the head of the Hiroshima Court of Appeals rejected Katō's moderate divorce law reform proposal in *Hōritsu shinbun*.[53] Why change the civil code if in practice the wife was already able to sue for divorce due to adultery? Ichinose Yūzaburō pointed to the grave cruelty paragraph (Art. 813.5) and declared that, according to his interpretation, adultery constituted cruelty since it was an insult to the "honor" of the wife. After addressing concerns for chaos in the family, order of the state, organization of society, duty and love between spouses, and mutual harmony, Ichinose declared that it would be desirable to eliminate the adultery provision from the penal law.[54] In the same year two more articles on adultery law reform appeared in *Hōritsu Shinbun,* and over a decade later reform was considered in the respective committees. While the promulgation of the Meiji penal code had induced the earlier adultery debate, when several law scholars published again on these issues twenty years later, they mostly intended to justify their work in committees aiming to reform the older legal consensus.

As law professor Hozumi Shigetō (1883–1951) suggested in the title "Adultery of the Husband," adultery continued to be associated with female conduct. Even more than previous legal experts, his major concern in 1937 was male behavior.[55] After discussing Ogawa's and Katō's views he surveyed the broadening of the definition of adultery through Japanese legal precedents and the movement toward spousal equality in various European laws (France in 1884, Germany in 1919, and

England in 1923). Hozumi defended his committee's proposal to permit a woman to divorce a husband due to adultery, as advocated by Katō, but mentions that distinctive legal language was adopted in the draft depending on the sex of the spouse.

His systematic analysis of divorce cases showed what aggravated adultery meant in court practice: fathering a child with an adoptive daughter, redeeming a prostitute and living with her, cohabitation with the divorced wife when the new wife visited her natal family, putting a concubine in the family home, having a sexual relationship with a servant girl and treating her like a wife in family affairs, etc. The terms commonly appearing were cohabitation (*dōsei*), illegitimate child (*shiseiji*), and behaving toward a woman as if she were the wife (*tsuma*). Aggravated adultery (*kajū kantsū*) as the courts interpreted the concept, Hozumi argued, provided insufficient redress for wives. That is why he supported a reform of divorce laws, emphasizing that in Japan a husband could not be divorced for keeping a concubine. The legal reform committee, with a split vote of 9 versus 3, changed the adultery provision toward equality. His pragmatic attitude made him less eager to change the criminal code, which he believed was supported by public opinion.

Law professor Nakagawa Zennosuke (1897–1975), a former student of Hozumi Shigetō's, published "Adultery and Bigamy" in the same volume.[56] To him adultery was more explicitly a symbol, or "barometer" as he called it, of the development of women's culture and social position. Adultery infringed on "marital relations" through extramarital "sexual relations" of either spouse. Nakagawa found it incredible that in 1937 a traditional system persisted in which adultery was exclusively a female crime. Criticizing Katō and implicitly his own teacher for not wanting to change the penal law, he praised Ogawa for advocating gender equality across the board. More of a moralist than Ogawa, he preferred a version of equality whereby adultery became a punishable offense for both spouses.

According to Nakagawa, adultery was a violation of the basic duty of marriage and gender equality universally accepted throughout the world as a result of several thousand years of cultural progress, but Japan still needed to climb the last step. As the trendsetter he invoked Germany, which was debating whether to reinstitute the crime of adultery for either spouse. Included in a draft code of 1927, the clause was erased in the 1930 draft. A majority of a combined German-Austrian Criminal Code Conference supported the old provision, and the Nazis intended to recriminalize adultery. His implicit presentation of Nazi policies as the highest peak of progressive morality and gender equality looks strange in retrospect, but it should be considered in the context of a lack of deeper awareness of the political developments in a faraway country that for decades had served as a model for Japanese legal scholars. His desire to penalize husbands' adultery was in line with an increase in campaigns of moral suasion by many social groups in Japan during the 1930s and had been a standard part of the law revision movement since the 1890s.[57]

Japanese legal experts from the early twentieth century recognized that the laws contained a sexual double standard running counter to the greater principle of legal equality for every citizen. This understanding of inequality, however, did not automatically induce them to advocate reform; they argued that public opinion and social practice supported gender differences, especially in the penal code. Some expressed a strong reluctance to incarcerate husbands, though others thought it would enhance public morality and achieve gender equality. Interestingly enough a Taishō period penal code draft included such a penalty, as women's groups had demanded. By contrast, abolishing the penalty altogether for both spouses, mentioned as a theoretical possibility in the debate, appeared to receive scant support from elite lawyers, women's groups, and the political establishment. Divorce law reform seemed more appealing to a public interested in male morality. Lawyers broadly favored ideas enabling wives to sue their husbands in court for adultery, and court jurisdiction generally moved in that direction although political resistance in the Diet prevented actual revisions of the codes. If the key concern in the laws prior to the twentieth century was to control the sexuality of the wife, the scholarly and public debate on legal revision became increasingly obsessed with containing male sexuality and enforcing monogamy not only in law but also in practice.

While elite lawyers moralized more about husbands' sexuality, the population at large may, paradoxically, have become somewhat more forgiving toward female infidelity. After the implementation of the 1908 Criminal Code, the overall number of female convicts declined gradually, presumably due to the increased use of probation and parole. By 1931 there were only 582 women left in jail, or less than 1.4 percent of the total prison population.[58] Adjustment in adultery-related confinement, which in earlier times had been the most prevalent reason for incarcerating women, according to the French legal advisor Georges Bousquet, may have played a role in the long-term decline of the female prison population as state and society increasingly treated it as a private, personal problem.[59] Court statistics reflected a de facto decriminalization of female adultery after the introduction of the 1908 penal law. The number of aggrieved husbands suing for adultery dropped precipitously from 213 in 1913 to almost a tenth of that number (28) in 1937. The decline was most marked during the liberal Taishō years (1912–1926). The conviction rate plunged, too. As few as 21 percent of accused adulterers were given a prison sentence of more than six months between 1916 and 1940. By contrast, in 1880 89 percent of those prosecuted were sentenced to at least one year of penal servitude and the proportion of female inmates was accordingly much higher.[60] In a Diet hearing in 1947 Judge Miyake Masatarō confessed that during the ten years when he served on the Supreme Court not a single adultery case reached that institution. Moreover, in 1929–1930 lower courts only heard 48 adultery crime cases; 60 percent proceeded to a second trial but then were withdrawn before the verdict and "not a single person entered prison." For the prosecution to succeed the husband needed to sever his marital ties and sue not only the lover but also his wife. Since the suit could be withdrawn any time, the accused usually pleaded with the wronged husband when threatened with a prison sentence.[61] Even before the elimination of adultery from the penal law, popular practice no longer treated it as a crime. This shift did not necessarily signify greater tolerance in moral affairs; rather, the decline in the number of adultery convictions and the length of sentences ran counter to a general trend toward enhanced conservative moral and sexual values in society, as seen by its declining divorce rate, fewer children born out of wedlock, and spreading concern with premarital virginity.[62]

Despite intermittent reform attempts in the prewar period, the double shock of defeat and the American Occupation was necessary to overhaul the legal system and finally eradicate legal gender discrimination. Even if one has to take the bragging accounts of self-styled American liberators of Japanese women with a grain of salt, legal reforms from the constitution to the civil code often had a remarkably strange taste: Japanese newspapers referred to them as "smelling of butter," a shorthand for things foreign. General MacArthur reminisced that he considered the liberation of Japanese women his greatest achievement, and in the early years Americans emphasized social reform through the purge of "feudalism" from society and the family. Occupation authorities provided political muscle to support revisions of adultery legislation that Japanese legal experts and courts had been advocating since the turn of the century. In the name of "gender equality" they removed adultery from the criminal code and revised the grounds for divorce in the civil code, concluding a process toward narrowing the gender gap in Japanese law and making the sexual double standard disappear.

The new constitution of May 3, 1947, served as the legal basis for adultery reform. The crucial provision was the principle of the essential equality between men and women that had been inserted by a young female staff member of the Occupation administration.[63] Article 24 stipulated the equal rights of husband and wife, equality of the sexes, and the inviolability of the individual. Article 14 emphasized the principle of equality for all persons before the law.[64]

Adultery was only one of two alterations of the criminal code, the other being lèse-majesté. The reason why the criminal code was not subject to a more radical overhaul was that reformers thought of it as a relatively advanced piece of legislation leaning "heavily on European models" and containing little that appeared unconstitutional.[65] Alfred Oppler, a German lawyer who had immigrated to the United States in the 1930s and whose knowledge of European law qualified him to become one of the key American legal experts during the Occupation, subtitled his chapter on legal reforms "a cooperative effort," but when discussing criminal code reform, he said "we insisted" on changing the adultery provisions because

> the violation of the Constitution was so clear that it was even not necessary to bring the matter to the attention of SCAP. The existing law provided for punishment of the wife and of the other party to the adultery. A husband who was unfaithful with an unmarried woman was not subject to punishment. The principle of equality of the sexes, we told the Japanese, left them the alternative of either making adultery equally punishable for both sexes, or of abolishing it as a criminal offence. Characteristically enough, the Diet decided in favor of abolition. After all, it consisted mostly of males, and the habit of keeping a mistress was probably more customary in the case of Japan's married men than in other nations, since the choice of spouse was made by the family elders and often not based on mutual affection.[66]

Oppler's casual dismissal of the criminal code's adultery regulations as a remnant of male chauvinism was not fully shared by Japanese observers. Although they recognized a "disparity" in the criminal law, they explained that "extramarital intercourse by a married man with an unmarried woman was no crime because it would not affect the purity of the family lineage." Article 183 was repealed by law number 124 effective October 14, 1947.[67]

Civil law reforms followed similar basic principles, especially concerning marriage and divorce, which was now explicitly based on the mutual will of the spouses without the need of parental consent for adults. Oppler said that "equalization has been adopted in this field, too."[68] According to Article 770.1, adultery of either spouse became a ground for legal divorce. But a spouse's adultery no longer entitled a husband to a divorce; it merely became one piece of evidence that the marital spirit had evaporated.

Gender, Law, and History

During the eighty years from 1868 to 1948, adultery moved from being a capital offense to decriminalization in the penal code and becoming a ground for judicial divorce in the civil code. What does this process tell us about the connection between law and gender in imperial Japan?

First, as generations of scholars have shown, the influence of Western legal concepts transformed traditional Japanese notions of how to regulate society. After 1868, the modernizing nation-state established basic legal institutions we now take for granted, including a national legislature, universal codes, and a countrywide system of courts. But some legal principles, such as the essential equality of individuals before the law, were not fully implemented until after World War II. There is no doubt that the introduction of foreign models supported Japan's modernization by establishing more of what is known as "the rule of law" and restricting arbitrary decision making by powerful institutions, groups, and individuals. Analysts and policy makers frequently attributed gender inequalities to the inclusion of "customary" or "feudal" practices in prewar Japanese law.[69] What has often been overlooked even by historians is that rules enshrining inequality were often taken word for word from contemporary European legislation and that Japan was absorbing and selecting from what were then legitimately considered international best practices. Some of the foreign male legal advisors in Japan supported and justified sex-differentiated adultery provisions as either natural or rational and equitable. Reliance on or reference to European codes may have perpetuated and reinforced differential treatment of men and women as part of the legal gendering of Japanese society. After the turn of the century, European legal changes or continuities served as a source of reference for Japanese to contextualize their own points of view as being part of the trends of the times and in placing Japan within the trajectory of progress of civilization symbolized by the inferior legal position of women. Interestingly enough, Japanese scholars paid scant attention to the United States, which appeared to be of little relevance in the discussion of the revision of the codes because they had originally been modeled on Continental European laws and some of the most influential experts were themselves trained in Europe. Even during the American Occupation, Japanese discussed adultery with reference to Europe, and key legal personnel in the American administration had been dispatched to Japan because of their background in German law.

Second, a new state-sanctioned ideal of a monogamous marriage created by blending legal models from abroad with Japanese popular practices served as ideological background for adultery legislation in the eighty years under investigation. With the advent of the Meiji period, the state propagated a nationwide legal definition of marriage as part of its policies of nation building, encompassing issues that during the Tokugawa period had been regulated and defined by status-based rules and local customs. When a state-sanctioned marriage recorded in official family registration documents became a hegemonic ideal, other relationships were characterized as lesser, marginal, or undesirable. By the early twentieth century, adultery legislation became one of the publicly contested parts of the process of reshaping notions of matrimony, conjugal expectations, and public morality because it served as a visible symbol of customary hierarchy in the patriarchal family and as a sign of legal and actual gender inequality and prevalent sexual double standards in society.

Third, although or because adultery laws were traditionally concerned with wives' behavior as well as with the male intruder into the family order, during the early twentieth century the crucial legal and popular controversies were about husbands' behavior and whether maintaining such striking legal inequality was still justifiable in a society aspiring to modernity. Jurisdiction was slowly moving toward mitigating the gender gap in divorce by extending the meaning of grave cruelty to encompass married men engaging in long-term sexual relationships with other women. Critics frequently singled out the institution of concubines as a unique Japanese social problem and chastised wanton male sexuality. By contrast, there appears less unity in reforming the penal law because the desire for gender equality was often trumped by the desire for a more moral society. As a result, a series of penal law proposals shows no consistent trend. Some would punish husbands and wives equally, while others would reduce the gender gap while recognizing only aggravated adultery by the husband. Despite the increasing scarcity of criminal convictions, no prewar state committee proposed to decriminalize adultery.

Fourth, adultery laws were not the only or even the most important legislation that treated women differently from men in modern Japan. Some were petty regulations of everyday life, such as the early Meiji period ban on women cutting their hair, which was encouraged for men. Other laws excluded women from enrolling at public universities and gaining access to the professions. A bill to grant women the vote in local elections in 1931 was defeated in the upper house, despite the fact that universal manhood suffrage had been introduced in 1925. When the public was envisioned as predominantly a sphere of men, and the home a female domain, challenging adultery legislation turned into an attack on arbitrary male authority in the family.[70] The American Occupation in that sense "liberated" Japanese women from a broad set of traditional gendered laws of inequality, but few people then and now were aware how closely adultery legislation was modeled after France's legal tradition, which already at the time of its adoption in Meiji Japan was seen as backward in the European context. Indeed, we could go so far as to claim that adultery law was one of the French contributions to maintaining legal inequality in modernizing Japan.

Notes

1. Arne Dunker, *Gleichheit und Ungleichheit in der Ehe: Persönliche Stellung von Frau und Mann im Recht der ehelichen Lebensgemeinschaft 1700–1914* (Köln: Böhlau Verlag, 2003), 677–695.

2. Kasumi Nobuhiko, *Meiji shoki keijihō no kisoteki kenkyū* (Keiō Gijuku Daigaku Hōgaku Kenkyūkai, 1990), 3–62.

3. Sheldon Garon, *Molding Japanese Minds: The State in Everyday Life* (Princeton, NJ: Princeton University Press, 1997), 94–95, 102.

4. Joan W. Scott, "Gender: A Useful Category of Historical Analysis," in Joan W. Scott, *Gender and the Politics of History* (New York: Columbia University Press, 1988), 171.

5. Harald Fuess, *Divorce in Japan: Family, Gender and the State* (Stanford, CA: Stanford University Press, 2004), 1–15, 172.

6. *Kujikata* articles reprinted in Ono Takeo, ed., *Edo jidai keibatsu fūzoku saiken* (Tenbōsha, 1976), 311; Iyoku Hideaki, ed., *Hōsei shiryō kenkyū*, vol. 1 (Gannandō, 1994), 349–375.

7. Tsuji Tatsuya, ed., *Sen'yō ruishū*, vol. 1 (Zoku Gunsho Ruijū Kanseikai, 1967), 166–168.

8. For a fuller discussion of Tokugawa period adultery laws and their application see Amy Stanley, "Adultery, Punishment, and Reconciliation in Tokugawa Japan," *Journal of Japanese Studies* 33, no. 2 (Summer 2007): 309–335; and Harald Fuess, "Ehebruch als Verbrechen: Der europäische Beitrag zur Frauendiskriminierung in Japan," *Zeitschrift für japanisches Recht* 24, no. 1 (2007): 108–136. Some of the discussions in this chapter on the legal development since the Meiji period are also to be found in my earlier German-language article.

9. Mega Atsuko, *Hankachō no naka no onna-tachi* (Heibonsha, 1995), 10, 167; Daniel V. Botsman, *Punishment and Power in the Making of Modern Japan* (Princeton, NJ: Princeton University Press, 2005), 73.

10. Ryosuke Ishii, *Japanese Legislation in the Meiji Era*, trans. and adapted by William Chambliss (Tokyo: Pan-Pacific Press, 1958), 339–341.

11. Paul Heng-chao Ch'en, *The Formation of the Early Meiji Legal Order: The Japanese Code of 1871 and Its Chinese Foundation* (New York: Oxford University Press, 1981), 71.

12. Ishii, *Japanese Legislation*, 348.

13. English translation of code in Ch'en, *Formation of the Early Meiji Legal Order*, 168. Japanese original text in *Shihō shiryō, bessatsu* 17, 1, in Shihōshō, ed., *Nihon kindai keiji hōreishū* 3 (Shihōshō Hishoka, 1945).

14. Ch'en, *Formation of the Early Meiji Legal Order*, 92, 137.

15. Ibid., 170; George Thomas Staunton, *Ta Tsing Leu Lee; Being the Fundamental Laws and a Selection from the Supplementary Statutes of the Penal Code of China; Originally Printed and Published in Pekin, in Various Successive Editions, Under the Sanction, and by the Authority, of the Several Emperors of the Ta Tsing, or Present Dynasty* (Taipei: Ch'eng-Wen Publishing, 1966), 404–410; M. J. Meijer, *Murder and Adultery in Late Imperial China: A Study of Law and Morality* (Leiden: Brill, 1991), 39–48; Geoffrey MacCormack, *Traditional Chinese Penal Law* (Edinburgh: Edinburgh University Press, 1990), 280–282.

16. Ch'en, *Formation of the Early Meiji Legal Order*, 28, 63.

17. Ishii, *Japanese Legislation*, 345.

18. Draft of 1877, Article 353. *Projet de code pénal pour l'empire du Japon présenté au sénat par le ministere de la justice le 8e mois de la 10e année de Meiji (Août 1879)* (Kokubunsha, 1879), 93.

19. F. C. Jones, *Extraterritoriality in Japan and the Diplomatic Relations Resulting in Its Abolition, 1853–1899* (New Haven, CT: Yale University Press, 1931), 111.

20. Gustave Emil Boissonade, *Projet révisé de code pénal pour l'empire du Japon accompagné d'un commentaire par Mr. Gve Boissonade* (Kokubunsha, 1886), 1033.

21. Nihon kirisutokyō fujin kyōfūkai, ed., *Nihon kirisutokyō fujin kyōfūkai hyakunenshi* (Domesu Shuppan, 1986), 77.

22. Karl-Friedrich Lenz, "Penal Law," in *History of Law in Japan since 1868*, ed. Wilhelm Röhl (Leiden: Brill, 2005), 614.

23. Ujiie Mikito, *Fugi mittsū: Kinjirareta koi no Edo* (Kōdansha, 1996), 5.

24. Ibid., 221.

25. Ibid., 225.

26. Ibid., 228.

27. Boissonade, *Projet révisé de code pénal*, 900, 908–912.

28. Ujiie, *Fugi mittsū*, 227.

29. Boissonade, *Projet révisé de code pénal*, 1015. He adapted articles 813–822 of the French criminal code on pp. 1031–1032.

30. Ibid., 1032, 1033, 1035.

31. J. E. De Becker, *The Annotated Civil Code of Japan*, vol. 3 (London: Butterworth and Co., 1909–1910), 75.

32. More critical foreign views existed to be sure, especially when linking the issues to public morality and male depravity. A newspaper article cites the Dutch Jurist G. A. van Hamel: "Adultery is treated according to the system of the French Code: it is only punished when it is committed by the woman; and this inequality is even augmented, for the provision of the French Code, feeble as it is, against the husband who has kept a concubine in the conjugal house, is wanting in the Code of Japan." The unsigned article then continues with claims that in Japan wives were "virtually at the mercy of their husbands" and raves on about the toleration of concubines, which "formerly" were legally recognized. Ironically its main trust was to interpret the existence of French-inspired adultery clauses as a sign of how women's status remained little changed despite "contact with foreign civilization." *Japan Weekly Mail*, June 9, 1883, 128.

33. Nobushige Hozumi, *Lectures on the New Japanese Civil Code as Material for the Study of Comparative Jurisprudence* (Maruzen Kabushiki-Kaisha, 1912), 70–74.

34. Okamura Tsukasa, *Minpō shinzokuhen,* in *Nihon rippō shiryō zenshū, bekkan* 339 (1898; reprint, Shinzansha Shuppan, 2005), 505–507.

35. Nishimura Kannosuke and Iwano Shinpei, *Shin keihō gige,* 7th ed. (Shimizu Shoten, 1912), 528–530.

36. Sharon H. Nolte and Sally Ann Hastings, "The Meiji State's Policy Towards Women, 1890–1910," in *Recreating Japanese Women, 1600–1945,* ed. Gail Lee Bernstein (Berkeley: University of California Press, 1991), 155; Garon, *Molding Japanese Minds,* 115–145.

37. Hozumi Shigetō, "Otto no kantsū," in *Kazoku seido zenshū shironhen,* vol. 2, *Rikon,* ed. Hozumi Shigetō and Nakagawa Zennosuke (Kawade Shobō, 1937), 155–156.

38. Okamura, *Minpō shinzokuhen,* 507.

39. Hozumi, "Otto no kantsū," 188.

40. Tanaka Sumie, "Kantsū," in *Gendai kyōyō zenshū,* vol. 9, *Yūjō, ren'ai, kekkon* (Chikuma Shobō, 1959), 305.

41. Nihon kirisutokyō, ed., *Nihon kirisutokyō,* 331. For recent, more detailed studies of the WCTU and the women's movement, see Elizabeth Dorn Lublin, *Reforming Japan: The Woman's Christian Temperance Union in the Meiji Period* (Vancouver: University of British Columbia Press, 2010); Marnie S. Anderson, *A Place in Public: Women's Rights in Meiji Japan* (Cambridge, MA: Harvard University Asia Center, 2010); and Barbara Molony, "The Quest for Women's Rights in Turn-of-the-Century Japan," in *Gendering Modern Japanese History,* ed. Barbara Molony and Kathleen Uno (Cambridge, MA: Harvard University Asia Center, 2008), 463–492.

42. Nihon kirisutokyō, ed., *Nihon kirisutokyō,* 78.

43. *Shin shin fujin,* which advertised itself as the first magazine of the women's movement in Japan, ran several issues on the husband's promiscuity and the wife's adultery. Nishikawa Kōjirō was one of the few contributors who explicitly supported the Women Christian Temperance Union's desire for legal reform. Ulrike Wöhr, *Frauen zwischen Rollenerwartung und Selbstdeutung: Ehe, Mutterschaft und Liebe im Spiegel der japanischen Frauenzeitschrift Shin shin fujin von 1913 bis 1916* (Wiesbaden: Harrassowitz, 1997), 230, 246, 268, 280–281.

44. Tamura Gorō, *Katei no saiban: Fūfu* (Nihon Hyōronsha 1985), 1–2.

45. Wöhr, *Frauen zwischen Rollenerwartung und Selbstdeutung,* 230–231.

46. Iida versus Iida, Supreme Court, Civil Affairs Section, *Shinbun* 2976,

March 1, 1929; Yozo Watanabe, "The Family and the Law: The Individualist Premise and Modern Japanese Family Law," in *Law in Japan: The Legal Order in a Changing Society*, ed. Arthur Taylor von Mehren (Cambridge, MA: Harvard University Press, 1963), 371–372; Ōno Fumio and Yano Masanori, *Sei no saiban kiroku: Kantsū, teisō shingai (gōkan, kyōsei waisetsu, kekkonsagi) seiteiki bujoku, seiki kison* (Sakai Shoten, 1975).

47. Tamura, *Katei no saiban*, 7–9; Watanabe, "Family and the Law," 371–372.

48. "Kantsū hikoku jiken," *Shinbun* 1518 (January 30, 1936), 45–53.

49. Preliminary decision, July 20, 1926, First Criminal Branch Supreme Court Decision (re) 233; "Kyōkatsu hikoku jiken," in Daishin'in, comp., *Daishin'in keiji hanreishū*, vol. 5 (Hosokai, 1927), 318–325; final verdict on May 27, 1927. Discussed also in Nakagawa Zennosuke, "Kantsū oyobi jūkon," in *Kazoku seido zenshū shironhen*, vol. 2, *Rikon*, ed. Hozumi Shigetō and Nakagawa Zennosuke (Kawade Shobō, 1937), 257; and Hozumi, "Otto no kantsū," 184.

50. Temporary Council on the Legal System. Watanabe, "Family and the Law," 371.

51. Also quoted in Katō Hiroyuki, "Kantsū ni tsuite," *Hōgaku kyōkai zasshi* 26 (1908): 1; Nakagawa, "Kantsū oyobi jūkon," 255; and Hozumi, "Otto no kantsū," 153.

52. Katō, "Kantsū ni tsuite," 1–6.

53. Ichinose Yūzaburō, "Danshaku Katō sensei no kantsūron o haidoku shi 'Minpō dai 113 jō keihō dai 354 jō' kaitei 'Keihō dai 184 jō' ni oyobu," *Hōritsu shinbun* 476 (January 30, 1908), 165–166.

54. Ibid., February 5, 1908: 197–199.

55. Hozumi, "Otto no kantsū," 151–188.

56. Nakagawa, "Kantsū oyobi jūkon," 253–266.

57. Garon, *Molding Japanese Minds*, 106–114.

58. See Botsman, *Punishment and Power*, and his essay "Of Pity and Poison," in this volume.

59. Georges Bousquet, *Le Japon de nos jours et les échelles de l'extrême orient* (Paris: Librairie Hachette, 1877), 103.

60. Hayashi Hiromasa, *Kaisei keihō karian seiritsu katei no kenkyū* (Seibundō, 2003), 312–314. On October 26, 2006, the *TKC hōritsu jōhō* legal database yielded 57 *Daishin'in* cases related to the keywords *mittsū, kantsū,* and *yūfukan* for 1899–1943.

61. Miyake Masatarō, "Atte yō nashi," in Hokkaidō hōsha, ed., *Kantsū*

zai o dōsuru? Shūgiin hatsu no kōchōkai kara (Sapporo: Hokkaidō hōsha, 1947), 23–24.

62. Fuess, *Divorce in Japan*, 128–143.

63. Beate Shirota Gordon, *The Only Woman in the Room: A Memoir* (Tokyo: Kodansha International, 1997).

64. Watanabc, "Family and thc Law," 373.

65. Alfred Oppler, *Legal Reform in Occupied Japan: A Participant Looks Back* (Princeton, NJ: Princeton University Press, 1976), 120–121.

66. Ibid., 74–75.

67. Watanabe, "Family and the Law," 366.

68. Oppler, *Legal Reform in Occupied Japan*, 118. See also Kurt Steiner, "The Revision of the Civil Code of Japan: Provisions Affecting the Family," *Far Eastern Quarterly* 9 (November 1949–August 1950): 182.

69. Steiner, "The Revision of the Civil Code of Japan," 169–183.

70. Harald Fuess, "Men in the Women's Kingdom," in *Public Spheres, Private Lives in Modern Japan, 1600–1950*, ed. Gail Bernstein, Andrew Gordon, and Kate Wildman Nakai (Cambridge, MA: Harvard University Asia Center, 2005), 259–292.

CHAPTER 5

Of Pity and Poison

Imprisoning Women in Modern Japan

Daniel Botsman

ALTHOUGH THE "REVISIONIST" scholars who rekindled widespread interest in the history of punishment in the 1970s were largely oblivious to questions of gender, the decades since have seen the publication of a series of important studies (all by women) that call attention to the way in which the punishment of men and women has differed significantly in various Western societies.[1] Unfortunately, the same trend has not been apparent in Japan, where, with the exception of a few valuable but short essays by prison historian Shigematsu Kazuyoshi, the history of women's prisons and the punishment of women have been almost entirely neglected in the scholarly literature.[2] One possible explanation for this neglect is that women have constituted only a very small portion of those sentenced to judicial punishment. This is the case in most modern societies, but it is especially true for modern Japan. As we shall see in more detail below, in the period since the Meiji Restoration, Japanese prison populations have rarely been more than 5 percent female. While this, in itself, raises interesting questions about the relationship between gender and crime, it has also made it easy for scholars to treat the punishment of women as, at best, a side issue. Yet, historians do not usually approach the study of the human past as if it were a numbers game—if they did we would presumably have many more histories of women and many more of the non-Western world. The real question is whether the study of a particular problem has anything important to tell us about the past, and as the work of Estelle Freedman, Nicole Hahn Rafter, Patricia O'Brien, and Lucia Zedner makes clear, the punishment of women has the potential to be an especially fruitful topic in this regard.

To begin with, a consideration of the punishment of women provides us with a useful corrective to any simplistic equation of mass incarceration with modernity. In the case of Japan, imprisonment was already a relatively important form of punishment for women in the late Tokugawa period, and although the creation of a network of modern prisons in the early Meiji period initially led to a sharp increase in the total number of women in state custody, the first half of the twentieth century brought an equally sudden and dramatic *decline* in numbers. In addition, and perhaps more importantly, the special rules and (eventually) special institutions that were created for female convicts can provide us with a useful window through which to consider the development of state attitudes about gender roles and, in particular of course, the proper role of women in society.[3] Even more than girls' schools, women's prisons were, after all, "total institutions," in which the state could, in theory, try to impose its vision of "proper behavior" on virtually every aspect of an inmate's life.

Moreover, while Sharon Nolte and Sally Ann Hastings are undoubtedly right to suggest that "most government policies [in the Meiji era] addressed just women of a particular class" (i.e., the middle), the prison was one institutional space in which the question of what constituted an appropriate role for women who were *not* from middle-class or elite backgrounds had to be addressed.[4] Indeed, as Japanese penologists and bureaucrats began to engage the new eugenicist theories of criminality that were being developed in the West from the late nineteenth century, they quickly came to see such women and their likely impact on the future of "the race" as an issue of real concern. In this sense, the punishment of women and, in particular, the development of specialist institutions for imprisoning and "treating" them is an issue that can also help throw new light on the history of what Foucault famously termed "governmentality" (i.e., an approach to governance based on the study and management of populations) in modern Japan.[5]

Although a full examination of the history of women in prison in Japan will not be possible without considerably more archival research, this essay will elaborate upon some of the key issues outlined above in the hope that it may at least provide a starting point for future explorations of this important topic. In order to provide a basis for understanding the changes that followed the Meiji Restoration, the essay begins with a brief discussion of the punishment of women in the Tokugawa period. After considering the place of women in the "great confinement" of the early Meiji period, we then turn to a more focused examination of Japan's first specialist "women's prison" and the reasons for its establishment in 1903. Finally, the chapter concludes with an overview of the "great decarceration" of the late Taishō and early Shōwa periods, and a tentative discussion of some possible explanations for this remarkable reversal of earlier trends.[6]

Punishing Women in Tokugawa Japan

Given that the punishment of women has so often been treated as a footnote in dominant narratives of the history of punishment, it is perhaps appropriate to begin with a case drawn from an actual footnote in an article published in the 1950s by the great legal historian Hiramatsu Yoshirō. The case concerns a thirty-four-year-old woman named Tetsu, who, in the summer of 1865, just a few years before the collapse of the Tokugawa shogunate, was brought in for questioning by one of the Edo Town Governor's (*Edo machi bugyō*) regular police patrols.[7] The officers in the patrol did not have any particular reason for arresting Tetsu. She had simply caught their attention with her "suspicious" behavior. No doubt the sight of the patrol had been enough to make her nervous because, as it turned out, this was not her first run-in with the shogun's officers. Under interrogation she confessed that when she was younger she had been arrested for a minor offense and that as part of her punishment she had been tattooed on her arm. This, in itself, would not have been a problem for Tetsu, but at some point after her initial punishment she had met and married a man named Iwajirō, and because she feared that he would abandon her if he saw the tattoo, she had secretly used moxa to burn it off. For this attempt to defy the authority of the shogunate and, quite literally, erase her criminal past, Tetsu was sentenced to the standard punishment stipulated under bakufu law for such offenses: her original tattoo was re-inscribed and she was banished from the city of Edo.

At one level then, Tetsu's case provides us with a clear example of two quintessentially *pre*-modern (or perhaps it would be better just to say *un*-modern) strategies of punishment that continued to be used right up until the final years of the Tokugawa period: her body was first physically marked as criminal, and then later, when she was found to have resisted her official branding, she was expelled from her home place and, in a sense, "set free" to wander the countryside, surviving as best she could without the support of an established community. Following a "pop Foucaultian" formula, we might well contrast all of this with the new system of punishment that was to emerge in the wake of the Restoration—in which, in theory at least, the main target of punishment was no longer the criminal body, but her "soul," and the primary mode of punishment was not expulsion but confinement and "discipline." Yet, while it is true that punishments such as banishment and tattooing disappeared quickly after the Restoration, a closer examination of Tetsu's case records also reminds us that even in the Tokugawa period imprisonment was not unknown as a form of official punishment: in addition to tattooing, her original sentence had also stipulated that she should serve a short term at the bakufu's official jailhouse. It was almost certainly because she was a woman that she was given this particular punishment. In order to understand why this was the case we must briefly consider the history of corporal punishment under the Tokugawa.

In the early decades of Tokugawa rule, bodily mutilation (most notably, severing of the ears and/or nose) was a common form of punishment for various kinds of petty crime. By the end of the seventeenth century, however, this practice, which was associated with the earlier "Warring States" (*Sengoku*) period, had largely fallen out of use. Eventually, under the eighth shogun, Yoshimune (r. 1716–1745), who was determined to find ways to bolster respect for warrior authority, the bakufu introduced flogging and tattooing as official replacements for the older, defunct forms of corporal punishment. As we already know from the case of Tetsu, tattooing continued to be used to punish women for the remainder of the Tokugawa period, and initially flogging too may have been applied equally to both men and women. In 1789, however, during Matsudaira Sadanobu's Kansei Reforms, a special rule was issued banning the use of flogging for women.[8] In future, it was ordered, women who committed crimes for which a man would ordinarily have been punished with a "severe flogging" of 100 lashes were instead to serve 100 days in the jailhouse; while those whose crimes warranted a "light flogging" (= 50 lashes) were to be imprisoned for 50 days. This is significant because flogging quickly became the bakufu's standard penalty for petty theft and most other minor crimes. According to statistics compiled by Hiramatsu, by the end of the Tokugawa period it accounted for more than 70 percent of all punishments ordered by the authorities in the city of Edo.[9] By mandating that imprisonment replace flogging for women, therefore, the bakufu effectively ensured that any woman found guilty of a petty crime in the late Tokugawa period would be sentenced to a short jail term.

Even prior to these reforms women had sometimes been sent to the jailhouse as a form of punishment. From early in the period the warrior authorities had maintained a number of "special" punishments for women. Hitomi Tonomura has written, for example, about the practice of cutting off a woman's hair in order to shame and humiliate her.[10] This practice, which has its origins in the medieval past, continued to be used in the Tokugawa period, but by far the most severe of all the special punishments for women dispensed by the Tokugawa authorities was "slavery" (*nuhi-kei*). In some cases those who were sentenced to this punishment were actually assigned to the household of a warrior "master," but more often it meant a life of permanent confinement and menial service within the grounds of a Tokugawa jail. In effect, then, it can be considered to have been a form of life imprisonment.[11] After the completion of the Rules for Determining Criminal Matters (*Kujikata osadamegaki*), a basic law code compiled under Yoshimune in the mid-eighteenth century, the use of "slavery" was restricted to cases of women who secretly passed through or around one of the bakufu's official checkpoints, but in the early half of the period it had been commonly used to punish (by association) the female relatives of men who committed a broad range of serious crimes. Partly for this reason, no doubt, the Tokugawa bakufu's main jailhouse at Kodemmachō in Edo had always had special rooms for the separate confinement of women. In the latter half of the period, the ban on flogging as a punishment for women and its replacement with short-term jail sentences must have helped ensure that these rooms remained full with a steady stream of petty criminals.

None of this is to suggest that the inmate populations of Tokugawa jails were ever overwhelmingly female. The primary purpose of these jails, after all, was to hold criminal suspects while they were being investigated and judged, and then, as now, the vast majority of criminal suspects were men.[12] It is also true that in some cases men too were given jail terms as a form of punishment. These cases, however, were quite exceptional, and overall it is safe to say that in the late Tokugawa period imprisonment was a significantly more important form of punishment for women than it was for men. This is especially the case if we are willing to take into consideration the special system for policing unlicensed prostitution in cities like Edo. The notion that Yoshiwara and the other so-called "pleasure quarters" of the Tokugawa period were prison-*like* in the sense that they were cut off from the surrounding cities by a moat and that the women inside were prevented from leaving is by now something of a cliché. What is less well known, however, is that from the late seventeenth century licensed brothel owners had been given the right to hunt down and arrest prostitutes working illegally in other parts of the city and that the standard bakufu punishment for those who were caught in these "whore hunts" was three and a half years of unpaid service (i.e., hard labor) in the "licensed quarters."[13] From time to time bakufu officials also conducted their own "roundups" of prostitutes and female entertainers. During the Tempō Reforms of the 1840s, for example, the rooms for women prisoners at the Kodemmachō jailhouse are said to have been full of female performers (*musume gidayū*) and geisha as a result of Mizuno Tadakuni's infamous campaign to crack down on vice and immorality in the city.[14] It is also worth noting that in 1876, when the Meiji government finally replaced the Kodemmachō jailhouse with a newly completed prison at Ichigaya, the old jail buildings continued to be used for a short time as a special detention center for prostitutes.[15]

Overall then, there is considerable evidence to suggest that imprisonment was already a relatively familiar form of punishment for women in the late Tokugawa period, especially poor, working women in large cities like Edo.

Gendering the "Great Confinement"

The first decade of the Meiji era witnessed a veritable revolution in official methods of punishment. Old forms of "warrior" execution such as crucifixion, burning alive, and eventually even beheading were replaced with the more "civilized" (i.e., British) method of hanging, and the overall use of capital punishment was greatly curtailed. Banishment was officially abolished, as were the old corporal punishments of tattooing and flogging, which had been completely phased out by the end of the 1870s. The great void left by these rapid changes was, of course, filled by a new emphasis on incarceration, and it was not long before prison populations across the country began to rise dramatically. By 1883, when the pioneering female activist and writer Kishida Toshiko (1863–1901) was thrown in jail in Ōtsu for making one of her famous "political" speeches about the need to educate women, she was able to console herself by noting in her diary that "these days . . . to live in jail is all the fashion in society"—and, indeed, in the ten years between 1876 and 1885 the total number of convicts in prison in Japan increased by more than 500 percent, jumping from just under 13,000 to just over 63,000 people.[16] (This is more than twice the total number of convicts in English prisons in the same period.)[17]

Unfortunately, national statistics for women prisoners are not available for the period before the mid-1880s, but at the end of 1885 Japan had around 2,800 women convicts, which was the equivalent of about 4.5 percent of the total convict population. In the ten years that followed, the overall convict population dipped and then rose back to around the same level, but the number of women in prison increased steadily, so that by 1894 there were a total of roughly 4,600 women convicts nationwide. This represented about 6.8 percent of all convicts. This is the largest that the female convict population has ever been in Japan, both in terms of absolute numbers and as a percentage of the total prison population.[18] There are a number of possible explanations for this dramatic peak in female convict numbers in the middle of the Meiji era. One important factor may have been the government's 1890 ban on political activity by women. It is also possible that legal changes ushered in under the 1882 Penal Code were significant, and that the Meiji government's campaign to "civilize" the manners and mores of everyday life led to much tighter policing of the behavior of women. Finally, there is a good chance that the economic upheavals of the 1880s and early 1890s led to a rise in female poverty and therefore also petty crime. An examination of police statistics from this period should eventually help throw more light on this question.

Needless to say, just as the laws that could lead to incarceration changed considerably in this period, so too did the rules and regulations governing life in prison. Within just a few years of the Restoration members of the new government began carefully studying various Western judicial and penal systems. During their trip abroad in 1871–1872 members of the celebrated Iwakura mission visited the renowned Eastern State Penitentiary in Philadelphia, and in England they inspected the Manchester prison, where Kume Kunitake (1839–1931), the mission's official diarist, made a special note of the arrangements in place there for female inmates.[19] Even prior to this an official named Ohara Shigechika (1834–1902) had been sent to Hong Kong and Singapore to study the British colonial prisons and courts there, and upon his return to Japan in 1871 he was given the task of drawing up the country's first set of "Prison Rules" (*kangoku soku*) on the basis of what he had observed.[20] One of the basic ideas that prison reformers in nineteenth-century England had fought hard to establish was that women inmates should be kept away from their male counterparts and supervised only by members of their own sex.[21] This idea was also clearly reflected in Ohara's Rules. Already in the Tokugawa period it had been standard practice to confine women inmates in separate rooms, but the new Rules went one step further than this, stipulating that women prisoners should be housed in special buildings, entirely separate from those used to imprison men (Art. 8). The Rules also required the appointment of special women guards, presumably modeled after the "matrons" of nineteenth-century English women's prisons, who were to be responsible for all searches of female inmates. Later, under a revised set of Prison Rules issued in 1889, all men other than the warden, the chief of guards, priests, and doctors were formally banned from entering the women's section of a prison (Arts. 10, 15).

British influence was also evident in early Meiji guidelines governing the internal discipline of troublesome prisoners: just as in Britain, women inmates could be placed in a dark isolation cell for periods of up to a week, but unlike men they could not be subjected to leg irons or chains.[22] The notion that these kinds of physical restraint were inappropriate for women inmates also had implications for their work regimen. In general, the single biggest difference between Meiji prisons and the old Tokugawa jails was that convicts were now expected to work, and Ohara's 1872 Prison Rules laid out a system of five different stages of labor through which inmates were expected to progress over time. Men were expected to begin their sentences in "stage five," wearing heavy irons and performing backbreaking physical labor. As they graduated to higher "stages" they would be rewarded with less punishing forms of work and lighter irons, but it was not until they reached "stage one" that their final set of chains was removed. In contrast to this, women inmates were never required to wear chains, and "because their bodies are particularly weak" they were only expected to pass through the two final stages of labor.[23] Unfortunately little is known about the kinds of work that women inmates performed in the early decades of the Meiji period, but it is certainly worth noting that as early as 1881 a special textile factory for women prisoners had been established within the grounds of the Kajibashi prison in Tokyo.[24] This predates most of the private textile factories established in the Meiji period and suggests that female prisoners may well have formed part of the vanguard labor force in Japan's industrial revolution.

As Christine Marran has pointed out in her fascinating study of the figure of the "poison woman" in early Meiji literature, throughout this period Japan's reading public were regularly entertained by dramatic stories of wicked female criminals.[25] The best known of all of the so-called "poison women" (*dokufu*) was undoubtedly Takahashi Oden, who, in 1879, became the last person to be beheaded in Tokyo, but readers were kept enthralled long after her death by the stories of other criminal women such as the murderess Hanai Oume, who was sentenced to life in prison in 1887, and the infamous gang leader Suzuki Matsu, who was arrested in Asakusa in 1899. Occasionally there were also stories of dramatic escapes. In 1883, for example, a group of four women in the Tokushima prison managed to escape by tying their *fundoshi*-style underwear together and then using it as a rope to climb over the wall.[26]

In spite of the general public's fascination with the figure of the "poison woman," and the steady increase in female convict numbers in the 1880s and 1890s, Japan's male penologists and policy makers showed very little interest in issues relating to the treatment of women prisoners in this period. In 1894, for example, when Ogawa Shigejirō (1863–1924), the Home Ministry's resident expert on prison policy, published his massive one-thousand-page textbook on penology (*Kangokugaku*) it included a grand total of seven pages on women prisoners.[27] He briefly noted that it was difficult ("in reality almost impossible") to find women who were well suited to serve as guards and was otherwise content simply to state that many experts considered the "reform of women prisoners easier than men" and that the key was to "make use of their sharply developed emotions."[28]

In some ways, perhaps, the indifference of male officials to the question of women in prison is not so surprising. As Freedman and Zedner have pointed out, in both England and America concern about the situation of women inmates was sparked largely by the efforts of women reformers from elite or middle-class backgrounds.[29] By far the best known of the early women reformers was a wealthy English Quaker named Elizabeth Fry ("the more than female Howard"—after John Howard, England's most famous male prisoner reformer), who found her calling in 1813 after observing firsthand "the appalling conditions of 'riot, licentiousness, and filth' suffered by women in the female wards" of London's Newgate prison.[30] In addition to her own activities in prisons all over the British Isles she also played a key role in the establishment of the British Ladies' Society for the Reformation of Female Prisoners and wrote an influential book arguing that the prison regime for women should be fundamentally different from that which contemporary male reformers, such as Jeremy Bentham, prescribed for men: "Whereas Bentham's scheme advocated uniform treatment, formal direction, rigid adherence to rules, and no individual differentiation between prisoners, Fry went so far as to suggest that willing co-operation and cheerful submission to the rules by the women was a prerequisite to their reform."[31] In the latter half of the nineteenth century Fry's ideas and personal example provided the primary source of inspiration for the American women behind the establishment of the first reformatories for female offenders in New York, Massachusetts, and Indiana.[32]

In Japan there was never any equivalent attempt by middle-class women to become involved in prison work, but from around the turn of the century the accomplishments of Elizabeth Fry and others began to be discussed by prominent male figures such as the Protestant social reformer Tomeoka Kōsuke (1864–1934).[33] Tomeoka had established his reputation as an authority on penal affairs while serving as a prison chaplain in Hokkaidō in the early 1890s, and in 1899, when the Home Ministry opened a special school for training police officers and prison officials in Tokyo, he was given a teaching post there. The next year he published a collection of his lectures on the history of prison systems in the West, presumably for use as a textbook. Following a pattern common to most contemporary Western accounts, he devoted the first half of the book entirely to the life and achievements of John Howard, but his subsequent discussion of developments after Howard also included a detailed description of the activities of early English women reformers such as Sarah Martin and, of course, Fry—whose contributions, he suggested, were comparable to those of Howard himself.[34] This seems to have created some interest in Fry, for just a few months after the appearance of Tomeoka's book an article about her life was also published as a special preface to the influential *Prisons Association Journal* (*Kangoku kyōkai zasshi*).[35] Tomeoka was concerned with more than just providing hagiographies of important Western reformers, however. His book also included descriptions of a number of "model" prisons from around the world, and he pointed out that it was the United States, particularly

Massachusetts and Indiana, which had now taken the lead with regard to the creation of specialist prisons for women. He wrote that he himself had been duly impressed by the Massachusetts women's prison when he inspected it on his travels in America, and was later assured by experts that there was no finer institution of its kind to be found anywhere in Europe.[36]

Home Ministry bureaucrats were, of course, always keen to learn from the latest trends and developments in the West, and in July 1903, Japan opened a specialist women's prison of its own at Hachiōji on the outskirts of Tokyo. In the years that followed, Tochigi (1906) and Yonezawa (1907) prisons were also designated as special women's facilities, and new areas for women were created within existing prisons in Yokohama (1904) and Osaka (Horikawa) (1906). Tomeoka's glowing description of the work of Elizabeth Fry and others may have been one factor in prompting these changes, but there was clearly more to it than this alone. As Carol Gluck pointed out some two decades ago, the period immediately following the first Sino-Japanese War of 1894–1895 was one in which members of the Japanese bureaucracy and elite began to discover a range of new "social problems" that plagued the nation.[37] More specifically, this was a time when concerns about poverty, juvenile delinquency, and the overall health and well-being of "the race" began being acted upon with a new sense of urgency. Predictably enough, the same kinds of concern also turn out to have been central factors in the push to create new facilities for women prisoners.

Women Prisoners as "Social Problem"

In September 1903, just a few months after the opening of the new women's prison at Hachiōji, the *Prisons Association Journal* published its first full-length article about "the treatment of women prisoners."[38] The author, Innami Otokichi (n.d.), was a regular contributor to the journal, well versed in various aspects of Western social policy, including the new field of eugenics.[39] From as early as 1898, in fact, he had begun publishing translations of work by Havelock Ellis, the English author whose 1890 book, *The Criminal,* helped popularize Cesare Lombroso's theories of "criminal anthropology" in both Britain and the United States.[40] Not surprisingly then, his views on women prisoners also clearly suggest a familiarity with the latest eugenicist theories. He began his article by emphasizing the great gulf that separated the "fallen women" in prison from the "good women" in mainstream society, which was even greater than the divide separating men and women. Not only were these "fallen women" rough and uneducated, most had defiled their own virtue by pursuing illicit sexual relations with men, and, in the worst cases, had lost all fear of authority in the process. Such women, he suggested, had generally been raised in terrible conditions on the very bottom rungs of the social ladder and could, in effect, be thought of as "natural born criminals." If there was to be any hope of reforming them, he argued, they would have to be forced to submit to the strictest regime of discipline and made to recognize the futility of resisting the power of the state. They would also have to be put to work, so that they could come to understand "the sanctity of labor," and they would need to be given education and training in order to correct their irrational and unreasonable ways. Finally, as women, they would have to be shown the meaning of love—not the kind of "perverted love" that so many of them had pursued in the past, but rather the true, pure love that could only come from religion and god (presumably the Christian god).

Yet, if the task of reforming these "natural born criminals" was really so difficult, why should the government bother to devote precious resources to it? Innami's answer to this question comes toward the end of the article when he writes, "Truly, women prisoners are the future mothers of our country." Cross-referencing the new discourse on juvenile delinquency that David Ambaras' work has done so much to illuminate, Innami agreed that it was, of course, important to find ways to reform child offenders. He also insisted, however, that unless steps were taken to correct the failings of the women who gave birth to these children it would not be possible to destroy the root cause of crime.[41] The "criminal classes" would simply continue to reproduce themselves. In the end, therefore, Innami's view was that the primary role of a women's prison should be to prepare female prisoners for a life in the home, as "wise mothers and good wives." And he argued that both their work and their educational activities in prison should be tailored to this goal.

With the establishment of the Hachiōji prison, Japanese bureaucrats and reformers could do more than just write about the latest Western theories. They now had a laboratory in which to conduct their own studies of a population of "degenerate" women. Not surprisingly, then, about a year after Innami's article appeared, the *Prisons Association Journal* began publishing a series of articles describing conditions at Hachiōji and documenting the situation of its inmates.[42] The author of the articles, writing under the pseudonym Hachi-jo-sei (perhaps for Hachiōji joshū kenkyūsei—"student of the Hachiōji women prisoners"?), clearly shared many of Innami's basic ideas, but presented a somewhat less ambitious agenda. Doubting that it would be possible to ever properly transform the prisoners into "wise mothers and good wives," he suggested the main goal should simply be to prevent them from "spreading their poison through society."[43]

One key for success in this regard, Hachi-jo-sei suggested, was to ensure that women prisoners were properly equipped with the basic skills needed to run a household or find work as maids after their release. To this end, he noted, the warden at Hachiōji had been quick to introduce night classes, in which prisoners were taught reading, writing, arithmetic (each one night a week), and, most important, sewing (three nights a week). Because of limited resources, the prison was only able to provide places for 32 of the 60 women who applied to attend these classes. Basic primary education was also provided for children in prison (according to the article, Hachiōji's inmate population of 150 women in the summer of 1904 included 4 girls, presumably under the age of twelve or thirteen, and another 15 minors under the age of twenty).

With regard to sewing, Hachi-jo-sei writes that only four or five of the inmates at the Hachiōji women's prison in 1904 were able to sew properly—a fact that he took as the clearest evidence of all that they had been raised in "imperfect homes." While the state of women's education in Japan was not good, he argued, sewing had long been one of the basic skills that every woman needed to learn. For this reason he was convinced that the inability to sew would be a far greater source of embarrassment for a woman than the inability to read or write. Yet, to his surprise, he had learned that sewing was by far the least popular of the lessons taught in the prison.[44] Several years later, singing was also added to the curriculum because, as the resident teacher at the prison explained in a separate article, it helped provide moral fortification against a life of boredom and drudgery and was a useful skill for those who were likely to work as *komori* nursemaids after their release.[45]

Clearly then, the project of the women's prison was, in large part, about class. It was an attempt to impose at least a smattering of middle-class respectability on the poorest segments of society. In this regard, it is hardly surprising that in his discussion of the women who had been imprisoned at Hachiōji for theft (40 out of 150 in July 1904), Hachi-jo-sei emphasized the fact that most of them came from the dreaded slums of Tokyo's Shitaya district: "Ah!," he wrote, "Mannenchō in Shitaya is a nest of paupers and a nest of criminals. The majority of Tokyo's female shop-lifters and other petty thieves are drawn from the ranks of those living in Mannenchō" and a few other famous slums.[46]

In addition to the issue of class, Hachi-jo-sei's careful analysis of the crimes of inmates at Hachiōji is interesting for other reasons. He found, for example, that although only one of 150 inmates had been imprisoned for having an abortion, 18 of the 25 women who were in prison at Hachiōji for murder had killed their own babies soon after giving birth. Rather than simply condemn these women, Hachi-jo-sei, who never uses the phrase "fallen woman," instead emphasized the unfortunate circumstances that had led them to their crimes—portraying them as victims of a combination of illicit sexuality, "imperfect homes," and a lack of parental supervision. "While these women must be hated [for their crimes]," he summed up, "surely they must also be pitied." This was a theme that Hachi-jo-sei also developed in his discussion of arson, which turned out to be the most common of all the crimes committed by women inmates at Hachiōji. It was, in fact, even more common than theft—accounting for an astounding 42 inmates out of 150. In explaining this, Hachi-jo-sei argued that whereas a man might grab a sword or just hit someone in a moment of rage, arson was an easy way for women, whose bodies were smaller and weaker than men, to express their anger and exact revenge on those around them. It was, in other words, a classic "weapon of the weak," but in the end, because the potential damage caused by a fire was so great, women who committed arson in an act of momentary rage were inevitably punished more severely than men who, in similar situations, tended to commit less serious crimes. In this regard too, he suggested, the inmates at Hachiōji were truly piteous and unfortunate women.

In the end, there is no easy way to gauge how representative the writings of Innami and Hachi-jo-sei were of the broader views of prison officials and bureaucrats in the early twentieth century. Nor is it possible at this point to judge how representative the inmates at Hachiōji were of the total population of female prisoners nationwide. What is clear, however, is that in the decades immediately following the establishment of the Hachiōji prison that population was to undergo some dramatic changes.

The Great Decarceration of Taishō/Shōwa Japan

In general terms, we are used to thinking of the early decades of the twentieth century as a time when Japanese society was increasingly haunted by the specter of the *modan gaaru,* rampant sexuality, and gender ambivalence.[47] Given this, we might well have expected to find that the number of women in prison continued to rise steadily in this period. In fact, the opposite was true. With the exception of one sharp jump after the introduction of a new criminal code in 1908 (from around 2,500 in 1908 to some 3,750 in 1909) the population of female convicts declined steadily—and in the years immediately following World War I, dramatically. At the end of 1918 Japan had a total of 1,964 female convicts, which was the equivalent of roughly 3.7 percent of the overall convict population. By 1926 there were only 786 women convicts nationwide, or just under 2 percent of the total. Given this change, it is perhaps not surprising that in the middle of the 1920s the Home Ministry decided to convert the Hachiōji women's prison into a boys' reformatory—a move that is suggestive of both the considerable overlap in ideas about the proper treatment of women offenders and male juvenile delinquents, and the ongoing sense of urgency with which the latter group were viewed.[48] Even after the abandonment of the experiment at Hachiōji there were still a number of prisons with special facilities for women inmates. At the end of 1924 the Home Ministry gave primary responsibility for the incarceration of female convicts to five institutions, the most important of which were at Tochigi in Kantō, and Miyazu in Kansai.[49] Arrangements for the women at these institutions remained somewhat makeshift in nature, however, and it was not until 1932 that a new, purpose-built prison for women was completed in Wakayama.[50] Just a few months earlier, at the end of 1931, the total population of female convicts nationwide fell to an all-time low of only 582, which was less than 1.4 percent of the total convict population. Over the course of the 1930s, numbers began to rise again, but they did so very slowly, and judging from the available national statistics, it was not until the end of the 1970s that Japan's prison system again held a total of more than 1,000 female convicts. It was, moreover, only in the 1990s that the number of women convicts began to approach 5 percent of the total convict population—a figure that had been typical for the period between 1880 and 1910.

As noted at the beginning of this chapter, the dramatic drop in the number of women in prison in twentieth-century Japan clearly provides us with another reason to be cautious about equating "modernity" with incarceration in any simple, linear way. In this regard, it is also worth noting that although the drop in numbers experienced in Japan was particularly sharp, it was by no means unique. In her survey of the history of women's prisons in the West, Zedner notes that "the most important change in women's prisons in the first half of the twentieth century was the staggering decline in their populations. In Britain, for example, more than 33,000 convicted women had been imprisoned in 1913; by 1921, this number had fallen to 11,000, and by the 1960s, to less than 2,000."[51] Zedner posits two main reasons for this change: the steady "medicalization" of ideas about the causes and treatment of female crime in the twentieth century and, more generally, a "declining faith in the value of imprisonment" for women.

Without further investigation it is not possible to confirm whether these factors were as important in Japan as they were in Britain, France, and the United States, but a quick perusal of the articles about women and crime that appeared in the *Prisons Association Journal* in the 1910s, '20s, and '30s certainly suggests that they may have been. From the earlier discussion of Hachi-jo-sei's descriptions of the women inmates at Hachiōji we have seen that already in 1904 there was a tendency to see female criminals as victims of circumstance who were not fully responsible for their actions. This theme was clearly also taken up in later articles with titles such as "The ability of females to bear criminal responsibility" (1915), "Should the sexual functions of women be seen as motives for crime?" (1915), "On the reformability of female criminals" (1917), and "On the relationship between female crimes and menstruation/pregnancy" (1913). These are clearly suggestive of the same kind of medicalization of female crime that Zedner has detected elsewhere. That Sawada Junjirō, a noted sexologist, contributed a series of five essays on "Female crime" in 1915, is also striking.[52] There were also essays on the "Psychology of female crime" (1917) by Kojima Saburō, and a number of more general reports regarding "research on female prisoners." Clearly then, declining numbers did not mean a lack of interest in the question of women prisoners among bureaucrats and social reformers, and a thorough investigation of these texts should reveal a great deal, not only about the reasons for the dramatic decline in inmate numbers, but also more generally about conceptions of femininity, gender, class, and crime in the prewar period.

Notes

1. The key "revisionist" studies of the 1970s were David J. Rothman, *The Discovery of the Asylum: Social Order and Disorder in the New Republic* (Boston: Little, Brown and Co., 1971); Michel Foucault, *Discipline and Punish: The Birth of the Prison* (London: Peregrine Books, 1977); and Michael Ignatieff, *A Just Measure of Pain: The Penitentiary in the Industrial Revolution, 1750–1850* (London: Macmillan, 1978). More recent studies that have either focused specifically on women in prison or included a significant discussion of the punishment of women include Estelle B. Freedman, *Their Sisters' Keepers: Women's Prison Reform in America, 1830–1930* (Ann Arbor: University of Michigan Press, 1981); Patricia O'Brien, *The Promise of Punishment: Prisons in Nineteenth Century France* (Princeton, NJ: Princeton University Press, 1982); Nicole Hahn Rafter, *Partial Justice: Women, Prisons, and Social Control* (New Brunswick, NJ: Transaction Publishers, 1990); Lucia Zedner, *Women, Crime, and Custody in Victorian England* (Oxford: Clarendon Press, 1991). On black women in prisons and custodial institutions in the United States, see Cheryl D. Hicks, "'In Danger of Becoming Morally Depraved': Single Black Women, Working-Class Black Families, and New York State's Wayward Minor Laws, 1917–1928," *University of Pennsylvania Law Review* 151, no. 6 (June 2003): 2077–2121. For an attempt to develop an overarching theoretical framework for studying gender and punishment, see Adrian Howe, *Punish and Critique: Towards a Feminist Analysis of Penality* (London: Routledge, 1994). A useful overview of the literature on Britain, France, and the United States is also provided by Lucia Zedner, "Wayward Sisters: The Prison for Women," in *The Oxford History of the Prison,* ed. Norval Morris and David J. Rothman (New York: Oxford University Press, 1995), 329–361.

2. In addition to the brief, but valuable, accounts in his *Zukan Nihon no kangokushi* (Yūzankaku, 1985) and *Sekai no kangokushi* (Kashiwa Shobō, 2001), Shigematsu has also written a series of five articles about the development of women's prisons in postwar Japan. They appear under the title "Joshi keimusho rekibōki" in *Hōgaku seminaa* 254 (May 1976): 84–88; 255 (June 1976): 98–102; 256 (July 1976): 122–128; 257 (August 1976): 130–134, 258 (September 1976): 76–83. The usual tendency to neglect the situation of women has been illustrated recently by Kikuta Kōichi's otherwise useful study of Japanese prisons today, *Nihon no keimusho* (Iwanami Shinsho, 2002), which devotes little more than half a page to the question of women in prison.

3. As Nicole Hahn Rafter has noted in her critique of Rothman's work, an awareness of the special arrangements that have been made for the punishment of women can also highlight the way in which assumptions about *masculinity* have shaped modern penal systems. See Hahn Rafter, "Gender, Prisons, and Prison History," *Social Science History* 9, no. 3 (Summer 1985): 233–234; and *Partial Justice*, xii–xiii.

4. Sharon H. Nolte and Sally Ann Hastings, "The Meiji State's Policy Towards Women, 1890–1910," in *Recreating Japanese Women, 1600–1945*, ed. Gail Lee Bernstein (Berkeley: University of California Press, 1991), 157.

5. For Foucault's explanation of this concept, see his "Governmentality," in *The Foucault Effect: Studies in Governmentality*, ed. Graham Burchell, Colin Gordon, and Peter Miller (Chicago: University of Chicago Press, 1991), 87–104.

6. This article has not attempted to recover the voices of women prisoners, primarily because of the difficulty of finding appropriate sources. There are a small number of well-known prison diaries and memoirs written by Japanese women (most notably, Kishida Toshiko's "Goku no kidan" [1883], Fukuda Hideko's "Warawa no hanseigai" [1904], and Kaneko Fumiko's "Nani ga watakushi o kō saseta ka" [1926]). Given that these were written by "political criminals," there are questions about how representative they are of the experience of female prisoners more generally. Even more importantly, these "prison diaries" are not so much about life in prison as they are records of the events leading up to the imprisonment of the authors. For partial translations of prison writings by Fukuda, Kaneko, and Kanno Suga, see Mikiso Hane, *Reflections on the Way to the Gallows: Rebel Women in Prewar Japan* (Berkeley: University of California Press, 1993). For a full translation of Kaneko Fumiko, see Jean English, trans., *The Prison Memoirs of a Japanese Woman* (London: M. E. Sharpe, 1991).

7. Hiramatsu Yoshirō, "Bakumatsu-ki ni okeru hanzai to keibatsu no jittai—Edo Kodemmachō rōya kiroku ni yoru," *Kokka gakkai zasshi* 71, no. 3 (March 1957): 104 n. 6.

8. Hiramatsu Yoshirō, *Kinsei keiji soshō hō no kenkyū* (Sōbunsha, 1960), 973. On corporal punishment generally, see also Daniel V. Botsman, *Punishment and Power in the Making of Modern Japan* (Princeton, NJ: Princeton University Press, 2005), 27.

9. Hiramatsu, "Bakumatsu-ki ni okeru hanzai to keibatsu no jittai," 92–95.

10. Hitomi Tonomura, "Sexual Violence against Women: Legal and Extralegal Treatment in Premodern Warrior Societies," in *Women and*

Class in Japanese History, ed. Hitomi Tonomura, Anne Walthall, and Wakita Haruko (Ann Arbor: Center for Japanese Studies, University of Michigan, 1999), 146.

11. Ishii Ryōsuke, *Edo no keibatsu* (Chuō Kōronsha, 1964), 87–88.

12. On Tokugawa jails, see Botsman, *Punishment and Power*, 61–69.

13. Tsukada Takashi, *Mibunsei shakai to shimin shakai* (Kashiwa Shobō, 1992), 129–132; Miyachi Masatō, *Bakumatsu Ishin-ki no bunka to jōhō* (Meicho Kankōkai, 1994), 44.

14. Nawa Fumio, *Gōmon keibatsu shi* (Oyamakaku, 1987), 68–69. According to Lucia Zedner, in eighteenth-century England, "The governors of the London Bridewell . . . ran their prison as a highly profitable brothel by persuading their inmates to provide sexual services" ("Wayward Sisters," 329). I have found no comparable examples for Tokugawa Japan, and at Kodemmachō the bakufu authorities did take some steps to protect women prisoners against sexual exploitation by male guards. For example, all searches of female prisoners had to be conducted by women "helpers," who were appointed from the neighboring "outcast" (i.e., *hinin*) community. Of course, sexual exploitation could also come from within the inmate population. According to Nawa (who does not give his sources), during the Tempō reforms the women's room at Kodemmachō was ruled over by an inmate boss named Ōsakaya Hanatori, who had herself been an *oiran*, and who unleashed her "abnormal" (i.e., lesbian) sexual desires on the younger women who were imprisoned during Mizuno's crackdown.

15. "Ichigaya kangoku enkaku shi, Kodenmachō rōyashiki no zu," unpublished manuscript, Kyōsei kyōkai archives.

16. Kishida Toshiko, "Goku no kidan (1883)," in *Sabetsu no shosō*, ed. Hirota Masaki (Iwanami Shoten, 1990), 411. All prison statistics are from Naikaku tōkei kyoku, ed., *Nihon teikoku tōkei nenkan*, published annually by the Japansese government from 1882. Prison populations in the prewar period were given as recorded on December 31 of each year. They are not daily averages. The total number of people being held in prison (including suspects as well as convicts) in 1885 was even higher than this—reaching almost 80,000 people.

17. Zedner, *Women, Crime and Custody*, 317, 323 (tables 5 and 9).

18. In comparison with the situation in Western societies in the early nineteenth century this number still appears low: according to Zedner, in Britain in this period women made up about 20 percent of the overall prison population, in France about 14–20 percent, and in the United States "as little as 4–19% were women." Zedner, "Wayward Sisters," 331. From the

late nineteenth century, however, a figure of about 5 percent seems to have been more typical.

19. Kume Kunitake, ed., *Tokumei zenken taishi Beiō kairan jikki,* vol. 2 (Iwanami Shoten, 1978), 166–168. According to Kume's notes there were 196 female and 470 male inmates in the Manchester prison at the time of the visit. The men and women's prisons were in separate areas, but were linked by an underground tunnel. He also noted that all of the guards in the women's prison were female, and he seems to have been particularly impressed by a "matron" in her sixties who had been working at the prison for some thirty years.

20. For the full text of Ohara's 1872 Prison Rules, see Naikaku kiroku-kyoku, ed., *Hōki bunrui taizen,* vol. 57 (Hara shobō, 1980), 62–105.

21. Zedner, "Wayward Sisters," 336.

22. Shigematsu, *Sekai no kangokushi,* 248–249. For Britain, see Zedner, "Wayward Sisters," 350. According to Shigematsu, in the early Meiji period arguments and fights between women prisoners were the main reason for disciplinary action, but he also notes that there were a considerable number of "homosexual incidents" (*dōseiai jiken*), in which predatory women prison bosses reportedly preyed on their fellow inmates.

23. See the "Prison labor chart" (*chōekihyō*) provided in the 1872 Prison Rules.

24. Shigematsu Kazuyoshi, "Ninsoku yoseba to Ishiawajima kangoku," in *Ninsoku Yoseba shi,* ed. Ninsoku Yoseba Kenshōkai (Sōbunsha, 1974), 357.

25. Christine L. Marran, "'Poison Woman' Takahashi Oden and the Spectacle of Female Deviance in Early Meiji," *U.S.-Japan Women's Journal, English Supplement,* no. 9 (1995): 93–110. For a fuller treatment of the subject, see Christine L. Marran, *Poison Woman: Figuring Female Transgression in Modern Japanese Culture* (Minneapolis: University of Minnesota Press, 2007).

26. Shigematsu, *Sekai no kangokushi,* 249.

27. Ogawa Shigejirō, *Kangokugaku* (Keisatsu Kangoku Gakkai, 1894), 909–916. Prior to the publication of Ogawa's textbook there were a small number of articles relating to the women prisoners published in the *Dai Nihon kangoku kyōkai zasshi* (Great Japan Prisons' Association Journal), but these too were very short (one or two pages), and only one (by Yoshimoto Takejirō in July 1889) was actually about the proper treatment of women in prison. Unfortunately I have not been able to obtain a copy of this article.

28. Ogawa, *Kangokugaku,* 909–911. He also claimed that, because of their long hair, extra care should be taken to police the personal hygiene of

women convicts who were more likely than men to become a source of filth. Cf. *Kangoku kyōkai zasshi* 88 (M28.9): 6; 90 (M28.11): 65.

29. Freedman, *Their Sisters' Keepers*, 7–67; Zedner, *Women, Crime, and Custody*, 93–130.

30. Zedner, *Women, Crime, and Custody*, 118.

31. Ibid., 119–20.

32. Freedman, *Their Sisters' Keepers*, 22.

33. Elite women did become involved in other kinds of social reform movements. Kathleen S. Uno has discussed the role that such women played in the creation of Japan's first modern day care facilities in the early twentieth century. See her *Passages to Modernity: Motherhood, Childhood, and Social Reform in Early Twentieth-Century Japan* (Honolulu: University of Hawai'i Press, 1999). For a broad ranging discussion of women, social reform, and the state, see Sheldon Garon, *Molding Japanese Minds: The State in Everyday Life* (Princeton, NJ: Princeton University Press, 1997), 115–145.

34. Tomeoka Kōsuke, *Gokusei enkakushi* (Isomura Masatomi, 1900), 114–117.

35. Mongaikan, "Jogō Erizabesu Furai," *Kangoku kyōkai zasshi* 13, no. 5 (May 1900): i–iv.

36. Tomeoka, *Gokusei*, 122.

37. Carol Gluck, *Japan's Modern Myths* (Princeton, NJ: Princeton University Press, 1985), chs. 4, 5, 6. See also W. Dean Kinzley, "Japan's Discovery of Poverty: Changing Views of Poverty and Social Welfare in the Nineteenth Century," *Journal of Asian History* 22, no. 1 (1988): 1–24.

38. Innami Otokichi, "Joshū shogū ron," *Kangoku kyōkai zasshi* 16, no. 9 (September 1903): 16–25.

39. On the development of eugenics in Japan, see Sumiko Otsubo and James Bartholomew, "Eugenics in Japan: Some Ironies of Modernity, 1883–1945," *Science in Context* 11, nos. 3–4 (1998): 545–565; and Sumiko Otsubo, "Feminist Material Eugenics in Wartime Japan," *U.S.-Japan Women's Journal, English Supplement* no. 17 (1999): 39–76. See also Jennifer Robertson, "Blood Talks: Eugenic Modernity and the Creation of New Japanese," *History and Anthropology* 13, no. 3 (2002): 1–26.

40. For one example of Innami's early translations of Ellis, see "Hannin no shintai gokan no kankaku," *Dai Nihon kangoku kyōkai zasshi* 127 (December 1898), 9–18. On Ellis' role in the spread of "criminal anthropology," see Nicole Hahn Rafter, *Creating Born Criminals* (Urbana: University of Illinois Press, 1997), 115. As Sabine Frühstück has noted, Ellis was also an important figure in the early development of sexology. See Frühstück, *Colonizing*

Sex: Sexology and Social Control in Modern Japan (Berkeley: University of California Press, 2003), 82, 84–85. It is perhaps also worth noting that the first response to Lombroso's theories appeared in the Prisons Association Journal as early as 1892. See Ume Kenjirō, "Romburoso o yomu—zainin-sokubyōnin setsu o sessu," *Dai Nihon kangoku kyōkai zasshi* 45 (January 1892), 19–27; 46 (February 1892), 25–32.

41. David R. Ambaras, *Bad Youth: Juvenile Delinquency and the Politics of Everyday Life in Modern Japan* (Berkeley: University of California Press, 2006). Innami himself had published a series of articles on juvenile delinquency and prisons in 1901 under the title "Furyō shōnen ni kansuru kangoku mondai," *Kangoku kyōkai zasshi* 14, nos. 5–7 (1901).

42. The eight articles appeared between August 1904 and August 1905 under the title "Hachiōji jokan no kako oyobi genzai no jōkyō."

43. Hachi-jo-sei, "Hachiōji jokan no kako oyobi genzai no jōkyō," *Kangoku kyokai zasshi* 18, no. 8 (August 1905): 46.

44. *Kangoku kyōkai zasshi* 18, no. 4 (April 1905): 50. The women's active dislike for sewing was confirmed again in 1909 by the resident teacher, Chiba Takeno, in her article "Joshū no kyōiku ni tsuite," *Kangoku kyōkai zasshi* 22, no. 6 (July 1909): 27.

45. Chiba, "Joshū no kyōiku," 27. On the culture of singing among nursemaids in this period, see Mariko Asano Tamanoi, "Songs as Weapons: The Culture and History of Komori (Nursemaids) in Modern Japan," *Journal of Asian Studies* 50, no. 4 (November 1991): 793–817.

46. Hachi-jo-sei, "Hachiōji jokan no kako oyobi genzai no jōkyō," *Kangoku kyokai zasshi* 18, no. 3 (March 1905): 54. More generally, Hachi-jo-sei's discussion of the gangs of female shoplifters that operated out of Shitaya closely overlaps with that of other contemporary middle-class observers. See Ambaras, *Bad Youth*, 37–39.

47. There is now a considerable body of work on the rising tide of concern about these issues, but some of the most important studies include Donald Roden, "Taishō Culture and the Problem of Gender Ambivalence," in *Culture and Identity: Japanese Intellectuals during the Interwar Years*, ed. J. Thomas Rimer (Princeton, NJ: Princeton University Press, 1990), 37–55; Miriam Silverberg, "The Modern Girl as Militant," in *Recreating Japanese Women, 1600–1945*, ed. Gail Lee Bernstein (Berkeley: University of California Press, 1991), 239–266; Narita Ryūichi, "The Overflourishing of Sexuality in 1920s Japan," in *Gender and Japanese History*, vol. 1, *Religion and Customs, The Body and Sexuality*, ed. Wakita Haruko, Anne Bouchy, and Ueno Chizuko (Osaka: Osaka University Press, 1999), 345–371; Barbara Sato, *The*

New Japanese Woman: Modernity, Media, and Woman in Interwar Japan (Durham, NC: Duke University Press, 2003).

48. On male juvenile delinquents, see Ambaras, *Bad Youth,* esp. chap. 3.

49. The other three prisons given responsibility for women convicts at this time were Sanji (Hiroshima), Saga (Kyūshū), and Ōdōri (Sapporo) in Hokkaidō. Special reformatory areas for women were also established at the Miyagi and Nagoya prisons. Shigematsu, *Sekai no kangokushi,* 250.

50. Shigematsu, *Sekai no kangokushi,* 251.

51. Zedner, "Wayward Sisters," 359. These figures, it should be noted, cannot be compared directly to those given here for Japan, which are for the number of female convicts in prison at the end of each calendar year, not the number newly admitted over the course of the year.

52. On Sawada, see Früstück, *Colonizing Sex,* 103, 106.

CHAPTER 6

Burning Down the House

Gender and Jury in a Tokyo Courtroom, 1928

Darryl Flaherty

WHO WAS YAMAFUJI KANKO? This was the riddle that the daily papers presented to their readers on the occasion of the "Yamafuji Kanko Arson Trial" or "Kanko Jury Trial." Taken separately, attempted arson, female criminality, or the defendant's beauty did not win front-page coverage in the Tokyo *Asahi shinbun*. Yet in 1928 these factors, combined with the convening of the imperial capital's first jury, made Yamafuji Kanko, aged twenty-one, more than front-page news. Yamafuji Kanko's jury trial created a legal context in which male jurors, justices, procurators, attorneys, along with men and women in the general public measured and judged the feminine identity of a young woman before them. In the courtroom, the jurors addressed more than the question of guilt or innocence. They served as proxies for society by adjudicating the applicability to the defendant of the competing labels for women of the day such as the "new woman," the modern girl, along with gender norms for members of the new and old middle classes. During the trial, prosecution and defense crafted stories of a Yamafuji Kanko that sought resonance with jurors and echoed beyond the courtroom.

In addition to gender and legal judgment, economic and political issues were also at stake. Yamafuji was a sweets shop proprietor in an economic downturn when she appeared before judge, jurors, and the public on December 17, 1928. The trial was not only about Yamafuji. The proceedings also put the male jurors and the jury system itself on trial. In the process, it revealed some of the fissures of early Shōwa society along lines of wealth and class and between national government and local community. These questions had their gendered elements too. Yamafuji Kanko's alleged crime seized national attention because it wove together broad social concern about feminine identity with the political question of the capacity of the Japanese subject to serve as a juror. The trial and its coverage exposed the ironies of contemporaneous forms of female empowerment and powerlessness. The state prescribed women, particularly mothers, key positions as unequal partners in the project of cultivating loyal and able imperial subjects. In the meantime, male jurors who stood in for the public sought to apply the narrowing logic of a legal trial to the facts. Even while the law called on the jurors to weigh evidence impartially, the jury showed little sign of ignoring gender differences or expectations and other considerations of class and status in its deliberations.

In the end, for Yamafuji Kanko the trial was a struggle to escape conviction. And while proponents hoped that the jury room would become a site of rational deliberation in the interest of creating a reformed democratic subject, the first trial in Tokyo suggested that their hopes were in vain.

A Woman on Trial, Women on Trial

With the trial taking place in the context of social anxiety about femininity, expressed in discourses on the "new woman" and the "modern girl," Yamafuji's gender took center stage.[1] While a young, female defendant added an element of intrigue to an arson-for-insurance case, intense national interest exceeded that explained by gender and crime alone. Like other criminal proceedings that had captured national attention, the Yamafuji Kanko trial offered participants a chance to evaluate the state of society through the lens of a legal trial. It was this opportunity that drew men and women, young and old to the observers' gallery in the courtroom and to news articles in the daily papers. At the same time, lawyers and criminologists offered themselves as critical interpreters and explainers of the context of female criminality. On the subject of the fragile feminine psyche, Yamafuji's defense attorney claimed particular expertise.

Going into the trial, the facts revealed a narrative with multiple levels. At its most basic, the trial focused on the question of alleged arson. In July 1927, Yamafuji Kanko and her husband, Uichi, rented a two-story building inclusive of a sweets shop.[2] Yamafuji assumed the shop's debt of around 600 yen in lieu of rent. By March 1928, the debt had compounded to 900 yen. A fire broke out in the building on March 15.

On top of this the prosecution suggested that Yamafuji had set the fire herself to collect insurance. A few days previous, Yamafuji had secured renter's insurance for 8,000 yen: 3,000 yen of coverage from Imperial Fire Insurance and another 5,000 yen from the Chiyoda Fire Insurance Company. Everyone involved agreed that there had been a fire in the Yamafuji house, that Yamafuji's business had been in debt, and that Yamafuji had secured insurance. Yet Yamafuji's contradictory statements about that night confounded the certainty of these facts. She confessed and then recanted a confession. Yamafuji first told police that someone had set the fire "from outside."[3] Then in a subsequent statement she said that around 2 a.m. on March 15, she had soaked sheets of newspaper with a solvent to start a fire but then extinguished the flames as they spread. She later repudiated this statement claiming that it was the result of police pressure. Other questions and inconsistencies aided the defense on one side and the prosecution on the other. While the facts pointed to a motive for arson, what the defense identified as police excesses during the investigation and the reliance on Yamafuji's repudiated confession introduced further measures of ambiguity.

Compounding the tension between a charge of guilt and protestations of innocence, broader social interest in questions of female criminality and gender identity drove the proceedings into the ranks of other celebrated and infamous trials. In the words of contemporaries, Yamafuji's trial was "the object of all of Japan's anticipation." In this, it joined legal proceedings that had previously received national attention in the press for a different kind of politics, a politics of radical activism and direct political action. The Fukushima Incident Trial of 1884 saw the state charge male Jiyūtō party activists with attempted overthrow of the Meiji regime.[4] The trial in the Fukushima Incident received nearly daily coverage in newspapers such as the *Chōya shinbun* and was Japan's first national trial. Political trials with female defendants also received widespread media attention in the late nineteenth and early twentieth centuries. Kageyama Hideko received a three-year prison sentence for her involvement in the Osaka Incident, the 1885 plot to invade Korea.[5] In 1911, the trial of Kanno Suga resulted in execution for involvement in the High Treason Incident.[6] While Yamafuji had not attempted a coup, a foreign invasion, or an assassination, she appeared before a jury of men in a moment of gender upheaval. The jury trial created a legal venue for social interrogation of feminine identity more broadly, a venue that in December 1928 focused on the young, urban Yamafuji.

Who was this Yamafuji? Was she a paragon of the state orthodoxy of "good wife and wise mother"? Was she a new kind of politicized woman (*shin fujin*)? Or was she an irresponsible and irrepressible modern girl (*modan gaaru* or *moga*)? Was she on the vanguard of a new, education-oriented middle class or a remnant of the respectable but stagnant old bourgeoisie? The defense went to great pains to identify Yamafuji with conventional ideas of femininity grounded in Yamafuji's identity as a mother and filial daughter. Through testimony during the trial, it located her within an extended and supportive family. Her appearance indicated that she was not a modern girl. She wore her hair in a traditional coif, not in a short bob.[7] Yamafuji's self-presentation during the trial included no hint of the urban cafe hostess, not a whiff of a young woman in the thrall of the erotic, the grotesque, or the nonsensical. There was nothing overtly political in the defense's representation of Yamafuji. Her attorneys did not suggest that her long pretrial detention was a metaphor for female subordination. Nor did they identify her as an object of the systematic oppression of women. Yamafuji was no Kanno Suga—who in the Great Treason Trial planned to blow up the emperor for the sake of the nation while asserting that he "must be killed."[8] In the words of her lead attorney, Tsukasaki Naoyoshi, Yamafuji Kanko was "a female of refinement."[9]

Along with the competing feminine identities offered by the media at the time, the state promoted a vision of wives and mothers that was equally ubiquitous and of longer standing. It was a reductive vision promoting, as Kathleen Uno has described it, a "single-minded view of adult women as socializers of children [that] overrode alternative visions of women as direct participants in the world of paid labor and public affairs."[10] There was a tension between the state's narrow view of motherhood and the reality of women who raised children while also engaging in financially productive labor. Yamafuji was more than a "socializer of children" as were so many other women who balanced home responsibilities with work in a small store or on the farm. Yet Yamafuji's central position in the sweets shop was at odds with an increasingly idealized and constraining idea promoted by the state. This was a vision of women's work orbiting around childrearing, to the exclusion of external activities.

An unintended consequence of the state's designation of women as partners in cultivating imperial subjects was an extension of a degree of social power. Those who subscribed to state orthodoxy by supporting imperial ambitions, including groups such as the Patriotic Women's Association (Aikoku fujinkai), wielded social and, later, political leverage. Yet in supporting the state, they diminished the fluidity and freedom of constructing and occupying a range of identities. Calls for submission to an orthodox identity of "good wife and wise mother" contended with clearly heterodox identities including the modern girl and more ambiguous positions on the margins of old and new middle-class respectability. With women so central to the construction and extension of Japan's male-dominated imperial modernity, wholesale and widespread rejection of the orthodoxy constituted a challenge to the status quo.

By the end of the 1920s, anxieties about the threat of wayward women meant that an attempted female arsonist was as potentially alarming to society as an avowed bomb thrower. This stoked interest in the Yamafuji Kanko trial well beyond criminologists, lawyers, the media, politicians, and Ministry of Justice bureaucrats. On December 17, on its first day, potential observers representing all sectors of society defied a morning chill and pressed in on the bailiffs who managed the crowd. Those who won coveted seats included male and female high school students, businessmen in frock coats, and women with long hair, coiffed carefully atop their heads. One of the earliest arrivals was a "company man" who had boarded the first train to guarantee a seat in the gallery.[11] Proponents of juries hoping for political transformation would have been delighted to hear that for him the trial represented the "trend of democratization."[12] Yet he was in the minority. Most of those seeking a place in the gallery came to see great drama, "a theater."[13] When the bailiffs opened the doors "an avalanche descended on the courtroom with a throng of observers, male and female rushing in."[14] Spectators exceeded capacity by 6 a.m.[15] Legal drama had become mass spectacle.

Lawyers and criminologists offered themselves as social scientific interpreters of the proceedings, giving a decorous sheen to the voyeurism. At the same time, they heightened the sense of drama in the Yamafuji case by claiming that all young women teetered on the precipice of evil. Tsukasaki Naoyoshi, attorney for the defense, was a leading purveyor of this notion. Tsukasaki's criminological expertise rested on theories of female criminality then current worldwide. Tokyo Imperial University professor Terada Seiichi's 1916 work, *Women and Crime* (*Fujin to hanzai*), took a social approach to the question of female criminality that drew on the writing of late nineteenth-century Italian criminologist Cesare Lombroso.[16] Writing on feminine criminality in an essay published before the Yamafuji trial, Tsukasaki opined that women "committed crimes when they were right around twenty years old" because coming of age meant encounters with men, and such encounters were ripe for criminality.[17] Going further, Tsukasaki stated, "there are many criminals among the beauties."[18] He concluded that beautiful women sought to enhance their appearance with expensive cosmetics and the latest fashions, thus the poorer among them turned to shoplifting. Lombroso, like Tsukasaki, argued that female vanity led to criminality. If one succumbed to the temptations of vanity and became corrupted, then a woman "learned to walk in the shadows of society."[19] In the minds of these male observers, young women struggled to navigate the treacherous passage to married adulthood, imperiled by their vanity and facing potential corruption in mind and body by immoral men. Thus, popularity with men was "the first step toward criminality."[20] Media accounts stressed Yamafuji's beauty and trial testimony pointed to her indebtedness; by these accounts she was particularly susceptible to the temptations of crime.

In his writing on female criminality, Tsukasaki foregrounded a fatal combination of beauty and weakness. His essays on gender and law, along with the defense's strategy employed during Yamafuji's trial, enforced the idea of the woman as victim. Such thinking had a logic of its own. If women were consumers to be consumed, shoplifting cosmetics one moment and being seduced the next, defined in society by their appearance, they dropped from the realm of accountability. Theories of woman's lack of accountability, emotionalism, and subservient place in a patriarchal society served as the grounds on which the state denied women the vote, the right to organize, and the right to express controversial political ideas in print. Tsukasaki's own profession had long rejected the inclusion of women in the bar, only considering the license of women lawyers some years after the establishment of the jury in 1933. While the question of Yamafuji's identification with a particular gender identity was left to the jury to puzzle out, the trial closely tracked the predominant academic assumptions about female criminality. As the trial proceedings revealed, Tsukasaki exploited the ambiguities of contemporary theories on women. On one side, Tsukasaki suggested that her femininity reduced Yamafuji's accountability for her actions in the sphere of business. On the other side, he stressed that she fulfilled the obligations of good mother and filial daughter within the home.

Jurors on Trial, the Jury on Trial

After 1928, the presence of the jury as an arbiter of truth in criminal trials shifted the legal landscape. Proceedings before judge and jury had to attend to both the black letter of the law and the layperson's commonsense perspective.[21] Under the new Jury Law, three professional judges presided in the presence of twelve jurors who stood in for the (male) public. In Yamafuji's trial, ideas about women, a woman's place in society, and a female defendant's potential for criminality likely shaped they jury's consideration of the charge against Yamafuji. At the same time, the jurors themselves were on trial. As stand-ins for the general public, expectations about their performance were high, and the trial's initial days suggested that the jury might fall short. The state was present as an in-court observer, highlighting the various individual/state and local/national tensions that at times polarized Japanese subjects in the late 1920s. These included high-profile political issues such as universal manhood suffrage and the Peace Preservation Law and less familiar but important economic questions of the containment of proliferating department stores. In a fast-changing political and economic environment, proponents of the jury system had posited that the jury would embody new possibilities for Japanese democracy.[22] These hopes added to the excitement of Yamafuji's trial.

Despite hopes for democratic change in the form of popular participation in the judicial process, jurors represented only the narrowest slice of Japanese society. It fell on the exclusive, all-male body of the jury to serves as "the honorary representatives of the people."[23] Lawmakers justified limitations on the jury pool with claims that educated, older members of a community with means would be in a position to think rationally and independently. Those eligible included: (1) male subjects, aged thirty or older; (2) who had lived in the same city, town, or village for two years or more; (3) who had paid three yen or more in direct national taxes for two continuous years; and (4) who were functionally literate.[24] In addition to women, the law also excluded men who were deaf, mute, blind, or convicted and sentenced to six years or more in prison.[25] In other words, Japanese subjects with a stake in reform rather than radical change filled juries. Tellingly, local and national court administrators, working in tandem, identified those chosen to serve as jurors. Regional courts selected jurors by lot from a list prepared by local officials.

Well before the Tokyo Regional Court called candidates for jury duty in Yamafuji's trial, the state had been preparing jurors for their role in the new system.[26] To guarantee that potential jurors were well versed in the deliberative process, the Ministry of Justice delayed the institution of the jury system for five years from the time of the passage of the Jury Law in 1923. The interim period saw the construction not only of courtrooms but also spartan, dorm-style lodgings for jurors at the nation's seventy-one regional courts, moot court proceedings, orientation speeches and films, and the distribution of written materials to educate potential jurors about the system.[27] The Ministry of Justice sought to ensure that jurors would successfully serve as representatives of the public in the grand experiment of reforming the judiciary and democratizing the Japanese subject.

While the state may have had high hopes for how a jury trial would shape Japanese law and politics, those called on to serve responded with different ideas and a range of experiences. After five years of preparation, doubts remained about the capacity of the jurors themselves. Both the process of selection, which was random, and each juror's varied approach to service, interpreted in the media by their appearance, intensified speculation about the jury's ability to perform its assigned duty. On the first day of Yamafuji's trial, the jurors began to arrive around 8 a.m., after the observers but before the lawyers, prosecutors, and judges. Narrowing down the thirty-two candidates for jury duty to twelve jurors (and two alternates) took place behind closed doors. In camera, the judge drew name cards for each juror out of a box and allowed the prosecution and defense to make their challenges. When fourteen remained, the process was over. The court preserved an element of anonymity during the selection process, which was further strengthened by prohibitions on jurors discussing their participation in the trial. Yet the media "read" the clothing of the jurors as a guide to their feelings about service and their range of responses to being called to serve. One juror appeared in high collar and frock coat out of respect for the court as an august body. Another juror, embracing the description of juries as "the people's court," showed up as a *furoshiki*-bearing petty bourgeois.[28] The youngest in the assembled pool was thirty-three years old; the oldest, fifty-four.[29] All potential jurors arrived at the court with their own supply of canned food.[30] While they had prepared sustenance for their time in the jury box, the jury's readiness to be an active participant in the trial was an open question.

Eagerness to witness the jury's performance gripped the observers' gallery as jurors took their seats. When seated, the jurors took an oath of impartiality and fairness. The chief judge then spoke about the honor and privilege of serving in Tokyo's first jury trial and the obligation to deliberate with "sincerity."[31] The jurors listened on the edge of their seats. Throughout the trial, the jurors had the opportunity to question witnesses through the judge. Since the 1880s, Japan's criminal justice system had relied heavily on Continental European models, including the inquisitorial system of the French criminal justice process. As in a French courtroom, the judge questioned the witnesses nearly as much as the prosecution and defense. This allowance for questioning of witnesses during the trial also extended to the jurors. Yet the first day of the trial did not see any questions from the jury. On adjourning for the day, the judge chastised the jurors for not availing themselves of the opportunity to question the day's witnesses, including the defendant. The judge commented that he had only received one communication from a juror. The note read, "I have to go the toilet."[32]

As an experiment in the readiness of the Japanese subject to engage in this new participatory site of democratic self-governance, the trial would be a failure without the jury's full participation. Optimism and pessimism about juries hinged on the observer's reading of Japanese culture. Some analysts thought Japanese were better suited to jury duty than their European counterparts. Other analysts concluded the opposite. Even before his involvement in the Yamafuji Kanko trial, Tsukasaki Naoyoshi made favorable comparisons between the Japanese and French psyche in relation to participation in a jury. Critiquing the overly emotional French, Tsukasaki held high expectations for his fellow Japanese when they entered the jury box. He arrived at his conclusion from a reading of a Paris trial fourteen years previous. In March 1914, coverage of the case of Henriette Caillaux transfixed all of France. Caillaux, the wife of a finance minister who had killed one of her husband's critics, fainted repeatedly during her trial and her defense appealed to the all-male jury's sympathies.[33] This led to an acquittal that hinged on her emotional (in)stability at the time of the shooting. Coincidentally, well before he knew that he would become Yamafuji's attorney—but the same month that fire had threatened the Yamafuji residence—Tsukasaki had written that the Japanese mentality was well suited to jury deliberations. Commenting on the future of the jury in Japan as a former chair of the Tokyo Bar Association, Tsukasaki derided the jurors in the Caillaux trial. He wrote that in "foreign countries, there are many examples of the tendency for emotion to control the jury."[34] In the Caillaux case, he argued that the jury "forgot justice for emotion."[35] Of course, "juries in the Japanese empire will never engage in such shameful proceedings."[36] The examination of Tsukasaki's trial strategy below will reveal the irony of this claim.

Others believed that Japan's national character was too deferential for the jury system. The chief judge in the Yamafuji case, Toyomizu Dōun, shared these concerns, which were justified by the seeming passivity of the jurors during the first days of the trial. At the start of the second day, the chief judge was very solicitous of the jury. Before questioning he urged their fortitude in facing one more night of canned food because witness questioning would "take one more day of your labor."[37] Again, during this second day of witness testimony, the jurors were silent.[38] This did not mean that the jury was inactive, just not active in the manner prescribed. When questioning turned to key matters in the case, jurors leaned forward to better see and hear. They became animated and their eyes opened wide as testimony shifted in favor of or against the defendant. During emotional outbursts, they were visibly "moved."[39] This was after all, "a very touching arson case," as noted by the press.[40] On the third day of the trial, the jurors did ask questions of witnesses, particularly regarding a box of matches that the police had offered as evidence of arson.[41] While the jurors had taken some time to warm to their task, it appeared that their participation in the proceedings would not end in farce.

Ministry of Justice bureaucrats and other representatives of the state had great stakes in this Tokyo trial, a trial that had attracted so much attention. They made their presence known. From a special, separate entry government observers took places on a dais in front of and above the observers and the prosecution and defense.[42] They were joined by other officials in places of honor behind the panel of three judges.[43] Official observers included the past president of the Japan Lawyers' Association and current Minister of Justice Hara Yoshimichi, who had campaigned ardently for passage of a jury law.[44] He sat alongside Ohara Naoshi, a former procurator and longtime judicial bureaucrat known for his conservatism. In the process of instituting the jury system, its architects envisioned it as an incremental step toward general democratization. Former prime minister Hara Kei pushed the jury law with the belief that a jury should precede universal manhood suffrage and instruct the Japanese subject in the workings of the state.[45] Yet in the five years between the Diet's passage of the Jury Law in 1923 and its implementation in 1928, the Diet had passed universal manhood suffrage legislation. The jury system was a costly venture whose rationale had been bypassed by larger political trends. By their presence, Ministry of Justice officials pressured the presiding judge and jurors to perform; at the same time, they were expressing the state's hopes and fears about the jury. They provided both imprimatur and judgment of the proceedings. If the democratic subject did emerge, it would do so under the watchful eye of the state.

The hortatory and supervisory messages sent by the presence of officialdom at Yamafuji's trial echoed the 1925 laws that had passed since the jury system's establishment, the Peace Preservation Law and universal manhood suffrage. While the suffrage law gave the male population an opportunity to participate in politics in new and expansive ways, the Peace Preservation Law extended the power of the state to police those practices. In a sense, all three measures tied Japanese subjects closer to the affairs of the nation. Lawyer proponents of the jury system such as Usawa Fusaaki hoped that juries would effectively instruct Japanese subjects in state processes. The courts would benefit too. According to Usawa, the jury system would "introduce the will of the people into the judicial process and infuse the courts with new vigor."[46] While jury proponents celebrated expanding state involvement in its subjects' everyday affairs, others were less enthusiastic. In politics as well as economics, some parties at the local level, including the small shopkeepers—whose ranks yielded many jurors—resented the increasing omnipresence of the nation-state in their daily lives. They carried this resentment when they were called to sit on the jury.

In addition to questions of gender, local reactions to national economics and politics also informed jury trials. Accounts from jury trials of the late 1920s and early 1930s reveal that a measure of parochialism shaped how members of juries viewed their service to the state. Participants told of jurors tweaking the central authorities during jury trial proceedings.[47] In a trial in Fukuoka, a centrally appointed public procurator from Tokyo complained of how he had to "stick to the facts" when making his case while local defense attorneys "freely narrated the facts through symbols and allusions, and a number of defense attorneys would then continue the narrative, swaying the jurors."[48] Defense lawyers described how they included local lawyer-politicians on their defense teams in jury trials and allowed the local lawyer-politician to make closing arguments. The leader of a prosecution team felt that lawyers for the defense did more than simply appeal to the jurors with a more compelling narrative; they relied on personal ties as members of the same community. "Because many of the lawyers were local politicians or Diet members, the jury trial was also wrapped up in politics, and the [lawyer-politicians] moved the juror-voters with great effect by appealing to feelings of obligation."[49] Local political affinities confounded Ministry of Justice officials who imagined that juries would tie Japanese subjects to the nation-state through participation in the administration of justice.

National/local tensions were pronounced in Tokyo, where economic strain had brought conflict between large capital and its allies in the national government into conflict with smaller enterprises. The politics of retail stores influenced the work of juries in that many jurors were drawn from the ranks of small shopkeepers. Paralleling the contested nature of female gender identity in 1928, the identity of the local, small retailer was also under siege. Tokyo's first jury trial took place in a moment of antagonism toward the central government from the street, where proprietors of small and medium stores rioted against the intrusion of large, national businesses.[50] By the late 1920s, small retailers of urban shopping districts called on the Diet to pass laws akin to those passed or under consideration in Europe that would protect small retail against competition from department stores.[51] At least half of the jurors in the Yamafuji trial were owners of small or medium-sized businesses. The jury consisted of a pharmacist, a company employee, a vendor of art supplies, two equipment salesmen, a tailor, two men without occupation (presumably independently wealthy), two sellers of *konnyaku* (a gelatinous food made from a powdered tuber), and purveyors of soba, dried fish, and sake. And while Yamafuji Kanko was neither able to vote nor sit on a jury, she was a shopkeeper. While the outcome of the trial gave some indication of how their occupations may have shaped the sympathies and animosities of the jurors, their reticence during the trial and laws prohibiting discussion after the trial rendered the grounds for the jury's reasoning somewhat opaque. Even so, in society at large small shopkeepers resented large stores and their perceived ties to national politicians. The Yamafuji Kanko Trial cannot have been immune to national/local tensions along lines of economics or politics.

Critiques of creeping national power on the street may have provoked the juror's pique, but the jury courtroom did not unleash the power of the layperson. Rather, the prosecution and judges used procedures designed for their benefit to shape outcomes. During the Yamafuji proceeding, the judge gave the defense little quarter. Whenever the defense tried to suppress evidence or contest a line of questioning, the chief judge ruled in favor of the prosecution. The court's sympathies appeared allied with the prosecution against the defense. The judge's instructions to the jurors also echoed the appeals of the prosecution. If the outcome of the case according to the jurors was contrary to what the panel of judges expected, the judges could retry the case. Twenty-four cases that went before juries were retried by judge's order.[52] Of those, seventeen ended in a guilty verdict, six ended in innocent verdicts, and one was dismissed. The possibility of a retrial was one of two provisions that answered concerns about the constitutionality of the Jury Law. First, because the constitution only allowed judges to try a person "in the name of the emperor," jurors did not issue rulings on guilt or innocence. Juries only determined whether or not the defendant had committed the act outlined in the charges. However, when the jury did submit its findings, those were subject to the second provision designed to preserve the constitutionality of the Jury Law, that if a jury ruled in a manner inconsistent with the findings of the judges, then the trial could be held again. Even so, the national attention to the Yamafuji case and an interest on the part of the judges in ruling according to the findings of the jurors likely benefited Yamafuji.

Despite shortcomings and idiosyncrasies, contemporaries saw the jury system as a step toward greater democracy. In a February 1929 article on jury trials published in the journal *Kaizō,* Tsukasaki wrote that the Yamafuji trial had been "a step toward closing a curtain on infringements of human rights, such as coerced testimony."[53] In 1929, legal scholar Suehiro Izutarō wrote, "politicians . . . have produced the [jury] system to protect the interests of the people (*minshū*)."[54] If one equated "defense of human rights" with leniency, then the jury was an improvement over a judicial process that had yielded a high rate of convictions. The jury system only remained in effect for fifteen years, from 1928 to 1943. During that period, juries acquitted 17 percent of defendants.

The rate of acquittal in cases going before panels of judges was a little more than 1 percent.[55]

Telling Stories of Guilt and Innocence

In the Yamafuji case, each side presented a skewed narrative that measured Yamafuji Kanko against the image of an ideal (Japanese) woman on one side and the narrow question of the commission of arson on the other. The prosecution took a dual tack; it suggested that jurors should ignore Yamafuji's gender, but even as it did so, it put her feminine character on trial. It highlighted conflict in her marriage and potential extramarital affairs. In contrast, the defense unapologetically placed a very different vision of Yamafuji's gender front and center. Yamafuji's lawyers ensured that she was tried not as an adulterous, craven liar, but as a young mother, a devoted daughter, and a wife. Newspapers of the day played on the confluence of confection and beauty in Yamafuji, the proprietor of a small sweets shop.

Of the many kinds of cases that might have been heard before this first jury in the imperial capital, statistical probability favored an arson or murder trial.[56] By law, juries heard only criminal, not civil, matters. Nearly half of the 484 cases tried while the jury system was in effect from 1928 to 1943 were for arson (214). Another 215 were for murder with the remaining cases roughly distributed among trials for manslaughter, rape, assault, perjury, and counterfeiting.[57] Arson cases went before juries in disproportionate numbers because fire often destroyed evidence. Bringing one's case before a jury was entirely voluntary. The principle that trial by jury was a reform in the interest of the defendant meant that the defendant could opt out of a jury trial if she deemed it contrary to her interests; Article 24 of the Meiji Constitution guaranteed that judges would rule in criminal matters.[58]

In the Yamafuji Trial, fear of fire joined with fear of the female criminal. Among crimes committed by women, arson had its own, deeply gendered history. In cities built from wood, arson had an extensive lore grounded in its terrors. From the Meireki Fire of 1657 to the conflagration following the Great Kanto Earthquake of 1923, raging flames had repeatedly devastated the capital.[59] In this trial only five years after the great quake, memories of the flames were still fresh. Tsukasaki connected fire and gender in an essay titled "Characteristics and Motives of Feminine Criminality" in the following way: "Because women are physically weak . . . from times past arson has been a specialty for women; the burning of the green-market in Edo at the hand of greengrocer O-Shichi is a famous example."[60] As Daniel Botsman notes elsewhere in this volume, women convicted for arson outnumbered convicted thieves at Hachiōji prison, reflecting the harsh penalties for a crime that had the potential to inflict widespread destruction. In light of the punishment that would likely follow a conviction, Yamafuji elected to have her case heard before a jury.

The trial began with the bailiff shouting "all rise" to the appearance of the chief judge, Toyomizu, followed by an opening statement from the prosecution. When the prosecutor asserted that there was no doubt this was arson, "Kanko began to sob."[61] This was the defense, working to conjure a fragile defendant. Yamafuji dabbed her face with a handkerchief and muttered inaudibly. Here, the judge pressed her to speak up. She stated louder that the prosecution had it all wrong. The courtroom buzzed with excitement.[62] The chief judge continued, "was not your *fusuma* on fire?" Her voice again softened, "it was."[63] The jury strained to hear, and Toyomizu somewhat solicitously offered the jurors that testimony could be repeated, "if they could not make out what was said."[64] Gaining her composure, Yamafuji described the night of the fire:

> That night, with my child crying I opened my eyes to hear a crackling sound. Two or three times before in the neighborhood and in our own house there had been fires, so I quickly woke up my husband and we put it out. . . . One can only think that the fire was started by someone.[65]

The prosecution's case for guilt included the defendant's confession on the night of the fire, inconsistent testimony from the defendant in previous proceedings, and a powerful motive. Much of the state's case rested on statements that Yamafuji had made when she was held at a local police box.

Could she have known how things would turn out as she walked away from her once smoldering then soaking home? After she filed her report, the police came to investigate. As they headed upstairs, they saw a jug on top of a shelf on the first floor. When they returned from the second floor, the jug was no longer there. It had disappeared into a cupboard. Inside the jug was benzene, a solvent or a flammable accelerant, depending on one's point of view. The patrolmen escorted Yamafuji back to the police box and began questioning her. As she described it at the trial:

> A fat patrolman came in and took me to another room just as I was saying, "I don't know [what happened]." He said, "It will go poorly if you're stubborn. Everyone knows what's going on. Go ahead and tell us again what happened." Because I was worried about my child and my home, I told a groundless lie: "I did it," I said.[66]

Yamafuji had no legal representation during this first encounter with police. Nor were the police obliged to make legal representation available to her. With her child in mind, Yamafuji trusted the police in their promise that a confession would allow her to return home. Instead, the police booked her and held her indefinitely at the police station.

Initially, Yamafuji claimed that someone outside the house had started the fire; then she stated that she had started the fire. She shifted her response again when faced with questions during a preliminary inquiry, a closed proceeding during which the bench determined whether she would be indicted, still without the assistance of counsel.[67] Again, Yamafuji confessed to setting the fire. But when the judge pressed her on the details, she reversed herself and denied culpability, stating that she had been cowed into a confession by the police.[68] At a subsequent inquiry, she maintained her innocence. The multiple contradictory statements varied largely on the question of her husband's involvement. The preliminary inquiry accepted Yamafuji's protestations of innocence. A subsequent proceeding dismissed the case on the basis of insufficient evidence. Yet the prosecution, undaunted by the dismissal, appealed the ruling, and the Tokyo Court of Appeals found sufficient grounds to prosecute for arson before a jury.

On the second day of the trial, the prosecution's case focused on motive, showing why Yamafuji might have set her house and business on fire.[69] The first witness was an agent from Chiyoda Fire Insurance who had issued a policy to Kanko and her husband for 5,000 yen of coverage just before the incident on March 15. The prosecution's effort to show that Yamufuji had secured inflated coverage for her sweets business fell flat when, in response to the prosecutor's question of who had recommended the sum of 5,000 yen, the agent replied that the suggestion was his. The prosecution called a stream of persons who did business with Yamafuji to show that she was chronically in debt. "Gentleman after gentleman took the stand and recounted how around the time before the fire from month to month they had extended credit" to Yamafuji's enterprise.[70] Yet their testimony also yielded ambiguity. A sweets wholesaler who had "standing business with Yamafuji of about 200 yen each month" stated that a month or two before the fire he had extended goods to Yamafuji on credit. Yet he was unable to state an exact sum, and was reluctant to estimate, even when pressed by the judge.[71] Unwittingly, as the prosecution crafted its story of deceit, penury, and greed, it had also written a story that could be read as an account of victimization in which Yamafuji struggled against the elements, the authorities, and a dismal economy. The defense exploited these openings.

The defense focused on Yamafuji's desire to see her child as the reason for her initial confession and pointed to inconsistencies in the prosecution's case while introducing other inconsistencies that favored the defense. At the same time, the defense emphasized Yamafuji's filial qualities as wife and daughter and grounded her defense in her identity as a mother. At critical turning points during the trial, Yamafuji shouted for her child. The defense did not go so far as to physically bring her daughter, three-year-old Hatsue, to the courtroom. Nor did Hatsue appear prominently in the daily coverage of the trial or profiles of the defendant in the mainstream press. Nonetheless, Yamafuji-as-mother occupied center stage. With her child in the background, Yamafuji could fill the category "mother" without clouding the minds of the jurors with details of actual motherhood.

Her explanation for her false confession was her desire to see her child. In probing her confession, the chief judge asked Yamafuji, "why did you tell [the patrolman] you started the fire?"[72] Yamafuji answered, "The patrolman pressed me 'You probably started it to collect insurance money.' . . . I believed if I said I started the fire I would be allowed to go home."[73] Yamafuji's suggestion that the police pressured her was consistent with the experience of other defendants in state custody. Contemporaries argued that defendants faced systemic abuses. In a 1919 study arising from a case involving a prefectural governor, the national lawyers' association revealed that the criminally accused often experienced psychological manipulation and physical deprivation during police custody—even torture. The association found that the accused person who refused to cooperate with the police might end up in a narrow box as part of interrogation, denied food and water, or be told that the police would arrest family members.[74] While the record is unclear about the degree to which Yamafuji suffered such treatment, she was detained from the time that she appeared at the local precinct through her trial, 280 days in all.

While Yamafuji languished in pretrial detention, her attorneys prepared for her defense.[75] Their preparation yielded various questions and concerns. Although the police said the fire came from inside because the gate was locked, the gate was in fact open the night of the fire.[76] A spent match was found in the ashes. According to the police, this was the match that started the fire. Yet while the discovery of the match may have been dramatic, it raised its own questions. "When the patrolman arrived, the whole scene was drenched [with water], yet this match was dry."[77] One hope surrounding the establishment of juries was that public involvement in the judicial process would contribute to reform of the police. During the trial, the lawyers for the defense argued that "here again, one could see the police's usual practice of inventing [evidence]."[78] In addition to the various forensic elements of the case, the investigation and trial also revealed the existence of a lover from Yamafuji's past who even after her marriage "passed back and forth in front of her house."[79] Testimony at the trial suggested that a young man from the neighborhood, Shimizu Taizō, was an object of her affection. He had been called as a witness, but it was said that he was in hiding in the Kansai area with a pistol, "his whereabouts unknown."[80] The defense did not delve into this relationship.

Yamafuji Kanko's husband, Uichi, was called as a witness on the second day.[81] After opening with questions about his life and relationship to the defendant, the prosecution abruptly asked who first knew of the fire on that early morning of March 15.[82] Uichi answered, "the defendant and the maidservant."[83] Next to take the witness stand was Kanko's maidservant, Shiosawa Tomi. She too stated that she "knew [of the fire] when awoken by my master."[84] To all other questions, she was singularly unresponsive, answering "I forget" or "I don't know."[85] Then the prosecution produced a jug, asserting that the contents were used to start the fire. The maidservant stated that, at Yamafuji's request, she had purchased the jug and its contents the day before the fire. Asked how much liquid was in the bottle at the time of purchase she "repeated over and over that she could not remember."[86] At the time of the trial, there was a very small amount in the bottle. Lawyers for Yamafuji implied that the prosecution drained liquid from the bottle after the preliminary inquiry, when it had been fuller. This remained a point of contention.

Yamafuji explained that she had purchased solvent to clean a metal hair ornament that she had received from her mother-in-law. Her mother-in-law's testimony confirmed that she had in fact recently given Yamafuji such an ornament and Yamafuji had spoken of using benzene to clean it.[87] While this provided an explanation for the timing and purchase of an accelerant, why did Yamafuji hide the jug after the policeman went upstairs? Yamafuji said that anxiety from her initial encounter with the police caused her to put the jug away to allay suspicion. Lawyers for the defense argued that if the contents of the jug had been used to start the fire, Yamafuji would certainly have concealed it in the first place, not left it on the shelf. Placing the bottle in plain sight was like cutting someone down, and having "murdered them, leaving the blood-soaked sword on display."[88] The question of the contents of the jug continued to hang over the trial.

Finally Yamafuji's elderly father took the stand to vouch for his daughter's financial situation and her virtues as a daughter and as a mother, now persecuted by the state. A man of some means, he stated that even with the debt she had incurred, his daughter had no need to commit arson.[89] "There was never an instance in which Kanko spoke of being troubled by debts," he said in response to defense attorney questioning.[90] He then described, in a trembling voice, what happened after the police detained Yamafuji. "That night . . . my grandchild, and I . . . I held my crying grandchild all night" [ellipsis in the original].[91] Hearing this, Yamafuji "suddenly threw herself from her perch in the defendant's box onto the floor—all of her pent up suffering bursting forth."[92] In response to her cries of anguish, her father began wailing too. According to reports in the *Asahi shinbun,* the jurors, particularly the "*konnyaku* vendors and the soba vendor were clearly moved."[93] Others wrote of how the sobbing of the spectators echoed from the gallery and lawyers for the defense cried "silent tears."[94] The court adjourned for the day. Bailiffs forcibly removed the defendant, whose cries were punctuated with the plea: "Please let me see my child."[95] Her father again broke down in tears. The testimony of Yamafuji's father brought into stark relief the familial bonds that had been severed by the state. His testimony pointed to the poignant absence of Yamafuji in Hatsue's daily life and the hardship this caused.[96] Yamafuji's outburst was a demonstration worthy of Henriette Caillaux.

While the defense focused on Yamafuji's exemplary femininity, the prosecution sought a conviction based on a competing narrative of Yamafuji as a fallen woman. As part of its story, the prosecution equated the indebtedness of her shop with Yamafuji's profligacy. In doing so, the state failed to consider the multiple identities ascribable to Yamafuji at the time of the trial. In particular, the prosecution's description of Yamafuji paid insufficient heed to the larger economic and political context that made life difficult for Yamafuji and other small retailers. This was a startling oversight considering that nearly half of the occupants of the jury box were small-business owners themselves. Yamafuji was not simply mother-wife-daughter; she too was struggling in the strained economy of the late 1920s.[97] Despite this, the state rested much of its case against Yamafuji on a belief that its prescriptive view of women's work as socializers of children was conventional wisdom. Yamafuji's function as the proprietor of a sweets shop only entered the equation as an explanation for the fraudulent procuring of insurance. By arguing that indebtedness was another feature of Yamafuji's flawed femininity, the prosecution unwittingly scripted an alternative narrative in which Yamafuji was again an unwitting victim of forces beyond her control. Nearly two-thirds of the almost thirty witnesses that testified at her trial were businessmen with connections to Yamafuji's sweets shop. While these witnesses often testified that the shop owed them money, they confirmed Yamafuji's identity as a fellow small shopkeeper.

As the trial drew to a close, the prosecution and defense summed up their stories of Yamafuji Kanko and the fire on March 15, 1928. "As usual, the observers' gallery was full, persevering until this, the final day."[98] The prosecution painted Yamafuji as a common criminal. Newspaper headlines read, "Prosecution Pleads with Jurors—'Do Not Err Because She Is a Woman.'"[99] The lead procurator argued that the financial difficulties at the sweets shop, the defendant's character, and the purchase of insurance coverage all pointed to the commission of the crime by the defendant.[100] Throughout the trial, the prosecution had attacked Yamafuji's character. She was excitable, "throwing a tangerine box at her husband during a fight . . . tearing up letters [from her lover] that had been discovered."[101] Finally, the prosecution spoke about the defendant's gender:

> If the gentlemen of the jury were not here, and a panel of judges was, no one would think, 'perhaps she committed the crime but, because she is a woman then we should say she did not.' A crime is a crime. The facts are the facts. . . . There is sufficient evidence to show that this is the case. So definitely, without error, and particularly in accord with the high expectations for this, Tokyo's first jury trial, deliberate in an appropriate manner.[102]

Yet the prosecution's attempt to color jury perception of Yamafuji's character cut multiple ways. In a sense, the prosecution made the case that Yamafuji should be measured by her gender and that she was above all an emotional woman. The defense responded that the state had not answered the many questions raised by the evidence, highlighting all of the ambiguities in the state's case. Tsukasaki laid out eighteen elements that pointed to Yamafuji's innocence.[103]

After witness testimony and closing statements had concluded in the Yamafuji Kanko Jury Trial, the judge turned to the jurors and in his instructions in essence reiterated what the prosecutor had said. The jury was to deliberate on the question:

> Did the defendant, on March 15, 1928 at 2 a.m., with the intention of burning down the two-story, tile-roofed, wood house occupied by her husband Uichi and others, approach the paper of the sliding door adjacent to the kitchen—separating the same from her shop—with a newspaper soaked in benzene and then take a match to the newspaper?[104]

He recognized that the jurors had already heard this question discussed from many perspectives but stressed that "there is only one reality."[105]

The defense countered that a shopkeeper and mother of a three-year-old baby girl sat before the court. She was married. Her father was demonstrably supportive and involved in her life. Her mother-in-law testified on her behalf. The defense attorney Tsukasaki entertained multiple story lines of a young woman potentially victimized by others. Perhaps there was a spurned lover who tried to burn the house down. Perhaps the police, taken by her beauty, exploited her, promising her release. One might even ask why was Kanko, not Uichi, on the stand? Was her husband exploiting her? According to the defense, Yamafuji Kanko lived surrounded by forces of malice beyond her control. The defense suggested that, as a woman, she was not accountable beyond her actions as daughter, wife, and mother.

With their charge, the jurors retired to the deliberation room. As a first step, they elected a foreman from among themselves, the company employee. More than an hour later, the jurors returned to the courtroom. The jury foreman had paper in hand. He passed the finding to the judge, and the court reporter read out, "She did not do it."[106] All eyes turned toward the defendant, who "buried her face in her handkerchief."[107] As for the jurors, "having completed their momentous task," they were a picture of relief.[108] While weighing and measuring the actions of one woman, they had also heard arguments about the qualities of good Japanese women, women who were filial daughters and good mothers. Perhaps they were also celebrating fellow entrepreneurs and working wives. The judges disappeared into a separate room, appearing again moments later. Toyomizu called Yamafuji to the stand and stated that the court found her innocent. He thanked the jurors for their exertions and then the court adjourned. Due to an electrical outage, candles illuminated the courtroom. "With her profile bathed in the flame's glow, tears glistened in Kanko's eyes."[109]

Beyond its meanings in contemporary society and history, the Yamafuji Arson Trial was, for its defendant, a quest for acquittal. Reformers had hoped that the search for truth and justice in jury trials would create a new site for rational discourse about society and law, a place of democratic transformation. In the Yamafuji Kanko trial, and many other trials like it, the courtroom instead became a site for male Japanese subjects to affirm widely held social norms about appropriate behavior. For those defendants, male and female, who could craft a legal defense that resonated with jurors, early jury trials introduced an element of leniency into the justice system; this was a goal of some reformers. Yet rather than being a catalyst for a new kind of democratic society, the outcome in the Yamafuji Kanko trial turned on competing narratives of Yamafuji's personality, a woman's lack of accountability, and the erosion of the prosecution's case in the face of sympathy for the defendant and questions about evidence and motive. As for Yamafuji Kanko, aside from intermittent statements refuting earlier confessions and responses to queries from the judge, her voice was largely absent from the trial. She left it to her defense attorneys, her father, the insurance salesmen, numerous creditors, and other witnesses to define her. After closing arguments, the judge gave her a final opportunity to contribute to the competing narratives of identity that the male-dominated proceedings had brought forward. When asked if she had anything to add, Yamafuji "thought in earnest and after a while, from her quivering lips came the words: 'No, nothing at all.'"[110]

Notes

1. Barbara Sato provides an overview of the discourses on a range of feminine identities, including the new woman and the modern girl in *The New Japanese Woman: Modernity, Media, and Women in Interwar Japan* (Durham, NC: Duke University Press, 2003).

2. "Kono jiken no arasuji," *Asahi shinbun,* December 17, 1928, 1. See also Tsukasaki Naoyoshi, *Bengo sanjūnen* (Okakura Shobō, 1937), 172–175.

3. Ibid.

4. "Kono jiken no arasuji," *Asahi shinbun.*

5. On Kageyama (Fukuda) Hideko see Mikiso Hane, ed. and trans., *Reflections on the Way to the Gallows: Rebel Women in Prewar Japan* (Berkeley: University of California Press, 1988). See also Vera Mackie, *Creating Socialist Women in Japan: Gender, Labour, and Activism, 1900–1937* (Cambridge: Cambridge University Press, 1997).

6. See Hane, *Reflections on the Way to the Gallows;* and Helene Bowen-Raddeker, *Treacherous Women of Imperial Japan: Patriarchal Fictions, Patricidal Fantasies* (New York: Routledge, 1997).

7. During the trial, Yamafuji Kanko sported the *sokuhatsu* hairstyle. On the social meaning of hairstyles during the 1920s and 1930s, see Sato, *The New Japanese Woman,* 51–56.

8. Hane, *Reflections on the Way to the Gallows,* 56.

9. Tsukasaki Naoyoshi, "Kanko hōka jiken no baishin saiban," *Kaizō* 7 (February 1929): 49–53.

10. In the early 1920s, there was an increasingly reductive ideology of motherhood that focused on caregiving and cultivation of upwardly mobile children at the expense of a multiform feminine identity. See Kathleen S. Uno, "Womanhood, War, and Empire: Transmutations of 'Good Wife, Wise Mother' before 1931," in *Gendering Modern Japanese History,* ed. Barbara Molony and Kathleen Uno (Cambridge, MA: Harvard University Press, 2005), 508; and Mark Jones, *Children as Treasures: Childhood and the Middle Class in Early Twentieth Century Japan* (Cambridge, MA: Harvard University Asia Center, 2010).

11. "Hōtei o megutte, shobaishin no hi no zakkan," *Asahi shinbun,*

December 17, 1928, 1. The trial was covered in other daily papers. For a summary of the trial, see "Tantei teki kyōmi o sosoru, Tokyo no sho baishin," *Hōritsu shinbun,* December 30, 1928, 20–22.

12. "Kyō ha hōtei ni, igai! koi monogatari, Kanko baishin no mikkame, hikitsuzuite shōnin no jinmon," *Asahi shinbun,* December 20, 1928, 2.

13. Ibid.

14. "Mazu baishin kōsei de, senshutsu sareta jūnimei," *Asahi shinbun,* December 17, 1928, 1.

15. Tsukasaki, "Kanko hōka jiken no baishin saiban," 50.

16. Terada Seiichi, *Fujin to hanzai* (Dai Nihon Bunmei Kyōkai Jimusho, 1916) as cited in Janice Matsumura, "Unfaithful Wives and Dissolute Labourers: Moral Panic and the Mobilisation of Women into the Japanese Workforce, 1931–45," *Gender & History* 19, no. 1 (April 2007): 78–100.

17. Tsukasaki, *Bengo sanjūnen,* 185–186.

18. Ibid.

19. Ibid., 186.

20. Ibid.

21. For a history of the establishment of the jury system, see Mitani Taichirō, *Kindai Nihon no shihōken to seitō: baishinsei seiritsu no seijishi* (Hanawa Shobō, 1980). Osatake Takeki offers a history of the idea of the jury during the Meiji period in his *Meiji bunkashi toshite no Nihon baishinshi* (Hōkōdō Shoten, 1926). Lawyer proponents of the establishment of the jury penned books too. Hara Yoshimichi, Egi Makoto, and Hanai Takuzō edited *Baishin seido hōrikan* (Hiramatsu Ichizō, 1921).

22. On the jury system and hopes for democratization see, Darryl Flaherty, "Democratization, 1919, and Lawyer Advocacy for a Japanese Jury," *Journal of Japanese Studies* 37, no. 2 (Summer 2011): 257–287.

23. "Mazu baishin kōsei de," *Asahi shinbun.*

24. Maruta Takashi, *Baishin saiban o kangaeru: Hōtei ni miru Nichibei Bunka hikaku* (Chūō Kōronsha, 1990), 10–11.

25. In addition, the following could exercise a special exemption: (1) ministers of state; (2) Ministry of Justice officials and other national government officials; (3) military personnel; (4) postal and transport workers; (5) local government officials; (6) legal practitioners (such as lawyers and notaries); (7) monks and priests; (8) doctors and other medical personnel; and (9) students. Maruta, *Baishin saiban,* 10–11.

26. "Mazu baishin kōsei de," *Asahi shinbun.*

27. *Hōritsu shinbun,* September 3, 1923, cited by Maruta Takashi in *Baishin saiban o kangaeru,* 135. Anna Dobrovolskaia has translated into English

a guidebook written for jurors, "The Jury System in Pre-War Japan: An Annotated Translation of 'The Jury Guidebook' (*Baishin Tebiki*)," *Asian-Pacific Law & Policy Journal* 9, no. 2 (2008): 231–296.

28. Descriptions of the jurors appeared in Tsukasaki, "Kanko hōka jiken," 50; and "Mazu baishin kōsei de," *Asahi shinbun.* A *furoshiki* was a cloth traditionally used to wrap and carry objects.

29. Accounts of the ages of jury members varied. The *Asahi shinbun* in "Mazu baishin kōsei de" listed the oldest as fifty-four years of age. *Hōritsu shinbun* identified Satō Aizō as a sixty-five-year-old juror in "Tantei teki kyōmi," 20.

30. "Hōtei o megutte," *Asahi shinbun.*

31. Japan's first jury trials held after the Jury Law went into effect in October 1928 took place in regional courts at Ōita and Mito. Tsukasaki, *Bengo sanjūnen,* 95; "Mazu baishin kōsei de," *Asahi shinbun.*

32. "Baishinin ichigo mo hasshi sezu, kōhan daiichini ha owaru, hikoku no otto o hajime sō hito chikaku no shōnin shirabe ni tada mokumoku," *Asahi shinbun,* December 18, 1928, 2.

33. Edward Berenson, *The Trial of Madame Caillaux* (Berkeley: University of California Press, 1992), 99–101.

34. Tsukasaki, *Bengo sanjūnen,* 92.

35. Ibid., 93.

36. Ibid., 94.

37. "Baishin no hōtei ni oyako nakidasu, Kanko jiken daifutsuka no gogo, baishinintachi mo horori," *Asahi shinbun,* December 19, 1928, evening edition, 2.

38. "Kyō ha hōtei ni, igai! koi monogatari," *Asahi shinbun.*

39. "Baishin no hōtei ni oyako nakidasu," *Asahi shinbun.*

40. "Kono jiken no arasuji," *Asahi shinbun.*

41. "Tantei teki kyōmi," *Hōritsu shinbun,* 22.

42. Ibid.

43. "Mazu baishin kōsei de," *Asahi shinbun.* In preparation for Japan's jury trials, Toyomizu Dōun had observed criminal juries in England, contributing to the Ministry of Justice's report: Shihōshō, ed., *Baishin seido kansatsu hōkoku shoshū* (Shihōshō Saijin Kanbō Chōsaka, 1926).

44. For Hara on the jury system, see Hara Yoshimichi et al., *Baishin seido hōrikan.*

45. Hanai Takuzō, "Shiryō: Meiji shonen ni okeru sanza seido," *Hōgaku shinpō* 33, no. 7 (1923): 125.

46. Usawa Fusaaki, "Baishin hō to sengakusha," in *Kaigyō nijūnen kinenronbunshū,* ed. Amano Kōichi (Dōrōsha Kappanjo, 1923), 104.

47. Urabe Mamoru, *Wagakuni ni okeru baishin saiban no kenkyū—keikendan ni yoru jittai chōsa o chūshin toshite* (Shihō kenshūjo, 1968).

48. Statement of Yamai Hiroshi, former prosecutor general of Fukuoka, in ibid., 62.

49. Ibid.

50. For a first-person recollection of the violence that small stores directed against department stores in their midst, see Mizutani Chōzaburō's statement in a Diet committee meeting in 1947 in which he reflected on his anti–large store activism as a Labor and Farmer Party member. *Shūgiin, Shōkō iinkai gijiroku,* no. 9, September 23, 1947.

51. The reference here is to national/local tensions in the retail sector. See for example, Suzuki Yasuaki, *Shōwa shoki no kourishō mondai: hyakkaten to chūshō shōten no kakuchiku* (Nihon Keizai Shinbunsha, 1980), 296–300.

52. Cases would be retried under different judges and different jurors. Shihōshō Keijikyoku, *Baishin seido no hanashi* (Shihōshō Keijikyoku, 1926), 20. This was an expensive proposition for the notoriously underfunded Ministry of Justice.

53. Tsukasaki, "Kanko hōka jiken," 53.

54. Suehiro Izutarō, "Yamamoto Senji-shi kyōshi jiken—hōritsuka no tachiba yori," *Kaizō* 11, no. 4 (April 1929): 146. In 1928, a right-wing extremist stabbed and killed Yamamoto Senji, a member of the Diet in the Labor and Farmer Party and a critic of the government's China policy.

55. Saeki Chihiro, *Baishin saiban no fukkatsu* (Dai-ichi Hōki Shuppan, 1996), 12–16.

56. Judges automatically convened juries in capital cases and cases where a life sentence was possible. Juries also convened in response to a defendant's request, where the sentence might exceed three years. Hayashi Raizaburō, *Nihon baishinhō gikai* (Chūō Daigaku, 1926).

57. Okahara Masao, "Baishin teishi ni kansuru hōritsu ni tsuite," *Hōsōkai zasshi* 21, no. 4 (1943): 18–19.

58. Both in cases where a jury would be convened automatically and cases where the defendant requested a jury trial, the defendant could later submit a request to withdraw and instead be tried before a panel of judges. Shihōshō keiji kyoku, *Baishin seido no hanashi,* 25.

59. William Kelly, "Incendiary Actions: Fire and Firefighting in the Shogun's Capital and the People's City," in *Edo and Paris: Urban Life and the*

State in the Early Modern Era, ed. James McClain, John Merriman, and Ugawa Kaoru (Ithaca, NY: Cornell University Press, 1994), 310–330.

60. Tsukasaki, *Bengo sanjūnen,* 187.

61. "Kaikō ichiban . . . jijitsu o hinin, mattaku chigaimasu to nakidashita hikoku," *Asahi shinbun,* December 17, 1928, 1.

62. Ibid.

63. Ibid.

64. Ibid.

65. Ibid.

66. Ibid.

67. In contrast to the Anglo-American system of grand juries for felony indictments, there was no grand jury in Japan. This was an element of reform that some jury proponents sought without success before the passage of the Jury Law in the Diet. Mitani, *Kindai Nihon no shihōken to seitō.*

68. "Kaikō ichiban," *Asahi shinbun.*

69. "Seikaku na jikan de, baishin kaitei, iyoiyo daifutsuka no shōnin shirabe, mondō goto ni baishinin kinchō," *Asahi shinbun,* December 19, 1928, 2.

70. Ibid.

71. Ibid.

72. Ibid.

73. Ibid.

74. Darryl Flaherty, "Organizing for Influence: Lawyers Associations and Japanese Politics, 1868—1945" (PhD diss., Columbia University, 2001); and [Nihon Bengoshi Kyōkai] Kyoto Jinken Mondai Tokubetsu Iinkai, "Kyoto jinken mondai ni kansuru tenmatsu hōkoku," *Nihon bengoshi kyōkai rokuji* 24, no. 249 (February 1919): 49–110.

75. Tsukasaki, *Bengo sanjūnen,* 175–176.

76. Ibid.

77. Ibid.

78. Ibid.

79. Ibid.

80. Accounts of the proceedings are unclear about the relationship between Shimizu Taizō and Yamafuji Kanko. "Kyō ha hōtei ni, igai! koi monogatari," *Asahi shinbun.*

81. "Baishinin ichigo mo hasshi sezu, kōhan daiichini ha owaru, hikoku no otto o hajime sō hito chikaku no shōnin shirabe ni tada mokumoku," *Asahi shinbun,* December 18, 1928, 2.

82. Ibid.

83. Ibid.

84. Ibid.

85. Ibid.

86. Ibid.

87. "Tantei teki kyōmi," *Hōritsu shinbun,* 21.

88. Tsukasaki, *Bengo sanjūnen,* 176.

89. Ibid., 174.

90. "Baishin no hōtei ni oyako nakidasu, Kanko jiken daifutsuka no gogo, baishinintachi mo horori," *Asahi shinbun,* December 19, 1928, evening edition, 2.

91. Ibid.

92. Ibid.

93. Ibid.

94. Tsukasaki, "Kanko hōka jiken," 50.

95. "Baishin no hōtei ni oya ko nakidasu," *Asahi shinbun.*

96. "Aiji o hishi to ureshi naki, muzai to natta Kanko, hahaoya to kazoku ni kakomarete," *Asahi shinbun,* December 22, 1928, 2.

97. On questions of gender and economics in the late 1920s, see Mark Metzler, "Woman's Place in Japan's Great Depression: Reflections on the Moral Economy of Deflation," *Journal of Japanese Studies* 30, no. 2 (Summer 2004): 315–352.

98. "Baishin no tōshin kyō ni enki, onna yue ni hyōketsu o ayamaru na to, kenji baishinin ni nozomu," *Asahi shinbun,* December 21, 1928, 3.

99. Ibid.

100. Ibid.

101. Tsukasaki, *Bengo sanjūnen,* 176.

102. "Baishin no tōshin kyō ni enki," *Asahi shinbun.*

103. Tsukasaki, "Kanko hōka jiken," 52.

104. Ibid.

105. "Baishin no tōshin kyō ni enki," *Asahi shinbun.*

106. "Tsui ni baishinin kara unmei no sai," *Asahi shinbun.* See also "Tantei teki kyōmi," *Hōritsu shinbun,* 22.

107. "Baishinin no tōshin de Kanko ni muzai hanketsu, chūmoku sareta Tokyo saisho no kōhan ni, kinchō shita saigo no hi," *Asahi shinbun,* December 22, 1928, 2.

108. Ibid.

109. Ibid.

110. "Baishin no tōshin kyō ni enki," *Asahi shinbun.*

PART III

Colonial Law and the Problem of the Family

CHAPTER 7

Sim-pua under the Colonial Gaze

Gender, "Old Customs," and the Law in Taiwan under Japanese Imperialism

Chen Chao-ju

CHINESE WOMEN CRIPPLED by bound feet. Indian widows committing suttee on their husbands' funeral pyres. Women's subordination has long been treated as a core element of Asian tradition and viewed as a sign of Asian backwardness. The representation of Asian women as victims bound by tradition is part of the ideological construction of Western superiority and Asian inferiority. So is the representation of Asian legal traditions as "lagging" or deficient. What legal historian Teemu Ruskola identifies as legal Orientalism—the ways in which "the Orient" as well as "the West" have been co-produced through the rhetoric of law—has informed Western knowledge of Asian law.[1] Indeed, backwardness demonstrated by women's oppression under uncivilized law marks Asia's existence under Western eyes.

Colonialism manifests its power in representations of the subordination of women and the uncivilized state of law in the colony, and Japanese colonialism in Asia was no exception. The Japanese Empire expressed its domination over the colony of Taiwan by systematically portraying Taiwan's legal tradition as underdeveloped and Taiwanese women as oppressed by backward customs, thereby justifying its civilizing mission. As a study of feminist legal history, this essay investigates the institution of *sim-pua*—a local custom of trading daughters—in order to explore the interplay of gender, customs, and the law in Taiwan under Japanese colonialism.[2] As a critique of the Orientalist paradigm of legal history, this study does not consider Western law to be a natural, necessary, or progressive model.[3] I analyze how Japanese colonial legal policy in Taiwan, in particular its treatment of "old customs," was informed by deliberations on the state of civilization, the meanings and applicability of modern law in the colony, and Japan's own experience of westernization. Colonial courts' treatment of resistance to the institution of *sim-pua* demonstrates that law served as a contested site that produced complex effects in shaping and reshaping gender.

The essay begins by explaining the meanings of *sim-pua* from a feminist perspective. It then discusses Japan's initial colonial policy of recognizing family law as local customary law and the gradual shifts in its treatment of *sim-pua,* exploring how the practice was understood and represented by Japanese legal authorities. It then examines the work of the newly established colonial courts, which on the one hand served as a site of contestation where the colonized could challenge gender inequality and on the other carried out a civilizing mission. Finally, I demonstrate the "partial agency" of *sim-pua* who fought for freedom and equality under the shadow of patriarchy, both inside and outside the law.

Adopted by Parents-in-Law and Married to a Brother

In Han-Taiwanese society, as in many other societies, children, as juniors under parental and senior authorities, sometimes became "human commodities" traded for the sake of their family, a practice that was especially pronounced among the poor.[4] Wealthy families in Taiwan usually possessed a few male and female servant-slaves. Unlike many other instances of enslavement, however, in Han-Taiwanese households slaves and masters usually belonged to the same ethnic group. There were a variety of ways in which children were traded, and male as well as female children were objects of this practice at the hands of their parents or others in positions of authority. The treatment of children was by no means gender-neutral, in that parents were much more likely to sacrifice female than male children for the family. That female children could be subordinated is an instance of what Elisabeth Croll terms "daughter discrimination," which she identifies as a prevalent phenomenon in Asia:

> Female autobiographies in Asia document in great detail the secondary position of daughters as temporary members or outsiders estranged from the permanence of the family line and future, their own sense of exclusion from family genealogies and from ritual and practical definitions of the family, and the repercus-

> sions this has for representations of daughters and their own self-perceptions and self-representation as lesser or secondary beings. . . . It is these temporary and continuing assertions of gender difference, divisions, and complementarity, which emphasize gendered divisions of labour that are also hierarchical and most assuredly contribute to the cognitive conception that daughters cannot substitute for sons.[5]

The historical investigation of local specificities in Taiwan shows that the trade in daughters was one mode of daughter discrimination. It usually took the form of adoption. One form of adopting daughters, which was rooted in south China but then transmitted by emigrants to major Chinese settlements including Taiwan, Hong Kong, and Singapore, was known as *sim-pua* or *iu-shin* (literally, "little daughter-in-law" or "adopted daughter-in-law") in the Hakka or Holo Taiwanese dialect or *tong-yang-xi* (literally, "daughter-in-law raised from childhood") in Mandarin Chinese.[6] Although generalizations about the institution risk oversimplification, these terms denote a practice in which parents give a girl to another family that raises her and marries her to their son after the boy and girl reach maturity.[7] The girl, called a *sim-pua,* usually arrives at the boy's household as an infant or a young child through the services of a female intermediary or marriage broker. She is then raised to be a future daughter-in-law, to secure the marriage of the boy and continue the family line. Monetary payments are often involved in this type of adoption.

Through this trade in daughters, families raised wives for their sons and sent their own daughters to the families of future husbands. If the adoptive family had no son, they could give the girl away in marriage, take in a husband for her, return her to her natal family, make her a female servant-slave (called *ca-bo-kan* in Taiwanese dialect), or sell her to the entertainment trade. It is difficult to draw strict distinctions among a *sim-pua* (as a future daughter-in-law), an adopted daughter, and a female servant-slave. The status of a *sim-pua* did not define her ultimate position; she could end up as a daughter-in-law, an adopted daughter who married out or took in a husband, a female servant-slave, or a woman sold into prostitution.[8]

Twentieth–century anthropologists have posited a number of reasons families might want or need to raise a son's future wife: to economize by saving costs on marriage and raising children, in response to an unbalanced sex ratio and an affluent market economy, as a defensive strategy on the part of women to promote domestic harmony and secure their future, or as a solution to the problems posed by the incest taboo and maternal sentiments.[9] But they were not the first to have noticed this exotic custom and provided explanations for it. By the late nineteenth century, the custom had already caught the eyes of Western missionaries and Japanese colonizers in their encounters with Taiwanese society, and their understandings and regulation of *sim-pua* were products of Orientalist thinking.

In the late nineteenth century, the practice of *sim-pua* prevailed in Taiwan, especially in the north.[10] Taiwan (then called the island of Formosa) was under the rule of the Qing Empire, whose official law was silent on the matter of *sim-pua* but lent some degree of legitimacy to the sale of daughters by tolerating it in the name of compassion for the poor, and whose customary law recognized the validity of *sim-pua* practice.[11] George Leslie MacKay, a medical doctor and the first missionary commissioned by the Canada Presbyterian Church to visit Northern Taiwan in 1871, noted in his 1895 ethnography of Taiwan:

> The most common method is for the parents to purchase a young girl and bring her up in their own home to be a wife for their son. This is much cheaper, as she earns more than she costs, and no gifts or money need be paid her parents at the marriage. In such a case the girl is called Sim-pu [*sim-pua*], and is regarded as one of the family, but too often is treated with great harshness and cruelty.[12]

Though addressing the topic in a universal way, MacKay's description of *sim-pua* includes an account of his personal encounters. His supportive wife, Tiu Chhang-Mia, also known as Minnie, had been an ill-treated *sim-pua,* whose adoptive grandmother was the first female Christian in northern Taiwan. Tiu Chhang-Mia's natal family had given her to a family that was abusive. Her husband-to-be died when she was twelve. Tiu began attending a church's Roman alphabet literacy class and a Bible study class; the church provided a certain amount of money to attract students, so she was able to make money for her adoptive family. MacKay baptized and married Tiu Chhang-Mia in 1878, with the consent of her adoptive grandparents and parents and her natal parents. An interracial marriage was rare in Taiwan at that time, and this union was part of MacKay's mission to convert and civilize the natives.

A year before he married Tiu Chhang-Mia, MacKay wrote to the Foreign Mission Committee in Canada expressing his sympathy for victimized Taiwanese women and his determination to marry a local woman instead of a Canadian woman in order to enhance his ability to convert the natives:

> I have determined, God willing, to take a Chinese lady to become my helpmeet, and labor for these perishing thousands. She is a young, devoted, earnest Christian who will, I believe, labor until death for the salvation of souls. My great motive in this is that I may be more instrumental in the salvation of souls. . . . Brother R. just sent me a note saying there are "charming ladies in Canada, one of which would come out as my helpmeet." I am not thinking about "charming ladies." I am thinking how I can do most for Jesus. This is a trying climate for foreign ladies. A foreign lady cannot live in the chapels in the country, and she cannot reach the women by living in the port.[13]

By marrying an abused *sim-pua,* MacKay learned to speak Taiwanese fluently. He went on to baptize hundreds of Taiwanese Christians and establish churches, schools, and a hospital that practiced Western biomedicine.[14] Tiu Chhang-Mia contributed significantly to the mission, especially with regard to women's education. Through marriage to a white man and active participation in the Christian rescue mission, she transformed herself from a victim into a rescuer.

Although MacKay's generalization that *sim-pua* was "the most common method" of Taiwanese marriage might seem an overstatement, postwar anthropologists Arthur P. Wolf and Huang Chieh-shan verified the prevalence of *sim-pua* marriages in the two districts known to MacKay by examining Japanese household registration records.[15] Although MacKay noted that some *sim-pua* were treated kindly and loved like daughters, he may have exaggerated the extent to which *sim-pua* generally were "treated with great harshness and cruelty."[16] Historical discourses have reproduced the picture of *sim-pua* as abused victims, and today the *sim-pua* still symbolizes a life of misery.

In 1895, when MacKay's ethnography *From Far Formosa* was published in Toronto, the Chinese Qing Empire, which had ruled Taiwan for more than two hundred years, signed the Treaty of Shimonoseki and conceded to Japan full sovereignty over several territories, including Taiwan, making it the first colony of the Japanese Empire.[17] Postwar studies based on Japanese household registration records show that *sim-pua* practices persisted. In some northern areas, 65 to 72 percent of all girls born between 1891 and 1920 became *sim-pua*.[18] Studies done by the Japanese in the 1930s also indicate that the practice of *sim-pua* continued.[19] The institution cut across class lines: affluent families were almost as likely as poor ones to give daughters as *sim-pua*.[20] But the frequency of *sim-pua* marriages was lower and the age of adoption higher in southern Taiwan than in northern Taiwan.[21] Significantly, the prevalence of completed *sim-pua* marriages declined in the late 1920s and the early 1930s.[22]

Arthur Wolf attributes the change under Japanese colonial rule to an interaction between two chains of causation: a universal response to early childhood association between boys and girls that inhibits sexual attraction, and the consequences of social and economic shifts that stemmed from the Japanese colonial government's initiatives that weakened parental authority and strengthened young men's ability to resist arranged marriages.[23] He argues that Japanese colonial rule empowered Taiwanese youth by promising them an independent life and by suggesting that young men could resist *sim-pua* marriages. In turn, parents increasingly avoided adopting *sim-pua* for their sons.

The role of law and the issue of gender equality are, however, left untreated in Wolf's analysis. How did the law relate to the shaping and the reshaping of *sim-pua* practices? How did the law determine a *sim-pua*'s legal status and subsequent treatment? What were the implications of the legal treatment of *sim-pua* for the dynamics of gender relationships? Did legal reform promote equality or further the subordination of women by empowering men but not women? When young men were economically and legally empowered to revolt against arranged *sim-pua* marriages, were young women empowered as well? How were changes in local customs under colonialism used to signify the success of the Japanese civilizing mission? To answer these questions, we must first inquire into family law and the legal status of Taiwanese customs under Japanese colonial rule.

Family Law as Customary Law

In 1895, when Taiwan became a colony of Japan, the Meiji state had begun its endeavor to catch up with the West and to expand Japan's sway in the region. Shortly after the turn of the twentieth century, the influential politician and commentator Takekoshi Yosaburō declared:

> Western Nations have long believed that on their shoulders alone rests the responsibility of colonizing the yet unopened portions of the globe, and extending to the inhabitants the benefits of civilization; but now we Japanese, rising from the ocean in the extreme Orient, wish as a nation to take part in this great and glorious work. Some people, however, are inclined to question whether we possess the ability requisite for this task. I felt that these would doubt no longer, could they but read the account of our success in Formosa.[24]

In other words, Japan's successful governance in Taiwan would prove that Japan was able to exercise colonial rule.

This task included the civilization of law, that is, the imposition of modern law by the Japanese. Indeed, as legal anthropologist Sally Engle Merry has pointed out, "modern law itself is a creation of colonialism, developed during an era of mercantilism and imperial expansion and shaped by these conditions. . . . And modern law . . . has come to define the 'civilized' society."[25] Japan's colonial legal policy in Taiwan exemplifies this view.

During the first few years of Japanese rule in Taiwan, officials were uncertain about what kind of colonial policy to adopt. After several years of deliberation, the fourth governor-general of Taiwan, Kodama Gentarō, and his civil administrator, Gotō Shinpei, established the guiding principle of differential governance that recognized and accommodated colonial particularities, a concept they had learned from British colonial experiences in India. This policy was to prevail until the 1920s. In the arena of law, Taiwan, as a *gaichi* (outer area), was subject to a special regime under which the majority of laws were tailored to the unique circumstances of the colony. Japanese mainland law did not apply to Taiwan unless there was a *shikō chokurei* (an ordinance authorizing the application of law). Moreover, the governor-general of Taiwan was given the power to decide the content of law in Taiwan, subject to a degree of supervision by the central government.[26]

Taiwan became a special legal zone of the Japanese Empire. In establishing the foundation for colonial policy and legislation, Gotō Shinpei adopted the idea of *kyūkan onzon* (respecting and adopting old customs). A German-trained physician, he developed and practiced the theory of "scientific colonialism" in Asia, advocating that Japan adhere to policies that were suited to the abilities and characteristics of the colonized.[27] This social Darwinist celebration of colonial particularities was more an accommodation of the colony's perceived backwardness than an appreciation of its uniqueness. In an interview with journalists from the *Tokyo Daily News* (*Tōkyō nichi nichi shinbun*), Gotō described the Taiwanese as "a mix of barbarians and civilized people" and refused to apply Japanese law to the Taiwanese, because Japanese law—difficult even for the progressive Japanese people—would be an impossibility for the more conservative Taiwanese.[28]

Under this policy, "Taiwanese old customs" were to be the law in civil matters involving only the Taiwanese (or Chinese), unless there were laws that provided otherwise.[29] As a result, only a small portion of the Meiji Civil Code—enacted in mainland Japan in 1898, three years after Japan had acquired Taiwan—and other Japanese civil statutes were applicable to the Taiwanese. In regard to family relations and succession, "old customs" still governed. From a legal perspective, the term "old customs" referred to the official written law and customary law that had functioned in Taiwan under the Qing Empire. Written laws regulating civil matters were relatively few, so local common law served as the major source of law.[30] Customary law was not the equivalent of prevailing customs, however; only those customs that were recognized by the courts and other competent authorities constituted customary law. The identification of the contents of old customs is a process not of discovering static facts but of constructing or, in E. J. Hobsbawm's words, "inventing" tradition.[31]

The Japanese colonizers comprehended and constructed Taiwan's old customs, including the institution of *sim-pua,* through scientific colonialism. Gotō Shinpei stressed the importance of investigation and research into customs on the island, aiming to acquire a deep scholarly understanding of Taiwanese society. The resulting knowledge would serve as the foundation of colonial laws and guide the court system in resolving civil disputes. To carry out this plan, the civil administrator recruited outstanding Japanese scholars and established official institutions to investigate customs and law in Taiwan. The Commission for the Investigation of Old Laws and Customs in Taiwan (Rinji Taiwan kyūkan chōsakai) was established in 1901 as the research arm of the colonial government, and a monthly journal, *Records of Taiwanese Cus-*

toms (*Taiwan kanshū kiji*) was published by the Association for the Study of Taiwanese Customs (*Taiwan kanshū kenkyūkai*).[32] The courts made use of knowledge produced by Western-educated Japanese legal scholars through a methodology that combined textual scholarship and fieldwork carried out with the assistance of local informants. Both the colonizers and the colonized constructed and contested the old customs. On occasion, the courts invoked the concepts of "public order and good morals" and "the principle of law" to invalidate certain Taiwanese customs. The colonized also applied these concepts to their litigation against the old customs.

Sim-pua as Adopted Daughter and Daughter-in-Law

The policy of treating family law as customary law endorsed the institution of *sim-pua*. What did it look like under the colonial gaze? This culture-specific institution could not easily fit into the framework of modern European legal concepts adopted by Japanese legal scholars. Continental European laws had drawn a strict distinction between adoption and marriage and had forbidden any marriage between siblings. Was a *sim-pua* an adopted daughter, a daughter-in-law, or a combination of the two? Japanese legal scholars and judges had difficulty categorizing *sim-pua* within Japan's newly Westernized legal system. Yet Japanese people could understand the institution and the ideas behind it, because in the Japanese practice of *mukoyōshi* (adopted son-in-law), an adopted son-in-law married into his wife's natal family, took her family name, and became his father-in-law's successor. The Meiji Civil Code recognized adopted son-in-law practices and defined them as a special kind of adoption.[33]

In a similar fashion, colonial knowledge tended to define *sim-pua* as a special form of adoption.[34] The *Provisional Report on Investigations of Laws and Customs in the Island of Formosa*, published in Japanese in 1901 and in English in 1902, was compiled by Okamatsu Santarō, a German-educated law professor at Kyoto Imperial University, a student of German legal anthropologist Joseph Kohler, and the director-in-chief of the commission. Li Shaw-han, a former Qing functionary, assisted Okamatsu. The chapter on adoption distinguishes between the adoptions of males and of females. The section on adopted daughters recognizes the complexity of the position of a *sim-pua*, including the different terms used to describe her:

> In Formosa, when one adopts another's daughter as his own, such daughter is called *iu-shin* or simply *shin-pu*. In this case, it is also usual to pay for her, and when she attains her proper age, the adopted parents either get her married to their own son or else secure a husband for her from outside. . . . Sometimes they give the adopted daughter to another in marriage, and they even go to the extent of reselling her to a third person. The object in adopting girls is not always the same. Some buy girls for the purpose of using them as maid servants, but this is different from *iu-shin,* for in that case they do not consider the girls as a human being, and consequently such a girl has no family name. The people call them *chobo-kan,* and those who are adopted as *shin-pu* are called *chabo-kian*. Both words have a distinct sound but there are no Chinese characters corresponding to them.[35]

The report distinguishes between *sim-pua* and female family servants by categorizing the latter as a kind of slavery. It defines the conditions for the adoption of daughters: the absence of a son or a daughter in the adopting family was not a requirement, and the adoption of several daughters was permitted.

Sim-pua is described as "a peculiar custom which arose in Formosa for the purpose of making money through re-sales when the girls were grown up, especially if they were good-looking," which required an agreement between the adopting parents and the natal parents but not the consent of the adopted daughter or her future husband.[36] The report states that before an adopted daughter was married to a son in her new family, her position was "just as if she were a true child of the family." It recognizes no kinship between the girl's natal family and her adoptive family before she marries the son; after the marriage, the two families are relatives by marriage. It stipulates, "if a girl is adopted, the real parents lose all right to exercise any power or control over her person, and only in case of cruel treatment on the part of the adopted parent can the real parent protest against such treatment or demand the dissolution of adoption."[37] It recognizes dissolution by arrangement or due to such serious factors such as a *sim-pua*'s disobedience to her adoptive parents, but identifies no laws specifying the legitimate causes of dissolution.[38] The *Provisional Report* characterizes the *sim-pua* as a daughter transferred from the hands of her natal parents to those of her adoptive parents; after marrying the son, she becomes a daughter-in-law.

Knowledge about *sim-pua* was advanced by the commission's report on Han-Taiwanese civil customs, a thirteen-volume text entitled *Taiwan shihō* (Taiwanese Private Law) published more than ten years later. In addition to the distinction between *sim-pua* and female family servants, *Taiwanese Private Law* draws a further distinction between *u thau-tui* (matched) *sim-pua* and *bou-thau-tui* (unmatched) *sim-pua*. "Matched" refers to the situation in which the adoptive family intends to marry the *sim-pua* to their son and has a son to match with her at the time of adoption. "Unmatched" refers to the situation in which the adoptive family lacks a son to match with the *sim-pua* at the time of adoption. Recognizing the indefinite nature of this distinction and the interchangeability of these statuses, *Taiwanese Private Law* identifies unmatched *sim-pua* as *iong-lu* (adopted daughters) and matched *sim-pua* as *iu-shin* (adopted daughters-in-law). It also describes various grounds for the dissolution of the adoption before marriage and treats dissolution after marriage as divorce.[39] Thus, the concept of adopted daughters was divided into three subcategories: female servant-slaves, matched adopted daughters-in-law, and unmatched adopted daughters.

Taiwanese Private Law, along with the commission's other voluminous reports, served as a major reference for the courts. In addition, the commission was charged with drafting a Taiwanese civil code. Like Gotō Shinpei, Okamatsu Santarō was also a proponent of legislation tailored to colonial specificities, but he approached the matter differently. After discussing the shortcomings of the Japanese civil code, he expressed the hope that Taiwan could serve as a laboratory for progressive legislation.[40] In his view, the experimental legislation in colonial Taiwan could become a model for Japan. The legitimation of old customs would also facilitate the successful governance of Taiwan, which would demonstrate Japan's capacity as a colonial ruler and earn respect from the West.

Consequently, *Taiwanese Private Law* served as the foundation, but not the only source, for a series of Taiwanese civil codes (*Taiwan minjirei*), including the Taiwanese Family and Succession Code (*Taiwan shinzoku sōzoku rei*). The commission produced three drafts of this code. The first, issued in 1911, had only six articles (Arts. 96–101) on *sim-pua* adoption and treated the adoption of *sim-pua* as a special form of marriage.[41] The second draft, issued in 1912, stipulated the conditions, effects, and permitted dissolution of *sim-pua* adoption in more detail (Arts. 112–141).[42] The third draft, issued in 1914, was no different in substance from the second as regards the institution.[43]

According to the second and third drafts, *sim-pua* was a combination of adoption and marriage. The legislators sought to narrow the scope of *sim-pua* and to impose restrictions on it in an attempt to "reform" local customs while codifying them. The later drafts excluded female family servants and unmatched *sim-pua* from the category of *sim-pua*. A *sim-pua* adoption automatically dissolved upon the completion of marriage, so that the young woman became a regular daughter-in-law. These drafts also set an age limit: it was illegal for families to adopt girls younger than fourteen as *sim-pua* (Art. 113). They grounded the establishment and dissolution of *sim-pua* adoption principally on an agreement between the fathers of each of the two families (Arts. 115, 132, 134), but entitled a *sim-pua* and her prospective husband to agree on dissolution after they reached adulthood (Art. 133) and to sue for dissolution on grounds similar to those of divorce, such as bigamy, adultery, intolerable mistreatment, or serious insult (Arts. 138–141).

This proposed legislation on *sim-pua* did more than preserve "old customs" through codification. It also had the mission of civilizing the natives, a goal that was to be accomplished in a moderate and gradual manner. By narrowing the scope of the *sim-pua*'s legal status, the proposed legislation indirectly functioned to "normalize" adoption and to make explicit the hitherto blurred distinction between adoption and marriage. What is more, the draft legislation empowered a matched *sim-pua* and her prospective husband to terminate their arranged engagement under certain conditions.

This legislation gave rise to serious confrontations among the Japanese officials and legal scholars on the review committee. Most condemned *sim-pua* as an "undesirable custom," voted against its codification, and advocated the abolition of "compulsory marriages." Nonetheless, Okamatsu Santarō successfully defended the proposed draft.[44] Objections were also raised by the Taiwan chapter of the Japanese Bar Association, which supported the implementation of Japanese law on the island. A letter from this organization condemned the institution of *sim-pua* as a form of human trafficking that denied independent personhood and free will to those subject to it and demanded its abolition.[45] It viewed the codification of the institution of *sim-pua* as tantamount to an endorsement of a backward custom and as an obstacle to modernity.

In the end, the proposed legislation failed to obtain approval from the central government. It is reasonable to conclude that the post-1910 shift in Japan's colonial policy from an accommodation of colonial particularity toward the promotion of *dōka* (assimilation) led to this failure; critics feared that a law unique to Taiwan would undermine its integration into the empire.[46] Still, this legislative project reveals how scientific colonialism operated in the field of law and how the formation of colonial knowledge positioned freedom and equality in contrast to local cultural particularities.

The Controversy over the Extension of the Meiji Civil Code to Taiwan

The codification of "old customs," as a policy product of differential governance, was conditioned on the assumption that the colonized Taiwanese should be treated differently from Japanese. In contrast, the idea of assimilation demanded that treatment of the colonized mirror that of the colonizers. As Leo Ching has explained, the assimilation policy was the colonial authority's attempt to "contain and pacify the growing demands for political autonomy by the indigenous intellectual elites," an attempt that, "with its emphasis on cultural integration, conceals the fundamental social and political inequality between the colonizer and the colonized."[47] In the arena of law, the assimilation policy would require that Japanese law be extended to the colony.[48] The central government revised fundamental colonial law in 1919 and began to apply most types of Japanese law to Taiwan.[49] An ordinance extending the Meiji Civil Code and several other Japanese civil statutes to Taiwan took effect in 1923, but the codes on family relations and succession were exempt.[50]

The decision to make the Meiji Civil Code applicable to Taiwanese was made deliberately after heated debate. The controversy over whether or not Japan should apply a Western-style civil code to Taiwan was rooted in the nation's own experience. During the Meiji era, the drafting and adoption of a new civil code, especially that governing family relations and succession, had been a matter of great concern. The debate centered on the presumed conflict between Japanese culture and modern Western law: should a Western-style civil code trump Japanese tradition, or should Japanese tradition give way to modern Western law? The fact that family relationships were at stake made the controversy particularly sharp. Hozumi Yatsuka, a leading conservative legal scholar at Tokyo Imperial University, leveled an influential attack against the proposed civil code and deplored the situation of *minpō idete, chūkō horobu* (an enacted civil code would spell doom for loyalty and for filial piety).[51] Yet, as Ueno Chizuko has persuasively argued, the Japanese family tradition was, in fact, invented by the Meiji government and instituted through the Meiji Civil Code.[52] By contrasting Japanese family tradition with individualist Western law, the civil-code debate both reflected and created an Orientalist trap that forced legal scholars to choose between surrendering to Western modernity and betraying tradition or defending Japanese tradition and rejecting modernity.

The controversy over Japan's extension of the Meiji Civil Code to Taiwan in the late 1910s and early 1920s derived much of its content and form from views on colonial culture and gender order, as well as from Japan's varied experiences of importing and imposing Western-style law. Those involved in the controversy adopted one of two opposing positions, neither of which was unique to either the colonizer or the colonized. Proponents of the assimilation policy contended that Japan should apply the complete Meiji Civil Code to Taiwan, both to facilitate the integration of the colony into the empire and to promote the civilization of the colonized. In this view, the legal code symbolized the unification of the empire, the standard of civilization, and the emperor's benevolence toward the colonized. For example, Tanino Kaku, a Japanese judge serving on the Taiwan High Court, bluntly asserted that Japan ought to apply the Meiji Civil Code to Taiwan even though it would conflict with Taiwanese tradition. He grounded his argument on Japan's own reception of modern Continental European law, arguing that Japanese law was an imitation of German law and French law and that Japanese society had benefited significantly from this Westernization, even though the imported body of law often clashed with Japanese culture and tradition.[53] Huang Xin, an elite member of the consultative council of the government of Taiwan, also felt it was crucial to implement the civilized Japanese civil code in Taiwan, arguing that this would facilitate Taiwan's integration into the empire.[54] For the assimilationists, Taiwan's old customs needed to give way to Japan's modern law, which was a necessary step toward civilization.

Opponents of the assimilation policy sought to preserve Taiwanese tradition, the particularity and the uniqueness of colonial culture, and the convenience of colonial rule. Endorsing cultural relativism, they spoke against the superiority of Japanese law over Taiwanese customs and demanded that Taiwanese customary law remain the family law for Taiwanese. Zheng Song-yun, a Taiwanese lawyer and an advocate of the codification of Taiwanese customs, referred to the Japanese experience, noting that many Japanese disapproved of a Westernized family law contrary to traditional customs and that Japan's own codes on family and succession still preserved some Japanese particularities.[55] Lin Cheng-lu, a legal expert who advocated both universalism and cultural relativism, demanded that Japan implement the Japanese civil code in Taiwan to facilitate the development of modern capitalism there, but exclude the codes on family and succession so that the law would be tailored to folk customs. Contrasting the Han-Taiwanese custom in which all sons received equal shares of the inheritance with Japanese primogeniture, Lin contended that some Taiwanese customs regarding family and succession were closer to modern standards than were the corresponding Japanese customs.[56]

These opponents' celebration of colonial differences was not unqualified. Both Zheng and Lin contended that the law should not sustain Taiwanese customs contrary to "public order and good morals," although they identified different practices as problematic. Lin condemned concubinage and *sim-pua,* which he characterized as an extreme form of "compulsory marriage." Yet many other critics endorsed its legality. The *Taiwan Daily News* (*Taiwan nichi nichi shinpō*), the influential and popular newspaper supported by the government, hosted a heated discussion of possible exceptions to Japan's application of the Meiji Civil Code to Taiwan.[57] Unlike concubinage, which had attracted harsh criticism and strong demands for its abolition, a majority of the discussants approved of the custom of *sim-pua* in the name of Taiwanese tradition and in compliance with established standards of public order and good morals.

Those who invoked these standards to determine the acceptability of Taiwanese customs rarely delved into the question of gender equality. They either denied the legality of the *sim-pua* custom on the grounds of its backwardness or upheld its legality on the grounds that Taiwanese tradition was worthy of preservation. That participants in this debate rarely took gender into account suggests both the masculine viewpoint that informed the category of "Taiwanese" and the conservatism that dominated the discourse on public order and morality. Lin Cheng-lu, one of the few critics who raised objections to the institution of *sim-pua,* condemned it for its denial of individuals' freedom to choose their own marriage partners. Huang Xin, an assimilationist, described *sim-pua* as an institution that victimized women and transformed them into prostitutes and advocated its abolition.[58] Other critics disliked the custom but suggested that the colonial authorities preserve it to meet the needs of lower-class Taiwanese families.[59] According to these discussions, *sim-pua* were either passive victims to be rescued or a necessary component of the Taiwanese family. *Sim-pua*'s own voices were absent from the discussion.

Proponents of the extension of the Meiji Civil Code to Taiwan hoped that the application of identical bodies of law would encourage the Japanese to treat the Taiwanese as equals. Opponents demanded that Japan's treatment of Taiwanese differ so that the Taiwanese people could preserve their distinctive traditional interests. Advocates of both positions implied that Japanese law had become the standard to evaluate Taiwanese custom. But legalists also determined the superiority of Japanese law to Taiwanese customs, or vice versa, according to their approximation to modern Western law. In this way, Western modernity achieved hegemonic status over both Taiwanese and Japanese culture. Tanino Tadasu advocated the extension of Japanese law to Taiwan insofar as Japanese law best articulated Western-style law. Lin Cheng-lu preferred the succession system of the Han-Taiwanese over that of the Japanese because it exhibited greater "equality," a concept attributable largely to modern Western thought. What Lin failed to notice was its gender inequality: although all sons were entitled to an equal share, women remained excluded from inheritance.

The campaign to unify civil law in Taiwan and Japan was partially successful. In 1922, the central government in Japan decided to extend the Meiji Civil Code to Taiwan but exempted the codes on family relations and succession, allowing these Taiwanese customary laws to remain in place. Den Kenjirō, the first civilian governor-general of Taiwan, announced the decision to maintain customary law as the law for family affairs and explained that whether or not the Meiji Civil Code on family and succession should apply to Taiwanese depended on "the degree of progress in Taiwanese culture."[60] His remark carried a significant message: it was the backwardness of Taiwanese culture, not the discriminatory intent of the empire, that prevented the colonizer from applying its codes on family relations and succession to Taiwan. By positioning the colony as culturally inferior to Japan, this legal policy was more an exercise of colonial dominance than a sign of respect for colonial difference. The exception to discriminatory assimilation was no less discriminatory than assimilationism itself.

Civilizing the Natives

In the controversy over the application of Japanese laws to Taiwan, some critics employed the indefinite standard of "public order and good morals" to assess the validity of Taiwanese customs. Colonial courts, composed overwhelmingly of male Japanese judges, followed similar practices.[61] While family affairs were governed by Taiwanese customs throughout the period of Japanese rule, colonial courts, as agents of the empire and of modern law, also employed this standard in exercising their power of determining whether a Taiwanese custom at issue should be sustained or invalidated. In this way, colonial courts carried out their civilizing mission and regulated gender relations in the colony.

On a case-by-case basis, colonial courts constructed and contested the contents of Taiwanese customs, upholding some customs and terminating others. "Public order and good morals" was by no means a neutral standard; it was applied at the discretion of male Japanese judges, and its exercise displayed paradoxical gender politics. A Japanese lawyer, Yamada Tokiyuki, held the opinion that "public order and good morals" ought to be determined pursuant to Taiwan's standard, not Japan's.[62] But what was "Taiwan's standard"? An examination of court decisions regarding family and succession disputes among the Taiwanese shows that the courts tended to appeal to "the standard of a civilized society" when invalidating certain customs and to adopt "Taiwan's standard" when sustaining other customs.

As early as 1909, the courts invalidated the trafficking of wives and daughters on the grounds that such practices violated the "public order and good morals" of a modern civilized society.[63] For the same reason, the courts outlawed the recovery of "bridewealth" in the case of divorce because this practice commercialized marriage, and the practice of expelling a widow from her deceased husband's family because it denied women's personhood.[64] The courts also granted women rights relative to marriage, limiting parental power in the conclusion of a marriage contract,[65] giving wives the right to sue for divorce on specific grounds,[66] granting concubines the right to terminate the relationship without any causes for divorce,[67] and according girl servants the right to end this relationship because the practice was inhumane slavery.[68] These decisions treated girls and women as human beings to be neither traded for money nor disposed of as garbage, enabling wives and concubines to pursue independence by ending their relationships. But this reshaping of women's status was dependent on the dichotomy between colonial tradition and civilization. These court decisions described invalidated customs as undesirable carryovers from ancient times. By characterizing Taiwan's cultural and legal tradition as the sole source of oppression in the colony and by advancing a narrowly defined brand of civilization, the colonizers made themselves the saviors of victimized colonial women.

In other cases, the courts sustained certain Taiwanese customs in the name of respect for culture. One notable example is the courts' continuous refusal to invalidate concubinage. The courts repeatedly rejected requests by wives who sought a divorce on the basis of their husbands' concubine relationship, arguing that concubinage was a popularly recognized Taiwanese custom that did not violate "public order and good morals," although it would be unacceptable in a civilized society.[69] The courts permitted a Taiwanese man's multiple extramarital relationships by invoking "Taiwan's standard." It should be noted, however, that in a milestone decision the court granted a concubine the right to terminate the concubine relationships unilaterally, arguing that the practice violated the standard of "public order and good morals" as well as the natural right of freedom.[70] Many legal critics celebrated this decision as an invalidation of a practice that "no civilized countries" would tolerate and as bringing "blissful tidings of equality and freedom for Taiwanese women" who had "been oppressed for hundreds of years."[71] The legal liberation of women in Taiwan hinged on colonial Japan's depiction of local traditions as backward and of Japanese and Western-inspired civilization as progressive.

In spite of the colonial power's civilizing mission, the institution of *sim-pua* was upheld, with the exception of the custom of female servant-slave. Ever since the formation of colonial knowledge about *sim-pua,* discourses had distinguished female family servants from *sim-pua* by characterizing it as inhumane slavery. A police order prohibited the practice in 1916, after which time no registration of female family servants was permitted.[72] The courts invalidated female family servants in 1917. This prohibition did not put an end to the practice of female family servants, however, for they were adopted and registered under the title "adopted daughters."[73] In addition, household registration regulations enforced the distinction between matched *sim-pua* and unmatched *sim-pua* so as to draw a clear line between a daughter-in-law-to-be and an adopted daughter, making it a requirement for *sim-pua* registration that the family already have a son and declare their intention to make him the girl's husband; otherwise, the girl had to be registered as an "adopted daughter."[74] The courts, while requiring only that a family intend to marry the *sim-pua* to a son, regardless of whether or not they had a son at the time of the adoption, also acknowledged a strict distinction between *sim-pua* and adopted daughters, "civilizing" the institution of *sim-pua* by fitting it into the modern legal institutions of adoption and marriage.[75]

Resistance Inside and Outside the Law

In implementing their civilizing mission, colonial courts positioned themselves as the liberators of victimized colonial women. Native culture was considered the source of oppression, and native women awaited rescue. This view of colonial women overlooked one significant point: the courts would not have been able to rescue the victim without her own call for help. It was only when people brought their cases to the courts that the courts could intervene in civil disputes and exercise the power of defining customary law. Colonial women were not helpless victims of their culture; some *sim-pua* dissented from local customs and dared to assert themselves.

Their resistance took a variety of forms. One common strategy was for *sim-pua* to attempt to escape. The stories of two "women worthies"—Cai A-xin (1899–1990; also known as Sena Gibson), who was Taiwan's first female doctor and specialized in gynecology, and Xie Ah-nu (1901–1970; also known as Xie Xue-hong), who was one of the founders of the Taiwanese Communist Party—exemplify the escape strategy. Cai A-xin was born to an affluent family with strong ties to Dr. MacKay. Cai's father died of tuberculosis when she was five. Then, Cai recalled,

> Mother tried to give me away, but kept my little sister. She gave me to our church minister, with the hope that when I grew up the minister's son and I would be matched. I was only five years old, but I just would not live with my new parents although they were very kind to me and loved me. I would sometimes run away during the night and walk 30–40 minutes, rain or shine, to my

> mother's place. Finally the minister grew tired of chasing me and searching for me. He refused to keep me, saying that he could not handle this wild girl and did not want me to become his future daughter-in-law. From that time on, mother just had to have me with her.[76]

Cai was treated well, but she desperately wanted to be with her natal mother. She explained that her mother's decision to give her to the minister was influenced by the custom of *sim-pua,* in which families gave up young children because they had more children than they could afford. However, families rarely gave up boys.

Xie Ah-nu was born to a family so destitute that three of her siblings were sold. Her father died when she was eleven and her mother died the following year. Her relatives were planning to sell her in order to obtain the money needed for her mother's burial, but by threatening to commit suicide she averted that fate temporarily. The family eventually sold her to a family that virtually enslaved her. In her memoir, Xie describes in detail how she was abused and tortured. After a suicide attempt, Xie escaped from her adoptive family before she could be matched with the family's son. She became an influential communist activist, traveled and received an education in China and Russia, and founded the Taiwanese Communist Party with her comrades in 1928.[77]

The stories of Cai and Xie exemplify the diverse experiences of *sim-pua:* Cai was well treated, whereas Xie was an abused victim.[78] Their stories show that resistance to this system was possible, even for a five-year-old. To acknowledge that a *sim-pua* could sometimes successfully resist or escape is not to place blame on *sim-pua* who never escaped; rather, it subverts the image of *sim-pua* as passive victims incapable of exercising any agency. Agency and victimization are not dichotomous concepts but rather ends of a continuum. In the context of domestic violence, Kathryn Abrams outlines a form of agency that is "more partial and variable than the unitary, all-or-nothing agency of liberal theory."[79] The notion of partial agency is useful in recognizing various manifestations of resistance. Moreover, a victim's decision not to leave could also be an exercise of agency.[80] *Sim-pua* might remain in the adoptive family for various reasons. Some of them developed a detached and fatalistic attitude toward their situation, and many of them, especially those adopted at an early age, became attached to their foster mothers irrespective of bad treatment.[81] Nevertheless, for those *sim-pua* who suffered mistreatment, escape was one way out and was achievable particularly by means of laws and courts.

Reports on *sim-pua* in the *Taiwan Daily News* are full of accounts of how they were brutally abused, sexually violated, sold into prostitution, and even killed. They also describe how ill-treated *sim-pua* tried to save themselves by returning to their natal families. Natal families that offered their *sim-pua* daughters assistance sometimes sought legal remedies. Li Jin-ji, who was forced into prostitution and abused by her adoptive father, became ill, but her adoptive father refused to let her natal mother take her home to care for her. Li's mother turned to a male Japanese attorney for help and successfully obtained a court injunction allowing her to take Li home. The 1907 news report on this case praises the court's decision as a blessing for prostitutes and an example of the colonists' rescue of native *sim-pua.*[82]

Although some *sim-pua* and their natal parents obtained redress through litigation, the courts did not always offer a helping hand. The court first ruled in 1906 that the custom did not permit a *sim-pua* to ask her adoptive parents for termination of the *sim-pua* relationship.[83] A 1910 decision held that a *sim-pua* could not refuse to live with the adoptive family unless her adoptive father gave her permission to leave, even when she had suffered abuse.[84] The courts ruled in 1913 that a *sim-pua* could not leave the adoptive family after the death of her prospective husband but could be transferred to another family.[85] The adoptive parents were even allowed to chastise the *sim-pua* provided that the punishment was not unbearable. The court granted this permission on the grounds that "Taiwanese customs recognize the senior's right of chastisement of the junior, and it is a common practice that the ignorant underclass Taiwanese chasten their children to a certain degree."[86] Here, in the name of respect for Taiwanese customs that were constructed in an Orientalist fashion, the court turned a blind eye to the suffering *sim-pua* and denied her request to terminate the relationship on the grounds of unbearable abuse.

The courts later became more sympathetic to the suffering of *sim-pua.* A remarkable court decision in 1918 enabled a *sim-pua* who had been subjected to unbearable abuse to leave her adoptive family. An eleven-year-old *sim-pua,* whose adoptive mother had beaten and injured her, was entitled to terminate the relationship because the beating extended beyond reasonable chastisement.[87] This decision may well have had significant effects, for some time afterward a Taiwanese woman recalled a rumor that when a *sim-pua* was cruelly abused, her natal mother could bring a case to the court and take her daughter home.[88] In this view, the colonial courts served as rescuers for the colonized who were physically abused.

Men who opposed arranged marriages also raised their objections in court. In 1931, a court held that parents could not enforce a *sim-pua* marriage, so the prospective husband was free to marry another woman and the *sim-pua* relationship was terminated.[89] The decline of matched *sim-pua* marriages since the 1930s, as Arthur Wolf has observed, may be related to this legal entitlement for men to reject *sim-pua* marriages, although more evidence is required to prove this connection. I have, however, uncovered no court decision that awarded a *sim-pua* the right to decide whether she would marry her prospective husband or end the *sim-pua* relationship. The legal rejection of arranged *sim-pua* marriages was granted only to the prospective husband; indeed, the court gave him the unilateral right not only to determine his marriage but also to control the fate of the *sim-pua* in a way that only household heads had previously been able to. The court decision enhanced men's marriage freedom but turned a blind eye to the *sim-pua*'s lack of freedom. *Sim-pua* were empowered by courts when a *sim-pua* presented herself as a battered victim, but not when she acted as an independence-seeking subject.

Conclusion

Japanese colonial rule in Taiwan produced double effects in the shaping and reshaping of gender relationships in the legal arena. On the one hand, the colonial courts served as a site of contestation, a channel through which the colonized could challenge gender inequality. On the other hand, colonial legal policy carried out the Japanese Empire's mission to civilize the colonized, producing an Orientalist trap that identified Taiwanese society as the sole source of patriarchy, which enhanced the hegemony of Japan.

The influence of Japan's colonialist construction of *sim-pua,* which forced a choice between a *sim-pua*'s legal status as an adopted daughter or a daughter-to-be, survived the end of Japanese rule in Taiwan and has continued to dominate current understandings of the practice. Today, *sim-pua* continue to experience an indeterminate status under contemporary Taiwanese law, which draws a clear distinction between adoption and marriage. The legal system's failure to reconstruct a *sim-pua*'s relationships with her birth family and her foster family has produced a new form of oppression. A *sim-pua* may have established a substantial relationship with two families—her natal family and her adoptive family, that is, the family of her husband-to-be—or even with three families—her natal family, her adoptive family, and her husband's family if she marries outside the adoptive family. But it is not uncommon for contemporary Taiwanese courts, bound as they are both by modern legal concepts and a colonial legacy, to turn down a *sim-pua*'s request to confirm her membership in one of these families, thereby denying her the rights that would derive from family membership, particularly her right of inheritance. I hope that this legal history of *sim-pua* under the Japanese Empire invites more critical reflections on the nature and legacy of Japanese colonialism from a feminist perspective and facilitates collective efforts to rename the *sim-pua*'s existence to avoid the Orientalist trap, redress their suffering, and recognize their resistance to oppression.

Notes

1. Teemu Ruskola, "Legal Orientalism," *Michigan Law Review* 101, no. 1 (2002): 179–234.

2. Tracy A. Thomas and Tracey Jean Boisseau, "Introduction: Law, History, and Feminism," in *Feminist Legal History*, ed. Thomas and Boisseau (New York: New York University Press, 2011), 1–29.

3. Orientalist legal history identifies the development of law in advanced Western nations as a prototype of legal evolution and sees it as the task of law in non-Western nations to mimic this evolution. My definition of Orientalist legal history is similar to the dominant version of legal history that Robert W. Gordon has termed "evolutionary functionalism"; see Gordon, "Critical Legal Histories," *Stanford Law Review* 36 (1984): 59–67.

4. The phrase "adopted by parents-in-law and married a brother" is my adaptation of the title of Arthur P. Wolf's pioneering article on *sim-pua*. Wolf's title makes the adopting family and men the subject, whereas my version makes the female *sim-pua* the subject. See Wolf, "Adopt a Daughter-in-Law, Marry a Sister: A Chinese Solution to the Problem of Incest Taboo," *American Anthropologist* 70, no. 5 (1968): 864–874. See also Hill Gates, "The Commoditization of Chinese Women," *Signs: Journal of Women in Culture and Society* 14, no. 4 (1989): 799–832.

5. Elisabeth Croll coined the term "daughter discrimination" as an alternative to the concept of "son preference"; see Croll, *Endangered Daughters: Discrimination and Development in Asia* (London: Routledge, 2000), 18.

6. I use the term *sim-pua* rather than the popular English translations of this term, "child bride" or "adopted (foster) daughter-in-law," because neither accurately conveys its meaning. "Child bride" suggests that the girl is married to the boy when the relationship is established, which is not the case in *sim-pua.* "Adopted daughter-in-law" is equally misleading, because a *sim-pua* is not formally a daughter-in-law until a *sim-pua* marriage has been conducted in adulthood.

7. In some forms, the girl's ties with her natal family remain.

8. For a discussion on the blurred lines among *sim-pua, iong-lu* (adopted daughter), and *ca-bo-kan,* see Arthur P. Wolf and Chieh-shan Huang, *Marriage and Adoption in China, 1845–1945* (Stanford, CA: Stanford University Press, 1980), 113–117.

9. See, for example, Chieh-shan Huang and Arthur P. Wolf, "Marriage in Taiwan 1881–1905: An Example of Regional Diversity," *Journal of Asian Studies* 54, no. 3 (1995): 781–795; Arthur P. Wolf and Hill Gates, "Chinese Marriage Regimes," *Journal of Family History* 23, no. 1 (1998): 90–99; Wolf, "Adopt a Daughter-in-law, Marry a Sister"; Wolf and Huang, *Marriage and Adoption,* 272–281; and Arthur P. Wolf, "Maternal Sentiments: How Strong Are They?" *Current Anthropology* 44 (2003): S31–S49.

10. For example, see Ying-chang Chuang, "Chinese 'T'ung-yang-hsi' Marriage: The Ch'en Family of T'ou-fen, Taiwan," *Proceedings of National Science Council, Part C: Humanities and Social Sciences* 2, no. 1 (1991): 174–185. Most studies on *sim-pua* rely on contracts, census records, and household registrations. Rather than identifying the number of daughters who were given out, they often identify the number of sons who entered into *sim-pua* marriages.

11. Although the law officially banned the sale of a wife, concubine, or daughter, it allowed for "exceptions" because of poverty, and the practice was widespread. Philip C. Huang, *Code, Custom, and Legal Practice in China: The Qing and the Republic Compared* (Stanford, CA: Stanford University Press, 2001), 160–161.

12. George Leslie MacKay, *From Far Formosa: The Island, Its People, and Missions* (1895; 3rd ed., Taipei: SMC Publishing, 1991). According to Arthur Wolf, the institution of *sim-pua* in Han Chinese society was first described in English by a nineteenth-century visitor to Foochow, the Rev-

erend Justus Doolittle, in *Social Life of the Chinese: Daily Life in China* (New York: Harper and Brothers, 1865). Wolf, "Adopt a Daughter-in-Law, Marry a Sister," 864.

13. Robert Peter MacKay, *Life of George Leslie MacKay, D.D. 1844–1901* (Toronto: Board of Foreign Missions, Presbyterian Church in Canada, 1913), 33–34.

14. Marian Keith, *The Black-Bearded Barbarian: The Life of George Leslie MacKay of Formosa* (Toronto: Missionary Society of the Methodist Church, The Young People's Forward Movement Dept., 1912).

15. Wolf and Huang, *Marriage and Adoption,* 123–124.

16. MacKay, *From Far Formosa,* 121–122.

17. Japan is often considered the first and only Asian colonial power, but there are dissenting opinions; see Emma Teng, *Taiwan's Imagined Geography: Chinese Colonial Travel Writing and Pictures, 1683–1895* (Cambridge, MA: Harvard University Press, 2004).

18. Wolf and Huang, *Marriage and Adoption,* 305.

19. Okada Yuzuru's 1936 survey of 148 households in the Shihlin district of northern Taiwan reports that 179 of 388 women marrying into district families came as *sim-pua* and 291 of 387 marrying out left as *sim-pua.* Okada, *Kiso shakai* (Kōbundō, 1949), 15–16. Kajiwara Michiyoshi's 1934 investigation of nine villages in northern Taiwan listed 208 *sim-pua* in 809 households. Kajiwara, *Taiwan nōmin seikatsu kō* (Taipei: Ogata Taketoshi, 1941), 180–183.

20. Arthur P. Wolf, *Sexual Attraction and Childhood Association: A Chinese Brief for Edward Westermarck* (Stanford, CA: Stanford University Press, 1995), 28–29. For the story of a *sim-pua* who came from an elite family, see Fan Li-qing, *Tiansongbi zhi chun: Yiwei Taiwan funu de shenghuoshi* (Taipei: Zili Wanbao Press, 1995).

21. Huang and Wolf, "Marriage in Taiwan."

22. In northern Taiwan, for men who survived to the age of seventeen and for women who survived to age fifteen, the completion rates for intended *sim-pua* marriages declined from 81.2 percent for males born between 1891 to 1895 to 55.8 percent for males born between 1916 and 1920. In subsequent years, the proportion of male children matched with *sim-pua* at age five dropped significantly, from 31.8 percent for males born between 1926 and 1930 to 17.4 percent for males born between 1931 and 1935. Wolf and Huang, *Marriage and Adoption,* 195.

23. Wolf and Huang, *Marriage and Adoption,* 193–201, 302–312.

24. Yosaburo Takekoshi, *Japanese Colonial Rule in Formosa,* trans. George

Braithwaite (London: Longmans, Green, 1907), vii. Gotō Shinpei wrote the preface to this book.

25. Sally Engle Merry, *Colonizing Hawaii: The Cultural Power of Law* (Princeton, NJ: Princeton University Press, 2000), 19.

26. Title 63, The Law Relating to Laws and Ordinances to Be Enforced in Taiwan (1896–1906); Title 31, The Law Relating to Laws and Ordinances to Be Enforced in Taiwan (1906–1921). Tay-sheng Wang, *Legal Reform in Taiwan under Japanese Colonial Rule (1895–1945): The Reception of Western Law* (Seattle: University of Washington Press, 2000), 33–54.

27. Tsurumi Yusuke, *Gotō Shinpei den* (Gotō Shinpei Denki Hensankai, 1937–1938), vol. 2, 397.

28. Gotō Shinpei, "Taiwan keiei jō kyūkan seido no chōsa o hitsuyō to suru iken," *Taiwan kanshū kiji* 1, no. 5 (1901): 24–38; no. 6 (1901): 25–35.

29. The 1898 civil, commercial, and criminal laws; the 1908 Taiwan Civil Law.

30. Wang, *Legal Reform in Taiwan,* 144.

31. Eric Hobsbawm and Terence Ranger, eds., *The Invention of Tradition* (New York: Cambridge University Press, 1983).

32. Timothy Y. Tsu, "Japanese Colonialism and the Investigation of Taiwanese 'Old Customs,'" in *Anthropology and Colonialism in Asia and Oceania,* ed. Jan van Bremen and Akitoshi Shimizu (Richmond, Surrey: Curzon Press, 1999), 197–218.

33. The Meiji Civil Code stipulated that an adopted son-in-law became the son of his wife's parents (Art. 860) and that the status of the successor was transferred from the wife to the adopted son-in-law (Art. 970). The postwar Japanese civil code has denied the institution's legitimacy.

34. Shih Chi-yun, "Wuguo jindai tongyangxi zhi faluxue de yanjiu," *Shehui kexue luncong* 6 (1954): 91–137.

35. Santaro Okamatsu, *Provisional Report on Investigations of Laws and Customs in the Island of Formosa* (Kobe: Printed at the Kobe Herald office, 1902), xv. "In-shin," "shin-pu," "chobo-kan," and "chabo-kian" are romanizations of Taiwanese dialect. Okamatsu (known in Japanese as Okamatsu Santarō) tried to clarify the differences between these terms, defining "in-shin," "shin-pu," and "chabo-kian" as adopted daughter-in-law, and "chobo-kan" as female servant slave. In this essay, I use "ca-bo-kan" instead of "chobo-kan" because the former is a commonly used romanization for contemporary scholars.

36. Ibid., xvi.

37. Ibid., xvii.

38. Ibid., xviii.

39. Rinji Taiwan Kyūkan Chōsakai, *Taiwan shihō* (Taihoku: Rinji Taiwan Kyūkan Chōsakai, 1900–1911), vol. 2, 413–25.

40. Okamatsu Santarō, "Nihon minpō no ketten o ronjite Taiwan rippō ni taisuru kibō ni oyobu," *Taiwan kanshū kiji* 5, no. 3 (1905): 13–26.

41. Rinji Taiwan Kyūkan Chōsakai, *Taiwan shinzoku sōzoku rei daiichi sōan* (Taihoku: Rinji Taiwan Kyūkan Chōsakai, 1911), 21–22.

42. Rinji Taiwan Kyūkan Chōsakai, *Taiwan shinzoku sōzoku rei daini sōan* (Taihoku: Rinji Taiwan Kyūkan Chōsakai, 1912), 22–28

43. Rinji Taiwan Kyūkan Chōsakai, *Taiwan shinzoku sōzoku rei daisan sōan* (Taihoku: Rinji Taiwan Kyūkan Chōsakai, 1914), 33–43.

44. Rinji Taiwan Kyūkan Chōsakai, *Hōan shinsakai daiyonkai kaigigijiroku* (Taihoku: Rinji Taiwan Kyūkan Chōsakai, 1913), 24–27.

45. Nihon Bengoshi Kyōkai Taiwan Shibu, "Taiwan minjirei oyobi shinzoku sōzokurei ni taisuru kengisho," *Taiwan Sōtokufu kōbun ruisan,* 1915, fifteen-year preservation, vol. 6, part 1, no. 14 (original archive number 05921).

46. For discussions on the failure of the codification of Taiwanese old customs, see Haruyama Meitetsu, "Taiwan kyūkan chōsa to rippō kōsō; Okamatsu Santarō ni yoru chōsa to ritsu'an o chūshin ni," *Taiwan kin-gendaishi kenkyū* 6 (1988): 81–114.

47. Leo Ching, *Becoming Japanese: Colonial Taiwan and the Politics of Identity Formation* (Berkeley: University of California Press, 2001), 107. See also Mark R. Peattie, "Japanese Attitudes towards Colonialism, 1895–1945," in *The Japanese Colonial Empire, 1895–1945,* ed. Ramon H. Myers and Mark R. Peattie (Princeton, NJ: Princeton University Press, 1984), 80–127.

48. On colonial legislation under the assimilation policy, see Wang, *Legal Reform in Taiwan under Japanese Colonial Rule,* 52–54.

49. Law No. 3, The Law Relating to Laws and Ordinances to Be Enforced in Taiwan.

50. The 1922 Application of a Civil Statute Order (Ordinances No. 406 and No. 407, Art. 5).

51. Hozumi Yatsuka, "Minpō idete, chūkō horobu," *Hogaku shinpō* 5 (1891). For a discussion on the controversy, see John Owen Haley, *Authority without Power: Law and the Japanese Paradox* (New York: Oxford University Press, 1991), 75–77.

52. Ueno Chizuko, "Modern Patriarchy and the Formation of the Japanese Nation State," in *Multicultural Japan: Paleolithic to Postmodern,* ed. Donald Denoon et al. (Cambridge: Cambridge University Press, 1996), 235–244.

53. Tanino Kaku, *Taiwan shin minjihō* (Taihoku: Taiwan Jihō Hakkōsho, 1923).

54. Huang Xin, "Minshōhō shigyō ni stuite," *Taiwan nichi nichi shinpō,* July 9 and 12, 1921, 4th ed.

55. Zheng Song-yun, "Minshōhō shigyō ni tsuite," *Taiwan seinen* 3 (1922): 19–26.

56. Lin Cheng-lu, "Minhō shōhō shigyō ni tsukite wa yoroshiku jogairei o okubeshi," *Taiwan seinen* 3 (1922): 21–35.

57. Wang Kei-yun, "Minfa shixing yilun xiaoji," *Taiwan nichi nichi shinpō,* August 9, 1921, 5th ed.

58. Huang Xin, "Minshōhō shigyō ni stuite."

59. Yen Yun-nian, "Duiyu ziwen-an zhi guanjian," *Taiwan nichi nichi shinpō,* June 27, 1921, 4th ed.

60. "Den Sōtoku kunji," *Taiwan nichi nichi shinpō,* October 8, 1921, 5th ed.

61. Throughout the colonial period, all judges were male and most were Japanese. The first Taiwanese judge to serve in Taiwan in 1931 was a male graduate of Kyoto Imperial University. Wang, *Legal Reform in Taiwan,* 78–84.

62. Yamada Tokiyuki, "Kokuhō jo kyūkan no chi-i," *Taihō geppō* 9, no. 8 (1915): 23–30.

63. Judgment No. 567 of December 10, 1909, the Court of Appeal.

64. Judgment No. 720 of November 8, 1918, the Court of Appeal; Judgment No. 587 of October 8, 1918, the Court of Appeal.

65. In law and practice, *sim-pua* marriage and other forms of "minor marriages" (such as concubine marriage) were differentiated from so-called major marriage. The parental right to decide major marriage arrangements for their children was first upheld and then annulled by courts. In 1908, the court held that a contract of marriage could not be made merely on the agreement of the bride and groom but must be agreed upon by their parents (Judgment No. 288 of April 29, 1908, the Court of Appeal). In 1919, the court ruled that a marriage decided by the parents without the bride and groom's consent was invalid (Judgment No. 332 of August 9, 1919, the Court of Appeal). Yet it ruled again in 1937 that a marriage between a man younger than thirty and a woman younger than twenty-five without their parents' consent could be annulled (Judgment No. 106 of August 18, 1937, the Re-appeal Division of the Higher Court). The age requirement was not a Taiwanese custom but an element of the Japanese civil code.

66. Judgment No. 714 of March 10, 1908, the Court of Appeal; Judg-

ment No. 129 of August 17, 1910, the Court of Appeal; Judgment No. 63 of February 22, 1918, the Court of Appeal; Judgment No. 27 of April 22, 1922, Appellate Division of Higher Court; Judgment No. 61 of August 24, 1922, Re-appeal Division of Higher Court; Judgment No. 132 (1923) of February 14, 1924, Re-appeal Division of the Higher Court.

67. Judgment No. 853 of February 16, 1920, Appellate Division of the Higher Court; Judgment No. 774 of January 18, 1922, Appellate Division of Higher Court.

68. Judgment No. 557 of November 7, 1917, the Court of Appeal; Judgment No. 65 of February 22, 1918, the Court of Appeal; Judgment No. 414 of July 18, 1921, the Re-appeal Division of the Higher Court.

69. Judgment No. 294 of August 31, 1906, the Court of Appeal; Judgment No. 77 of October 20, 1921, the Re-appeal Division of the Higher Court; Judgment No. 387 of June 27, 1922, the Re-appeal Division of the Higher Court.

70. Judgment No. 853 of February 16, 1920, the Re-appeal Division of the Higher Court.

71. "Chikushō seido o yaburu shinhanketsu," *Taihō geppō* 14, no. 5 (1920): 90.

72. Wolf and Huang, *Marriage and Adoption,* 115.

73. Aneha Shohei, *Hontōjin nomi ni kansuru shinzokuhō oyobi sōzokuhō no taiyō* (Taihoku: Taihō Geppō Hakkōsho, 1938), 165.

74. Wolf and Huang, *Marriage and Adoption,* 113. Wolf and Huang report that this distinction was made to help control the sale of females into prostitution but might have reflected local custom in central and southern Taiwan.

75. Judgment No. 26 of February 28, 1924, the Re-appeal Division of the Higher Court; Judgment No. 102 of August 4, 1925, the Re-appeal Division of the Higher Court; Judgment No. 254 of March 11, 1931, the Re-appeal division of the Higher Court; Judgment No. 102 of August 4, 1925, the Re-appeal Division of the Higher Court.

76. Sena A. Gibson (Cai A-xin), *Pioneer Doctor's Adventures* (unpublished manuscript, on file with author), 7. (Cai A-xin used the name Sena A. Gibson when she lived with her second husband in Canada after the end of World War II.) Her maternal grandparents belonged to the first group of Christians who embraced MacKay's teachings. MacKay posted bail for her paternal grandfather after the Japanese jailed him for supplying materials for the guerillas. Her mother learned the Roman alphabet in a Bible school that MacKay had established and later became a trained midwife.

Her father learned medicine from MacKay and became a medical doctor as well as a pastor.

77. See Xie Xue-hong, *Wo de bansheng ji* (Taipei: Yang Cuihua, 1997).

78. For an account based on oral history, see Ceng Qiu-mei, *Taiwan Xifuzi [sim-pua]de shenghuo shijie* (Taipei: Yushanshe, 1998). The author Ceng's parents tried to give her away as a *sim-pua* in the 1970s, but failed to do so.

79. Kathryn Abrams, "Sex Wars Redux: Agency and Coercion in Feminist Legal Theory," *Columbia Law Review* 95 (1995): 304–376.

80. On this issue, see Elizabeth M. Schneider, "Feminism and the False Dichotomy of Victimization and Agency," *New York Law School Law Review* 38 (1993): 387–399, and Schneider, *Battered Women and Feminist Lawmaking* (New Haven, CT: Yale University Press, 2000).

81. See Wolf and Huang, *Marriage and Adoption,* 238–241.

82. "Shinjō karishobun meirei," *Taiwan nichi nichi shinpō,* 16 January 1907, 5th ed.

83. Judgment No. 129 of April 23, 1906, the Court of Appeal.

84. Judgment No. 621 of November 14, 1910, the Court of Appeal.

85. Judgment No. 765 of December 24, 1913, the Court of Appeal.

86. Judgment No. 554 of December 4, 1917, the Court of Appeal.

87. Judgment No. 608 of December 24, 1918, the Re-appeal Division of the Higher Court.

88. Jiang Wen-yu, *Xiaoshi zhong de Taiwan ama* (Taipei: Yushanshe, 1995), 102–103.

89. Judgment No. 254 of March 11, 1931, the Re-appeal Division of the Higher Court.

CHAPTER 8

Japanese Colonialism, Gender, and Household Registration

Legal Reconstruction of Boundaries

Barbara J. Brooks

THE WORKINGS OF POWER have always been at the center of the study of colonialism in its diverse manifestations. Much scholarly attention has recently addressed divisions between colonizer and colonized, both within colonial and metropolitan spaces, as a means of better grasping the nature of colonial rule and the culture of colonialism. In an important essay, Ann Stoler and Frederick Cooper call attention to the study of "the relationship between knowledge and rule" and "how a grammar of difference was continuously and vigilantly crafted" by empires that rhetorically claimed clear categories separating colonized from metropolitan subjects, while at the same time, in fact, boundaries were porous.[1] Studies in the culture of colonialisms have often focused on the nature of boundaries between categories and especially people in imperial spaces who fell between or crossed such boundaries, not so much for the proportions or numbers of people in such places, but for the telltale ways colonial and metropolitan states dealt with them.[2] As study of the Japanese Empire matures and grows more complex, more sources for the study of colonial power and knowledge undergo analysis, and within this enterprise, study of the legal classification of metropolitan vs. colonial subjects within the household registration systems of the empire begins to be possible.

This essay sketches a broad research agenda by first exploring the general landscape of the imperial population for which the Japanese Empire, beginning in Taiwan in 1895, built systems of laws that divided a large realm of metropolitan law applied to all subjects from the changing colonial realms of "customary law." It then offers an outline of the complexities of the movement of peoples, the distinctive gendering, and both discursive and legal complexities concerning the status of different subjects in the Japanese Empire, with particular attention to what can be discerned about cases of mixed-blood offspring. Discussion of mixed-blood offspring (those with both a metropolitan or *naichi* and a colonial or *gaichi* parent) has to be brought into the analysis of a vast and unwieldy, and changing, system of management and manipulation of categories of people across the empire.

Study of the evolving colonial systems of legal categorization of metropolitan and colonial subjects also demands broad, even international, contextualization. Japanese bureaucratic systems of registration in Japan proper did not arise in a solely domestic or national framework. The Japanese state encountered issues of extraterritoriality and citizenship from at least 1854. Its own modernization of a traditional system of household registration was accomplished with international issues regarding citizenship always lurking and threatening to undermine sovereignty. During the Meiji years, Japan's bureaucratic system of household registration (*koseki seido*) evolved, along with its taxation and military draft systems, to focus on the Japanese subjects at the individual and household level in their local jurisdictions. As Japan rose to consequence as a player in Great Power politics in East Asia and as a new colonial power, the state also emerged as a manipulator of categories of citizenship that classified subject peoples in household registration systems of the metropole (*naichi*) and colonial territories (*gaichi*). The first Japanese legal specialists went to Korea with the goal to create law codes "on par with the law codes of civilized countries," in order to abolish extraterritoriality in Korea, but also with the goal of aligning Korea closely with Japan's national interests.[3] Meiji jurists who had developed Japan's civil code after, but also despite, intense study of French civil law now came to Korea to compile the basis for the new Korean customary law. In both metropole and periphery, the jurists were also working toward modernizing the state in important areas of family law.

Recent scholarship, particularly on Korea, has clarified the nature of customary law as "invented" or in any case selectively encoded as law by Japanese legal experts based on Japanese scholarship on "customs" of the particular colonial society and actual courtroom challenges.[4] Customary law was civil law, and within that, law that ordered the Korean family system, including marriage and divorce, succession, adoption, and property inheritance in families. In effect, metropolitan Japan, with its household head and household registration system, had a different civil code than the ones that imperial jurists devised for colonial subjects in Taiwan and Korea. That numbers of individuals might, by their mixed heritage or their mixed marriages, challenge the household registration system would require evolving legal changes in colonial customary law to bring all *koseki* systems into closer alignment over time.

The Japanese Empire and Movements of Peoples

The period of Japan's imperial expansion in Manchuria coincided with a long period of migration into the region from China and Korea. As most of the people who moved to Manchuria from Korea were poor agricultural settlers, numbers are only crude estimates. C. Walter Young's 1932 study of Koreans as a factor in the Manchurian Incident cited Japanese Foreign Ministry figures of "one million at least," and others have estimated that up to two million Korean people had come to live in Manchukuo by the end of the war.[5] I have argued elsewhere that Japanese authorities were instrumental in their claims to include "compatriot" Koreans as part of the Japanese community in pre-1931 Manchuria. After 1931, Koreans, often thought to be one of the acclaimed "five races" that made up the rainbow community in Manchukuo, sometimes disappear as a category as their numbers were subsumed into head counts to inflate numbers of "Japanese" residents.[6] Similarly, ethnic Chinese residing in China sometimes maintained Japanese colonial citizenship through real or fictional ties to colonial Taiwan (these somewhat nominal Japanese subjects were termed "registered people" or *sekimin*).[7]

Recent scholarship on Japan in the period of empire has ignited debate over how (or even whether or not) the Japanese distinguished themselves from other ethnic groups in Northeast Asia. Evidence from multiple sources across Japanese society bolsters Oguma Eiji's argument that the concept of Japanese "homogeneity" is a product of the postwar period that must not be read back into the colonial era. Oguma also provides evidence of colonial authorities who resisted concepts of Japanese racial separateness or superiority.[8] The Japanese rhetorical embrace of diverse marginal subjects and the formulation of policies aimed at the manipulation of marginal peoples furthered imperialist ends, particularly the "Japanese" social and economic penetration into remote parts of China and Manchuria (often through illicit networks of drug trafficking and prostitution in which Japanese women and colonial subjects were embedded).

Japanese colonial policies of assimilation were founded on the belief that the Japanese people were themselves formed from a multicultural mixture of diverse ethnicities over time, with the core Japanese "forever assimilating surrounding ethnic groups without losing their own identity."[9] The colonial drive to assimilate was strongest in Korea, fueled in part by the belief, buttressed by modern Japanese archaeologists and anthropologists, that Koreans and Japanese shared the same ancestors (*dōsōron*) and that the colonization of Korea would return the "branch" family of Koreans to the "main" branch of the Japanese. The legal scholar Marie Seong-hak Kim has reminded us that for Japanese jurists in Korea, such as Ume Kenjirō, following French legal and colonial thought of the late nineteenth and early twentieth centuries, "the colonial theory of assimilation was framed mainly in terms of political and legal assimilation, as opposed to the cultural assimilation of the natives."[10] In contrast to jurists and policy makers, of course, resident Japanese in Manchuria and China articulated strong prejudices against Koreans and Chinese. Bigotry toward the colonized or semi-colonized was, as elsewhere in the colonial world, at the heart of colonial life and its discourses. What is different here is the degree to which this bigotry ran counter to official discourses of *sameness* between colonizer and colonized.

Scholars such as Peter Duus and Kimura Kenji have documented that the majority of Japanese who found their way to Korea in the early period of settlement were hard-pressed after losing their basis of livelihood at home or having it severely threatened.[11] The migration of struggling Japanese men to Korea and Manchuria must have had its impact on the nature of the settler community, but the story of Japanese women goes further to demonstrate how the gendering of the Japanese Empire produced this distinctive colonial culture.[12]

Proximity to the metropole may be the single best explanation for the large numbers of poor Japanese women who traveled to Northeast Asia and Siberia starting as early as the 1860s. Like the movement of poor Koreans, the global migration of women has often been invisible. Recently a new literature on development in the twentieth century is demonstrating that "women as migrants were largely invisible . . .

until the mid-1970s and, if mentioned at all, seen as dependents of men."[13] In the past, scholarship assumed that women migrated across political boundaries as economic dependents of men, but now a strand of scholarship on development argues that migration interrupts the patriarchal contract, that a "restructuring of gender relations" might take place, even if not on a permanent basis.[14] These insights help to explain the gender dynamics of the Japanese colonial frontier and even its largest settlements, which often seemed populated not just by Japanese women as dependents of Japanese men, but also by many "anomalous" women in a variety of trades of their own, the most prevalent being prostitution.

Ann Stoler's lucid analysis of the gendering of European colonial culture describes a rather different phenomenon, where European women were scarce commodities bound into a patriarchal system that exceeded the strictures of the metropole and above all policed the sexual divide between white women and colonized men. "European demographics in the colonies . . . were enormously skewed by sex. . . . In the late nineteenth and early twentieth centuries, the number of men was, at the very least, double that of the women, and sometimes exceeded the latter by twenty-five times."[15] In early Japanese settler communities, Japanese women often outnumbered Japanese men; when they were counted their numbers were always significant. In Vladivostok in 1884, for example, records indicate 276 resident Japanese women versus 119 Japanese males, a highly unusual ratio in comparison to any other national group. In other expatriate communities, men outnumbered women by a factor of at least three times. In 1915, a Foreign Ministry breakdown of resident Japanese in Manchuria by profession listed 7,122 women, with women in the entertainment business claiming the top numbers of all Japanese "professions" in the cities of Harbin and Tsitsihar.[16] Elsewhere in the far north of Manchuria (the area of the Chinese railway), statistics for 1915 reveal that there were 1543 Japanese women to 769 men.[17] The historian Kimura Kenji gives the official employed Japanese population of Korea in 1910 as 171,543, divided between 92,751 men and 78,792 women.[18]

That the sheer numbers of individuals was no indication of the settled or "respectable" population is evident in the fact that such statistics were always accompanied by numbers for households (in Korea in 1910, 50,992 households), and Japanese consuls in China noted with satisfaction the growing number of Japanese households in treaty port communities. Official numbers did not account for an unregistered and floating population of people, especially women, who although not considered "resident" were nevertheless there.

Japanese women were in spaces in the colonial/semi-colonial order that, in the European case, seem only to be populated by colonized men and women. They were domestics, mistresses of Japanese men, telephone operators, ticket punchers in the new streetcars and railways, hairdressers, and single shopkeepers, but above all, they were engaged in prostitution and the myriad jobs for women in the "entertainment" business. As in the metropole, the Japanese maintained licensed prostitution in Korea, the Kantōshū, Tianjin, and elsewhere, and some information is available on their numbers. The majority of women who worked in licensed prostitution on the continent were Japanese until late in the period. In 1923, according to governor-general statistics, the 7,540 licensed prostitutes in Korea included 4,651 Japanese, 2,876 Korean, and 13 foreign (probably Russian and Chinese) women, who received some 327,710 venereal inspections.[19] In 1938, after the second Sino-Japanese war had taken its toll, the ratio of Japanese to non-Japanese began to change: of 12,767 licensed prostitutes (in three categories), 4,510 were Japanese women.[20]

In 1931, the League of Nations Commission of Inquiry on Traffic in Women and Children in the East sent a delegation to inspect and probe the situation of international prostitution across the Middle East and Asia. Records in the Japanese Foreign Ministry Archives concerning this mission and the preparations and response of Japanese officials across China, Manchuria, Korea, and Japan proper reveal broad details of the invisible migration of women in the sex trade and the complicity of Japanese authorities in this trade.[21] In 1933 the Commission published its report and declared that "the bulk of this traffic is traffic in Asiatic women from one country in Asia to another; that the greatest number of such victims are of Chinese race; the next in numerical importance are women of Japanese nationality—that is, Japanese, Korean and Formosan."[22] The Foreign Ministry documents provoked by the League of Nations inquiry make visible to some extent the sizable movement of women from Japan and Korea to other parts of Northeast Asia during the period up to 1931. Perhaps just as significantly, in the testimony left behind by the members of the Commission, we can find that these European and American reformers left unchallenged assertions by various Japanese authorities that Japanese women traveling to China were not crossing "national" boundaries, for, after all, in China such women still fell under the protection of Japanese police authorities. Even in the context of this early human rights inquiry, the Japanese were able to manipulate the rules of extraterritoriality to claim that theirs was no "international" traffic.

This section has served to outline a general argument that the Japanese Empire tended to consciously manipulate categories of citizenship for perceived advantages of expansion, and that Great Power extraterritorial privileges in Korea (before 1910) and China were the creative framework that sponsored these policies and their multiple outcomes, not all of which were expected. Next, I will go further into uncharted territory to consider the Japanese policies that dealt with one aspect of the resulting hybridity in the empire.

Japanese Regulations and Mixed-Blood Offspring

The presence and the instrumental manipulation of Japanese colonial subjects in the context of extraterritoriality in China is remarkable enough, but Japanese imperialism went even further for the purposes of expansion of empire when it took advantage of the outflow from Japan of untold numbers of its own marginal metropolitan citizens, anomalous Japanese women. An important result of this outflow would also be the creation of sizable pool of mixed-blood offspring. We can contrast this with the case of European colonies, where offspring of colonizer and colonized were visible and feared, as Stoler has written:

> They were the "enemy within," those who might transgress the "interior frontiers" of the nation-state, who were the same but not quite, potentially more brazen in their claims to an equality of rights with "true" Europeans, but always suspect patriots of colonial rule.[23]

In the Japanese Empire, children of unions between Japanese and Koreans, Taiwanese, or Chinese were physically indistinguishable from purebred Japanese, and the evolving systems of categorizing them in the modern Japanese bureaucratic state bear study, as part of the quest to understand how Japanese governmentality worked across different administrative spaces in the complex world of citizenship and law in East Asia.

More specifically, we need to raise the question of what contradictions arose in the gap between Japanese, or *naichi,* and Korean, or *gaichi,* categories of subjects in the Japanese Empire. Japanese legal handbooks that concerned household registration were issued with some frequency in both colonial Korea (after annexation) and in metropolitan Japan to clarify the myriad complications that arose in relation to every aspect of registration—that is, registration of births, marriages, divorces, adoptions, deaths; issues of succession and inheritance; legal recognition of illegitimate offspring; formation and ending of households—into the metropolitan and colonial household registration systems of metropolitan Japan and its empire. These handbooks cite large numbers of individual cases, summaries of actual bureaucratic judgments regarding individuals—but without including their names—that concern ambiguities of status and registration. Issues between colonial and domestic systems are only a fraction of all types of registration issues set out in these books, which primarily address registration problems of segregated metropolitan or Korean subjects. The following section will summarize some of the individual findings, but I will begin by addressing the issues raised in contemporary scholarship on the issues of ethnicity and assimilation.

Colonial Policy and Assimilation

In recent years, significant scholarship in English and Japanese has analyzed the historical evidence that some Japanese intellectuals, policy makers, and colonial officials viewed the empire as a multi-ethnic polity and believed that eventual wartime exigency would hasten both assimilation and the legal rights of colonial subjects.[24] In Japanese, scholars such as Oguma Eiji and Suzuki Yūko have elaborated that the Japanese Empire was, from start to finish, assimilationist (as opposed to anti-miscegenationist) in nature.[25] Oguma has demonstrated that the theories of Japanese as a mixed-race (or mixed-nation) people and of the common ancestry of Koreans and Japanese were the context within which a strong assimilation policy in Korea took form. That policy included, though with varying degrees of strength and clarity at different times, promotion of intermarriage, Japanese language schooling for Koreans, and much more. Oguma's first book, *The Origin of the Myth of Homogeneity* (*Tanitsu minzoku shinwa no kigen*), offers a careful explication of opposing discourses of Japanese identity—mixed nation vs. pure blood theories. Although Oguma argues that the emergence of a belief in the latter theory of pure-blooded Japaneseness is mostly a postwar creation, he also devotes many pages to discussing the rise of the idea of a homogenous Japanese people in the work of several prominent prewar intellectuals, especially Tsuda Sōkichi. Certainly by the late 1930s there was a confluence of ideas, some old and some new, and many linked to the imperial house, that tended to celebrate the Japanese as a unique and master race.

But, from the location of the colonial site, or from the perspective of colonial officialdom and colonial *policy,* the goal of assimilation only grew stronger with time. Robert Young has written of assimilation in French colonial policy:

> There was a further paradox contained within the assimilation doctrine: on the one hand, it was the most progressive of all imperial ideologies, to the extent that it assumed the fundamental equality of all human beings, their common humanity . . . and considered. . . all native peoples could immediately benefit from the uniform imposition of French culture in its most advanced contemporary manifestation. On the other hand, this very assumption meant that the French model had the least respect and sympathy for the culture, language and institutions of the people being colonized—it saw difference, and sought to make it the same—what might be called the paradox of ethnocentric egalitarianism.[26]

Strong assimilationist policies in Korea were predicated on theories of sameness between Koreans and Japanese, but due to the Japanese version of the paradox described by Young for the French, the assimilationist drive was inherently contradicted in everyday life, and no less so, in rules and regulations concerning the status of metropolitan and colonial subjects of the Japanese Empire.

It is important to note that the late Chosŏn (Korean) government, in its "enlightenment movement" of the last few years of the nineteenth century, began the modernization of the Korean household registration system. A major focus of the reforms the new system implemented was the "leveling" of Korean society through the attempt to register the whole population and to deny previous categories of people, such as slaves. In his analysis of the 1896 and 1909 registration reforms and the numbers of people who were finally entered into the registries (and some given surnames for the first time), Kyung Moon Hwang asserts that Japanese rule brought about consolidation of previous Korean reforms with a great deal of continuity of purpose with the reformers of the previous native regime. The Japanese, however, in 1909 went further in their "governmentality" through the use of the police to effect household registrations, with the result that the numbers of Koreans registered increased considerably.[27] While undoubtedly the later, superior census of subjects in Korea aided Japanese control of the colony, Hwang is not alone in arguing that the Japanese did not simply impose their own experiences with household registration on to Korean society, but that they sought to codify previous Korean customs or, in his analysis, to further the spirit of Korean reforms begun under the native regime.

Chulwoo Lee has also noted that the Japanese civil code, introduced into Korea in 1912, was implemented in a limited fashion restricted by the Ordinance on Civil Matters in Korea (*Chōsen minjirei*). The ordinance served to preserve Korean customary law in matters such as inheritance, kinship, and family succession.[28] Marie Seong-hak Kim has gone further to show that, from the start, the colonial state's codification of Korean "customs" was a selective and inventive process that changed over time to better unify civil and customary law in both Korea and Japan.[29] In various ways, Korean customary law in these areas, from the period after annexation, differed from that of Japan, and Japanese administrators throughout the colonial period grappled with the difference in the two systems. Eventually, the reforms of 1939 sought to transform Korean customary law and patriarchal family nomenclature (the repertoire of the household registration system) to closely resemble that of Japan, as carefully explicated in Motokazu Matsutani's essay in this volume. These 1939 reforms are associated with the famous oppressive action of the colonial government to require Koreans to adopt Japanese surnames, but a closer look reveals that they were (or were also) steps to unify clan names (by, to cite one example, forcing Korean women to take the surnames of their spouses) and permit Koreans, like Japanese, to adopt sons or sons-in-law in cases where household succession was thwarted by the lack of a natural son and heir. Japanese rationality/governmentality was at work across the decades to bridge gaps between Korean (*gaichi*) and Japanese (*naichi*) categorizations, and changes in the ordinances signaled changing policies regarding distinctions between colonial and metropolitan subjects.

In the first decades of rule in Korea, as Japanese drew up legal categories and rules for status of colonial citizens in Korea, they could change their justifications of policy, that is, basing it alternatively on assimilation or, in contradiction, on respect for Korean customary law, in order to accomplish what they needed at a given time. In fact, although annexation took place in 1910, and the first decade of colonial rule operated on one set of household registration rules, the Japanese changed those rules in 1922, in part because they found this gave the state more control over both Japanese and Korean subjects. But the establishment of the new laws had the potential to wreak havoc on individual lives. Colonial officials justified the changes, in some cases at least, by insisting that they were doing it in the name of respect for Korean civil or customary law.

Oguma Eiji, in his second book, *The Borders of Japaneseness* (*Nihonjin no kyōkai*), discusses how the household registration system that evolved in Korea was, in his view, the means of maintaining difference between metropolitan and colonial subjects, between Japanese and Koreans. According to Oguma, annexation brought about the Japanese embrace of Koreans as Japanese citizens, and Japanese jurists such as Yamada Saburō (law professor at Tokyo Imperial University and later president of Keijō Imperial University) argued that Korean subjects, if they moved to Japan, had to be able to transfer their household registration (a transfer known as *tenseki* in Japanese) and obtain all the rights and duties of Japanese subjects. In 1922, the metropolitan court issued its well-known rule that proclaimed the legality of marriage and adoption between individuals in the colonial and metropolitan household registration systems. Nevertheless, Oguma states, especially after the Korean colonial government's belated 1923 promulgation of Korean household registration regulations, a gap arose between the Korean household registration system and that of the metropole. In effect, there was no apparent procedure for individuals to file the paperwork necessary to enter the metropolitan system and become Japanese subjects—at least, within colonial Korea, there was a lack of cooperation on the part of bureaucrats who might enable a movement between registries, or at least for those leaving the colonial and entering the metropolitan registries.[30] Oguma describes a situation where "the Japanese government cleverly avoided having to clarify in law the discrimination between Koreans and Japanese," that was, in effect, sustained through the household registration system. But a closer look does reveal some discriminatory judgments policing the evolving system of colonial vs. metropolitan registration.[31]

The Japanese press in colonial Korea offers tantalizing glimpses into a society where, in fact, there were a number of mixed marriages (legal or not) and hybrid families. In the 1910s, there were strident and articulate concerns that the assimilation policy could not work: rather than Koreans becoming "Japanized," Japanese would wind up "Koreanized." Indeed, one editor opined, this was already taking place, as proved by the lax character and laziness of so many Japanese in Korea.[32] Settlers opposed some policies of the Korean colonial government aimed at implementing "universal brotherhood" (*isshi dōjin*), a slogan that celebrated Koreans and Japanese equality in the new colony, even going so far as to accuse the government of providing better facilities for colonized subjects at the expense of poor settlers in Korea's interior.[33] A reading of Japanese-language journalism in colonial Korea illuminates the formation of Japanese popular racism against Koreans in the face of colonial policies that seem to threaten the cohesion of the Japanese community by offering Koreans new services and opportunities. One of them, which deserves a separate time for discussion, was the colonial government's threat to implement joint schooling of Korean and Japanese children (*kyōgaku*)—a system modified, perhaps because of popular settler resistance, very quickly in order to keep Japanese in the most privileged positions to benefit. As Ann Stoler has suggested, scholarship of colonialism and emerging modern states cannot forget that racism can arise directly at the point of most intense contact with colonizers and then can be imported back to the metropole.

Japanese-language journalism in Korea offers insight into the issue of mixed marriage and hybrid offspring. In August 1912, for example, one journal published a series entitled "Japanese-Korean love stories of men and women" that ran seven or eight times over a few years and featured biographical accounts of mixed Japanese-Korean couples in Seoul that included discussion of their courtship and relations with their extended families. Nearly all of them were Japanese women married to or living with Korean men; most were common-law wives (*nai-ensai*), and their children retained their mother's Japanese surname and metropolitan registration.[34] In the same journal in 1925 another article profiled Japanese men who had formally married Korean women, after lamenting the slow pace of intermarriage that could produce "an age of no discrimination between Koreans and Japanese, even in blood."[35] Adoption, often a by-product of uxorilocal marriage, conferred even more beneficial privileges on Korean men marrying into Japanese families. In 1923, one Japanese writer described with pride how he had arranged the marriage of a Korean graduate of Sapporo Agricultural College to the single daughter of a former samurai (*shizoku*) family. With the wedding, the young man at once became a superlative (*rippa na*) metropolitan Japanese subject and a nobleman![36] Thus, both marriage and adoption reveal that the boundaries between colonizer and colonized were anything but fixed or stable, as elsewhere in the colonial world.

The Korean colonial government stood out among global colonial governments for its promotion of intermarriage (termed *sōgo kekkon,* in its early years) as part of the policy of assimilation.[37] Another article from the Japanese settler community shows their resistance to this aspect of assimilation policy, taking up the issue of intermarriage and mixed-blood offspring with an interesting twist. The author argued that since Koreans had before the Heian period (pre–ninth century AD) intermarried with Japanese, there was no necessity for further mixing of the two peoples' blood. He next listed the known Japanese surnames associated with Korean ancestry and then proceeded to list dozens of Japanese residents with these surnames who were resident in Seoul, even giving their addresses, in order to emphasize that there was no fundamental difference for the government to pursue between metropolitan and Korean residents.[38] The vignettes and discussions of intermarriage (and its threat) that appear frequently in newspapers in the first decade after annexation illuminate a period of confusion over mixed marriage issues, but, at least from the settler point of view, no one seems to doubt that the Korean colonial government was promoting intermarriage and that it was, in fact, taking place. Motokazu Matsutani's chapter in this volume includes further details on intermarriage of Koreans and Japanese in Korea; the figures that he cites from his research substantiate a picture of intermarriage and cohabitation.

Consulting the Legal Handbooks

The confusion regarding intermarriage apparent in journalistic discourse is a persistent theme in legal handbooks that appeared in both the metropole and colonial sites, summarizing family law cases for consultation by bureaucrats charged with keeping household registration records. A legal handbook published bilingually in Seoul in 1915 reveals a series of regulations and cases that seem compatible with the settlers' views.[39] While the manual repeatedly reiterates that the Korean household registration law (*minseki hō*) has not yet been promulgated, it offers concrete advice for problems that arose concerning intermarriage, such as how to enter Korean individuals into Japanese household registries through adoption or marriage and how to register the offspring of Koreans and Japanese. It seems clear that in practice there was a mechanism for Koreans to lose their Korean household registration and colonial subject status, upon marriage or adoption into a Japanese family, even though the Japanese government continued to forbid Koreans to become naturalized citizens of any other foreign power.[40] However, because of the lack of a Korean household registration law, Japanese could not be entered into the Korean household registries and thus could not become Korean.[41] And while there were no legal barriers for Koreans to adopt Japanese names, they could not do so for the purposes of masquerading as Japanese, and there were complications if the Korean was a household head. Taken together, the cases detailed in the handbook suggest that marriage and adoption into Japanese registries was really the only path for a Korean to acquire a Japanese name.[42]

During this period, roughly 1910–1921, significant numbers of Japanese women (primarily marginal Japanese women) married Korean men and managed to have their Korean spouse's names added to their own household registry in their local villages in Japan.[43] As the anecdotal evidence from the Seoul-based popular press suggests, marriage or even cohabitation seems to have primarily been an affair between Japanese women and Korean men; what is much harder to determine is how many Korean men were also adopted as heirs (*iriyōshi*) and sons-in-law (*mukoyōshi*) into Japanese families. However, the number of judgments listed in the handbooks suggests that such mixed unions were relatively commonplace. The authorities, both in Korea and the metropole, must have observed these trends and sought to manipulate them in the civil laws they issued concerning intermarriage (1922) and Korean household registration (1923).

Evidence in support of this contention comes in a later legal handbook on household registration published in Japan proper. The handbook was published in 1928 in Tokyo, and it is a much more comprehensive compendium than the 1915 handbook with hundreds of civil court decisions regarding relations between Koreans and Japanese.[44]

It is clear here that there is another side to the celebrated 1921 action of the Japanese government to "legalize" marriage between metropolitan and colonial citizens, a move that was touted as a step toward the enlightened colonial policy of assimilation. The law rendered intermarriage "legal" but also delineated the new requirement that Japanese women marrying Korean men must transfer their household registration to the Korean, or colonial, household registries. The cases are extremely instructive. In one instance, a civil court decision directed a Japanese village head to remove the notation in the register of the marriage of a Japanese woman who had married a Korean man before July 1921 and subsequently had the marriage recorded in her family records. The officials not only had to remove her entire entry, with the notation, from the records, but were also instructed to write up a report and send the documentation to the village of the Korean man in question, for entry into his colonial household records. A further ruling stated that any children born of this union and previously noted in the women's registry (as an illegitimate child) must also be written out of the registry and the documents sent to the appropriate registry in Korea.[45] Japanese women married to Koreans were now to be cast from the metropolitan registries and clerically transformed into colonized subjects, and the offspring of such unions were to be entered into the colonial registers as well.

Another suggestive case from 1928, about a Taiwanese-Japanese union, offers more evidence that Japanese women might prefer to have illegitimate offspring if they formed relationships with colonized men. In this case, a Taiwanese man wished to legally recognize his illegitimate child, born of a Japanese women living in Japan. The court decided that this did not mean that the child's registration must be transferred to the Taiwan colonial household registry, but rather, as the child was already listed as an illegitimate child in the mother's metropolitan registry, a note to the effect that his father gave him recognition could simply be added.[46] This suggests the context for a phenomenon mentioned in settler journalism in the 1930s: one author estimated that the number of unmarried Korean-Japanese couples would swell the official numbers by at least a factor of four or five.[47] After 1921, there are also regulations that, citing Korean customary law, state that Japanese women wishing to divorce their husbands must have the permission of their Korean parents-in-law, which would further restrain their possible repatriation/re-entry into the metropolitan household registry system. In contrast, Korean women could now easily be removed from the colonial household registries and entered into the metropolitan registrations of their Japanese husbands. The absence of any cases on such unions, however, suggests more than just the ease of this transfer: it implies that marriages between a Japanese male and a Korean woman occurred infrequently.

The records from the mid-1920s are also lively on the subject of adopted sons (*yōshi*). One set of cases, for example, clearly indicates that if a Korean or Taiwanese male who had been properly entered into a Japanese household registry through adoption and also properly removed from or never entered into his corresponding colonial registers, were then to sever his relationship (*rien,* literally, "divorce") with his adopted Japanese family, he would be permitted to form his own new household in the metropolitan household system, the registry of his domicile in Japan proper.[48] In other cases of adopted sons, the authorities invoked Korean traditional or customary law to restrain the practice of Koreans adopting Japanese. Before 1922, Koreans could not adopt Japanese male heirs because the Korean civil regulations governing registration were not yet promulgated. After 1922, however, Koreans could not adopt Japanese because it went against Korean customary law that had ruled prior to annexation: Korean families traditionally did not adopt heirs, as adoption only occurred within the patrilineal clan or *sei* structure (and only agnatic or patrilineal adoption was permitted), nor did they have a method for ending a family line (*haike*), a procedure possible within the Japanese household registration system.[49]

These cases from the emergent colonial and metropolitan household register system in the late 1920s allow for three definite conclusions. First, the system encouraged Japanese women to transfer their registration to the colonial site through intermarriage with Korean men, although many couples chose not to formalize their unions and in this way managed to confer metropolitan status on offspring, as illegitimate children could simply be listed, with Japanese names, in the metropolitan household registries of their mothers. Second, the system permitted some Korean men to transfer their registration to the metropolitan registries through adoption (often accompanying uxorilocal marriage to a Japanese women). Korean women might become Japanese through marriage to Japanese men, though this seems a rare occurrence, which may have aided the authorities in making their decision to "legalize" intermarriage in 1921. Third, Japanese men were effectively barred from entry to the colonial household registration system through adoption. This last also conveniently coincided with the fears of Japanese authorities that metropolitan men might escape the draft by moving to the periphery and enlisting themselves in the colonial registries, thus becoming ineligible to serve as soldiers.[50]

What remains unclear is the fate of the large numbers of hybrid offspring that resulted from intermarriage. Did the Japanese Empire produce dramas of contested citizenship regarding mixed-blood offspring and the status of individuals under metropolitan vs. colonial civil codes? The cryptic entries in the household registration handbooks sketch out not just hybridities but individual life dramas that expand our understanding of how the Japanese Empire contorted notions of ethnicity and citizenship. Further analyses of these cases, if historical materials allow, might show the Japanese Empire for what it was: cosmopolitan, perhaps, but profoundly conflicted about the status of non-Japanese subjects, or alternately, assimilationist in the extreme, but shot through with qualifications that often took the outward stance of respect for the cultures of the peoples that Japan was trying to "imperialize."

Conclusion

In Korea and Taiwan under colonialism, a complex reading of assimilationist policies gave rise to rules about household registration that likely reinforced the movement of Japanese women from the metropole to the continent. Despite all that the state and bureaucratic rules might do, of course, individuals in the new legal spaces opened up by extraterritoriality and colonial regulations were often resourceful and creative. Individual stories can sometimes illuminate a remarkable cultural hybridity of empire, but they also may show us subversive, anticolonial actions and existences that further reveal just how dynamic, but unstable, it all was.

This essay has argued that, in the Japanese Empire, classification of subjects into metropolitan (*naichi*) and colonial (*gaichi*) household registers was an important aspect of colonial power. Close examination shows that there were many individuals who did indeed cross the registers during their lifetimes, and that determination of where a mixed-blood child might be registered—metropole or colony—was not as straightforward as expected. In the background of legal decisions rendered in civil proceedings, judgments that permitted a mixed-blood child to remain in his mother's metropolitan register, or even permitted a colonial husband of a metropolitan woman to assume metropolitan status after her death, reveal important aspects of imperial Japan's assimilationist drive that qualified its otherwise harsh or merely rhetorical manifestations. Sometimes, when an individual posed a challenge to the segregated household registration systems, the resolution of his or her status ended up reaffirming the general trend toward overall unification of civil and customary law systems across the empire.

Notes

1. Ann Stoler and Frederick Cooper, "Between Metropole and Colony: Rethinking a Research Agenda," in *Tensions of Empire: Colonial Cultures in a Bourgeois World,* ed. Ann Stoler and Frederick Cooper (Berkeley: University of California Press, 1997), 3–4.

2. Even prior to the advent of the recent academic work on imperial categorizations of subjects, authors of anticolonial fiction such as Pramoedya Ananta Toer employed the symbolic significance of colonial law and its treatment of mixed categories of subjects in works such as *This Earth of Mankind,* first published in Indonesian in 1975, and in English translation by Max Lane (New York: Penguin, 1996).

3. Ume Kenjirō, quoted in Marie Seong-Hak Kim, "Ume Kenjirō and the Making of Korean Civil Law, 1906–1910," *Journal of Japanese Studies* 34, no. 1 (2008): 10.

4. See Marie Seong-Hak Kim's important articles: "Law and Custom under the Choson Dynasty and Colonial Korea: A Comparative Perspective," *Journal of Asian Studies* 66, no. 4 (2007): 1067–1097; "Customary Law and Colonial Jurisprudence in Korea," *American Journal of Comparative Law* 57, no. 1 (2009): 205–247; and "Ume Kenjirō and the Making of Korean Civil Law, 1906–1910." In this volume, see the articles by Matsutani and Chen for careful studies of specific issues in evolving customary law in Korea and Taiwan under colonial rule.

5. C. Walter Young, "Korean Problems in Manchuria as Factors in the Sino-Japanese Dispute," *Supplementary Documents to the Report of the Commission of Inquiry,* Study No. 9, Geneva, 1932: 253. For extended treatment of Japan's Korean colonial subjects in China, see Barbara J. Brooks, "Peopling the Japanese Empire: The Koreans in Manchuria and the Rhetoric of Inclusion," in *Japan's Competing Modernities: Issues in Culture and Democracy, 1900–1930,* ed. Sharon Minichiello (Honolulu: University of Hawai'i Press,

1998), 25–44. See also Hyun Ok Park, *Two Dreams in One Bed* (Durham, NC: Duke University Press, 2005), esp. chaps. 1, 4–5.

6. See also Mariko Asano Tamanoi, "Knowledge, Power, and Racial Classifications: The 'Japanese' in 'Manchuria,'" *Journal of Asian Studies* 59 (2000): 248–276.

7. A preliminary study of *sekimin* issues is in Barbara J. Brooks, "Japanese Colonial Citizenship in Treaty Port China: The Location of Koreans and Taiwanese in the Imperial Order," in *New Frontiers: Imperialism's New Communities in East Asia, 1842–1952,* ed. Robert Bickers and Christian Henriot (Manchester: Manchester University Press, 2000), 109–125.

8. Oguma Eiji, *Tanitsu minzoku shinwa no kigen: "Nihonjin" no jigazō no keifu* (Shinyōsha, 1995). For example, he cites one Korean colonial official who was sharply critical of Nazi ideas of purebloodedness (241–243), articulating the often cited mixed racial background of the superior Japanese people as an argument. This work has been translated under the title *A Geneology of "Japanese" Self Images,* trans. David Askew (Melbourne: Transpacific Press, 2002).

9. Tessa Morris-Suzuki, "Becoming Japanese: Imperial Expansion and Identity Crises in the Early Twentieth Century," in *Japan's Competing Modernities.*

10. Kim, "Ume Kenjirō and the Making of Korean Civil Law, 1906–1910," 28.

11. Kimura Kenji, *Zai Chō Nihonjin no shakaishi* (Miraisha, 1989), 8.

12. Barbara J. Brooks, "Reading the Japanese Colonial Archive: Gender and Bourgeois Civility in Korea and Manchuria before 1932," in *Gendering Modern Japanese History,* ed. Kathleen Uno and Barbara Molony (Cambridge, MA: Harvard East Asian Monographs, 2005), 295–326.

13. Jacqueline Knorr and Barbara Meir, "Women and Migration: Anthropological Perspectives," in *Women and Migration: Anthropological Perspectives,* ed. Jacqueline Knorr and Barbara Meir (New York: St. Martin's Press, 2000), 9–20.

14. Giovanna Campani, "Present Trends in Women's Migration: The Emergence of Social Actors," in *Scapegoats and Social Actors: The Exclusion and Integration of Minorities in Western and Eastern Europe,* ed. Daniéle Joly (New York: St. Martin's Press, 1998), 192–217.

15. Ann Stoler, "Carnal Knowledge and Imperial Power: Gender, Race, and Morality in Colonial Asia," in *Gender at the Crossroads of Knowledge: Feminist Anthropology in a Postmodern Era,* ed. Micaela di Leonardo (Berkeley: University of California Press, 1991), 57–62.

16. Kanō Mikiyo, "Manshū to onnatachi," in *Iwanami kōza: Kindai Nihon to shokuminchi,* vol. 5, *Bōchōsuru teikoku no jinryū,* ed. Ōe Shinobu (Iwanami Shoten, 1993), 203, 205–206.

17. "HokuMan ni iru hōjin no sanpu jōtai," *Chōsen oyobi Manshū* 92 (March 1915): 36–37. The article notes that in the far north of Manchuria Russians welcomed Japanese women as domestics and child caretakers. (Hereafter this journal is abbreviated *COM.*)

18. Kimura, *Zai Chō Nihonjin no shakaishi,* 12.

19. Chōsen Sōtokufu, ed., *Chōsen Sōtokufu tōkei nenpō 1923, daigohen* (Keijō: Chōsen Sōtokufu, 1923), 76–77.

20. Chōsen Sōtokufu, ed., *Chōsen Sōtokufu tōkei nenpō 1938* (Keijō: Chōsen Sōtokufu 1938), 26–27.

21. Gaimushō Archives, B 9.10.0 1–1, *Kokusai renmei fujin jidō mondai ikken.*

22. League of Nations, *Commission of Enquiry into Traffic in Women and Children in the East. Report to the Council* (Geneva, 1933).

23. Ann Stoler, *Race and the Education of Desire* (Durham, NC: Duke University Press, 1995), 52.

24. See the powerful and nuanced analysis of Takashi Fujitani, *Race for Empire: Koreans as Japanese and Japanese as Americans in World War II* (Berkeley: University of California Press, 2011). Also Tessa Morris-Suzuki, "Debating Racial Science in Wartime Japan," *Osiris* 13 (1998): 354–375.

25. Suzuki Yūko, *Jūgun ianfu, naisen kekkon* (Miraisha, 1992).

26. Robert J. C. Young, *Postcolonialism: An Historical Introduction* (Malden, MA: Blackwell, 2001), 32.

27. Kyung Moon Hwang, "Citizenship, Social Equality and Government Reform: Changes in the Household Registration System in Korea, 1894–1910," *Modern Asian Studies* 38, no. 2 (2004): 355–387. See also Kyung Moon Hwang, *Beyond Birth: Social Status in the Emergence of Modern Korea* (Cambridge, MA: Harvard East Asian Monographs, 2005).

28. Chulwoo Lee, "Modernity, Legality and Power," in *Colonial Modernity in Korea,* ed. Gi-wook Shin and Michael Robinson (Cambridge, MA: Harvard Asian Monographs, 1999), 21–51.

29. Marie Seong-Hak Kim, "Law and Custom under the Choson Dynasy and Colonial Korea," 1089–1092.

30. Oguma Eiji, *"Nihonjin" no kyōkai: Okinawa, Ainu, Taiwan, Chōsen, Shokuminchi shihai kara fukki undō made* (Shinyōsha, 1998), 159–161.

31. Oguma Eiji, *"Nihonjin" no kyōkai,* 161.

32. "Chōsenka ron: Wa ga naichijin o keikoku," *COM* 130 (April 1918):

2–9. Similarly, "Chōsenjin no dōka mondai to Nihon," *COM* 133 (July 1918): 13–15.

33. See "Sōtokufu seiji ni okeru Chōsenjin to Nihonjin," *COM* 84 (July 1914), 2–6, which documents discrimination by the colonial governor-general against Japanese in favor of Koreans. See also Peter Duus, *The Abacus and the Sword: The Japanese Penetration of Korea, 1895–1910* (Berkeley: University of California Press, 1995), 358–363

34. "NisSen danjo tsuya monogatari," *COM* 57 (May 1912): 28–29.

35. "Kekkon kara mita naiSen yūwa," *COM* 206 (January 1925): 156–159.

36. "Chōsen mondai ni tsuite," *COM* 182 (January 1923): 37–40.

37. Intermarriage would also be promoted in Manchukuo; I have even found advertisements for a school to train Chinese women to become wives for Japanese settlers.

38. "Chōsenjin ni en no aru sei o motsu Keijō zaijū no naichijin," *COM* 109 (August 1917); Ann Stoler and Frederick Cooper, "Between Metropole and Colony: Rethinking a Research Agenda," in *Tensions of Empire: Colonial Cultures in a Bourgeois World*, 3–4.

39. Chōsen Sotokufu Keimukanbu, ed., *Chōsen minseki yōran* (Keijō: Shidokan, 1915).

40. See Brooks, "Peopling the Japanese Empire."

41. Chōsen sotokufu keimukanbu, ed., *Chōsen minseki yōran*, 65.

42. Ibid., 265–266.

43. See Brooks, "Reading the Japanese Colonial Archive."

44. Hōrei Kenkyūkai, ed., *Jitsurei hanrei bunrei jinjihō sōran* (Keibunsha Shuppanbu, 1928). The examples are drawn from section 4, entitled "Kosekihō ki."

45. Ibid., 446.

46. Ibid., 336.

47. "Nai Senjin no tsūkon jōtai," *COM* 326 (January 1935): 32–35.

48. Hōrei Kenkyūkai, ed., *Jitsurei hanrei bunrei jinjihō sōran*, 762.

49. Marie Seong-hak Kim explains further that the postcolonial Korean government struck down Japanese-imposed laws permitting adoptions of persons of different surnames and struck such adoptions from the records in 1952; the prohibition lasted until 1960. Similarly a ban on same-surname and same place of origin marriages was reissued after Korean independence and remained until 2005. Marie Seong-hak Kim, "Customary Law and Colonial Jurisprudence in Korea," 243–244.

50. Oguma, *Nihonjin no kyōkai*, 164–165.

CHAPTER 9

A New Perspective on the "Name-Changing Policy" in Korea

Matsutani Motokazu

THE "NAME-CHANGING POLICY" (*sōshi kaimei*) that forced Koreans to adopt Japanese names has been known as the most oppressive Japanese colonial policy in Korea. According to a standard textbook, "the forced assimilation policy of the 1930s reached its apex on the eve of the outbreak of the wider war in the Pacific. . . . A year earlier, however, the Japanese had struck at the most personal, and perhaps the most cherished, source of Korean identity, family and personal names. The Name Order promulgated in late 1939 'graciously allowed' all Koreans to change their names to Japanese-style surnames and given names."[1]

This conventional narrative may well represent the collective memory of the Korean people, but it vastly oversimplifies what actually happened in 1939. As Miyata Setsuko and Kim Yŏngdal detailed in their pioneering works, the colonial government did not actually issue a "Name Order" to change Korean names into Japanese style. Instead, it promulgated substantial revisions of the colonial civil laws and extended the Japanese family system into Korea.[2] In other words, the name-changing policy was not intended merely to Japanize Korean names, but to transform the Korean family system as a whole. Despite this important discovery, Miyata and Kim did not provide a sufficient account of why the colonial government combined these two distinct policies. They concentrated on the name-changing policy and devoted little attention to the more comprehensive family policy.

This essay pays primary attention to family policy, investigating why it was formulated and combined with the name-changing policy. Historically, the family policy agenda was developed in the 1920s as a means of lessening the importance of lineage in the traditional Korean family system and permitting more adoptions from outside the lineage; the idea of Japanizing Korean names was entirely absent from this plan. The name-changing policy was grafted onto it later, in the context of Japanese assimilation efforts in the 1930s. Because the two policy agendas were merged and became known as the name-changing policy, their significance for the family was obscured and ultimately misperceived. Building upon these new findings, this essay argues that the colonial government's priority was the family policy, which was designed to weaken the traditional Korean lineage system and replace it with the Japanese family system, while the naming policy agenda was less important.

Revision of the Colonial Family Laws in 1939

In late 1939, the Japanese colonial government issued a set of ordinances (*seirei*) and orders (*sōtokufurei*) to revise the Ordinance on Civil Matters in Korea (*Chōsen minjirei*) and the Ordinance on Korean Household Registration (*Chōsen kosekirei*) that had defined and governed the Korean family system.[3] These orders, hereafter referred to as the "1939 Amendment," constituted what later came to be known as *sōshi kaimei,* the name-changing policy. But Ordinance 19, clumsily entitled "On the Partial Revision of the Ordinance on Civil Matters in Korea," clearly demonstrates the interconnection between the name-changing policy and family policy.

Ordinance 19 stipulated several new legal terms and concepts to be added to the current family law (i.e., *Chōsen minjirei*) and granted them a legal effect. Space does not permit a detailed textual analysis, but the consequential changes were that (1) Koreans were obligated to have a "family name" (*shi*), which is conceptually differentiated from the Korean "clan name" (*sei*); (2) the Japanese custom of *mukoyōshi,* the adoption by parents of a boy who would simultaneously be married to their daughter,[4] was introduced to Korea and became practicable for Koreans; (3) the legal prohibition of *iseiyōshi*—adopting a child who has a different "clan name"—by the Korean customary laws was abolished. Without understanding their social context, it might be difficult to see the significance of these measures, but the 1939 Amendment intended to introduce several Japanese family practices into Korea and change the traditional Korean family system.

On the other hand, the obligation to have a "family name" did not mean that all Koreans were required to change their names into Japanese-style names. The supplementary provision of the ordinance stipulated:

> The Korean household head is required to make a new family name (*shi*) and report it to the mayor, or the town or village magistrate. . . . If it is not reported, the "clan name" (*sei*) of the household head shall become the family name on the enforcement date of this Ordinance. In case the household head is female . . . the clan name of the previous male household head shall become the family name.[5]

In sum, Koreans were required to create a "family name" rather than to change their "clan names," and only the household head was required to register the family name. Moreover, if the household head did not register the new family name, his clan name automatically became his family name; in this way, the clan name could become a Korean-style family name.

What was the rationale for the colonial government's conceptual distinction between the family name, *shi,* and the clan name, *sei* (hereafter referred to as the "*sei-shi* distinction"), and its order for Koreans to create *shi* rather than change *sei?* The answer lies in the fact that both *shi* and *sei* had a distinctive social function in the respective family systems of Japan and Korea.

Family Names and Clan Names

The Chinese characters for *shi* and *sei* commonly mean a person's surname and can be used interchangeably in both the Korean and Japanese languages today. However, in prewar Japan and colonial Korea, these terms were clearly distinguished as two different legal concepts. In the Japanese family system defined by the civil code, "family name," *shi,* is a title or identification attached to every household, called *ie,* and all members of a single household must bear the same family name. Thus, when someone left his or her natal household and entered another by marriage or adoption, he or she had to take the family name of the new household. Since this rule applied to everyone regardless of gender, even a male Japanese could change his family name, typically by adoption or becoming *mukoyōshi* of another household. In sum, *shi* identifies the household to which one currently belongs, and therefore it is subject to change as household affiliations change over the life course. (Hereafter, the system centered around the notion of "family name" is referred to as the "*shi*-system.")

In contrast, in the Korean system, "clan name," *sei,* identified a person's patrilineage and was typically presented in combination with another identifier, called "clan seat" (J. *hongan*/ K. *pon'gwan*), the alleged clan founder's original place of residence (e.g., Kim of Kyŏngju, Kim of Kimhae, Yi of Chŏnju), and those who shared the same clan name and seat were regarded as the member of the same clan, which was often referred to as "lineage." Korean children, both male and female, inherit their biological father's *sei* and clan seat name at birth and retain it throughout their lives. For this reason, a Korean woman retains her *sei* even after marriage, but she cannot pass it on to her children since *sei* by definition represents only patrilineal descent. This naming tradition originated from and was underpinned by Neo-Confucian ideology, especially the notion of patrilineal succession, which held considerable sway over Korean society in the latter half of the Chosŏn dynasty (1392–1910).[6]

Another distinctive feature of the clan name is that it was used as the legal standard to ban certain kinds of marriage and adoption. First, marriage between people who held the same clan name was prohibited as a consanguineous marriage, since having the same *sei* meant they were members of the same lineage, however remote the genealogical connection. (Hereafter, this rule is referred to as the "ban on same-*sei* marriage.") Similarly, adopting a child of a different clan name (i.e., *iseiyōshi*) was prohibited because the different *sei* signified the absence of the common patrilineal descent that was an absolute condition for family membership. Adoption was practiced only within the same lineage. (Hereafter, this naming tradition and the customary taboos are called the "*sei*-system.")

With this *sei-shi* distinction in mind, we can more clearly see the impact of Ordinance 19 on the Korean family system. The introduction of "family name" to Korea meant transplanting the household-centered Japanese *shi*-system into Korean society and transforming its family system based on the lineage-centered *sei*-system. It was not merely the name style that the Japanese wanted to change, but the family system as a whole.

Therefore, once the new concept of *shi* became a legal basis to define a family household, there was no need to retain the ban on same-*sei* marriage or *iseiyōshi* intended to exclude anyone who had no direct patrilineal connection from family membership. Thus, it was a logical consequence that *mukoyōshi* and *iseiyōshi* were legalized together with the introduction of the *shi*-system.

The 1939 Policy: Regulating Family and Personal Names

While Korean household heads were mandated to register a new "family name" there was no legal requirement as to its style. In theory, Koreans could register any name of their choice, but there were a few restrictions. Ordinance 20 stipulated that "the names of the late [Japanese] emperors shall not be used for either family or personal names." Another restriction is that "one cannot use a clan name for family name, unless it was his own clan name." Thus, a Kim could register Kim as his family name, but could not use other Korean clan names such as Pak or Yi for his new family name.[7]

On January 16, 1940, the colonial government added to the prohibition list the names of Korean imperial family members, famous Japanese shrines (e.g., Ise, Yasukuni), prominent Japanese aristocrats (e.g., Konoe, Ōji), and distinctive historical figures (e.g., Tōgō, Nogi).[8] This regulation was intended to keep Koreans from desecrating imperial authority, whether Japanese or Korean, and from passing themselves off as members of noble Japanese families.[9]

Orders 220 and 221 and Notice 77 described how to correct Korean household registration when the new name was registered. Importantly, the Korean clan name was not erased from the record, even when the new family name was registered. Instead, it was relocated to a different column where the *hongan* used to be recorded and was renamed "clan name and clan seat column" (*sei oyobi hongan*) to show both. This rule applied to all female members of the household, typically the mother, the wife, and the daughter-in-law, who had to take the family name that the household head newly registered.

When the household head did not report a new family name, his clan name automatically became the family name as stipulated in Ordinance 19, and the household registration officer took the liberty of changing the record. In this case, the *sei* and *shi* became identical and there was no change in terms of the name style. However, the female members of the household, who had a different *sei* from the household head, had to take the household head's *sei*-turned-*shi,* making their *sei* and *shi* different. For example, Kim Chŏngja, the wife of Yi Kwangu, came to have the *shi* Yi and became Yi Chŏngja, though her *sei,* Kim, was preserved on the record.

The conventional view holds that Koreans were coerced into changing their personal names as well as their clan names, but the truth is quite different. Order 222 stipulated that "a person who wants to change . . . their personal name should submit an application to the local court . . . and receive approval" as well as "pay the application fee of 50 sen." If the application was rejected by the local court, the person could not appeal to a higher court to reverse the decision.[10] This legal procedure was completely separate from the one for reporting the new family name, and even non–household heads could apply on an individual basis. Because changing one's personal name required payment of a fee, Koreans were discouraged from applying. In sum, changing a personal name was a legal choice, whereas creating a *shi* was an obligation. And here lies the reason why this policy was called *sōshi kaimei*—"creating family name, changing personal name"—in Japanese. In this sense, its common English translation, "name-changing policy," is not an accurate translation because it does not convey any sense that the two names were treated quite differently.

This analysis reveals that the 1939 Amendment was intended primarily to introduce the *shi*-system, which included the practice of *mukoyōshi* and *iseiyōshi,* while obligating all Koreans to have a *shi* in addition to a *sei.* This change was legally mandated, and Koreans had no choice but to accept it. What kind of *shi* they had depended on the individual choice of the household head. There was no provision mandating that Koreans take a Japanese-style *shi.* Significantly, however, there was a legal way to have a Korean-style *shi,* and the original Korean *sei* was not erased from the record.

In this sense, it can be said that the introduction of the *shi*-system was of primary importance as it was legally mandatory, while the Japanization of Korean names was somewhat secondary, not only because it was not legally mandated but also because it only became an option as a result of introducing the *shi*-system. The 1939 Amendment had two distinct policy agendas, and changing the Korean family system was more important than changing the style of Korean names. So, we must now ask why these two different agendas were conflated into a single set of rules.

Different Family Systems under Different Laws

By the time Japan annexed Korea in 1910, the Japanese government had substantial knowledge about the differences between Korean and Japanese family traditions. When Japan made Korea a protectorate in 1905, government experts undertook research on Korean social and legal customs in order to draft an independent Korean civil code, separated from the Japanese civil code. This work documented the fact that the Korean *sei* name had a very different social and legal function from the Japanese *shi.*[11]

The ambitious project to draft a separate Korean civil code was aborted when Korea lost its status as a sovereign state. The annexation did not result in the immediate extension of the Japanese civil code to Korea, however. Instead, the Japanese government decided to use Korean customary laws. As a result, Koreans remained subject to different civil laws from Japanese, even after annexation, and the distinctive Korean family system remained intact.

In 1912, the colonial government promulgated the Ordinance on the Civil Matters in Korea (*Chōsen minjirei*), which extended selected articles of the Japanese civil code to Korea as a first step toward integrating the two legal systems. However, those articles regarding legal capacity, kinship, and succession were excluded from extension.[12] Korean customary laws continued to provide the legal standards for governing the Korean family system.

The continuation of Korean customary laws and the continued separation of the two family systems were justified in the name of the "preservation of traditional customs" (*kyūkan onzon*).[13] This policy protected the Korean family tradition and quelled the concerns of conservative Koreans who feared that the Japanese might change their family traditions. Conversely, though, it kept Koreans bound by the old customs, many of which were constructed to buttress Neo-Confucian family values, especially the perpetuation of patrilineal succession, during the previous dynasty. Koreans were not allowed to challenge the customary ban on same-*sei* marriage and *iseiyōshi,* even if they disagreed with them. Women's rights remained strictly limited as well. They were disqualified from succession to family headship and from the inheritance of property and had no legal right to initiate divorce.[14]

The household registration systems in Korea and Japan were also governed by different laws. Upon annexation, the Japanese government decided not to unite the existing Korean household registration system (J. *minseki*/K. *minjŏk*)[15] with the Japanese system (J. *koseki*/K. *hojŏk*) and used the different systems as a legal standard to define Japanese and Korean nationality—that is, those on the Japanese household registration record were Japanese nationals and those on the Korean registration record were Korean nationals. Since household registration was of crucial importance in legally differentiating the two nationalities, transferring one's household from one system to the other was prohibited. This provision also meant that intermarriage and adoption between Japanese and Koreans were not legally practicable because such a transaction had to involve the transfer of registration from one household and nationality to the other.[16] In fact, this problem was considered a serious defect of the Japanese legal system by contemporary legalists, who urged the adoption of a new law enabling transfers of registration.[17]

In reality, the growing Japanese presence in Korea produced many de facto intermarriages between members of the two national groups, as discussed in Barbara Brooks' essay in this volume. According to an early colonial police survey, there were around one hundred Japanese-Korean couples without legal endorsement throughout the 1910s. Between 1912 and 1917, at least 275 Japanese men married Korean women and 360 Korean men married Japanese women. What also deserves attention is the fact that there were 9 cases of Koreans adopted into Japanese households and 11 cases in which Japanese men were adopted as *mukoyōshi* (*irimuko*) into Korean households, in clear violation of the Korean customary law prohibiting the adoption of anyone from outside the lineage, let alone a foreign Japanese. Although the numbers of intermarriages and instances of *mukoyōshi* were very small, they indicate that some Koreans had begun to seek a new style of marriage and adoption beyond the traditional social norms as early as the 1910s.

To respond to this changing social reality, the Japanese government issued the Compatibility Law (*kyōtsūhō*) in 1917 legalizing the transfer of household registration between Japan Proper (*naichi*), Korea, and Taiwan so that marriage and adoption were practicable between any two families in the Japanese Empire. The only qualification to exercise this right was that Japanese men must first fulfill their military duty. It aimed to prevent young Japanese nationals from evading conscription by becoming Korean or Taiwanese, which was now legally possible by transferring one's name from the Japanese household registration to the Korean or Taiwanese registration by means of mixed marriage or adoption.

The metropole–colony and colony–metropole transfer of household registration was now possible in theory, but additional revisions of the Korean household registration law (*minsekihō*) were required to make it practicable. The necessary revisions were made in 1922 by Order 99, and at last mixed marriages and adoptions by Japanese and Koreans became possible.

At the same time, the colonial government applied several additional provisions of the Japanese civil code to Korea as a first step toward integrating the two legal systems. Japanese laws regarding the minimum age of marriage, the right to initiate divorce, and the recognition of illegitimate children replaced Korean customary laws, giving Korean women the same legal rights as Japanese women.[18] Finally, the colonial government promulgated the Korean Household Registration Law (*Chōsen kosekirei*) and replaced the old Korean household registration (*minseki*) with a new registration system (*Chōsen koseki*) modeled after the Japanese system.[19]

Once these basic legal frameworks had been put in place, the numbers of intermarriages and adoptions gradually began to increase. The table below summarizes the totals for 1923–1937.[20]

The differences that are visible in this data reflect the distinctive features of the Japanese and Korean family systems. In Japan, common ancestry was not an absolute condition for family membership, so Koreans could enter Japanese households as wives, adoptees, *mukoyōshi,* and *nyūfu. Nyūfu* refers to another form of uxorilocal marriage in which the son-in-law does not became the legal son of the household nor take the

Table 1 Registration Transfers between Japanese and Korean Households

	Koreans who entered Japanese households				Japanese who entered Korean households			
Year	Korean wife	Korean *nyūfu*	Korean *mukoyōshi*	Korean adoptee	Japanese wife	Japanese *nyūfu*	Japanese *mukoyōshi*	Adoption
1921–1929	21	49	36	47	339	0	0	
1930–1939	158	413	138	399	1682	0	0	3
Total	179	462	174	446	2021	0	0	3

family name of the *ie*.[21] In contrast, in the Korean system one had to share a patrilineal connection to be eligible for adoption, so no Japanese could legally enter Korean households except as a wife.[22] Korean customary laws that banned *iseiyōshi* and *mukoyōshi* were still in effect throughout the 1920s and 1930s.

Actual family practices differed from officially sanctioned relationships, however. As mentioned before, the colonial police survey from the 1910s shows that there were de facto Japanese *mukoyōshi* in a few Korean households. Presumably some Koreans no longer viewed a patrilineal connection as an absolute precondition for family formation and even incorporated Japanese men into their families despite the lack of legal endorsement. The traditional notion of a Korean family or lineage bonded by patrilineal descent was slowly but steadily undermined by the interactions between Koreans and Japanese.

The Matsudera Plan of 1924

In this social context, the colonial government submitted a proposal in 1924 to the Korean Advisory Council (J. *chūsūin*/K. *chungch'uwŏn*), a consultative body consisting of Korean aristocrats and notables, to introduce *mukoyōshi* in Korea. Matsudera Takeo, the director of the Legal Affairs Bureau, explained the purpose of the proposal:

> In Korean custom, the person who takes charge of ancestral worship has to be selected from the same bloodline (*kettō*), specifically, the son of the same paternal bloodline. This originates from the idea of patrilineal succession (*fukei shugi*) that views blood as something that is passed from the father to the sons. As a result, even when you have your own child, if it is a girl, you must adopt a boy who has the same clan name and clan seat, while marrying off your own daughter. This is a completely logical and natural consequence of the principle of patrilineal succession. . . .
>
> However, would it not go against the human emotions that you must adopt someone else's child . . . despite having your own child [i.e., daughter] . . . and that you must give away your social status and property to someone else's child? . . . [This Korean custom] does not give enough consideration to the human emotion and human nature because it is excessively loyal to the formality of patrilineal succession.

> Thus, the Japanese civil code, though it also holds the patrilineal succession on principle . . . recognizes *mukoyōshi* as an exception so that theory (*riron*) and human emotion (*ninjō*) would be harmonized. Accordingly, the same exception should also be permitted in Korea. . . . I hear, in these days, there are some people who want to have *mukoyōshi.* If that is the case, it is the way to adapt to the trend of time to make an exception to the traditional custom.[23]

Matsudera did not specify who actually wanted to have *mukoyōshi,* but the example he used indicates that he had Korean cases in mind. Doubtless some Koreans wanted to adopt other Koreans as *mukoyōshi.* Introducing *mukoyōshi* in Korea was not an easy task, however. Matsudera was well aware that *mukoyōshi* was incompatible with Korean customary law. Not only was adopting a child who had a different clan name prohibited, but if the household head adopted a child who had the same clan name, his daughter and his adopted son could not marry because they had the same *sei;* same-*sei* marriage was also prohibited. *Mukoyōshi* was only practicable under the Japanese family system, where common ancestry was not a required condition for adoption and a family name could be changed and inherited by anyone.

Therefore, Matsudera proposed to introduce the institution of "family name" to Korea together with the institution of *mukoyōshi.*

> In Korea, there is no title for the household (*ie*). Even though there is a so-called clan name, it only identifies one's paternal bloodline. . . . Even when someone enters another's household upon marriage, the person's clan name does not change. . . . Thus, it is very common to see different clan names in a single household. . . . In such a case when a widow inherits the family property and becomes the household head, it has to cause a discrepancy between the clan name of the inheritor [the widow] and that of the [husband's] ancestor, which is very inconvenient.
>
> In Japan . . . Article 746 of the civil code stipulates that the household head and his family members must share the same family name. . . . So, I would suggest that you should attach a title to each household in Korea, too. If the household head is a female, let her take the clan name of the previous male household head for the title of the household. . . . But her clan name

> and clan seat should be properly kept on the household registration documents. . . .
>
> This plan . . . may sound like an idea to fundamentally transform the [family] system, but the actual change that will take place is that someone who enters one household from another has to take the clan name of the household head [as family name] . . . . The custom of the [Korean] nation should be respected, but if there is any inconvenience, it is necessary for the sake of national progress to make a slight modification so that it should fit our reality.[24]

The two policies that Matusdera proposed, the introduction of "family name" and of *mukoyōshi* (hereafter, the Matsudera Plan), perfectly coincide with the 1939 Amendment, even down to technical details such as showing both clan name and family name on the household registration or mandating that the female household head use the previous male household head's clan name for her new family name.

However, one major difference is that the Matsudera Plan did not have any intention of allowing Koreans to devise a new family name of their choice. His plan was to turn the household head's *sei* into the *shi* of the household, so the Japanization of the Korean name was not an issue. The important thing was to ensure that all Koreans had a *shi* as a new identification of the household, as distinguished from *sei,* the identification of their lineage. As long as the Koreans accepted *shi* as a new legal standard to define family membership and tolerated the practice of *mukoyōshi,* the style of *shi* did not have to be Japanese. What Matsudera wanted to change was the function of the name vis-à-vis the Korean family system, not the Korean name style.

In 1924 the Korean Advisory Council approved the Matsudera Plan and endorsed a study by the colonial government on how to implement the policy.[25] These decisions were not made in secret. For example, *Keijō nippō,* the Japanese newspaper in Korea, reported in June 1926 that *mukoyōshi* would soon become legalized in Korea by the revision of the Ordinance on the Civil Matters in Korea.[26] In 1927, the governor-general established a Committee for Judicial Revisions (*shihōhōki kaisei iinkai*) consisting of legal experts to deliberate on the technical details.[27]

In response to these proposed reforms of the Korean family system, the Korean Bar Association (Chōsen bengoshi kyōkai) held an emergency conference in early 1927 and discussed forwarding a proposal to the government so that their ideas might be reflected in the revision of the colonial family laws.[28] Interestingly, the topics they considered were not limited to the legalization of *mukoyōshi,* but also included the abolition of the customary law that prohibited marriage between persons with the same clan names. Indeed, they sought to change the Korean family traditions more radically than the government and to abolish the taboos on both adoption and marriage based on the notion of the clan name.

However, the government's proposal aroused strong opposition from conservative Koreans. According to the Korean media, the major opposition came from the "old-generation people" both within and outside the Korean Advisory Council. They held that the *sei*-system was the "beautiful custom of Korea" and stood against the penetration of Japanese customs into Korea.[29] Considering that the Advisory Council included many Korean *yangban* aristocrats who adhered to Neo-Confucian values and took pride in their renowned pedigrees, it is not surprising that they perceived the legalization of *mukoyōshi* and same-*sei* marriage as threats to the traditional social order in which patrilineal descent was the source of social status. The Korean Advisory Council evidently rescinded its agreement to the introduction of the "family name system" and *mukoyōshi* in 1928 or 1929. Fukasawa Shin'ichirō, director of the Legal Affairs Bureau, resubmitted the Matsudera Plan to that body in 1930.[30] In 1932, the Committee for Judicial Revision was dissolved as a result of governmental restructuring following the arrival of Ugaki Kazushige as the new governor-general.[31] It seems that the colonial government had failed to create a consensus and gave up the proposal entirely. The long-discussed plan to revise colonial family laws came to a complete halt.

The colonial government's surrender to conservatives frustrated Korean progressives who wanted to reform family traditions. Many young Korean intellectuals who had received a modern education came to view the traditional family system as a sign of Korea's backwardness. Popular Korean journals and magazines throughout the 1920s and the 1930s were flooded with articles urging Koreans to rid themselves of old family customs. Their most common targets were the extended family system that ignored individual freedom, the low status of women, the abusive treatment of wives by mothers-in-law, and the primacy of family over the state.[32]

Yi In, one of the first Koreans who passed the Japanese bar exam, believed that *mukoyōshi* should be legalized in Korea as it would prevent succession struggles in heirless Korean families.[33] Yi In did not have a pro-Japanese political orientation; he was a well-known anti-Japanese patriot who often volunteered to defend leaders of the independence movement and did not hesitate to criticize colonial misgovernment. He presented his argument for legalizing *mukoyōshi* as part of his critique of the colonial government for failing to respond to Koreans' desire for reform. His other demands included guaranteeing full freedom of speech and publication for Koreans, abolishing the Police Security Law (*hoanhō*), and treating Korean political prisoners properly. He saw the Japanese failure to institutionalize *mukoyōshi* as a sign of Japanese neglect of Koreans' human rights, and he characterized this as a failure as serious as the Japanese police's maltreatment of Koreans.[34]

This position won broad support from progressives. For example, *Tonga ilbo,* the most popular Korean newspaper and a stronghold of cultural nationalists, criticized the colonial government's abandonment of legalizing *mukoyōshi* in a front-page editorial: "the government's respect for the Korean custom is greatly appreciated," but an exception should be made for *mukoyōshi* because it would benefit Koreans. As the newspaper saw the situation, "the major cause of disharmony in a Korean family is the custom to adopt [someone else's] son despite the presence of a real daughter," so *mukoyōshi* was a way "to avoid ugly family disputes." Furthermore, it argued for abolition of the ban on same-*sei* marriage, stating that "there were many clans that had a membership of more than a million people" in Korea and the actual kin connections between clan members were often attenuated, so these marriages would not cause any problem "from a eugenic point of view."[35]

The Korean modern nationalists represented by the *Tonga ilbo* group thought that the traditional ban on same-*sei* marriage and *iseiyōshi* had no scientific basis and there was no need to cling to the narrow definition of family based on the notion of *sei*. They did not intend to blindly copy the Japanese family model, but they thought that some of its features could be of practical use to Koreans in reforming their own family system. The only problem was that Koreans had no right to revise the existing customary laws and draft new laws. Hence, they claimed that it was the Japanese colonial government's responsibility to heed Koreans' wishes and take the necessary legal measures to institute the reform plan immediately.

Nevertheless, the conservatives' opposition was stronger than the progressives' demand for reform. When the colonial government consulted the Korean Advisory Council about the possibility of legalizing same-*sei* marriage, providing statistical evidence that there were already 3,868 de facto marriages among spouses with the same clan name and that 3,437 of those couples had sought legal recognition, the council bluntly rejected the idea and contended that these figures were unreliable.[36] To the dismay of the Korean progressives, the conservatives in the Korean Advisory Council had more sway in the colonial government.

The Emergence of a New Plan

Proposals to install the *shi*-system and allow *mukoyōshi* resurfaced in the late 1930s and were finally realized by the 1939 Amendment. By then, however, the reform had been modified to include two new measures: to give a legal option for Korean household heads to create a family name in the Japanese style, and to allow Koreans to change their personal names upon judicial permission. How did this new plan emerge and become incorporated into the preexisting plan that aimed to introduce the *shi*-system and *mukoyōshi?* Currently available sources do not include any documentary evidence to answer the question, but the circumstantial evidence indicates that the new agenda emerged as a result of the dramatic sociopolitical changes of the late 1930s.

As is widely known, Korea gained a new strategic importance as Japan began its invasion of Manchuria and China. In particular, the arrival of Minami Jirō, the powerful Japanese military leader, as the new governor-general in 1936 and the outbreak of the Second Sino-Japanese War in 1937 accelerated the militarization of Korean society. In 1938, the Spiritual Mobilization Law was implemented both in Japan and in Korea, and a large number of Koreans were mobilized to work for the Japanese war machine.[37]

Amidst the growing militarization of Korea, the Minami administration reestablished the Committee for Judicial Revision in April 1937 and resumed studies on how to install the suspended plan for introducing the *shi*-system and *mukoyōshi*.[38] It is highly likely that the new idea of allowing Koreans to have Japanese-style names was proposed in one of these meetings. As Mizuno Naoki has pointed out, for decades the colonial government had not allowed Koreans to have Japanese-style names. As early as 1911, the colonial government prohibited Koreans from changing their clan names into "look-like-Japanese names" (*naichijin ni magirawashiki sei*) and from registering their newborns with Japanese-style names, and it kept this policy in place until 1939.[39] Allowing Koreans to have Japanese-style names represented a radical departure from previous policy.

The reason for this important policy change remains to be studied, but Miyata Setsuko suggests that it was to prepare for Korean conscription. She points out that there was strong opposition within the Japanese military to allowing Koreans to retain their names after they were enlisted in the Japanese Imperial Army.[40] The colonial government began considering the conscription of Koreans in the summer of 1937.[41] This timing coincides with the reopening of the Committee for Judicial Revision, where the idea of Japanizing Korean names might have been discussed.

Nevertheless, Japanese propaganda at that time stressed a more ideological reason for persuading Koreans to adopt Japanese names. It often noted that having a Japanese-style name helped Koreans escape from Chinese cultural bondage and return to the pre-Sinified stage of Korean history when Japan and Korean formed one nation.[42] In other words, the Japanization of Korean names signified severing Korea's historic ties with China and uniting it more closely with Japan. The Japanese authorities were rather insecure about Korean loyalty in the wake of the war with China and encouraged Koreans to bear Japanese names.

There is no reason to doubt that the idea of Japanizing Korean names surfaced as a new policy agenda in response to the growing Japanese demand for Korean human resources and loyalty in wartime. This idea was grafted on to the preexisting plan to introduce the *shi*-system, as both had to do with Korean names, and implemented as the 1939 Amendment. The dual character of the plan was the result of the conflation of the two different policy agendas that were developed separately for different purposes.

Japanese propaganda officers were well aware that the 1939 Amendment had two policy agendas, and they tried to explain the significance of both to the Korean public. The government emphasized the merits of the *shi*-system and *mukoyōshi,* presenting the 1939 Amendment as an epoch-making reform of the Korean family system. At the same time, it also stressed the merit of all imperial Japanese subjects having Japanese names.

When the colonial government first publicized the 1939 Amendment, the major headlines of the *Maeil sinbo,* the government's Korean-language newspaper, was "Korean Family System Reform" and "*Shi*-system for Koreans." The articles quoted Cho Kwangjo, a religious leader of Chŏndogyo, and Kim Hwallan (Helen Kim), the most prominent female educator and the president of Ewha Women's College, as saying that "*mukoyōshi* (*sawi yangja* in Korean) is very rational" and "we can search more broadly for a better adoptee and a better son-in-law."[43] *Chosŏn ilbo,* the popular Korean newspaper, headlined "Epoch-Making Change in Korean Family System: Civil Laws Revised in January" and "*Shi* Is the Title of Households—Koreans Use *Shi* like Japanese," and featured explanatory articles on the significance of the *shi*-system, *mukoyōshi,* and *iseiyōshi* by the director of the Legal Affairs Bureau.[44] The initial media attention was directed toward the family policy component of the 1939 Amendment.

The next day, Governor-General Minami Jirō issued a statement about the aims of the 1939 Amendment. He encouraged Koreans to have a Japanese-style family name to advance the idea of *naisen ittai*—the popular slogan that meant "Japan and Korea are one body"—and stressed the ideological significance of doing so. He did not forget, however, that the 1939 Amendment was aimed more broadly at uniting the family systems in Japan and Korea:

> I think the three things—1) Japanese and Koreans having family names and personal name in common, 2) intermarriage and 3) adoption with each other—will contribute to the realization of *naisen ittai* in the legal realm. . . . It is phenomenal that the number of Japanese-Korean intermarriages and adoptions has been rapidly increasing these days, and the revision of the Ordinance on the Civil Matters of Korea will allow Koreans to have a family name just like the Japanese and enable Koreans to adopt *iseiyōshi* and even a Japanese child.[45]

Despite governmental publicity on the merits of reforming family policy, this aspect of the 1939 Amendment was not fully understood or appreciated by the Korean public. The major reason is that the conceptual separation of *sei* and *shi* was incomprehensible to many Koreans who had little knowledge about the distinction between the Korean and Japanese family systems. Both Japanese and Korean mass media often failed to distinguish between the two concepts and thus contributed to popular confusion. For instance, *Keijō nippō* reported that Koreans were "granted freedom to change *sei,*"[46] when the government had actually ordered them "to create *shi*." Similarly, *Chosŏn ilbo* explained that "the wife should follow the husband's *sei*" and "*sei* should be identical within the family,"[47] as if Korean women had to adopt the husband's *sei* when it was actually the *shi* that had to be shared by family members.

The colonial government was very concerned about the erroneous reporting by the mass media. It was well aware that such misunderstandings would lead Koreans to believe that the purpose of the 1939 Amendment was to erase Korean *sei*, which would precipitate strong objections. It immediately issued a public statement that "your clan name will never disappear even if you create a new family name"[48] and that "your clan name and clan seat will stay on the family registration as before"[49] and reemphasized later that "it was not mandatory" to have a new family name that is different from one's clan name.[50] On another occasion, a Japanese legal expert gave a lecture on the *sei-shi* distinction to influential Korean leaders in order to secure their endorsement. However, it was difficult even for Yun Ch'iho, the renowned Korean Christian intellectual, to grasp the significance of the conceptual distinction between *shi* and *sei*. He recorded his response in his diary:

> Under the auspices of Dong-Nim-Hoi [sic],[51] a kind of round-table dinner party was given for a large number of Koreans and Japanese. The chief guests were Hon. Miyamoto, the Director of the Law Bureau and Captain Muratani. After the dinner, Mr. Miyamoto gave a lecture on the establishment of *shi* or family names in Korea. I can't understand the distinction between *shi* and *sei*. The Koreans have had their surnames or *sei* handed down from father to son for last 1,000 years. Why this change? To make the oneness of the Korean and the Japanese more concrete and closer.[52]

The general public could not be expected to understand something that was difficult for Yun Ch'iho to comprehend, and the common perception that the 1939 Amendment meant to change *sei* spread.

In fact, in many cases Japanese police, schoolteachers, and other governmental functionaries pressed Koreans to register a Japanese-style family name as if it were legally mandatory.[53] This kind of unjust and extralegal coercion reinforced the popular Korean opinion that the sole purpose of the 1939 Amendment was the annihilation of the Korean *sei* and led many Koreans to take defensive measures. The common tactic was to call for a "lineage meeting" (J. *monchū kaigi*/K. *munjung hoeŭi*) to devise a common family name, typically using one of the Chinese characters of their clan seat. They thought that they could sustain lineage unity by sharing the same *shi,* even if they lost the Korean *sei.* The collective registration of the family name on a lineage basis was widely and favorably reported by the press: "Common Family Name Created: The Yu of Chŏnju to Have Yanagisawa, and Yu of Chinju, Yanagimura."[54] In some cases, a lineage organization posted a classified advertisement appealing to lineage members to register the same family name: "To All the Members of Chŏn of Tanyang, Let's Have Tamura Together."[55]

The Japanese media praised the collective registration of the same family name on a lineage basis, believing that the higher the number of Japanese-style names registered, the more effectively colonial policy goals would be served.[56] The colonial government disagreed with this view, however. It judged that if Korean lineage members ended up having the same Japanese-style family name it would help them retain their collective identity and reinforce their allegiance to the patrilineage. The governmental legal guidebook on the 1939 Amendment strongly criticized the Japanese media for its lack of understanding of the real policy aim and warned Koreans not to take such action.

> We hear of cases where all members of a lineage came to have the same family name . . . but since a family name should be the title to identify the *ie,* it is desirable for each *ie* to have a different family name. Thus, it goes against the idea of "family name" when lineage members share the same family name. . . . In that connection, it must be said that some newspapers committed the greatest crime by praising and promoting such a practice.[57]

The Response of Korean Women

While Korea's male household heads were trying to protect their lineage identity by recycling a part of their clan name or clan seat in devising a new family name, the female members of the household—wives, mothers, and daughters-in-law—who came from different lineages and therefore had different clan names had no choice but to follow the husband's family name. What family name their household head created and registered was not a matter of interest for women, since they were given no legal right to devise their own family name. Amidst the prevailing confusion over the *sei-shi* distinction, many Korean women believed that they had to lose their own *sei* when they adopted the household head's *sei*. But for women the real issue was that they were forced to adopt their husband's family name. As the 1939 Amendment affected women differently than men, their responses to the name controversy also differed from that of men.

When a popular Korean magazine, *Chogwang*, interviewed several prominent Korean women about their views on the "wife's taking of husband's clan name" and their feelings about losing their own clan name, Yun Sŏngsang gave a rather cynical answer.

> According to Mendel's law, the offspring between Kim [male] and Yi [female] had to be either Kim or Yi or Kim-Yi. [However,] the clan name only represents the paternal bloodline. As a result, Kim could be born from Yi, but Yi would never be born from Yi. This is a big contradiction we should be aware of. . . . Since the clan name does not follow the [Mendel's] law, I wouldn't miss it, even if it was changed into a new one.[58]

Yun was aware that the clan name was the product of the male-centered lineage system in traditional Korean society and was frustrated by the fact that the woman's clan name was not heritable by her descendants. She did not recognize any positive meaning in her clan name and did not care to protect it when it was changed or lost.[59]

Ch'oe Igwŏn, a famous female educator whose husband, Paek Nakchun (George L. Paik), was the president of Yonsei University, offered a similar but more practical explanation for why the clan name had little significance for women: "I have not been called by my clan name for many years. Nor would my children ever inherit my clan name. Is it not the same since I have already lost my clan name? [Even if my clan name were changed] it would not bring me any new feeling." Ch'oe's response was rooted in her experience as a Korean wife and mother. Married women were not called by their clan name once they were married, even though they did not bear their husband's *sei;* instead, they were usually called "*samonim*" (missus) or "*ŏmŏni* (mother) of so-and-so (her child's name)." Women's clan names had no function in Korean society, so Ch'oe did not feel enthusiastic about protecting hers.

Of course, some women wanted to keep their own clan name. Chang

Mun'gyŏng, one of the earliest Korean female medical doctors, said: "If this small symbol of my personal identity were gone, and if I had to take my husband's [name], I would feel as sorry as if I were to lose my property."[60] Ch'oe Chŏnghŭi declared that "For a female writer, her clan name and personal name is the lifeline and the 'price tag.' I have been polishing my name for the past twenty or thirty years and it is hard to abandon it overnight."[61] Mo Yunsuk, a leading female poet, put it more emotionally: "If Mo Yunsuk is going to be called An Yunsuk,[62] it will bring an odd feeling. . . . I feel I am losing myself."[63] Women who opposed the idea of changing their clan name to their husband's family name cherished their names not because of their allegiance to their lineage but because of their desire to protect their personal identity. These prominent female professionals were known by their clan names, which gave their clan names social value. For most Korean women, their *sei* had much less significance because it was neglected in daily life and not inherited by their children. After all, the Korean *sei* was a meaningful sign only for men; women had little interest in protecting the Korean *sei* and fighting against the Japanese policy.

Conclusion

Previous scholarship has generally treated the name-changing policy as one of many Japanese policies designed to deprive Koreans of their distinct identity. While this policy was indeed aimed at assimilation, it was not the Korean name per se but the Korean family system as a whole that the colonial government wanted Koreans to adopt. The radical element of the policy was not the changing of Korean names but its aim of disestablishing the traditional Korean family system and the integration of Koreans into the Japanese family system.

The failure to notice that the name-changing policy was part of a larger colonial family policy has led many previous scholars to overstate the Japanese desire for Koreans to adopt Japanese-style names. But, once we realize that the policy had more to do with the family system than with names, we can provide a more persuasive account of the complex and confusing way the Japanese policy implemented this policy. This analysis suggests the following corrections to the conventional account of Japanese intentions.

First, it has often been said that the Japanese hypocritically left Korean clan names on the registration record to mask their goal of assimilation. Instead, this measure was necessary because the Japanese intention was not to erase the Korean *sei,* which would have aroused serious objections from Koreans, but rather to introduce the *shi*-system.

Second, Wan-you Chou has argued that the *sei-shi* distinction was merely a rhetorical device designed to persuade Koreans to change their names to Japanese style.[64] But *sei* and *shi* had different social functions in the Korean and Japanese family systems and were distinct legal concepts. Moreover, the *sei-shi* distinction was already emphasized in the 1920s when the colonial government considered introducing the *shi*-system and legalizing *mukoyōshi* in Korea. The *sei-shi* distinction was crucial to the implementation of Japanese family policy, not as a means to deceive Koreans.

Third, the conventional assumption that the Japanese were obsessed with imposing Japanese names upon Korean names does not explain why the colonial government did not simply coerce Koreans into adopting Japanese-style names. Moreover, it cannot account for the fact that the Japanese authority laid out different legal procedures for registering a new family name and for changing personal name and discouraged the latter by making the application process very onerous. In fact, less than 10 percent of Koreans had changed their personal names by the end of 1941.[65] Korean personal names had no significance in the Korean lineage system that the Japanese wanted to reform, so it is understandable that the Japanese had little interest in changing Korean names. Since the Japanese aimed to replace the *sei*-system with the *shi*-system, personal name changing had no direct service to the proposed aim and thus received scant attention.

Fourth, many Korean historians believe that they can judge their ancestors' loyalty to the Korean nation by checking whether or not they had a Japanese-style family name. However, it must be remembered that the colonial government granted the legal right to register a new family name only to the household head and that other members of the household had no choice but to adopt whatever family name the household head registered. Moreover, even household heads often followed a decision made by the lineage organization, which selected one family name to be used by all lineage members. Thus, it is impossible to judge anyone's loyalty to the Korean nation only by looking at the style of his or her name.

This essay has presented preliminary research and a new analysis of the historical link between the name-changing policy and colonial family policy. Many issues remain unresolved and require further study with additional evidence. Yet, it is clear that the historical development of the name-changing policy was closely connected with colonial family policy. The name-changing policy and the reform of the family were originally different policy goals, but the 1939 Amendment merged the two, creating confusion that continues until the present.

Notes

1. Carter J. Eckert and Ki–baek Yi, eds., *Korea, Old and New: A History* (Seoul: Ilchokak; distributed by Harvard University Press, 1990), 318.

2. For the representatives works on the policy, see Miyata Setsuko, "Sōshi kaimei ni tsuite, jō," *Rekishi hyōron* 486 (1990); Miyata Setsuko, "Sōshi kaimei ni tsuite, ge," *Rekishi hyōron* 487 (1990); Miyata Setsuko et al., *Sōshi kaimei* (Akashi Shoten, 1992); and Kim Yŏngdal, *Sōshikaimei no kenkyū* (Miraisha, 1997).

3. The orders for the legal revisions (in chronological order) were November 10, 1939, Ordinance 19, "On the Partial Revision of the Ordinance on Civil Matters in Korea," and Ordinance 20, "On the Korean Family Names and Personal Names"; December 26, 1939, Order 219, "On the Enforcement Date of the Ordinances [10 and 20]"; Order 220, "On the Partial Revision of Korean Household Registration Law"; Order 221, "On the Household Registration Filing Procedures to Reflect the Created Family Names of Koreans"; Order 222, "On Koreans Who Change Family Names and Personal Names"; and Notice 77, "On Administrative Details of Household Registration to Reflect the Created Korean Family Names." For the summary of these legal texts, see Nagumo Kōkichi, *Sōshi oyobi shimei henkō tetsuzuki to todokede shoshiki* (Keijō: Osakayagō Shoten, 1940), appendix (*furoku*).

4. By doing so, the parents are able to keep their daughter home, while securing a legal male heir who is supposed to succeed to their household and family property together with the daughter. This custom did not exist in Korea.

5. Nagumo Kōkichi, *Sōshi oyobi shimei henkō tetsuzuki to todokede shoshiki,* appendix 5.

6. For the Confucianization of the Chosŏn society and its impact on the family system, see Martina Deuchler, *The Confucian Transformation of Korea: A Study of Society and Ideology* (Cambridge, MA: Harvard University Press, 1992); and Mark A. Peterson, *Korean Adoption and Inheritance: Case Studies*

in the Creation of a Classic Confucian Society (Ithaca, NY: Cornell University Press, 1996).

7. Kim Yŏngdal claims that this regulation was a sneaky legal trick to leave Koreans no choice but to choose a Japanese-style name when they created the new family name (Kim, *Sōshikaimei no kenkyū,* 26). This contention is questionable, however, because taking someone's clan name was already taboo in traditional Korean society as it was regarded as a way of counterfeiting one's patrilineage and stealing a different pedigree by disguising one's origin. If a Korean was proud of his name and genealogy, he would have chosen to use his clan name for his family name, and it is less likely that he would have wanted to use someone's clan name for his family name. It seems more likely that the regulation was an extension of the customary rule intended to prevent social confusion and identity theft.

8. "Kaku chihōinchō shichō jōseki matawa hitori no hanji ate Chōsen sōtokufu hōmukyoku tsūchō" (January 16, 1940). For the full text, see Miyata Setsuko et al., *Sōshi kaimei,* 219–220.

9. There is a popular anecdote in Korea that some Koreans registered such names as *dennōheika* (which sounds similar to "emperor" in Japanese) or *inukuso kurae* ("eat bullshit") as a means of resistance. As Kim Yŏngdal has persuasively argued, however, registration officers were instructed to reject any names that breached the rules described above, and it is highly unlikely that such names were officially permitted and registered. In fact, no documentary evidence has been found to prove the case. Rather, the very fact that such rumors circulated widely is revealing of Korean sentiments. See Kim, *Sōshikaimei no kenkyū,* 26.

10. See Article 1 of Order 220.

11. Chōsen Sōtokufu Torishirabe Kyoku, ed., *Kanshūchōsa hōkokusho* (Keijō: Chōsen Sōtokufu, 1912), 290.

12. Chulwoo Lee, "Modernity, Legality, and Power in Korea under Japanese Rule," in *Colonial Modernity in Korea,* ed. Gi-Wook and Michael Edson Robinson (Cambridge, MA: Harvard University Press, 1999), 26.

13. Oguma Eiji, *"Nihonjin" no kyōkai: Okinawa, Ainu, Taiwan, Chōsen shokuminchi shihai kara fukki undo made* (Shinyōsha, 1998), chaps. 3–4.

14. Korean women had inheritance rights before the seventeenth century, but they were gradually lost. For more details about Korean women's status in patrilineal tradition, see Lee, "Modernity, Legality, and Power in Korea under Japanese Rule," 3–5.

15. Minseki were established in 1909 before the annexation. For more details on this registration system, see Sakamoto Shin'ichi, "Haisenzen

nihonkoku ni okeru Chōsen koseki no kenkyū," *Seikyūronshū* 10 (1997): 246–248.

16. For early colonial policy defining the Koreans' legal status vis-à-vis the Japanese, see Oguma Eiji, *"Nihonjin" no kyōkai,* 154–161.

17. Hozumi Shigetō, *Shinzokuhō taii* (Iwanami Shoten, 1917), 72–73. The information on the colonial police survey that follows is from Chōsen Chūsatsu Kenpei Shireibu, *Keisatsu tōkei* (Taisho 5–6 nen), cited in Kim Yŏngdal, "Nihon no Chōson tōchika ni okeru 'tsūkon' to 'konketsu,'" *Kansai Daigaku Jinken Mondai Kenkyūjo kiyo* 39 (July 1997): 31.

18. Chŏng Kwang-hyŏn, *Sŏngssi Nongo: Chosŏn Kajokpŏp Nongo* (Kyngsŏng: Tonggwangdang Sŏjŏm, 1940), 108.

19. Sakamoto Shin'ichi, "Haisenzen Nihonkoku ni okeru Chōsen koseki no kenkyū," 248–251,

20. On the legal rights of *nyūfu,* see Ume Kenjirō, *Minpōyōgi* (Yūhikaku, 1912), 115–116.

21. However, if family members later agree, a *nyūfu* may succeed the household head.

22. It is puzzling that Korean families adopted three Japanese children, since Korean customary laws did not legally sanction the adoption of nonlineage members. The only possibility is that a Korean widow with her son entered the Japanese household at her remarriage and later her son was adopted by his biological father's relative in Korea. Since he was originally born of a Korean father, his clan name was recorded on the Korean household registration before it was transferred to the Japanese registration and he could prove his Korean ancestry despite his Japanese nationality.

23. Nagumo Kōkichi, *Sōshi oyobi shimei henkō tetsuzuki to todokede shoshiki,* 24–27.

24. Ibid., 29–30. There is no doubt that it was a Japan-centric idea, based on the *ie* system, to think that name and ancestry can be separated and "family name" can be passed on to anyone without an actual patrilineal connection. In Korea, where the name and descent were tied together—in fact, the clan name and patrilineage were the two sides of the same coin—and people believed in only the succession of lineal descendents, distinguishing between the family name and the clan name would not make much sense.

25. Nagumo, *Sōshi oyobi shimei henkō tetsuzuki to todokede shoshiki,* 31.

26. *Keijō nippō,* June 23, 1926.

27. Aono Masaaki, "Chōsen sōtokufu no sōshi kōsō," *Momoyamagakuin Daigaku sōgōkenkyūjo kiyō* 28 (2002): 195–196.

28. *Chosŏn ilbo,* January 31, 1927, 2.

29. *Tonga ilbo,* June 29, 1932, 2.

30. For his explanation, see Nagumo, *Sōshi oyobi shimei henkō tetsuzuki to todokede shoshiki,* 31–34.

31. *Tonga ilbo,* June 29, 1932, 2.

32. See, for example, *Kaebyŏk* 3 (1920): 23–28; *Pyŏlgŏngŭn* 18 (1929): 62–68; *Samch'ŏlli* 3 (1929): 22–25.

33. Yi In, "Pomnyul chŏnsŏn ŭi uri ŭi ch'eso yogu," *Tonggwang* (December 1931): 22–25.

34. Ibid., 25.

35. *Tonga ilbo,* February 17, 1933, 1.

36. Chōsen chūsūin dai 299 gō, "Dōseidōhonjakan no kon'in ni kansuru ken" (June 10, 1936) in the online database at http://db.history.go.kr/.

37. Miyata et al., *Sōshi kaimei,* 23.

38. Ibid., 25.

39. Mizuno Naoki, "Chōsen shokuminchi shihai to namae no 'saika,'" in *Shokuminchishugi to jinruigaku,* ed. Yamaji Katsuhiko (Nishinomiya: Kansai Gakuin Daigaku Shuppankai, 2002), 146–158. Before 1911, there were several cases in which Koreans were legally allowed to change their clan names into Japanese, but later this decision was reversed. The prohibition of naming Korean children in Japanese style was lifted in 1937.

40. Miyata et al., *Sōshi kaimei,* 39–40.

41. Ibid., 25.

42. Morita Yoshio, ed., *Shisōsetsu no shinseishin to sono tetsuzuki* (Keijō: Ryokki Renmei, 1940), 18–19, 42–52; Nagumo, *Sōshi oyobi shimei henkō tetsuzuki to todokede shoshiki,* 12–13, 72. These materials are prefaced by the governor-general or the director of the Legal Affairs Bureau and therefore characterized as "governmental."

43. "Chosŏn kajok chedo ŭi pyŏnhyŏk," *Maeil sinbo,* November 10, 1939, 3.

44. *Chosŏn ilbo,* November 19, 1939, 2.

45. Quoted in Nagumo, *Sōshi oyobi shimei henkō tetsuzuki to todokede shoshiki,* 35–38.

46. *Keijō nippō,* November 10, 1940, quoted in Kim Yŏngdal, *Sōshikaimei no kenkyū,* 51.

47. *Chosŏn ilbo,* November 10, 1939, 2,

48. *Maeil sinbo,* November 19, 1939, 2.

49. Ibid., December 28, 1939, 2.

50. Ibid., February 11, 1940, 5.

51. Yun must have meant Dōminkai (K. Dongminhoe), a Korean private organization to promote the idea of Japanese-Korean Unity (*naisen ittai*) at the grassroots level.

52. Yun Ch'i-ho, *Yun Ch'i-Ho Ilgi,* vol. 11 (Seoul: Kuksa P'yonch'an Wiwŏnhoe, 1989), 263. However, he created the new family name Itō. Ibid., 310–311.

53. On Japanese coercion, see Richard E. Kim, *Lost Names: Scenes from a Korean Boyhood* (New York: Praeger, 1970), 100–106.

54. *Maeil sinbo,* February 21, 1940, 4.

55. Ibid., 1.

56. Kim, *Sōshikaimei no kenkyū,* 62–67.

57. Morita, ed., *Shisōsetsu no shinseishin to sono tetsuzuki,* 117.

58. *Chogwang,* January 1940, 382.

59. The only exception was another female writer, Chŏng Ch'angyŏng. She stated that "according to the tradition . . . the clan name is [to show] the bloodline of my father and mother, and to abandon it to take my husband's . . . is a very sorry thing. Born a girl, I have to cry." Here, she is concerned with the clan name as a matter of the preservation of the lineage. Nevertheless, her statement was based on the incorrect assumption that the clan name also shows the mother's lineage. The clan name only passes down the father's lineage, which is why other professional women criticized the clan name as a manifestation of the male-centered ideological construction of the family. *Chogwang,* January 1940, 383.

60. Ibid., 382.

61. *Samch'ŏlli,* March 1940, 239.

62. Her husband was An Hosang, a well-known scholar of philosophy and an educator.

63. Dōminkai Honbu, ed., *Sōshi kinen meishi kōkankai meibo* (Keijō: Taikaidō Insatsu, 1940), 382.

64. Wany-ao Chou, "The Kōminka Movement in Taiwan and Korea: Comparisons and Interpretations," in *The Japanese Wartime Empire, 1931–1945,* ed. Peter Duus, Ramon Hawlyer Myers, and Mark R. Peattie (Princeton, NJ: Princeton University Press, 1996), 58–59.

65. Out of the total 24,053,530 Korean population in 1940, only 2,311,263 changed their personal names (less than 10 percent); Yŏngdal, *Sōshikaime no kenkyū,* 33.

Bibliography

Serial Publications

Asahi shinbun
Chosŏn ilbo
Chōsen oyobi Manshū
Hōritsu shinbun
The Japan Weekly Mail
Kaebyŏk
Maeil sinbo
Nippon Times
Pyŏlgŏngŭn
Samch'ŏlli
Shūgiin, Shōkō iinkai gijiroku
Taiwan nichi nichi shinpō
Tonggwang
Tonga ilbo
Yomiuri shinbun

Books and Articles

The place of publication of all Japanese-language works is Tokyo unless otherwise noted.

Abrams, Kathryn. "Sex Wars Redux: Agency and Coercion in Feminist Legal Theory," *Columbia Law Review* 95 (1995), 304–376.

Alexander, M. Jacqui. "Erotic Autonomy as a Politics of Decolonization." In *Feminist Genealogies, Colonial Legacies, Democratic Futures,* edited by M. Jacqui Alexander and Chandra Mohanty, 63–100. New York: Routledge, 1997.

Ambaras, David R. *Bad Youth: Juvenile Delinquency and the Politics of Everyday Life in Modern Japan.* Berkeley: University of California Press, 2006.

American Diplomatic and Public Papers: The United States and China, Ser. II,

The United States, China, and Imperial Rivalries, 1861–1893. Vol. 12, *The Coolie Trade and Outrages against the Chinese,* edited by Jules Davids. Wilmington, DE: Scholarly Resources, 1979.

Anderson, Marnie S. *A Place in Public: Women's Rights in Meiji Japan.* Cambridge, MA: Harvard University Asia Center, 2010.

Aneha Shohei. *Hontōjin nomi ni kansuru shinzokuhō oyobi sōzokuhō no taiyō.* Taihoku: Taihō Geppō Hakkōsho, 1938.

Aono Masaaki. "Chōsen sōtokufu no sōshi kōsō." *Momoyamagakuin Daigaku sōgōkenkyūjo kiyō* 28 (2002): 187–198.

Asano Tamanoi, Mariko. "Songs as Weapons: The Culture and History of Komori (Nursemaids) in Modern Japan." *Journal of Asian Studies* 50, no. 4 (November 1991): 793–817.

Berenson, Edward. *The Trial of Madame Caillaux.* Berkeley: University of California Press, 1992.

Bessei soshō o sasaeru kai, web site accessed July 9, 2012, http://www.asahi-net.or.jp/~dv3m-ymsk/index.html.

Black, John R. *Young Japan: Yokohama and Yedo.* 2 vols. London: Trubner & Co.; Yokohama: Kelly & Co., 1880–1881.

Boissonade, Gustave Emil. *Projet révisé de code pénal pour l'empire du Japon accompagné d'un commentaire par Mr. Gve Boissonade.* Kokubunsha, 1886.

Botsman, Daniel. "Freedom without Slavery? 'Coolies,' Prostitutes, and Outcastes in Meiji Japan's 'Emancipation Moment,'" *American Historical Review* 116, no. 5 (2011): 1323–1347.

———. *Punishment and Power in the Making of Modern Japan.* Princeton, NJ: Princeton University Press, 2005.

Bousquet, Georges. *Le Japon de nos jours et les échelles de l'extrême orient.* Paris: Librairie Hachette, 1877.

Bowen-Raddeker, Helene. *Treacherous Women of Imperial Japan: Patriarchal Fictions, Patricidal Fantasies.* New York: Routledge, 1997.

Brodie, Janet Farrell. *Contraception and Abortion in Nineteenth Century America.* Ithaca, NY: Cornell University Press, 1994.

Brooks, Barbara J. "Japanese Colonial Citizenship in Treaty Port China: The Location of Koreans and Taiwanese in the Imperial Order." In *New Frontiers: Imperialism's New Communities in East Asia, 1842–1952,* edited by Robert Bickers and Christian Henriot, 109–125. Manchester: Manchester University Press, 2000.

———. "Peopling the Japanese Empire: The Koreans in Manchuria and the Rhetoric of Inclusion. In *Japan's Competing Modernities: Issues in Culture and Democracy, 1900–1930,* edited by Sharon Minichiello, 25–44. Honolulu: University of Hawai'i Press, 1998.

———. "Reading the Japanese Colonial Archive: Gender and Bourgeois Civility in Korea and Manchuria before 1932." In *Gendering Mod-*

ern Japanese History, edited by Kathleen Uno and Barbara Molony, 295–326. Cambridge, MA: Harvard East Asian Monographs, 2005.

Burns, Susan L. "The Body as Text: Confucianism, Reproduction, and Gender in Early Modern Japan." In *Rethinking Confucianism: Past and Present in China, Japan, Korea and Vietnam,* edited by Benjamin Elman, Herman Ooms, and John Duncan, 178–219. Los Angeles: UCLA Asia Pacific Monograph Series, 2002.

———. "Local Courts, National Laws, and the Problem of Patriarchy in Meiji Japan: Reading 'Records of Civil Rulings' from the Perspective of Gender History." In *Interdisciplinary Studies on the Taiwan Colonial Court Records Archive,* edited by Wang Tay-sheng, 285–309. Taipei: Angle Publishing, 2009.

Campani, Giovanna. "Present Trends in Women's Migration: The Emergence of Social Actors." In *Scapegoats and Social Actors: The Exclusion and Integration of Minorities in Western and Eastern Europe,* edited by Daniéle Joly, 192–217. New York: St. Martin's Press, 1998.

Canning, Kathleen. *Gender History in Practice.* Baltimore: Johns Hopkins University Press, 2006.

Case of the Peruvian Barque Maria Luz; with Appendix. Yokohama: n.p., 1872.

Ceng Qiu-mei. *Taiwan Xifuzi [sim-pua] de shenghao shijie.* Taipei: Yushanshe, 1998.

Ch'en, Paul Heng-chao. *The Formation of the Early Meiji Legal Order: The Japanese Code of 1871 and its Chinese Foundation.* New York: Oxford University Press, 1981.

Chen Zexian. "Shijiu shiji shengxing de qiyue huagong shi." *Lishi yanjiu* no. 1 (1963): 161–179.

Chiba Takeno. "Joshū no kyōiku ni tsuite." *Kangoku kyōkai zasshi* 22, no. 6 (July 1909): 24–28.

Childers, Kristen. *Fathers, Families, and the State in France, 1914–1945.* Ithaca, NY: Cornell University Press, 2003.

Ching, Leo. *Becoming Japanese: Colonial Taiwan and the Politics of Identity Formation.* Berkeley: University of California Press, 2001.

Chŏng Kwang-hyŏn. *Sŏngssi nongo: Chosŏn kajokpŏp nongo.* Kyŏngsŏng: Tonggwangdang Sŏjŏm,1940.

Chōsen Sōtokufu, ed. *Chōsen Sōtokufu tōkei nenpō 1923, daigohen.* Keijō: Chōsen Sōtokufu, 1923.

———. *Chōsen Sōtokufu tōkei nenpō 1938.* Keijō: Chōsen Sōtokufu, 1938.

Chōsen Sotokufu Keimukanbu, ed. *Chōsen minseki yōran.* Keijō: Shidokan, 1915.

Chōsen Sōtokufu Torishirabekyoku, ed. *Kanshūchōsa hōkokusho.* Keijō: Chōsen Sōtokufu, 1912.

Chou, Wan-yao. "The Kōminka Movement in Taiwan and Korea: Comparisons and Interpretations." In *The Japanese Wartime Empire, 1931–1945*, edited by Peter Duus, Ramon Hawlyer Myers, and Mark R. Peattie, 40–68. Princeton, NJ: Princeton University Press, 1996.

Chuang, Ying-chang. "Chinese 'T'ung-yang-hsi' Marriage: The Ch'en Family of T'ou-fen, Taiwan." *Proceedings of National Science Council, Part C: Humanities and Social Sciences* 2, no. 1 (1991): 174–185.

Connelly, Mark Thomas. *The Response to Prostitution in the Progressive Era.* Chapel Hill: University of North Carolina Press, 1980.

Corbitt, Duvon Clough. *A Study of the Chinese in Cuba, 1847–1947.* Wilmore, KY: Asbury College, 1971.

Cott, Nancy. *Public Vows: A History of Marriage and the Nation.* Cambridge, MA: Harvard University Press, 2002.

Crawford, Suzanne. "The *Maria Luz* Affair." *The Historian* 46, no. 4 (1984): 583–596.

Croll, Elisabeth. *Endangered Daughters: Discrimination and Development in Asia.* London: Routledge, 2000.

Cuba Commission. *Chinese Emigration: Report of the Commission Sent by China to Ascertain the Condition of Chinese Coolies in Cuba.* Shanghai: Imperial Maritime Customs Press, 1876.

Daishin'in, ed. *Meiji zenki Daishin'in keiji hanketsu roku.* 29 vols. Shihōsho, 1875–1887; repr., Bunsei Shoin, 1987–1989.

Dana, Richard Henry, Jr. *To Cuba and Back* [1859]. In *Two Years before the Mast and Other Voyages,* edited by Thomas L. Philbrick. New York: Library of America, 2005.

Davis, Natalie Zemon. *Fiction in the Archives: Pardon Tales and Their Tellers in Sixteenth Century France.* Stanford, CA: Stanford University Press, 1987.

De Becker, J. E. *The Annotated Civil Code of Japan,* vol. 3. London: Butterworth and Co., 1909–1910.

———. *The Nightless City, or the History of the Yoshiwara Yūkwaku,* 5th ed., revised [1905]. Rutland: Tuttle, 1971.

Desan, Suzanne. *The Family on Trial in Revolutionary France.* Berkeley: University of California Press, 2004.

Deuchler, Martina. *The Confucian Transformation of Korea: A Study of Society and Ideology.* Cambridge, MA: Harvard University Press, 1992.

Dobrovolskaia, Anna. "The Jury System in Pre-War Japan: An Annotated Translation of 'The Jury Guidebook' (*Baishin Tebiki*)." *Asian-Pacific Law & Policy Journal* 9, no. 2 (2008): 231–296.

Dōminkai Honbu, ed. Sōshi kinen meishi kōkankai meibo. Keijō: Taikaidō Insatsu, 1940.

Donzelot, Jacques. *The Policing of Families.* Baltimore: Johns Hopkins University Press, 1997.

Doolittle, Reverend Justus. *Social Life of the Chinese: Daily Life in China.* New York: Harper and Brothers, 1865.

Dorn Lublin, Elizabeth. *Reforming Japan: The Woman's Christian Temperance Union in the Meiji Period.* Vancouver: University of British Columbia Press, 2010.

Drixler, Fabian. Infanticide and Fertility in Eastern Japan: Discourse and Demography, 1660–1880. PhD diss., Harvard University, 2008.

Dunker, Arne. *Gleichheit und Ungleichheit in der Ehe: Persönliche Stellung von Frau und Mann im Recht der ehelichen Lebensgemeinschaft 1700–1914.* Köln: Böhlau Verlag, 2003.

Duus, Peter. *The Abacus and the Sword: The Japanese Penetration of Korea, 1895–1910.* Berkeley: University of California Press, 1995.

Eckert, Carter J., and Yi, Ki-baek, eds. *Korea, Old and New: A History.* Seoul: Ilchokak, 1990.

Engle, Sally. *Colonizing Hawai'i: The Cultural Power of Law.* Princeton, NJ: Princeton University Press, 2000.

English, Jean, trans. *The Prison Memoirs of a Japanese Woman.* London: M. E. Sharpe, 1991.

Enloe, Cynthia. *The Morning After: Sexual Politics at the End of the Cold War.* Berkeley: University of California Press, 1993.

Fan, Li-qing. *Tiansongbi zhi chun: Yiwei Taiwan funu de shenghuoshi.* Taipei: Zili Wanbao Press, 1995.

Farley, M. Foster. "The Chinese Coolie Trade, 1845–1875." *Journal of Asian and African Studies* 3, nos. 3–4 (July & October 1968): 257–270.

Flaherty, Darryl. "Democratization, 1919, and Lawyer Advocacy for a Japanese Jury." *Journal of Japanese Studies* 37, no. 2 (Summer 2011): 257–287.

———. "Organizing for Influence: Lawyers Associations and Japanese Politics, 1868–1945." PhD diss., Columbia University, 2001.

Foreign Relations of the United States, 1873. Washington, DC: Government Printing Office, 1874.

Foreign Relations of the United States, 1874. Washington, DC: Government Printing Office, 1875.

Foucault, Michel. *Discipline and Punish: The Birth of the Prison.* London: Peregrine Books, 1977.

———. "Governmentality." In *The Foucault Effect: Studies in Governmentality,* edited by Graham Burchell, Colin Gordon, and Peter Miller, 87–104. Chicago: University of Chicago Press, 1991.

Freedman, Estelle B. *Their Sisters' Keepers: Women's Prison Reform in America, 1830–1930.* Ann Arbor: University of Michigan Press, 1981.

Frühstück, Sabine. *Colonizing Sex: Sexology and Social Control in Modern Japan.* Berkeley: University of California Press, 2003.

Fuess, Harald. *Divorce in Japan: Family, Gender, and the State.* Stanford, CA: Stanford University Press, 2004.

———. "Ehebruch als Verbrechen: Der europäische Beitrag zur Frauendiskriminierung in Japan." *Zeitschrift für japanisches Recht* 24, no. 1 (2007): 108–136.

———. "Men in the Women's Kingdom." In *Public Spheres, Private Lives in Modern Japan, 1600–1950,* edited by Gail Bernstein, Andrew Gordon, and Kate Wildman Nakai, 259–292. Cambridge, MA: Harvard University Asia Center, 2005.

Fujime Yuki. "The Licensed Prostitution System and the Prostitution Abolition Movement in Modern Japan." *positions: east asia cultures critique* 5, no. 1 (Spring 1997): 135–170.

———. *Sei no rekishigaku: Koshō seido, dataizai taisei kara baishun boshihō, yusei hogohō taisei e.* Fuji Shuppan, 1997.

Fujitani, Takashi. *Race for Empire: Koreans as Japanese and Japanese as Americans in World War II.* Berkeley: University of California, 2011.

Fukuzawa Yukichi. *Fukuzawa Yukichi on Japanese Women: Selected Works.* Translated by Eiichi Kiyooka. Tokyo: University of Tokyo Press, 1988.

Gaimushō, ed. *Nihon gaikō monjo,* reprint. Nihon Kokusai Rengō Kyōkai, 1950–1956.

Gaimushō Archives, B 9.10.0 1–1, *Kokusai renmei fujin jidō mondai ikken.*

Gardiner, C. Harvey. *The Japanese and Peru, 1873–1973.* Albuquerque: University of New Mexico Press, 1975.

Garon, Sheldon. *Molding Japanese Minds: The State in Everyday Life.* Princeton, NJ: Princeton University Press, 1997.

Gates, Hill. "The Commoditization of Chinese Women." *Signs: Journal of Women in Culture and Society* 14, no. 4 (1989): 799–832.

Ghosh, Durba. *Sex and the Family in Colonial India: The Making of Empire.* Cambridge: Cambridge University Press, 2008.

Gibson, A. Sena (Cai A-xin). *Pioneer Doctor's Adventures* (unpublished manuscript).

Gluck, Carol. *Japan's Modern Myths.* Princeton, NJ: Princeton University Press, 1985.

Gordon, Andrew. *A History of Modern Japan: From Tokugawa Times to the Present,* 2nd ed. New York: Oxford University Press, 2008.

Gordon, Beate Shirota. *The Only Woman in the Room: A Memoir.* Tokyo: Kodansha International, 1997.

Gordon, Robert W. "Critical Legal Histories." *Stanford Law Review* 36 (1984): 59–67.

Gotō Shinpei. "Taiwan keiei jō kyūkan seido no chōsa o hitsuyō to suru iken." *Taiwan kanshū kiji* 1, no. 5 (1901): 24–38; no. 6 (1901): 25–35.

Great Britain. Foreign Office Archives. F.O. 84/1442. "Slave Trade—Fugitive Slave Commission. No. 29. Escape of Coolie Emigrants from the Peruvian Ship 'Maria Luz' on Board Her Majesty's Ship 'Iron Duke' in Japan in 1872."

Great Britain. House of Commons. *China. No. 3 (1875). Correspondence Respecting the Macao Coolie Trade: 1874–1875.* London: Harrison and Sons, 1875.

———. *Coolie Emigration.* London: n.p., 1868.

———. *Hong Kong: Copies or extracts of correspondence between the Colonial Department and the governor of Hong Kong . . . on the subject of emigration from Hong Kong and from the Chinese Empire to the British West Indies . . . since the 1st day of January 1853. Part I.* London: n.p., 1858.

———. *Hong Kong Coolie Trade.* London: Wm. Clowes & Sons, 1873.

Griffin, Eldon. *Clippers and Consuls: American Consular and Commercial Relations with Eastern Asia, 1845–1860.* Ann Arbor, MI: Edwards Bros., 1938.

Gronewald, Sue. *Beautiful Merchandise: Prostitution in China, 1860–1936.* New York: Institute for Research in History and Hawthorne Press, 1982.

Grossberg, Michael. *Governing the Hearth: Law and the Family in Nineteenth-Century America.* Chapel Hill: University of North Carolina Press, 1985.

Hachi-jo-sei. "Hachiōji jokan no kako oyobi genzai no jōkyō." *Kangoku kyokai zasshi* 17, no. 8 (August 1904): 47–49; 17, no. 9 (September 1904): 47–48; 17, no. 10 (October 1904): 59–62; 17, no. 12 (December 1904): 58–60; 18, no. 2 (February 1905): 51–53; 18, no. 3 (March 1905): 44–46; 18, no. 4 (April 1905): 48–50; 18, no. 8 (August 1905): 43–45.

Haga Noboru. *Nihon josei jinmei jiten.* Nihon Toshō Sentaa, 1993.

Hager, Kelly. *Dickens and the Rise of Divorce.* Burlington, VT: Ashgate, 2010.

Hahn Rafter, Nicole. *Creating Born Criminals.* Urbana: University of Illinois Press, 1997.

———. "Gender, Prisons, and Prison History." *Social Science History* 9, no. 3 (Summer 1985): 233–234.

———. *Partial Justice: Women, Prisons, and Social Control.* New Brunswick, NJ: Transaction Publishers, 1990.

Haley, John Owen. *Authority without Power: Law and the Japanese Paradox.* New York: Oxford University Press, 1991.

Hanai Takuzō. "Shiryō: Meiji shonen ni okeru sanza-seido." *Hōgaku shinpō* 33, no. 7 (1923).

Hane, Mikiso. *Peasants, Rebels, and Outcastes: The Underside of Modern Japan.* New York: Pantheon, 1982.

———, ed. and trans. *Reflections on the Way to the Gallows: Rebel Women in Prewar Japan.* Berkeley: University of California Press, 1993.

Hara Yoshimichi, Egi Makoto (also Chū), and Hanai Takuzō, eds. *Baishin seido hōrikan.* Hiramatsu Ichizō, 1921.

Hartog, Hendrik. *Man and Wife in America: A History*. Cambridge, MA: Harvard University Press, 2000.

Haruyama Meitetsu. "Taiwan kyūkan chōsa to rippō kōsō; Okamatsu Santarō ni yoru chōsa to ritsu'an o chūshin ni." *Taiwan kin-gendaishi kenkyū* 6 (1988): 81–114.

Hayashi Hiromasa. *Kaisei keihō karian seiritsu katei no kenkyū*. Seibundō, 2003.

Hayashi Raizaburō. *Nihon baishinhō gikai*. Chūō Daigaku, 1926.

Hayashi Yōko. "Chūjōryū." *Joseishi kenkyuū* 20 (1985): 27–31.

Hayashiya Reiji. "Meiji Shonen no minji soshō shin jukensū no kōsatsu." In *Meiji zenki no hō to saiban*, edited by Hayashiya Reiji, Ishii Shirō, and Aoyama Yoshimitsu, 91–116. Shinsensha, 2002.

Hicks, Cheryl D. "'In Danger of Becoming Morally Depraved': Single Black Women, Working-Class Black Families, and New York State's Wayward Minor Laws, 1917–1928." *University of Pennsylvania Law Review* 151, no. 6 (June 2003): 2077–2121.

Hiramatsu Yoshirō. "Bakumatsu-ki ni okeru hanzai to keibatsu no jittai—Edo Kodemmachō rōya kiroku ni yoru." *Kokka gakkai zasshi* 71, no. 3 (March 1957): 76–130.

———. *Kinsei keiji soshō hō no kenkyū*. Sōbunsha, 1960.

Hirata, Lucie Cheng. "Free, Indentured, Enslaved: Chinese Prostitutes in Nineteenth-Century America." *Signs: Journal of Women in Culture and Society* 5, no. 1 (1979): 3–29.

Hirota Masaki, ed. *Sabetsu no shosō*. Iwanami Shoten, 1990.

Hobsbawm, Eric, and Terence Ranger, eds. *The Invention of Tradition*. New York: Cambridge University Press, 1983.

Hōmushō Chōsa Tōkeika, ed. *Kensatsu tōkei 100-nen*. Hōmusho, 1976.

Hōrei Kenkyūkai, ed. *Jitsurei hanrei bunrei jinjihō sōran*. Keibunsha Shuppanbu, 1928.

Hoshino Tōru, ed. *Minpōten ronsō shi*. Nihon Hyōronsha, 1944.

Howe, Adrian. *Punish and Critique: Towards a Feminist Analysis of Penality*. London: Routledge, 1994.

Howell, David L. *Geographies of Identity in Nineteenth-Century Japan*. Berkeley: University of California Press, 2005.

Hozumi, Nobushige. *Lectures on the New Japanese Civil Code as Material for the Study of Comparative Jurisprudence*. Maruzen Kabushiki-Kaisha, 1912.

Hozumi Shigetō. "Otto no kantsū." In *Kazoku seido zenshū shironhen*. Vol. 2, *Rikon*, edited by Hozumi Shigetō and Nakagawa Zennosuke. Kawade Shobō, 1937.

———. *Shinzokuhō taii*. Iwanami Shoten, 1917.

Hozumi Yatsuka. "Minpō idete, chūkō horobu." *Hogaku shinpō* 5 (1891).

Huang, Chieh-shan, and Arthur P. Wolf. "Marriage in Taiwan 1881–1905:

An Example of Regional Diversity." *Journal of Asian Studies* 54, no. 3 (1995): 781–795.

Huang, Philip C. *Code, Custom, and Legal Practice in China: The Qing and the Republic Compared.* Stanford, CA: Stanford University Press, 2001.

Hu-DeHart, Evelyn. "Chinese Coolie Labour in Cuba in the Nineteenth Century: Free Labour or Neo-slavery?" *Slavery and Abolition* 14, no. 1 (April 1993): 67–83.

Huen, Yuki P. "Workplace Sexual Harassment in Japan: A Review of Combating Measures Taken." *Asian Survey* 47, no. 5 (September/October 2007): 811–827.

Hwang, Kyung Moon. *Beyond Birth: Social Status in the Emergence of Modern Korea.* Cambridge, MA: Harvard East Asian Monographs, 2005.

———. "Citizenship, Social Equality and Government Reform: Changes in the Household Registration System in Korea, 1894–1910." *Modern Asian Studies* 38, no. 2 (2004): 355–387.

"Ichigaya kangoku enkaku shi, Kodenmachō rōyashiki no zu." Unpublished manuscript. Kyōsei kyōkai archives.

Ichikawa Fusae, ed. *Nihon fujin mondai shiryō shūsei.* Domesu Shuppan, 1976–1980.

Ichinose Yūzaburō. "Danshaku Katō sensei no kantsūron o haidoku shi 'Minpō dai 113 jō' kaitei "'Keihō dai 184' ni oyobu." *Hōritsu shinbun* 476 (January 30, 1908): 165–166.

Ignatieff, Michael. *A Just Measure of Pain: The Penitentiary in the Industrial Revolution 1750–1850.* London: Macmillan, 1978.

Iida versus Iida. Supreme Court, Civil Affairs Section, *Shinbun* 2976, March 1, 1929.

Innami Otokichi. "Furyō shōnen ni kansuru kangoku mondai." *Kangoku kyōkai zasshi* 14, nos. 5–7 (1901).

———. "Hannin no shintai gokan no kankaku." *Dai Nihon kangoku kyōkai zasshi* 127 (December 1898): 9–18.

———. "Joshū shogū ron." *Kangoku kyōkai zasshi* 16, no. 9 (September 1903): 16–25.

Irick, Robert L. *Ch'ing Policy toward the Coolie Trade, 1847–1878.* Taipei: Chinese Materials Center, 1982.

Ishii, Ryosuke. *Japanese Legislation in the Meiji Era,* translated and adapted by William J. Chambliss. Tokyo: Pan-Pacific Press, 1958.

Ishii Ryōsuke. *Edo no keibatsu.* Chuō Kōronsha, 1964.

Ishii Shirō and Mizubayashi Takeshi, eds. *Nihon kindai shisō taikei.* Vol. 7, *Hō to chitsujo,* Iwanami Shoten, 1992.

Ishimoto, Yasuo. "International Arbitration in the Meiji Era." *Japan Annual of International Law* 7 (1963): 30–37.

———. "Meijiki ni okeru chūsai saiban no senrei (1)." *Ōsaka shiritsu daigaku hōgaku zasshi* 7, no. 4 (1961): 50–78.

Ishizaki Shōko. "Kindai Nihon no sanji chōsetsu to kokkai seisaku." *Sōgo joseishi kenkyū* 15 (1998): 15–32.

———. "Meiji Ishin to seishoku rinri." In *Esunishiti, jenda kara miru Nihon no rekishi,* edited by Kuroda Hiroko and Nagano Hiroko, 313–337. Yoshikawa Kōbunkan, 2002.

———. "Nihon dataizai no seiritsu." *Reikishi hyōron* 571 (1997): 53–70.

Itō, Hidekichi. *Nihon haishō undōshi.* Fuji Shuppan, 1931.

Iwata Shigenori. *"Inochi" wo meguru kindaishi: Datai kara jinkō ninshin chūzetsu e.* Yoshikawa Kōbunkan, 2009.

Iyoku Hideaki, ed. *Hōsei shiryō kenkyū,* vol. 1. Gannandō, 1994.

Jenkins, Edward. *The Coolie, His Rights and Wrongs.* London: Strahan & Co., 1871.

Jiang Wen-yu. *Xioshi zhong de Taiwan ama.* Taipei: Yushanshe, 1995.

Johnston, William. *Geisha, Harlot, Stranger, Star: A Woman, Sex, and Morality in Modern Japan.* New York: Columbia University Press, 2004.

Jones, F. C. *Extraterritoriality in Japan and the Diplomatic Relations Resulting in its Abolition, 1853–1899.* New Haven, CT: Yale University Press, 1931.

Jones, Mark. *Children as Treasures: Childhood and the Middle Class in Early Twentieth Century Japan.* Cambridge, MA: Harvard University Asia Center, 2010.

Jung, Moon-Ho. *Coolies and Cane: Race, Labor and Sugar in the Age of Emancipation.* Baltimore: Johns Hopkins University Press, 2006.

Kajiwara Michiyoshi. *Taiwan nōmin seikatsu kō.* Taipei: Ogata Taketoshi, 1941.

Kamichika Ichiko. "Baishun nado shobatsu hōan wa naze fuketsu sareta." *Fujin kōron* 40, no. 9 (September 1955): 66–68.

———. "Fujin wa heiwa e no suishinryoku de aru." *Shakai kyōiku* 8, no. 3 (March 1953): 8–11.

———. "'Matsumoto jiken' to chihō seiji no fuhai." *Fujin kōron* 40, no. 7 (July 1955): 201.

———. *Sayonara ningen baibai.* Gendaisha, 1956.

———. "Shin no tsukareru sōron: Baishun shobatsu hōan no teiansha to shite." *Toki no hōrei* no. 138 (July 3, 1954): 20–23.

———. *Waga seishun no kokuhaku.* Mainichi Shinbunsha, 1957.

Kanazu Hidemi. "Kindai Nihon ni okeru 'datai no tsumi' no seiritsu." *Josei shigaku* 16 (1996): 26–43.

Kanō Mikiyo. "Manshū to onnatachi." In *Iwanami kōza: Kindai Nihon to shokuminchi.* Vol. 5, *Bōchōsuru teikoku no jinryū,* edited by Ōe Shinobu, 199–222. Iwanami Shoten, 1993.

Kanzaki Kiyoshi. *Baishun Ketteiban Kanzaki repōto.* Gendaishi Shuppankai, 1974.

Kasahara Hidehiko. Maria Rusu gō jiken no saikentō: Gaimushō 'inen' to chūsai saiban." *Hōgaku kenkyū* 69, no. 12 (1996): 117–138.

Kasumi Nobuhiko, *Meiji shoki keijihō no kisoteki kenkyū.* Keiō Gijuku Daigaku Hōgaku Kenkyūkai, 1990.

Katō Hiroyuki. "Kantsū ni tsuite." *Hōgaku kyōkai zasshi* 26 (1908): 1–6.

Kaufmann, Chaim D., and Robert A. Pape. "Explaining Costly International Moral Action: Britain's Sixty-year Campaign Against the Atlantic Slave Trade." *International Organization* 53, no. 4 (1999): 631–668.

Keith, Marian. *The Black-Bearded Barbarian: The Life of George Leslie MacKay of Formosa.* Toronto: Missionary Society of the Methodist Church, The Young People's Forward Movement Dept., 1912.

Kelly, William. "Incendiary Actions: Fire and Firefighting in the Shogun's Capital and the People's City." In *Edo and Paris: Urban Life and the State in the Early Modern Era,* edited by James McClain, John Merriman, and Ugawa Kaoru, 310–330. Ithaca, NY: Cornell University Press, 1994.

Kikuta Kōichi. *Nihon no keimusho.* Iwanami Shinsho, 2002.

Kim, Marie Seong-Hak. "Customary Law and Colonial Jurisprudence in Korea." *American Journal of Comparative Law* 57, no. 1 (2009): 205–247.

———. "Law and Custom under the Choson Dynasty and Colonial Korea: A Comparative Perspective." *Journal of Asian Studies* 66, no. 4 (November 2007): 1067–1097.

———. "Ume Kenjirō and the Making of Korean Civil Law, 1906–1910." *Journal of Japanese Studies* 34, no. 1 (2008): 1–31.

Kim, Richard E. *Lost Names: Scenes from a Korean Boyhood.* New York: Praeger, 1970.

Kim Yŏngdal. "Nihon no Chōsen tōchika ni okeru 'tsūkon' to 'konketsu.'" *Kansei Daigaku Jinken Mondai Kenkyūjo kiyō* 39 (July 1997): 1–46.

———. *Sōshikaimei no kenkyū.* Miraisha, 1997.

Kimura Kenji. *Zai Chō Nihonjin no shakaishi.* Miraisha, 1989.

Kinzley, W. Dean. "Japan's Discovery of Poverty: Changing Views of Poverty and Social Welfare in the Nineteenth Century." *Journal of Asian History* 22, no. 1 (1988): 1–24.

Kirisutokyō jinmei jiten. Nihon Kirisutokyōdan Shuppankyoku, 1986.

Kiyoaki Murata. "Outlawing of Prostitution: Newly Passed Law Will Only Drive Prostitutes Underground." *Nippon Times,* May 28, 1956.

Knorr, Jacqueline, and Barbara Meir. "Women and Migration: Anthropological Perspectives." In *Women and Migration: Anthropological Perspectives,* edited by Knorr and Meir, 9–20. New York: St. Martin's Press, 2000.

Koizumi Eiichi. *Dataizai kenkyū*. Ganshōdō Shoten, 1934.

Kornicki, Peter F. "Frederick Victor Dickins (1838–1915)." In *Britain and Japan: Biographical Portraits,* vol. 3, edited by J. E. Hoare, 66–77. Richmond, Surrey: Japan Library, 1999.

———. "Introduction." In Frederick Victor Dickins, *Collected Works of Frederick Victor Dickins,* vol. 1, edited by Peter F. Kornicki, ix–xxxi. Bristol: Ganesha, 1999.

Kovner, Sarah C. "Prostitution in Postwar Japan: Sex Workers, Servicemen, and Social Activists, 1945–1956." PhD diss., Columbia University, 2004.

Kume Kunitake, ed. *Tokumei zenken taishi Beiō kairan jikki.* 2 vols. Iwanami Shoten, 1978.

"Kyōkatsu hikoku jiken." In Daishin'in, ed., *Daishin'in keiji hanreishū,* vol. 5, 318–325. Hosokai, 1927.

League of Nations. *Commission of Enquiry into Traffic in Women and Children in the East: Report to the Council.* Geneva, 1933.

Lee, Chulwoo. "Modernity, Legality and Power." In *Colonial Modernity in Korea,* edited by Gi-wook Shin and Michael Robinson, 21–51. Cambridge, MA: Harvard Asian Monographs, 1999.

Lenz, Karl–Friedrich. "Penal Law." In *History of Law in Japan since 1868,* edited by Wilhelm Röhl, 607–626. Leiden: Brill, 2005.

Lin Cheng-lu. "Minhō shōhō shigyō ni tsukite wa yoroshiku jogairei o okubeshi." *Taiwan seinen* 3 (1922): 21–35.

Locher-Scholten, Elsbeth. *Women and the Colonial State: Essays on Gender and Modernity in the Netherland Indies, 1900–1942.* Amsterdam: Amsterdam University Press. 2000.

Longford, Joseph H. "A Summary of the Japanese Penal Codes." *Transactions of the Asiatic Society of Japan* 5, part 2 (1877): 1–114.

Lublin, Elizabeth Dorn. *Reforming Japan: The Woman's Christian Temperance Union in the Meiji Period.* Vancouver: University of British Columbia Press, 2010.

MacCormack, Geoffrey. *Traditional Chinese Penal Law.* Edinburgh: Edinburgh University Press, 1990.

MacKay, George Leslie. *From Far Formosa: The Island, Its People, and Missions* [1895]. 3rd ed. Taipei: SMC Publishing, 1991.

MacKay, Robert Peter. *Life of George Leslie MacKay, D.D. 1844–1901.* Toronto: Board of Foreign Missions, Presbyterian Church in Canada, 1913.

Mackie, Vera. *Creating Socialist Women in Japan: Gender, Labour, and Activism, 1900–1937.* Cambridge: Cambridge University Press, 1997.

MacNair, Harley Farnsworth. *The Chinese Abroad: Their Position and Protection, A Study in International Law and Relations.* Shanghai: Commercial Press, 1933.

Majumdar, Rochona. *Marriage and Modernity: Family Values in Colonial Bengal.* Durham, NC: Duke University Press, 2009.

Maki, Hidemasa. *Jinshin baibai.* Iwanami Shoten, 1971.

Marran, Christine L. *Poison Woman: Figuring Female Transgression in Modern Japanese Culture.* Minneapolis: University of Minnesota Press, 2007.

———. "'Poison Woman' Takahashi Oden and the Spectacle of Female Deviance in Early Meiji." *U.S.-Japan Women's Journal, English Supplement* no. 9 (1995): 93–110.

Maruta Takashi. *Baishin saiban o kangaeru: Hōtei ni miru NichiBei bunka hikaku.* Chūō Kōronsha, 1990.

Masada Sayo. *Autobiography of a Geisha,* trans. G. G. Rowley. New York: Columbia University Press, 2003.

Matsumura, Janice. "Unfaithful Wives and Dissolute Labourers: Moral Panic and the Mobilisation of Women into the Japanese Workforce, 1931–45." *Gender & History* 19, no. 1 (April 2007): 78–100.

Matsumura Masayoshi. "Maria Rusu gō jiken no kōhō gaikō teki seikaku." *Teikyō kokusai bunka* no. 9 (1996): 1–52.

McClain, James L. *Japan: A Modern History.* New York: W. W. Norton and Company, 2002.

McWilliams, Wayne C. "East Meets West: The Soejima Mission to China, 1873." *Monumenta Nipponica* 30, no. 3 (1975): 237–275.

———. "Soejima Taneomi: Statesman of Early Meiji Japan, 1868–1874." PhD diss., University of Kansas, 1973.

Meagher, Arnold J. *The Coolie Trade: The Traffic in Chinese Laborers to Latin America, 1847–1874.* N.p.: Xlibris, 2008.

Mega Atsuko. *Hankachō no naka no onna-tachi.* Heibonsha, 1995.

Meijer, M. J. *Murder and Adultery in Late Imperial China: A Study of Law and Morality.* Leiden: Brill, 1991.

Meiroku Zasshi: Journal of the Japanese Enlightenment. Translated by William Reynolds Braisted. Cambridge, MA: Harvard University Press, 1976.

Mendel, Douglas H., Jr. "Japanese Attitudes toward American Military Bases." *Far Eastern Survey* 28, no. 9 (September 1959): 129–134.

Merry, Sally Engle. *Colonizing Hawai'i: The Cultural Power of Law.* Princeton, NJ: Princeton University Press, 2000.

Metzler, Mark. "Woman's Place in Japan's Great Depression: Reflections on the Moral Economy of Deflation." *Journal of Japanese Studies* 30, no. 2 (Summer 2004): 315–352.

Michie, Alexander. *The Englishman in China.* 2 vols. Edinburgh: Blackwood & Sons, 1900.

Mitani, Hiroshi. *Maria Luz Affair and Public Opinion in the World.* Nagoya: Nanzan University, Centro de Estudios de America Latina, 1985.

Mitani Taichirō. *Kindai Nihon no shihōken to seitō: Baishinsei seiritsu no seijishi.* Hanawa shobō, 1980.

Mitsunari Miho. *Jendā no hikakuhō shigaku: Kindaihō chitsujo no saikentō.* Suita: Osaka Daigaku Shuppankai, 2006.

Miyachi Masatō. *Bakumatsu Ishin-ki no bunka to jōhō.* Meicho Kankōkai, 1994.

Miyake Masatarō. "Atte yō nashi." In *Kantsū zai o dōsuru? Shūgiin hatsu no kōchōkai kara,* edited by Hokkaidō Hōsha, 23–24. Sapporo: Hokkaidō Hōsha 1947.

Miyata Setsuko. "Sōshi kaimei ni tsuite, jō." *Rekishi hyōron* 486 (1990).

Miyata Setsuko, Kim Yondaru, and Yan Teho. *Sōshi kaimei.* Akashi Shoten, 1992.

Mizubayashi Takeshi. "Shinritsu kōryō to Kaitei ritsurei no seikai." In *Nihon kindai shisō taikei.* Vol. 7, *Hō to chitsujo.* Iwanami Shoten, 1992.

Mizuno Naoki. "Chōsen shokuminchi shihai to namae no 'saika.'" In *Shokuminchishugi to jinruigaku,* edited by Yamaji Katsuhiko. Nishinomiya: Kansai Gakuin Daigaku Shuppankai, 2002.

Mogi Yōichi. "Kindai Mie-ken iki in okeru datai torishimari no suii nit suite." *Chiken nenpō* 13 (2007): 1–22.

Mohanty, Chandra. "Introduction: Cartographies of Struggle." In *Third World Women and the Politics of Feminism,* edited by Chandra Mohanty, Ann Russo, and Lourdes Torres, 1–47. Bloomington: Indiana University Press, 1991.

Mohr, James C. *Abortion in America.* New York: Oxford University Press, 1978.

Molony, Barbara, "Activism among Women in the Taishō Cotton Textile Industry." In *Recreating Japanese Women, 1600–1945,* edited by Gail Lee Bernstein, 216–238. Berkeley: University of California Press, 1991.

———. "The Quest for Women's Rights in Turn-of-the-Century Japan." In *Gendering Modern Japanese History,* edited by Barbara Molony and Kathleen Uno, 463–492. Cambridge, MA: Harvard University Asia Center, 2008.

Mongaikan. "Jogō Erizabesu Rurai." *Kangoku kyōkai zasshi* 13, no. 5 (May 1900): i–iv.

Moon, Katharine H. S. *Sex among Allies: Military Prostitution in U.S.-Korea Relations.* New York: Columbia University Press, 1997.

Moore, John Bassett. *History and Digest of the International Arbitrations to which the United States has been a Party.* Washington, DC: Government Printing Office, 1898.

Morikawa Yasutaka. "Kakuron: Gōkanzai no mondaiten." *Hōgaku seminā* 43, no. 10 (October 1998): 29–32.

Morinaga Eisaburō. "Dataizai shikō, ge." *Nihon hanzai gakkai zasshi* 2, no. 2 (1936): 52–62.

Morita Tomoko. *Kaikoku to chigai hōken.* Yoshikawa Kōbunkan, 2005.

———. "Maria Rusu gō jiken to geishōgi kaihō rei." In *Onna to shakai shi,* edited by Ōguchi Yujirō, 245–264. Yamakawa Shuppansha, 2001.

Morita Yoshio, ed. *Shisōsetsu no shinseishin to sono tetsuzuki.* Keijō: Ryokki Renmei, 1940.

Morris-Suzuki, Tessa. "Becoming Japanese: Imperial Expansion and Identity Crises in the Early Twentieth Century." In *Japan's Competing Modernities,* edited by Sharon Minichiello, 157–180. Honolulu: University of Hawai'i Press, 1998.

———. "Debating Racial Science in Wartime Japan." *Osiris* 13 (1998): 354–375.

Morse, Hosea Ballou. *The International Relations of the Chinese Empire.* 3 vols. New York: Longmans, Green, & Co., 1910–1918.

Murakami Kazuhiro. *Nihon kindai kekkonhō shiron.* Kyoto: Hōritsu Bunkasha, 2003.

Murphy, U. G. *The Social Evil in Japan,* 4th ed., revised. Tokyo: Methodist House, 1908.

Nagumo Kōkichi. *Sōshi oyobi shimei henkō tetsuzuki to todokede shoshiki.* Keijō: Osakayagō Shoten, 1940.

Naikaku kirokukyoku, ed. *Hōki bunrui taizen,* vol. 57. Hara Shobō, 1980.

Naikaku tōkei kyoku, ed. *Nihon teikoku tōkei nenkan.* Naikaku Tōkei Kyoku, 1882.

Naimushō, ed. *Naimushō nenpō hōkokusho,* bekkan 1. San'ichi Shobō, 1982.

Nakagawa Zennosuke. "Kantsū oyobi jūkon." In *Kazoku seido zenshū shironhen.* Vol. 2, *Rikon,* edited by Hozumi Shigetō and Nakagawa Zennosuke, 253–266. Kawade Shobō, 1937.

Narita Ryūichi. "The Overflourishing of Sexuality in 1920s Japan." In *Gender and Japanese History.* Vol. 1, *Religion, and Customs, the Body and Sexuality,* edited by Wakita Haruko, Anne Bouchy, and Ueno Chizuko, 345–371. Osaka: Osaka University Press, 1999.

Nawa Fumio. *Gōmon keibatsu shi.* Oyamakaku, 1987.

[Nihon Bengoshi Kyōkai] Kyōto Jinken Mondai Tokubetsu Iinkai. "Kyoto jinken mondai ni kansuru tenmatsu hōkoku." *Nihon bengoshi kyōkai rokuji* 24, no. 249 (February 1919): 49–110.

Nihon Bengoshi Kyōkai Taiwan Shibu. "Taiwan minjirei oyobi shinzoku sōzokurei ni taisuru kengisho." In *Taiwan Sōtokufu kōbun ruisan,* vol. 6, part 1, no. 14 (1915). Original archive number 05921.

Nihon kirisutokyō fujin kyofūkai, ed. *Nihon kirisutokyō fujin kyōfūkai hyakunenshi.* Domesu Shuppan, 1986.

Nishimura Kannosuke and Iwano Shinpei. *Shin keihō gige.* 7th ed. Shimizu Shoten, 1912.

Nishimura Nobuo. *Sengo Nihon no kazokuhō no minshūka,* 2 vols. Kyoto: Hōritsu Bunkasha, 1978–1991.

Nobuhiko Kasumi. *Meiji shoki keijihō no kiso kenkyū.* Keiō Gijutsu Daigaku Hōgaku Kenkyūkai, 1990.

Nolte, Sharon H., and Sally Ann Hastings. "The Meiji State's Policy towards Women, 1890–1910." In *Recreating Japanese Women, 1600–1945,* edited by Gail Lee Bernstein, 151–174. Berkeley: University of California Press, 1991.

Norgren, Tiana. *Abortion before Birth Control: The Politics of Reproduction in Postwar Japan.* Princeton, NJ: Princeton University Press, 2001.

O'Brien, Patricia. *The Promise of Punishment: Prisons in Nineteenth Century France.* Princeton, NJ: Princeton University Press, 1982.

Ōe Taku. "Baido no heifū sainen semugosuru o fusegubeshi." *Kakusei / The Purity* 1.4 (October 1911): 18–25.

Ogawa Shigejirō. *Kangokugaku.* Keisatsu Kangoku Gakkai, 1894.

Oguma, Eiji. *A Geneology of "Japanese" Self Images.* Translated by David Askew. Melbourne: Transpacific Press, 2002.

Oguma Eiji. *"Nihonjin" no kyōkai: Okinawa, Ainu, Taiwan, Chōsen, shokuminchi shihai kara fukki undō made.* Shinyōsha, 1998.

———. *Tanitsu minzoku shinwa no kigen: "Nihonjin" no jigazō no keifu.* Shinyōsha, 1995.

Oikata Sumio. "Nihon kindai kokka no seiritsu to baishō mondai." In *Nihon joseishi ronshū.* Vol. 9, *Sei to karada,* edited by Sōgō joseishi kenkyūkai, 75–109. Yoshikawa Kōbunkan, 1998.

Okada Yuzuru. *Kiso shakai.* Kōbundō, 1949.

Okahara Masao. "Baishinhō teishi ni kansuru hōritsu ni tsuite." *Hōsōkai zasshi* 21, no. 4 (1943): 18–19.

Okamatsu Santarō. "Nihon minpō no ketten o ronjite Taiwan rippō ni taisuru kibō ni oyobu." *Taiwan kanshū kiji 5,* no. 3 (1905): 13–26.

———. *Provisional Report on Investigations of Laws and Customs in the Island of Formosa.* Kobe: Printed at the Kobe Herald office, 1902.

Okamoto Harimatsu. "Honkoku ni okeru datai ni kansuru tōkeiteki chōsa no ippan." *Kyōto igakkai zasshi* 26, no. 8 (1929): 551–581; no. 9 (1929): 778–794; no. 10 (1929): 861–878.

Okamura Tsukasa. *Minpō shinzokuhen.* In *Nihon rippō shiryō zenshū, bekkan* 339. 1898; reprint, Shinzansha Shuppan, 2005.

Ōno Fumio, and Yano Masanori. *Sei no saiban kiroku: Kantsū, teisō shingai (gōkan, kyōsei waisetsu, kekkonsagi) seiteiki bujoku, seiki kison.* Sakai Shoten, 1975.

Ono Takeo, ed. *Edo jidai keibatsu fūzoku saiken.* Tenbōsha, 1976.

Oppler, Alfred. *Legal Reform in Occupied Japan: A Participant Looks Back.* Princeton, NJ: Princeton University Press, 1976.

Osatake Takeki. *Meiji bunkashi toshite no Nihon baishinshi.* Hōkōdō Shoten, 1926.

———. *Peirokoku Maria Roshi sen saiban ryakki*. In *Meiji bunka zenshū*. Vol. 11, *Gaikō hen*, edited by Meiji Bunka Kenkyūkai, 6–10. Nihon Hyōronsha, 1968.

Ōta Motoko. *Mabiki kankō shiryō shūsei*. Tōsui Shobō, 1997.

Ōta Tenrei. *Datai kinshi to yūsei hogohō*. Ningen Kagakusha, 1976.

Otsubo, Sumiko. "Feminist Material Eugenics in Wartime Japan." *U.S.-Japan Women's Journal, English Supplement* no. 17 (1999): 39–76.

Otsubo, Sumiko, and James Bartholomew. "Eugenics in Japan: Some Ironies of Modernity, 1883–1945." *Science in Context* 11, nos. 3–4 (1998): 545–565.

Ōyama Azusa. "Maria Rūsu gō jiken to saiban tetsuzuki." In *Nihon gaikōshi kenkyū*, 55–79. Ryōsho Fukyūkai, 1980.

Park, Hyun Ok. *Two Dreams in One Bed*. Durham, NC: Duke University Press, 2005.

Pascoe, Peggy. *What Comes Naturally: Miscegenation Law and the Making of Race in America*. New York: Oxford University Press, 2010.

Pateman, Carole. *The Sexual Contract*. Stanford, CA: Stanford University Press, 1988.

Pateman, Carole, and Charles Mills. *Contract and Domination*. Cambridge: Polity, 2007.

Peattie, Mark R. "Japanese Attitudes towards Colonialism, 1895–1945." In *The Japanese Colonial Empire, 1895–1945*, edited by Ramon H. Myers and Mark R. Peattie, 80–127. Princeton, NJ: Princeton University Press, 1984.

Peirokoku Maria Roshi sen saiban ryakki. [Kanagawa]: Kanagawa kenchō, 1874. Reprinted in *Meiji bunka zenshū*. Vol. 11, *Gaikō hen*, edited by Meiji Bunka Kenkyūkai, 29–60. Nihon Hyōronsha, 1968.

The Peruvian Barque "Maria Luz": A Short Account of the Cases Tried in the Kanagawa Kencho. [Kanagawa]: Kanagawa Kenchō, 1874.

Peterson, Mark A. *Korean Adoption and Inheritance: Case Studies in the Creation of a Classic Confucian Society*. Ithaca, NY: Cornell University Press, 1996.

Pramoedya, Ananta Toer. *This Earth of Mankind*. Translated by Max Lane. New York: Penguin, 1996.

Projet de code pénal pour l'empire du Japon présenté au sénat par le ministere de la justice le 8e mois de la 10e année de Meiji (Août 1879). Kokubunsha, 1879.

Ramseyer, J. Mark. "Indentured Prostitution in Imperial Japan: Credible Commitments in the Commercial Sex Industry." *Journal of Law, Economics, and Organization* 7, no. 1 (Spring 1991): 87–116.

Republica del Peru. *Colección de los tratados, convenciones capitulaciones, armisticios, y otros actos diplomáticos y políticos celebrados desde la independencia hasta el día, precedida de una introducción que comprende la época colonial*, edited by Ricardo Aranda. Lima: Imprenta del estado, 1890–1911.

Rinji Taiwan kyūkan chōsakai. *Hōan shinsakai daiyonkai kaigigijiroku.* Taihoku: Rinji Taiwan Kyōka Chōsakai, 1913.

———. *Taiwan Shihō.* Taihoku: Rinji Taiwan Kyūkan Chōsakai, 1900–1911.

———. *Taiwan shinzoku sōzoku rei daiichi sōan.* Taihoku: Rinji Taiwan Kyūkan Chōsakai, 1911.

———. *Taiwan shinzoku sōzoku rei daini sōan.* Taihoku: Rinji Taiwan Kyūkan Chōsakai, 1912.

———. *Taiwan shinzoku sōzoku rei daisan sōan.* Taihoku: Rinji Taiwan Kyūkan Chōsakai, 1914

Roberts, Richard L. *Litigants and Households: African Disputes and Colonial Courts in the French Soudan, 1858–1912.* Portsmouth, NH: Heinemann Educational Books, 2005.

Robertson, Jennifer. "Blood Talks: Eugenic Modernity and the Creation of New Japanese." *History and Anthropology* 13, no. 3 (2002): 1–26.

Roden, Donald. "Taishō Culture and the Problem of Gender Ambivalence." In *Culture and Identity: Japanese Intellectuals during the Interwar Years,* edited by J. Thomas Rimer, 37–55. Princeton, NJ: Princeton University Press, 1990.

Röhl, Wilhelm, ed. *History of Law in Japan since 1868.* Leiden: Brill, 2005.

Rothman, David J. *The Discovery of the Asylum: Social Order and Disorder in the New Republic.* Boston: Little, Brown and Co., 1971.

Rowley, G. G. "Prostitutes against the Prostitution Prevention Act of 1956." *U.S.-Japan Women's Journal, English Supplement* no. 23 (2002): 39–56.

Ruskola, Teemu. "Legal Orientalism." *Michigan Law Review* 101, no. 1 (2002): 179–234.

Saeki Chihiro. *Baishin saiban no fukkatsu.* Dai-ichi Hōki Shuppan, 1996.

Sakamoto Shin'ichi. "Haisenzen nihonkoku ni okeru Chōsen koseki no kenkyū." *Seikyūronshū* 10 (1997): 231–293.

Sakurai Yuki. "Mabiki to datai." In *Nihon no kinsei.* Vol. 15, *Josei no kinsei,* edited by Hayashi Reiko, 97–128. Chūō Kōronsha, 1993.

Sanders, Holly Vincele. "Prostitution in Postwar Japan: Debt and Labor." PhD diss., Princeton University, 2005.

Sato, Barbara. *The New Japanese Woman: Modernity, Media, and Women in Interwar Japan.* Durham, NC: Duke University Press, 2003.

Sawayama Mikako. *Shussan to shintai no kinsei.* Keisō Shobō, 1998.

———. "Umukoto/umanaikoto: Datai mabiki wo meguru kenryoku." In *Ningen keisei no zentai shi: Hikaku hattatsu shakaishi e no michi,* edited by Nakauchi Toshio et al. Ōtsuka Shoten, 1998.

Schneider, Elizabeth M. *Battered Women and Feminist Lawmaking.* New Haven, CT: Yale University Press, 2000.

———. "Feminism and the False Dichotomy of Victimization and Agency." *New York Law School Law Review* 38 (1993): 387–399.

Scott, Joan W. *Gender and the Politics of History.* New York: Columbia University Press, 1988.

Shiga-Fujime, Yuki. "The Prostitutes' Union and the Impact of the 1956 Anti-Prostitution Law in Japan." *U.S.-Japan Women's Journal, English Supplement* no. 5 (1993): 3–27.

Shigematsu Kazuyoshi. "Joshi keimusho rekibōki," *Hōgaku seminaa* 254 (May 1976): 84–88; 255 (June 1976): 98–102; 256 (July 1976): 122–128; 257 (August 1976): 130–134; 258 (September 1976): 76–83.

———. "Ninsoku yoseba to Ishiawajima kangoku." In *Ninsoku Yoseba shi,* edited by Ninsoku Yoseba Kenshōkai, 329–344. Sōbunsha, 1974.

———. *Sekai no kangokushi.* Kashiwa Shobō, 2001.

———. *Zukan Nihon no kangokushi.* Yūzankaku, 1985.

Shih Chi-yun. "Wuguo jindai tongyangxi zhi faluxue de yanjiu." *Shehui kexue luncong* 6 (1954): 91–137.

Shihōshō, ed. *Baishin seido kansatsu hōkoku.* Shihōshō Daijin Kanbō Chōsaka, 1926.

———. *Nihon kindai keiji hōreishū* 3. Shihōshō Hishoka, 1945.

Shihōshō keijikyoku. *Baishin seido no hanashi.* Shihōshō Keijikyoku, 1926.

Shiina Takashi. *Dai nijūni tokubetsu kokkai baishun mondai.* Yōyōsha, 1955.

Shimomura Fujio. *Meiji ishin no gaikō.* Ōyasu Shuppan, 1948.

Shinohara, Chika, and Christopher Uggen. "Sexual Harassment: The Emergence of Legal Consciousness in Japan and the U.S." *Sociological Quarterly* 50, no. 2 (2009): 201–234.

Sievers, Sharon L. *Flowers in Salt: The Beginnings of Feminist Consciousness in Modern Japan.* Stanford, CA: Stanford University Press, 1983.

Silverberg, Miriam. "The Modern Girl as Militant." In *Recreating Japanese Women, 1600–1945,* edited by Gail Lee Bernstein, 239–266. Berkeley: University of California Press, 1991.

Sotozaki Mitsuhiro. *Nihon fujinron shi.* Domesu Shuppan, 1986.

Spinney, Robert G. "Municipal Government in Nashville, Tennessee, 1938–1951: World War II and the Growth of the Public Sector." *Journal of Southern History* 61, no. 1 (1995): 77–112.

Sreenivas, Mytheli. *Wives, Widows, and Concubines: The Conjugal Family Ideal in Colonial India.* Bloomington: Indiana University Press, 2008.

Stanley, Amy. "Adultery, Punishment, and Reconciliation in Tokugawa Japan." *Journal of Japanese Studies* 33, no. 2 (Summer 2007): 309–335.

Staunton, George Thomas. *Ta Tsing Leu Lee; Being the Fundamental Laws and a Selection from the Supplementary Statutes of the Penal Code of China; Originally Printed and Published in Pekin, in Various Successive Editions, Under the Sanction, and by the Authority, of the Several Emperors of the Ta Tsing, or Present Dynasty.* Taipei: Ch'eng-Wen Publishing, 1966.

Steiner, Kurt. "The Revision of the Civil Code of Japan: Provisions Affecting the Family." *Far Eastern Quarterly* 9 (November 1949–August 1950), 169–183.

Stewart, Watt. *Chinese Bondage in Peru: A History of the Chinese Coolie in Peru, 1849–1874.* Durham, NC: Duke University Press, 1951.

Stoler, Ann. "Carnal Knowledge and Imperial Power: Gender, Race, and Morality in Colonial Asia." In *Gender at the Crossroads of Knowledge: Feminist Anthropology in a Postmodern Era,* edited by Micaela di Leonardo, 57–62. Berkeley: University of California Press, 1991.

———. *Race and the Education of Desire.* Durham, NC: Duke University Press, 1995.

Stoler, Ann Laura. *Carnal Knowledge and Imperial Power: Race and the Intimate in Colonial Rule.* Berkeley: University of California Press, 2002.

Stoler, Ann, and Frederick Cooper. "Between Metropole and Colony: Rethinking a Research Agenda." In *Tensions of Empire: Colonial Cultures in a Bourgeois World,* edited by Ann Stoler and Frederick Cooper, 1–57. Berkeley: University of California, 1997.

Suehiro Izutarō. "Yamamoto Senji-shi kyōshi jiken—hōritsuka no tachiba yori." *Kaizō* 11, no. 4 (April 1929): 146–147.

Suzuki Yasuaki. *Showa shoki no kourisho mondai: Hyakkaten to chūshō shōten no kakuchiku.* Nihon Keizai Shinbunsha, 1980.

Suzuki Yūko, *Jūgun ianfu, naisen kekkon.* Miraisha, 1992.

Tabohashi Kiyoshi. "Meiji gonen no 'Maria Rusu' jiken." *Shigaku zasshi* (1929): 40, no. 1: 98–114; 40, no. 3: 102–113; 40, no. 4: 87–112.

Takahashi Bonsen. *Datai mabiki no kenkyū.* Dai'ichi Shobō, 1981.

Takeda Yasumi. *Maria Rusu jiken: Ōe Taku to dorei kaihō.* Yokohama: Yurindō, 1981.

Takekoshi, Yosaburo. *Japanese Colonial Rule in Formosa.* Translated by George Braithwaite. London: Longmans, Green, 1907.

Tama Yasuko. "Datai to satsujin no aida: Senzen ni okeru datai eijisatsu no hanketsu kara." In *Kindai Nihon no bunkaron.* Vol. 6, *Hanzai to fūzoku,* edited by Aoki Tamotsu et al., 179–209. Iwanami Shoten, 2000.

Tamanoi, Mariko Asano, "Knowledge, Power, and Racial Classifications: The 'Japanese' in 'Manchuria.'" *Journal of Asian Studies* 59 (2000): 248–276.

———. "Songs as Weapons: The Culture and History of Komori (Nursemaids) in Modern Japan." *Journal of Asian Studies* 50, no. 4 (November 1991): 793–817.

Tamura Gorō. *Katei no saiban: Fūfu.* Nihon Hyōronsha 1985.

Tanaka Sumie. "Kantsū." In *Gendai kyōyō zenshū.* Vol. 9, *Yūjō, ren'ai, kekkon,* 302–307. Chikuma Shobō, 1959.

Tanaka Tokihiko. "Maria Ruzu gō jiken." In *Nihon seiji saiban shiroku.* Vol.

1, *Meiji zen*, edited by Wagatsuma Sakae, 273–298. Daiichi Hōki Shuppan, 1968.
Tanaka, Yuki. *Japan's Comfort Women: Sexual Slavery and Prostitution during World War II and the US Occupation*. London: Routledge, 2002.
Tanino Kaku. *Taiwan shin minjihō*. Taihoku: Taiwan Jihō Hakkōsho, 1923.
Teng, Emma. *Taiwan's Imagined Geography: Chinese Colonial Travel Writing and Pictures, 1683–1895*. Cambridge, MA: Harvard University Press, 2004.
Tezuka Yutaka. *Meiji shoki keihō shi no kenkyū*. Keiō Gijuku Daigaku Hōseigaku Kenkyūkai, 1956.
Thomas, Tracy A., and Tracey Jean Boisseau. "Introduction: Law, History, and Feminism." In *Feminist Legal History*, edited by Thomas and Boisseau, 1–29. New York: New York University Press, 2011.
TKC hōritsu jōhō legal database, accessed on October 26, 2006.
Tomeoka Kōsuke. *Gokusei enkakushi*. Isomura Masatomi, 1900.
Tonomura, Hitomi. "Sexual Violence against Women: Legal and Extralegal Treatment in Premodern Warrior Societies." In *Women and Class in Japanese History*, edited by Hitomi Tonomura, Anne Walthall, and Wakita Haruko, 135–152. Ann Arbor: Center for Japanese Studies, University of Michigan, 1999.
Treat, Payson. *Diplomatic Relations between the United States and Japan, 1853–1895*. 2 vols. Stanford, CA: Stanford University Press, 1932.
Triana, Mauro García, and Pedro Eng Herrera. *The Chinese in Cuba, 1847–Now*, edited and trans. by Gregor Benton. Lanham, MD: Rowman & Littlefield, 2009.
Tsu, Timothy Y. "Japanese Colonialism and the Investigation of Taiwanese 'Old Customs.'" In *Anthropology and Colonialism in Asia and Oceania*, edited by Jan van Bremen and Akitoshi Shimizu, 197–218. Richmond, Surrey: Curzon Press, 1999.
Tsuji Tatsuya. ed. *Sen'yō ruishū*, vol. 1. Zoku Gunsho Ruijū Kanseikai, 1967.
Tsukada Takashi. *Mibunsei shakai to shimin shakai*. Kashiwa Shobō, 1992.
Tsukasaki Naoyoshi. *Bengo sanjūnen*. Okakura Shobō, 1937.
———. "Kanko hōka jiken no baishin saiban." *Kaizō* 7 (February 1929): 49–53.
Tsurumi, E. Patricia. *Factory Girls: Women in the Thread Mills of Meiji Japan*. Princeton, NJ: Princeton University Press, 1990.
Tsurumi Yusuke. *Gotō Shinpei den*. Gotō Shinpei Denki Hensankai, 1937–38.
Uematsu Tadashi. "Eijisatsu ni kansuru hanzaigakutekina kenkyū." In *Keijihō no riron to genri: Ono Hakushi kanreki kinen*, vol. 2, edited by Uematsu Tadashi and Ono Seiichirō, 181–231. Yuhikaku, 1951.
Ueno Chizuko. "Modern Patriarchy and the Formation of the Japanese Nation State." In *Multicultural Japan: Paleolithic to Postmodern*, edited by Donald Denoon, Mark Hudson, Gavan McCormack, and Tessa

Morris-Suzuki, 213–233. Cambridge: Cambridge University Press, 2001.
Ujiie Mikito. *Fugi mittsū: Kinjirareta koi no Edo.* Kōdansha, 1996.
Ume Kenjirō. *Minpōyōgi.* Yūhikaku, 1912.
———. "Romburoso o yomu—zainin-soku-byōnin setsu o sessu." *Dai Nihon kangoku kyōkai zasshi* 45 (January 1892): 19–27; 46 (February 1892): 25–32.
Uno, Kathleen S. *Passages to Modernity: Motherhood, Childhood, and Social Reform in Early Twentieth-Century Japan.* Honolulu: University of Hawai'i Press, 1999.
———. "Womanhood, War, and Empire: Transmutations of 'Good Wife, Wise Mother' before 1931." In *Gendering Modern Japanese History,* edited by Barbara Molony and Kathleen Uno, 493–519. Cambridge, MA: Harvard University Press, 2005
Urabe Mamoru. *Wagakuni ni okeru baishin saiban no kenkyū—keikendan ni yoru jittai chōsa o chūshin toshite.* Shihō kenshūjo, 1968.
Usawa Fusaaki. "Baishin hō to sengakusha." In *Kaigyō nijūnen kinenronbunshū,* edited by Amano Kōichi. Dōrōsha Kappanjo, 1923.
Walkowitz, Judith. *Prostitution and Victorian Society: Women, Class, and the State.* Cambridge: Cambridge University Press, 1982.
Wang, Tay-sheng. *Legal Reform in Taiwan under Japanese Colonial Rule (1895–1945): The Reception of Western Law.* Seattle: University of Washington Press, 2000.
Warren, James Francis. *Ah Ku and Karayuki-san: Prostitution in Singapore, 1870–1940.* New York: Oxford University Press, 1993.
Waseda Daigaku Tsuruta Bunsho Kenkyūkai, ed. *Nihon keihō sōan kaigi hikki,* vol. 3. Waseda Daigaku Shuppanbu, 1997.
Watanabe, Yozo. "The Family and the Law: The Individualist Premise and Modern Japanese Family Law." In *Law in Japan: The Legal Order in a Changing Society,* edited by Arthur Taylor von Mehren, 364–398. Cambridge, MA: Harvard University Press, 1963.
Wen Qing, ed. *Chouban yiwu shimo: Tongzhi chao.* Peiping: Palace Museum, 1929–1930.
West, Mark D. *Law in Everyday Japan: Sex, Sumo, Suicide, and Statutes.* Chicago: University of Chicago Press, 2005.
———. *Lovesick Japan: Sex/Marriage/Romance/Law.* Ithaca, NY: Cornell University Press, 2011.
White, Luise. *The Comforts of Home: Prostitution in Colonial Nairobi.* Chicago: University of Chicago Press, 1990.
Williams, Samuel Wells. *Chinese Immigration: A Paper Read before the Social Science Association of Saratoga, September 10, 1879.* New York: Scribner's Sons, 1879.

Wöhr, Ulrike. *Frauen zwischen Rollenerwartung und Selbstdeutung: Ehe, Mutterschaft und Liebe im Spiegel der japanischen Frauenzeitschrift Shin shin fujin von 1913 bis 1916.* Wiesbaden: Harrassowitz, 1997.

Wolf, Arthur P. "Adopt a Daughter-in-law, Marry a Sister: A Chinese Solution to the Problem of Incest Taboo." *American Anthropologist* 70, no. 5 (1968): 864–874.

———. "Maternal Sentiments: How Strong Are They?" *Current Anthropology* 44 (2003): S31–S49.

———. *Sexual Attraction and Childhood Association: A Chinese Brief for Edward Westermarck.* Stanford, CA: Stanford University Press, 1995.

Wolf, Arthur P., and Hill Gates. "Chinese Marriage Regimes." *Journal of Family History* 23, no. 1 (1998): 90–99.

Wolf, Arthur P., and Chieh-san Huang. *Marriage and Adoption in China, 1845–1945.* Stanford, CA: Stanford University Press, 1980.

Wu Jianxiong. *Haiwai yimin yu Huaren shehui.* Taibei: Yunchen Wenwhua Shiye Youxian Gongsi, 1993).

Xie, Xue-hong. *Wo de banshen ji.* Taipei: Yang Cuihua, 1997.

Yamada Tokiyuki. "Kokuhō jo kyūkan no chi-i." *Taihō geppō* 9, no. 8 (1915): 23–30.

Yamamoto Shun'ichi. *Nihon kōshō shi.* Chūō Hōki Shuppan, 1983.

Yamazaki, Tomoko. *Sandakan Brothel No. 8.* Translated by Karen Colligan-Taylor. Armonk, NY: M.E. Sharpe, 1999.

Yen, Ching-hwang. *Coolies and Mandarins: China's Protection of Overseas Chinese during the Late Ch'ing Period (1851–1911).* Singapore: Singapore University Press, 1985.

Yoshimi Kaneko. *Baishō no shakaishi,* rev. ed. Yūzankaku, 1992.

Young, C. Walter, "Korean Problems in Manchuria as Factors in the Sino-Japanese Dispute," *Supplementary Documents to the Report of the Commission of Inquiry.* Study No. 9. Geneva, 1932.

Young, Robert J. C. *Postcolonialism: An Historical Introduction.* Malden, MA: Blackwell, 2001.

Yun Ch'i-ho. *Yun Ch'i-ho Ilgi,* vol. 11. Seoul: Kuksa P'yŏnch'an Wiwŏnhoe, 1989.

Zedner, Lucia. "Wayward Sisters: The Prison for Women." In *The Oxford History of the Prison,* edited by Norval Morris and David J. Rothman, 329–361. New York: Oxford University Press, 1995.

———. *Women, Crime, and Custody in Victorian England.* Oxford: Clarendon Press, 1991.

Zheng Song-yun. "Minshōhō shigyō ni tsuite." *Taiwan seinen* 3 (1922): 19–26.

Contributors

Barbara J. Brooks (1953–2013) was an associate professor of East Asian history at the City College and Graduate Center, City University of New York, and the author of *Japan's Imperial Diplomacy: Consuls, Treaty Ports and War in China, 1895–1938* (University of Hawai'i Press, 2000). She is also the author of many articles on gender, marginality, and the international dimensions of the Japanese Empire in China and Northeast Asia.

Daniel Botsman is a professor of history at Yale University. His publications include a translation of the memoirs of a prominent postwar foreign minister, *Okita Saburo: A Life in Economic Diplomacy* (Australia-Japan Research Center, 1993), and a study of the history of punishment from the sixteenth to the twentieth century, *Punishment and Power in the Making of Modern Japan* (Princeton University Press, 2005), also available in Japanese as *Chi nurareta jihi, muchi utsu teikoku* (Intershift, 2009). His current research examines the impact that Western ideas about slavery and emancipation had on Japanese society in the second half of the nineteenth century, focusing particularly on the experiences of Japan's outcaste communities.

Susan L. Burns is an associate professor of Japanese history at the University of Chicago. She is the author of *Before the Nation: Kokugaku and the Imagining of Community in Early Modern Japan* (Duke University Press, 2003). Her recent work on gender history includes "Local Courts, National Laws, and the Problem of Patriarchy in Modern Japan," in *Interdisciplinary Studies on the Taiwan Colonial Court Records Archives,* ed. Wang Taisheng (Angles Publishing, 2009), and "Marketing 'Women's Medicines': Gender, OTC Herbal Medicines, and Medical Culture in Modern Japan," *Asian Medicine* 5, no. 1 (2009): 146–172.

Chen Chao-ju is an associate professor of law at National Taiwan University College of Law. Her recent publications include "Gendered Borders—The Historical Formation of Women's Nationality under Law in Taiwan," *positions: east asia cultures critique* 17, no. 2 (2009): 289–314, and "Bargaining with Patriarchy: Daughter's Right of Inheritance in Practice," *National Taiwan University Law Journal* 38, no. 4 (2009): 133–228 (in Chinese). She is actively involved in human rights NGOs, and is now the president of the Awakening Foundation, a major feminist NGO in Taiwan.

Darryl Flaherty is an associate professor of history at the University of Delaware. His publications include "Democratization, 1919, and Lawyer Advocacy for a Japanese Jury," *Journal of Japanese Studies* 37, no. 2 (Summer 2011): 257–287, and a forthcoming book on Japan's nineteenth-century legal transition. His research interests include questions of law and social change in Japan, U.S. military bases in East Asia, and how public spaces express ideology.

Harald Fuess is a professor at the Cluster of Excellence "Asia and Europe in a Global Context" at Heidelberg University and a past president of the European Association of Japanese Studies. He authored *Divorce in Japan: Gender, Family, and the State* (Stanford University Press, 2004) and edited *Japanese Imperialism and Its Postwar Legacy* (Iudicium, 1998). His English-language publications on gender issues in Japanese history include "Men in the Women's Kingdom: Fatherhood in Taishō Japan," in *Public Spheres, Private Lives in Modern Japan 1600–1950,* ed. Gail Lee Bernstein, Andrew Gordon, and Kate Nakai (Harvard University Press, 2005), and "A Golden Age of Fatherhood? Parent-Child Relations in Japanese Historiography," *Monumenta Nipponica* 52, no. 3 (1997): 381–397. He is currently working on transnationality and extraterritoriality in the long nineteenth century as part of a larger collaborative project on maritime history.

Sally A. Hastings is an associate professor of history at Purdue University and editor of the *U.S.-Japan Women's Journal.* Her publications include *Neighborhood and Nation in Tokyo, 1905–1937* (University of Pittsburgh Press, 1995), and several essays on the history of Japanese women, most recently "Empress Nagako and the Family State," in *Handbook of the Emperors of Modern Japan,* ed. Ben-Ami Shillony (Brill, 2008), and "Assassins, Madonnas, and Career Women: Reflections on Six Decades of Women's Suffrage in Japan," *Asian Cultural Studies* no. 35 (2009): 229–239. Her current research project is on gender in Japanese politics during the first decade of women's suffrage in Japan, 1946–1956.

Douglas Howland is the David D. Buck Professor of Chinese History at the University of Wisconsin–Milwaukee. He is the author of *Translating the West: Language and Political Reason in Nineteenth-Century Japan* (University of Hawai'i Press, 2002), and *Personal Liberty and Public Good: The Introduction of John Stuart Mill to Japan and China* (University of Toronto Press, 2005), and with Luise White edited *The State of Sovereignty: Territories, Laws, Populations* (Indiana University Press, 2009).

Matsutani Motokazu is an associate professor at the Graduate School of Economics and Management, Tōhoku University. His major publications include "Church over Nation: Christian Missionaries and Korean Christians in Colonial Korea" (PhD diss., Harvard University, 2012), and "Minami chōsen ni okeru beisenryōgun no Shintō seisaku" [The U.S. Occupation Policy on Shintō in South Korea], *Gendai Kankoku Chōsen Kenkyū* 3 (2003): 64–77.

Index

Note: Page numbers in italic refer to graphs and tables.

Production Notes for
Burns & Brooks/
Gender and Law in the Japanese Imperium

Jacket design by Julie Matsuo-Chun.

Interior design and composition by Josie Herr
with text and display in New Baskerville.

Printing and binding by Sheridan Books, Inc.

Printed on 60 lb. House Natural Smooth, 420 ppi.